GOD'S ENDGAME

GARY S. CANGELOSI

Copyright © 2018 Gary Cangelosi

Citizens Chapel Press
Cornelius, North Carolina

All rights reserved. Printed in the United States of America. No part of this book may be reproduced, stored in a retrieval system, or transmitted, in any form or by any means, electronic, mechanical, photocopying, recording, or otherwise, without the prior written permission of the publisher.

Cangelosi, Gary S., 1953-
    God's Endgame / Gary S. Cangelosi
    p.   cm.

    ISBN: 978-0-9846642-3-8
    1. Millennialism. I. Title

Unless otherwise indicated, all Scripture quotations are from The Holy Bible, English Standard Version™, copyright © 2001 by Crossway Bibles, a division of Good News Publishers. Used by permission. All rights reserved.

Scripture quotations marked NIV are taken from the HOLY BIBLE, NEW INTERNATIONAL VERSION®. Copyright © 1973, 1978, 1984 by International Bible Society. Used by permission of Zondervan Publishing House. All rights reserved.

The "NIV" and "New International Version" trademarks are registered in the United States Patent and Trademark Office by the International Bible Society. Use of either trademark requires the permission of the International Bible Society.

COVER DESIGN
    Creative Director: Terri Cangelosi
    Art Director: Terri Cangelosi

For individual orders of this book: www.godsendgame.net

With a little help from my friends and a lot of help from my wife, Terri.

Contents

Foreword 1

1. God's Plans for the Future 3
2. The Missing Messianic Kingdom 21
3. Method of Interpreting the Scriptures 41
4. The Two Kingdoms of God 73
5. A Chart of God's Endgame 89
6. A Critique of Premillennialism 119
7. A Critique of Amillennialism and Postmillennialism 145
8. A Case for Postrestorationalism 165
9. A Hundredfold Reward on a Restored Earth 193
10. The Gospel of the Kingdom 211
11. The Final Resurrection 217
12. The Second Coming on Judgment Day 231
13. The New Heavens and New Earth 243
14. The Great Tribulation 255
15. The Battle of Armageddon 271
16. Daniel and the Olivet Discourse 277
17. The Seventy Weeks in Daniel 289
18. This Generation 307
19. The Cosmic Changes in the Heavens 315
20. The Stealthy Restoration 323
21. The Early Church Millennialists 339

22	Irenaeus and the Two Resurrections	355
23	Lactantius and the Two Resurrections	367
24	Augustine's Theology of the Future	375
25	Calvin's Theology of the Future	387
26	The Future of Israel	401
27	The Four Forms of Resurrection	417
28	God's Plan of Redemption	427

Scripture Index 445

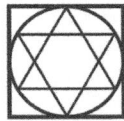

Foreword

www.godsendgame.net

Many verses quoted in this book will have interpretive comments located in brackets within the Scripture quotes. All italic or bold type in the Scripture quotes indicates emphasis added by the author.

This book is adapted from a lecture series that is available online on YouTube or Vimeo. These lectures are free, and you are welcome to download them from Vimeo and save them on your computer. You also have permission to show them to any small group or Sunday school class, or to any large group such as a conference.

Several chapters in this book are based on animated charts that are best understood by viewing the corresponding lecture. The charts are available online at www.godsendgame.net to download and print so that you can view them as you read these chapters. The charts are best viewed when printed on 11" x 17" paper, and you can freely print and distribute as many copies as needed.

1

God's Plans for the Future

This book is about God's endgame, or the biblical future. This is often referred to as "eschatology," or the study of end times. Many Christians associate the study of end times with interpreting the sensational events happening in the Middle East. But eschatology is an important subject because it is a biblical theology of the future and helps us understand God's plan of redemption.

The subject, however, can be controversial and divisive, and many pastors simply avoid the topic and teach that it will all just work out in the end. They prefer to focus their preaching on spiritual formation and how Christians should live today. Indeed, the Bible has plenty to say about how we should think and behave in everyday life. But as Christ said, we need to worship God in spirit and truth.

Most important, Christ and the apostles focus a great deal of their teachings on our future resurrection on Judgment Day, when we escape God's wrath and inherit the kingdom of heaven, which should greatly impact how we live today. Therefore, to live properly today, we need to understand God's plans for tomorrow.

The Bible is about what God has done in the past, is doing today, and *will do in the future*. As such, the study of God's plans for the future is an essential component of a Christian education so that we can develop a mature faith in God. In fact, faith in Christ requires that we have a good understanding of the biblical future in order to look forward to what God has in store for us: "Now faith is being sure of *what we hope for* and certain of what we do not see" (Heb. 11:1 NIV).

Unfortunately, conservative evangelical theologians, though in agreement on many core doctrines, have not been able to reach a consensus on eschatology. The different views are complex, confusing, and sometimes contradictory. The debate is often argumentative and contentious.

Some seminaries that advocate a particular eschatology will only seek faculty who adhere to and will teach the view they advocate. If professors shift their view, they are asked to leave. And although everyone wants a cordial discussion of the issues, most of the books written on the subject are hard-hitting rebuttals of the competing views. A great deal of biblical truth rides on the subject, so it necessitates a strong critique.

Evangelical theologians agree that Jesus of Nazareth is the Jewish Messiah who came into this world in the first century as the suffering servant to die for our sins and rescue us from God's wrath, reconcile us to God, and give us eternal life. But these theologians have never been able to reach a consensus on

- whether the Great Tribulation has already taken place or is a future event during the reign of the Antichrist,
- what transpires at Christ's second coming, or
- the meaning of the millennium as described by John in the book of Revelation, chapter 20.

As a result, many young Christians who want to be faithful to God's Word do not know what to hope for.

The Three Views on God's Endgame

Evangelical theologians are divided into three main camps, and there are many variations within each camp.

Amillennialists believe Christ is already ruling as King over his saints and that the millennium currently exists in the celestial or spiritual realm of heaven. When Christ comes again on Judgment Day to destroy (or purify) this Genesis earth, he will then rapture the saints and take them to the Father's eternal kingdom of heaven. Thus, there is no literal future paradise on this earth when Satan is totally removed from this world. The world remains in an evil age until the last day.

Postmillennialists also believe Christ returns on the last day to take us to heaven. But they believe that before Christ comes again to usher in the eternal kingdom, the church will evangelize and Christianize the nations. This will usher in a golden age of righteous humanity that may or may not last for a thousand years. Nations like North Korea and Iran will be led by Christian rulers, with their citizens living a Christian life of peace and righteousness. But Satan is not completely removed from this world.

Premillennialists believe Christ literally returns to this earth to establish a 1,000-year messianic kingdom before the saints inherit the Father's eternal kingdom. Satan is totally removed from this world, and the earth is restored to its Edenic condition of paradise. To inherit this millennial paradise, the saints are raptured either before the Tribulation, at the middle of the Tribulation, or at the end of the Tribulation. But all the raptured saints join Christ when he returns to this earth to establish his millennial kingdom.

The names themselves help identify these views.
- **A**-millennialism: *no* literal 1,000-year messianic kingdom before the eternal kingdom
- **Post**-millennialism: Christ returns *after* the thousand years of Christian civilization
- **Pre**-millennialism: Christ returns *before* a literal millennium to usher in his messianic kingdom

If you are new to the subject of eschatology and this information seems confusing and complicated, that is because it is. And believe it or not, this controversy over the millennium goes all the way back to the early church. But stay with me, and it will begin to make sense.

The Nature of Heaven

Theologians also do not agree on the nature of heaven. Some believe the Genesis earth will be annihilated on the last day of this age and will be replaced with a new heaven and a new earth as our eternal home. Others believe the earth is only purged by fire and remains the current planet, though totally renewed and restored to its Edenic condition. They believe Christ and his Father will come to dwell with the immortal saints on the renewed earth for eternity.

In this book I take the position that the earth will be destroyed on the last day. It will then be replaced with new heavens and a new earth. Just as Christ left his Father in heaven and came to dwell with us on this Genesis earth, one day he will take us to dwell with him and with his Father in his home on the eternal new earth. Throughout this book, the new heavens and new earth will also be referred to as the Father's kingdom of heaven, or simply, heaven. Heaven is the eternal home of the triune God where the raptured children of God will have eternal bodies and dwell with God forever in his eternal paradise. The saints are heirs of God himself in his eternal home.

A Biblical Theology of the Future

The purpose of this book is to take the strengths from each of the current views on the millennium and integrate them into an alternative understanding of the biblical future. Hopefully, this approach can help resolve the confusion that surrounds this subject. Then we can be certain of what we hope for.

We must be careful not to have a completely open mind. As Christians, our beliefs and way of life are bound by the Scriptures and should conform to them. We are also indebted to the historical teachings of wise and godly men throughout the history of the church, and we should be skeptical of any new doctrine.

But as the Reformation has taught us, we should have an open *biblical* mind. We should also evaluate any old, new, or modified doctrine based on its conformity to the Scriptures. For example, the Reformers did a good job of going back to the Scriptures and correcting the Catholic Church's flawed views on salvation (known as *soteriology*). But Calvin and the Reformers did not question the Catholic Church's doctrines on eschatology, which, after Saint Augustine, had become postmillennial.

And very little progress has been made on the subject during the last five hundred years; although premillennialism, which goes back to the early church, did experience a major revival in the late 1800s and is quite popular today. But premillennialists have been unable to persuade many Reformed brothers to accept their view, and the majority remain amillennial.

Books continue to be published on the subject, but each camp has been unable to persuade the others that their view is the correct biblical doctrine. Even after almost two thousand years of church history, the subject remains in a state of confusion and chaos. This is truly unfortunate, and it is a great disservice to all people—Christians and non-Christians alike—who are seeking to understand God's plans for the future. Something must be partially wrong with each of the current views on eschatology.

God is not the author of confusion. Thus, the confusing subject of eschatology is long overdue for a serious biblical analysis, reevaluation, correction, and reformulation. It is time for a reformation in the field of eschatology itself. So, I began an extensive study of eschatology and read numerous books by scholars from the different camps to better understand their biblical justification for their views. I had not settled on any one view, so I could make an honest assessment of all the views to see how well they conformed to the Scriptures and how rational and coherent they were.

I came away from this in-depth study deeply disappointed. As scholars constructed their respective views on eschatology from the biblical evidence, some Scriptures fit their overall framework quite well. But I also found that some Scriptures were distorted to force them to fit, which I found quite disturbing. I concluded that there were major design and structural flaws in all these views on eschatology, just as in a poorly designed and constructed house. I did not know the answer, but I knew something was not quite right with the prevailing views.

House of Ideas

In college, I studied architecture for several years before changing my major to history. I remember my professor of intellectual history saying that an ideology or worldview was like a house of ideas. People start with a basic set of ideas, which are then used to design and construct an entire ideology or philosophy of life. This ideology, in turn, can have either a positive or negative influence on a culture and civilization. For example, we studied the positive impact of the Puritan ideology on American society and government. The idea of a constitutional republic that guaranteed certain inalienable human rights and free enterprise grew out of the Puritan ideology.

We also studied the impact of Darwin's flawed ideas on evolution and natural selection on the Western world. During the Great Depression, for example, Germany experienced runaway inflation, which greatly destabilized the country. As the Nazis came to power during this period of turmoil, Hitler and his supporters developed a worldview that the Aryan race in Germany was a superior evolution of mankind. Influenced by this "survival of the fittest" principle, they believed that as the master race, it was their duty to rule over inferior nations and races and to prevent inferior races from contaminating the Aryan gene pool. They even decided that some inferior races or groups, such as the Jews, should be eliminated. Dump this ideology of a master race onto a disgruntled and industrious German people who had lost their Christian heritage, and you have a recipe for aggression, war, and genocide. Bad ideas and beliefs do have negative consequences. That is why the subject is called *intellectual* history. It is not just a history of dates and events. It is also the history of the ideologies that lead up to and cause historical events. Intellectuals and professors influence their students, who often become leaders. These leaders then build a house that we all must live in!

Flawed House Designs

I will never forget my college professor's metaphor of the house of ideas. Given my background in architecture and intellectual history, when I began reading and analyzing the various books on eschatology, I discovered some faulty house designs, with serious structural flaws in all the current views.

The Amillennial House: Amillennialists believe Satan is never totally removed from this world, and there is no literal 1,000-year age of righteous humanity. But they have a Messiah without his messianic kingdom, which seems like a contradiction in terms. They understand that Christ is capable of binding Satan so that he can save his elect from Satan's dominion of darkness. But is Christ not also capable of completely removing Satan from this world so that he can rule the world with absolute justice?

The Postmillennial House: Postmillennialists believe we can create a golden age of righteous humanity on this earth for a thousand years if we simply evangelize and Christianize the world. They admit, however, that Satan is not completely bound today and that he remains operational in this world until the last day. Do these theologians honestly believe we can create an age of righteous humanity while Satan remains operational in the world, influencing people to cheat, steal, and kill?

The Premillennial House: Premillennialists believe Christ returns to this earth with the raptured saints to establish his millennial kingdom. But what are the glorified sons of God doing on this earth comingling with natural human beings who survive the Great Tribulation? Don't the transformed children of God belong in heaven? And doesn't Peter teach that when Christ returns to take us to the imperishable kingdom of heaven, the earth is then destroyed (2 Peter 3:7–10)? How can Christ return to this earth if he destroys it when he returns?

I also discovered that each view has its strengths.

- **Amillennialists** make a good case that Christ comes again on the last day of this Genesis creation. He is the Alpha, the Omega, and judge of all mankind, after all.
- **Postmillennialists** make a good case that if Christ does rule the world for a thousand years, he can do so from his throne in heaven. He is God, after all.
- **Premillennialists** make a good case that there must be a 1,000-year messianic kingdom on this earth before we go to heaven. Jesus is the Messiah, after all.

Frustrated with the design flaws of these various views on God's endgame, I began to study the Scriptures in earnest, searching for an alternative design or structure that would make sense out of *all the relevant biblical data, from Genesis to Revelation*. I was not out to change the world; I just wanted to know the truth. And I believe that my background in architecture, as well as in intellectual history, not only helped me discern the design flaws in the current views, but it also enabled me to come up with a better framework for understanding God's endgame.

Endgame in Chess

When I began writing a book on the subject, a friend of mine who worked in strategic planning for the military suggested that I title it

God's Endgame. The term *endgame* comes from the game of chess, which is a game of war. It is used to describe the final stages of one's strategy to bring the game of war to a conclusive victory. Sometimes a king is held in "check," but since he has a means of escape, he can live on for another day. Only after a succession of strategic moves toward the end when he is held in "checkmate" is he without a means of escape, and he is destroyed and the game is over.

I thought my friend's suggestion was a great name for the book. Like a game of chess, the Bible reveals God's strategy for redeeming his people and defeating Satan and his demons. The garden of Eden was God's kingdom on this earth. But after the fall, Satan and his demons entered this world, and there has been spiritual warfare ever since. Premillennialists believe Satan will be held in "check" during the millennium, and the world will be under God's renewed Lordship. Amillennialists believe Satan remains the ruler of this world until he is held in "checkmate" on the last day of this evil age, when he is destroyed in the lake of fire.

The Rules of the Game

In the game of chess, there are rules that determine how the game should be played by the various pieces, such as bishops, rooks, knights, and pawns. When it comes to the process of understanding God's endgame, there are also rules of the game that students of the Bible should follow. Theologians call these rules "biblical hermeneutics." These are the principles of interpreting and organizing the Scriptures that should be followed when developing a proper view of God's plan of redemption.

For example, God's covenants with Abraham, Moses, and King David are guiding principles that determine how God will use Israel to one day crush Satan and bring about the redemption of mankind and this world. Through these covenants, God will use Israel to accomplish two very important missions: (1) to bring the Messiah into this world as the son of David, and (2) to usher in his messianic kingdom on this earth.

The Messiah was born of a Jew in Bethlehem of Judea, so Israel accomplished its first mission. But Israel rejected its own Messiah, and now theologians cannot agree on whether the remaining covenant with Israel to usher in the messianic kingdom is unconditional or conditional.

Premillennialists argue that the rules of the game have not changed and that Israel remains a strategic part of God's endgame. One day in the future, the Jews will indeed repent and believe in their own Messiah, just as many Gentiles have. They will again play a strategic role in God's endgame when Christ uses the nation of Israel to establish his messianic kingdom on this earth. In fact, all nations will want to go to Jerusalem with gifts to show their appreciation for the global peace and prosperity that the Jewish nation's Messiah has brought to the world.

Amillennialists, on the other hand, believe the rules of the game have changed. They assert that Israel's mission has been terminated because of their hard hearts and disobedience. Christ is now the new Israel. And even his mission has changed. Instead of ushering in the Jewish-led messianic kingdom when he returns, Christ's mission is to usher in the Father's eternal kingdom of heaven for all believers, Jew and Gentile. Thus, there is no future messianic kingdom on this earth.

Because of these two different interpretations of God's covenants with Israel, theologians cannot agree on the rules of the game. Examining these covenants has proven insufficient in helping to make the case for any particular eschatology.

But I believe the Bible itself reveals another set of rules as to how the game should be played that should get us beyond this impasse. When reading the Old Testament, I observed that the messianic kingdom is described by the prophets as a restoration of the Genesis creation to its Edenic condition. The wolf and the lamb graze together on a peaceful and prosperous earth. It is described as a kingdom where men and women marry, bear children, and experience an abundant life in a restored earthly paradise. The messianic kingdom is a restoration of our humanity as it was intended in the beginning before the fall. It is a restoration of the Adamic creation, or what I refer to as the Adamic order of being.

I further observed that the God of the Bible is a triune God and that within the Trinity this Genesis creation was uniquely created by, through, and for the Son of God. Christ was our Creator, who spoke this creation into existence. Before the fall, the garden of Eden was the Son's righteous kingdom. As such, he is the true Lord over all mankind. But when Satan came into this world, there was a regime change. The Son's dominion over righteous humanity became Satan's dominion of evil and darkness over unrighteous humanity.

When the Son of God came into this world to save us from Satan's dominion of darkness, he came as the son of David. Consequently, Jesus Christ was both the human Jewish Messiah *and* the incarnate Son of God. As the son of David, he had the right to rule over the nation of Israel. But as the Son of God, he has a divine right to rule over all the nations, for the whole Genesis creation rightly belongs to him.

Therefore, the 1,000-year messianic kingdom would simply be the Son's Genesis creation restored to him. It was his kingdom to begin with. In fact, God the Father has made an unconditional covenant with his eternal Son that one day he will remove all his enemies and restore this Genesis creation to him. Christ reveals this Trinitarian covenant between the Father and the Son when quoting from Psalm 110:

> Now while the Pharisees were gathered together, Jesus asked them a question, saying, "What do you think about the Christ? Whose son is he?" They said to him, "The son of David." He said to them, "How is it then that David, in the Spirit, calls him Lord, saying, 'The Lord [God the Father] said to my Lord [God the Son], "Sit at my right hand [on his divine throne in heaven], until I [the Father] put your enemies under your feet"? (Matt. 22:41–44)

After Christ ascended to his Father's right hand in heaven, he was given dominion over the world. As the Son of God, he has all the divine authority and power necessary to rule the world, but he is waiting on the Father to determine when his reign will begin. And the Father has promised his Son that one day he will rule over Israel *and* the whole world as King of kings and Lord of lords:

> "As for me, I have set my King on Zion, my holy hill [the kingdom starts in Israel]." I will tell of the decree: The LORD [the Father] said to me, "You are my Son; today I have begotten you. Ask of me, and *I will make the nations your heritage, and the ends of the earth your possession* [the kingdom extended throughout the world]." (Ps. 2:6–8)

All the nations of the world belong to Jesus Christ because, as the Son of God, he is the Creator of all mankind.

Amillennialists can argue that God's covenant with Israel was conditional based upon the nation receiving its Messiah. But this is an *unconditional* covenant between God the Father and God the Son. That is because Christ was always faithful to his Father, both as a human being and surely as the Son of God. When the Son ascended to heaven, he sat down at the Father's right hand. And one day the Father will remove all his enemies on this earth, demonic and human, and the Son will get his Genesis creation back. Then he will rule the world. God's plan of redemption includes a restoration of our humanity.

But in the New Testament, I also discovered that Christ introduced a new perspective on God's plan of redemption, which is also structured around the Trinity. The followers of Christ not only become men and women of God destined to inherit the restored Edenic earth during his messianic kingdom, but they also become born-again children of God the Father destined to inherit the Father's eternal kingdom of heaven. The followers of Christ become sons of God the Father, modeled after his Sonship. In the Father's imperishable kingdom, his children will no longer experience marriage and procreation. They will be a new creation that is neither male nor female. Jesus even taught us to address God as "Abba, Father," as he did, which is not how Adam, as a man of God, would have addressed his Creator.

The Son's messianic kingdom is described by the prophets as a restoration of our humanity, with marriage and reproduction on a restored Edenic earth. But the Father's eternal kingdom of heaven will not be a restoration of our humanity; otherwise, there would be marriage in heaven. In heaven, we will continue to be embodied creatures in a real place, but we will have immortal bodies that, like the angels, will not experience marriage. In an extraordinary revelation, Jesus taught:

> The sons of this age marry and are given in marriage [the Adamic order of being in this Genesis age], but those who are considered worthy to attain to that age [followers of Christ] and to the resurrection from the dead [in the eternal age to come] neither marry nor are given in marriage [the Adamic order of being as male and female comes to an end], for they cannot die anymore [an immortal body], because they are equal to angels and are sons of God, being sons of the resurrection [the new creation as eternal sons of God]. (Luke 20:34–36)

Christ and the apostles defined eternal life for the sons of God as an eternal, embodied life that is neither male nor female on an eternal new earth living in eternal fellowship with the triune God. And as fellow children of God, we will experience a new kind of companionship in heaven. In fact, **none** of the following forms of human companionship based on our human sexuality will exist in heaven:
- husband or wife
- father or mother
- son or daughter
- brother or sister
- grandfather or grandmother
- uncle or aunt
- nephew or niece, and so forth

These human relationships are all part of the human experience. When we are born again and become Christians, we become restored men and women of God in the Adamic order of being. My wife is my female companion in marriage, whom I am to love and serve. But in the new creation, my wife is also a fellow child of God in which there is neither male nor female. In heaven, she will no longer be my wife, and I will experience a new kind of companionship with her as a fellow child of God.

Theologians have done a poor job of integrating this revelation by Christ pertaining to the immortal bodies of the sons of God into their eschatology. I have read numerous books on the subject of God's plans for the future, but I do not recall any author taking this revelation seriously. Many ignore these Scriptures altogether. But understanding the two creations is critical to understanding God's plan of redemption.

As I studied the Bible, I observed that God's plan of redemption is designed and structured around these two kingdoms of the triune God and their corresponding creations:
- ***The Adamic creation*** as male and female is destined for the Son's restored earth for a restored humanity for a thousand years.
- ***The new creation*** as immortal sons of God is destined for the Father's heavenly kingdom on the eternal new earth.

The millennium is the Son's kingdom restored, and the new heavens and new earth is the Father's eternal kingdom.

According to the prophets, in the Son's messianic kingdom the people of God will continue to function as male and female in the image of God. Men and women will become one flesh, reproduce sons and daughters, and fill and subdue a restored Edenic earth with their offspring. The millennium will include a human society and civilization as it was intended to be in the beginning before the fall. But according to Christ and the apostles, when this Genesis earth perishes and we are taken to the Father's eternal kingdom of heaven, the eternal sons of God will no longer experience the Adamic functions of marriage and reproduction. And we will experience a new form of companionship as fellow children of God.

This is a Trinitarian eschatology. And these are the rules of the game that theologians should follow when constructing their version of God's endgame. In effect, these are the building codes as to how the house of ideas revealed in the Scriptures should be constructed.

When I embarked on a study of this subject, I began to use these principles of interpretation as design guidelines to organize the various biblical components into a well-constructed biblical theology of the future. For example, when I'm reading Isaiah and he describes a restored humanity with men and women experiencing marriage on a restored earthly paradise with a wolf living in peace with a lamb, then it obviously pertains to the Son's 1,000-year restoration of this Genesis creation.

Or, if I'm reading Paul's letter to the Philippians, and he describes our transformed immortal bodies inheriting our citizenship in heaven when Christ returns to take us to join him there, then it pertains to the Father's eternal kingdom of heaven. This method is an elegantly simple way to study the Scriptures in order to understand God's endgame.

Different Operating Systems

Jesus often used agrarian-based parables to help us understand the kingdom of God. Christ is portrayed as a planter, gardener, and reaper, and we are portrayed as his field, crop, and harvest. Most of us no longer live in an agrarian society, so to use an analogy from the modern age of computers, God's plan of redemption revolves around two very different computer operating systems. The operating system of the Son's 1,000-year restoration of this creation could be described as a reboot of the original computer with the corrupted operating system and software repaired. Satan, who hacked into the system and introduced malicious viruses and malware, would be removed and prevented from corrupting the system during Christ's reign. In contrast, the operating system of the Father's new creation could be described as a new computer with a very different operating system and software. This flawless system would operate forever without any interference, corruption, or breakdown.

I found that many of the mistakes made by theologians in describing God's endgame were the result of confusing these two operating systems. Since amillennialists do not believe in a future millennium, they sometimes impose the prophecies in Isaiah describing the Son's restored Genesis creation onto the Father's eternal kingdom of heaven, so that heaven is essentially a restored humanity on a restored Genesis earth. But how can heaven be a restored humanity if we will not experience marriage and reproduction? Marriage and procreation are fundamental to all the forms of human companionship that we experience on this earth. Being male and female gets to the very essence of our existence.

Premillennialists, on the other hand, make the mistake of having the raptured, glorified sons of God who no longer experience marriage coming back to the Son's restored natural earth during the millennium to live alongside human beings who continue to experience marriage. But this is another obvious design flaw. The eternal sons of God belong on the Father's eternal new earth—not on the Son's restored earth.

A Real Geopolitical Threat

The apostle Paul emphasized the eternal kingdom of heaven. And some amillennial theologians construe this lack of emphasis on Christ's earthly kingdom as an indication that God's plan of redemption no longer includes a restoration of this Genesis creation before the eternal kingdom.

But it is important to remember that Paul was a Jewish evangelist to the Gentiles operating in the hostile pagan Roman Empire. His main objective was to get the pagan Gentiles to believe in Christ so that they could inherit eternal life in the Father's kingdom of heaven. He knew these Gentile converts would be persecuted by the Roman authorities if they no longer worshiped the emperor or the pagan Roman gods. But he also knew that if his gospel message had included a clear vision of the earthly reign of Christ, it would have been perceived by the Roman authorities as a geopolitical threat to their empire, and they would needlessly be persecuted even more.

During the Roman Empire, all roads led to Rome, with soldiers bringing the spoils of war from other nations to enrich their great empire. But the Jewish prophets also foretold a Jewish Messiah who would destroy all the unrighteous kingdoms of sinful man and set up his messianic kingdom as a global empire. Then, they taught, instead of all roads leading to a pagan empire, all roads would lead to Jerusalem. The nations would bring gifts to Israel as a show of gratitude for the peace and prosperity the Jewish Messiah had brought to the world. King Herod, Pontius Pilate, and the Roman authorities were aware of these teachings, which is why they were paranoid of any Jew claiming to be the Messiah.

If Paul had articulated a clear message of Christ's future reign, the Romans would have no doubt set out to destroy the young church at the embryonic stage of its growth. Paul and the disciples were wise not to emphasize the earthly reign of Christ. When the Gentile Christians were persecuted for their faith in Christ, Paul taught them to remain focused on Christ's second coming, when their natural bodies would be transformed into eternal bodies and they would inherit their citizenship in heaven. Upon investigating these strange teachings, the Roman authorities might have thought Paul was out of his mind, but they would not have considered his gospel of a heavenly kingdom that is not of this world a real geopolitical threat.

This strategy helps explain the stealthy book of Revelation. It delivers the truth about the future millennial reign of Christ, cleverly hidden in a form of literature that made it almost impossible for the Romans to comprehend. If they had obtained a copy of the book, after reading a few chapters, they would have likely thrown it down in utter exasperation!

Even today theologians struggle to understand Revelation. But understanding Revelation is critical to understanding God's endgame. Revelation reveals that the saints will experience two resurrections: one at the beginning of the millennium, so they can inherit the Son's restored Genesis earth for a thousand years; and another at the end of the millennium when the earth perishes on Judgment Day, so they can inherit the Father's new heavens and new earth for eternity. Understanding the nature of these two resurrections and where Christ is when he rules the world are essential to understanding God's endgame.

Postrestorationalism

There are five key questions that need to be answered correctly to understand God's endgame:
1. What is the nature of the millennial reign of Christ?
2. Where is Christ if, and when, he rules the world?
3. What is the nature of the first resurrection at the beginning of the millennium?
4. What is the nature of the final or general resurrection after the millennium on the last day of this Genesis age?
5. When does Christ return?

In this book, I will make the biblical case that the millennium will be a restored Edenic paradise for a restored humanity. This occurs when Christ removes Satan, removes the curse, and reclaims his wonderful creation. But instead of Christ returning to this earth to establish his millennial kingdom, I will make the case that he rules the world from his throne in heaven at the right hand of God the Father. Since the beginning of the millennium is not his second coming, the first resurrection cannot be the rapture of the saints. Therefore, the first resurrection must be of the natural, Adamic bodies of the departed saints so they can inherit the Son's restored Edenic earth—restored natural bodies for a restored natural earth. Christ returns *after* the millennium at the final resurrection on Judgment Day to usher in the Father's eternal kingdom of heaven. The sons of God are then raptured into eternal bodies so they can inherit the Father's eternal new heavens and new earth—eternal bodies for an eternal kingdom. At the same time, unbelievers are resurrected from hades and sent to the lake of fire. Christ returns *after* (post-) a literal 1,000-year restoration of this Genesis creation. Thus, the name *postrestorationalism*.

Surprisingly, this view of God's endgame has never been considered. It is, however, very close to that of the early church millennialists. It is a modified form of historic millennialism. Some of the early church fathers in the first century knew John when he wrote the book of Revelation. They could ask John personally for his interpretation of the two resurrections. These church fathers claim that John and the apostles taught that the first resurrection will be of the natural bodies of the departed saints, similar to the resurrection of Lazarus, and that the final resurrection will be of the raptured, eternal bodies of the sons of God, as described by Jesus. Chapters 21–24 in this book are devoted to the important teachings of the early church millennialists. But most important, I will make a biblical case for this view of God's endgame.

Summary

The subject of eschatology is often considered as an esoteric topic. Pastors and theologians remain focused on a gospel message centered on sinful mankind's reconciliation with a holy God, redemption in this life, escaping God's wrath on Judgment Day, and eternal life in heaven. But understanding God's plans to restore mankind to an Edenic paradise during Christ's millennial reign before we are taken to heaven helps us grasp God's great love for sinful mankind. which is why the subject is so important to properly understand.

Unfortunately, theologians have offered different views on God's plan of redemption. But I will make the biblical case for postrestorationalism.

- During the millennium, Christ rules the restored Edenic earth *from his throne in heaven*.
- The *first resurrection* will be of the natural bodies of the departed saints because they are destined to inherit the Son's restored Genesis earth—natural human bodies for a restored natural earth.
- Christ returns *after the millennium* on the last day of this Genesis creation to usher in the eternal age to come.
- The *final resurrection* will be of the raptured, immortal bodies of the sons of God because they are destined to inherit the Father's kingdom of heaven—eternal bodies for an eternal kingdom.

2

The Missing Messianic Kingdom

Review

When we accept Christ, we become restored men and women of God in fellowship with our Creator. But we also become children of God the Father destined for eternal life on the new earth. In heaven, we will no longer be male or female, and we will no longer experience marriage and reproduction. When studying the Bible, I discovered that God's plan of redemption is based on these two creations and their corresponding kingdoms of the triune God:

- **The Adamic order of being** corresponds to the Son's 1,000-year restoration of the human experience on the restored Genesis earth.
- **The new creation as sons of God** corresponds to the Father's new heavens and new earth as the eternal home for the glorified sons of God.

Theologians have done a poor job of differentiating between the two orders of being and the two kingdoms of the triune God when formulating their theology of the future. This may explain why a consensus has never been reached on God's endgame.

Sharing the Gospel

When we share the gospel, I believe we should include a presentation of the Son's messianic kingdom as well as the promise of eternal life in the Father's eternal kingdom of heaven. Whenever I get a chance to share the gospel with a non-Christian friend, I always like to start with Genesis, which is the foundation to any biblical house of ideas. It not only reveals the origin of human life, but it also reveals the origin of sin and death, which is something we all need to understand.

Some theologians mate Darwinian evolution with the Genesis account of creation. But this creates a corrupted form of creation and Christianity. Darwin has humans surviving in a hostile environment with limited resources in a life-and-death struggle for the survival of their species. In stark contrast, in the garden of Eden, God has mankind thriving without death in a peaceful paradise with an abundance of food for all creatures. Darwin views death as the essential means of eliminating weaker organisms and advancing the evolution of man, while God says he imposed death on mankind as a result of the fall. The two versions of creation are polar opposites and cannot be blended. The hybrid views of creation are not only unbiblical, they are also irrational.

Although Genesis was written in the ancient world before modern science, that makes it no less historically accurate. Once the earth is created, Genesis reads like a history book, chronologically recording historical events beginning with Adam and Eve, then progressing to Cain and Abel, Seth and Enoch, Abraham and Sarah and ending with the life and death of Joseph. The last verse of the book states, "So Joseph died, being 110 years old. They embalmed him, and he was put in a coffin in Egypt" (Gen. 50:26). The way in which Adam and Eve lived and died is treated in the same manner as the way in which Joseph lived and died. They are not treated as mythical figures.

Moreover, the garden of Eden is not presented as a fantasyland, like C. S. Lewis's Narnia. Rather, it is presented as an actual historical place, just like Egypt is presented as a real place. The garden of Eden has identifiable rivers that the ancient world would have been familiar with: "A river flowed out of Eden to water the garden, and there it divided and became four rivers.... And the fourth river is the Euphrates" (Gen. 2:10–14). This is similar to the description of the land when Abraham and Lot were parting ways:

And Lot lifted up his eyes and saw that the Jordan Valley was well watered everywhere *like the garden of the* LORD, like the land of Egypt, in the direction of Zoar. (Gen. 13:10)

The land of Egypt was real, the Jordan Valley was real, and so was the garden of Eden. Some theologians seem embarrassed by the depiction of Adam and Eve in the garden of Eden. But the book of Genesis does not give us the option of treating Abraham and Lot as real people living in a real place and treating Adam and Eve as fictional characters living in a fantasyland.

I begin my presentation of the gospel with Adam and Eve living in fellowship with their Creator in the garden of Eden. As God ruled over them, they were to rule over and manage his wonderful creation. As they multiplied and developed the untamed regions of the earth, the garden of Eden would have spread to the whole world as an earthly paradise. The world would be God's wonderful kingdom on earth.

Paradise Lost

I then describe Satan's temptation of Adam and Eve to get them to reject God's dominion over them and set up their own autonomous kingdom. They succumbed to this temptation, which led to their subsequent insubordination, insurrection, and rebellion against God's rule over them. And they became isolated from their loving Creator.

This rebellion infuriated God and brought about his wrath and curse on mankind and the earth itself. Adam, Eve, and all their descendants would now experience a good bit of misery on a degenerate earth until their bodies died and decayed in the dirt. God also allowed Satan to enter our world and he became the false god of the world, usurping God as the true Lord of this creation. With this regime change, the world became Satan's dominion, and it has never been the same.

I then explain to my friend that Christians believe there are four fundamental problems with this world because of the fall:

Sinful humanity: Because we are all sinners, we all experience the loss of spiritual life that comes from the fact that we are disconnected from our Creator, who is Life. And our sinful nature affects all aspects of human behavior, civilization, and every occupation on this earth. There are wedding photographers, and there are photographers of pornography. There are doctors who help us give birth to children, and doctors who use their skills to abort children.

Unrighteous rulers: As sinful humans rise to positions of authority in government, unrighteous men and women rule the world. Some rulers are much worse than others, but they all have shortcomings. I then invite my friend to identify some of the worst characters in power in the world today, such as those leading countries like North Korea or Somalia.

A satanic world: Satan continues to be the false god of this fallen world, and his demons have a significant influence on the affairs of sinful mankind. Surprisingly, my non-Christian friend finds this reference to the presence of demons in this world credible. It helps explain some of the extreme inhumanity throughout history.

A cursed creation: The Genesis earth remains under God's curse, which is why there are so many natural disasters and humans experience so much hardship, sickness, and death.

My non-Christian friend can easily recognize that it is not paradise on the earth today. Yet, we all realize that, given the right circumstances, life on this earth can be deeply fulfilling. But people know that life on this cursed earth can be very fragile and circumstances can and will change over time. As we grow old, our bodies deteriorate. And the disparity between those who are blessed with good health, a great family, and prosperity and those who do not experience the good life is remarkable. But we will all experience death, which ends whatever joy and prosperity we may have obtained.

A lot of us are fortunate to experience times of great joy and beauty in our lives. But I believe we all subconsciously miss the garden of Eden. And if we take the time to assess our lives in this fallen world, we will realize that many of our human aspirations for a fulfilling life will go unfulfilled on this earth no matter how prosperous and fortunate we think we are. At any given time, circumstances in life can change dramatically.

My friend and I then identify many of the things that can go wrong in this world. Sudden earthquakes can cause massive destruction and generate gigantic tidal waves. Hurricanes like Katrina, Harvey, and Irma devastated the Gulf Coast and Caribbean islands. There are active volcanos around the world and hard-to-control forest fires. There are severe droughts in many parts of the world, as well as all kinds of diseases, some leading to horrible epidemics.

But natural disasters are not the only cause of our misery. There are numerous manmade disasters. Horrific terrorist attacks are occurring throughout the world, often where peaceful and festive crowds are gathered. Industrial pollution remains a problem when government leaders are not held accountable to their people. Many people are living in entrenched poverty, with more than 900 million people going to bed hungry and malnourished every night.

Yet, some people believe they can achieve an idyllic life. But we are only one heartbeat away from the end of life on this earth. And then there is the second death on Judgment Day, which I tell my friend he needs to avoid at all costs.

Deep down we wish the world was like the garden of Eden when it was God's kingdom on a good earth and mankind did not experience such misery and death.

The Promised Messiah

But I explain to my friend that because God so loved mankind, he initiated a plan of redemption immediately after the fall when he promised a redeemer who would one day crush Satan and restore humanity to its original glory. His plan continued to be revealed when he used Abraham as his means to bring the Jewish nation of Israel into existence and bring hope to all nations. And from the Jewish King David would come a son who would be the Messiah, who would restore the world to its Edenic paradise and create an age of righteous humanity once again. He surely did not use the Egyptian pharaohs or the pagan Babylonians to bring salvation to all humanity. The Jewish prophet Isaiah foretold of the coming Messiah and his messianic kingdom:

> For to us a child is born, to us a son is given; and the *government* shall be upon his shoulder, and his name shall be called Wonderful Counselor, Mighty God, Everlasting Father, Prince of *Peace*. Of the increase of his government and of peace there will be no end, on *the throne of David and over his kingdom*, to establish it and to uphold it with *justice* and with *righteousness* from this time forth and forevermore. The zeal of the Lord of hosts will do this. (Isa. 9:6–7)

According to the Jewish prophets, the Messiah will usher in God's kingdom once again as it was in the beginning, and Israel and the whole world will be characterized by peace, justice, righteousness, and abundant prosperity. The Messiah will establish a paradise on a restored earth during an age of righteous humanity.

When the Messiah came into this world, however, the Jews rejected him and had him crucified by the Romans. But he was resurrected, and instead of overthrowing the tyrannical Roman Empire and establishing his messianic kingdom on this earth as his disciples expected, he left this world and ascended into heaven. As my son likes to say, he split and left us in this rotten world!

As a result, the world remains characterized by strife and war instead of peace, unrighteousness instead of righteousness, injustice instead of justice, and systemic poverty instead of abundant prosperity. We continue to experience an age of unrighteous humanity on a cursed earth. And the world remains full of demons and the cosmic forces of evil.

The Son of God Incarnate

I further explain to my friend that Jesus Christ, as the human Jewish Messiah, was also the Son of God incarnate who created this Genesis creation. I then describe some of the many miracles Jesus performed to demonstrate his deity and his compassion for those suffering in this fallen world. He created food for thousands. He controlled nature at will and calmed a nasty storm on the Sea of Galilee with a simple command. He restored to health people who were diseased, blind, deaf, or paralyzed. He easily raised people from the dead. And he cast out legions of demons with merely a command.

My friend may then ask, so if Jesus of Nazareth is the Jewish Messiah, then why hasn't he established his messianic kingdom of peace, justice, and prosperity on this earth? And if he is God incarnate who created the heavens and the earth as you claim, then why hasn't he used his divine power to restore this Genesis earth to its Edenic paradise? Why aren't we experiencing an abundant life today?

I explain to my friend that this is one reason why many of the first-century Jews rejected Jesus of Nazareth as their Messiah. He refused to overthrow the tyrannical Roman rulers, liberate Israel, and set up his messianic kingdom, returning Israel to power and prosperity. He also claimed to be God, which they found highly offensive.

But his disciples, after listening to his extraordinary teachings and witnessing his amazing miracles, became convinced that he was indeed the Messiah and eventually understood that he was God incarnate. Yet they, too, were initially befuddled by his refusal to set up his kingdom in their lifetimes and were shocked by his eventual crucifixion and ascension to heaven. The disciples soon learned that his crucifixion and resurrection were critical to our redemption from our sinful nature and the restoration of true spiritual life with God.

As the prophets foretold, the sinless Christ had to first be sacrificed for our sins in order to reconcile us to a holy God and bring us back into his righteous kingdom. Through the cross, God devised a way to justify the ungodly so that we could be reconciled to our Creator and become members of his righteous kingdom again. If we are to spend eternity with a holy God in his paradise in heaven, then we first have to be made holy and righteous, as Christ was holy and righteous. Christ's death and resurrection give us that opportunity. We all need to repent of our sins, accept Christ and his sacrifice for our sins, be raised from spiritual death, and reconnect with our Creator, who is Life. The disciples eventually understood the necessity of Christ's crucifixion. But they still expected Christ to set up his messianic kingdom after his resurrection.

We live in a secular society that knows very little about the Bible. But the disciples lived in a deeply religious nation with priests, rabbis, Pharisees, and teachers of the law. The Jewish disciples grew up attending synagogues, where they were exposed to the prophecies of the coming Messiah and his messianic kingdom. And even though many of them were simple fishermen, they knew their Jewish Scriptures. Read what Philip said about Christ when he first met him:

> The next day Jesus decided to go to Galilee. He found Philip and said to him, "Follow me.". . . Philip found Nathanael and said to him, "We have found him of whom Moses in the Law and also the prophets wrote, Jesus of Nazareth, the son of Joseph." (John 1:43–45)

Philip and the disciples expected the Messiah to be a descendant of David, who would overthrow the tyrannical Roman authorities and become the king and ruler of Israel, restoring them to an abundant "promised land." And based on the following prophecy from Jeremiah, they expected Christ to set up his messianic kingdom in their lifetimes:

> The word that came to Jeremiah from the LORD: . . . "For behold, days are coming, declares the LORD, when I will restore the fortunes of my people, . . . I will bring them back to the land that I gave to their fathers, . . . I will break his yoke from off your neck, . . . and foreigners shall no more make a servant of him. . . . I will fulfill the promise I made to the house of Israel and the house of Judah. In those days and at that time I will cause a righteous Branch to spring up for David [the Messiah], and **he shall execute justice and righteousness in the land.** In those days Judah will be saved, and **Jerusalem will dwell securely.**" (Jer. 30:1, 3, 8–9; 33:14–16)

Jeremiah is not just speaking of the Messiah providing for the spiritual salvation of Israel. He is also describing the messianic kingdom, with real consequences on this earth. The Messiah will bring them back to the land promised to Abraham. He will liberate Israel from foreign occupation. He will establish justice and righteousness in the land. He will create peace in Jerusalem; they will "dwell securely," without fear of invasion by hostile enemies. The Messiah, by definition, will establish a messianic kingdom on this earth. The disciples' excitement and anticipation for his coming reign must have been quite intense. But the coming of the messianic kingdom did not go exactly as they thought it would.

John the Baptist's Confusion

One of the saddest events in the New Testament occurred when John the Baptist became so confused because of his imprisonment by King Herod that he began to have doubts that Jesus was the Christ. John baptized Christ and had the extraordinary experience of hearing God the Father's voice from heaven. Jesus even claimed to be a fulfillment of the prophecies found in Isaiah. At the beginning of his public ministry in the synagogue in Nazareth, Jesus read from the book of Isaiah:

> The Spirit of the Lord is upon me, because he has anointed me to proclaim good news to the poor. He has sent me **to proclaim liberty to the captives** and recovery of sight to the blind, **to set at liberty those who are oppressed**, to proclaim the year of the Lord's favor. (Luke 4:18–19)

Israel had been conquered by the pagan Romans, and the Jews were oppressed by their tyrannical rule. The Roman overlords appointed rulers such as Herod to impose their unjust regime over Israel, levying heavy taxes on the Jews to enrich themselves. But the Lord's favor had arrived with the coming of the Messiah, who had the power of the Holy Spirit to heal the blind, free prisoners, and liberate the oppressed!

Yet, while Christ was preaching the good news and demonstrating remarkable supernatural power through incredible miracles, John the Baptist remained imprisoned by a political tyrant ruling with only earthly powers. He must have been profoundly sad and disillusioned while he sat in prison thinking about these Scriptures. Where was the "liberty to the captives" that went along with this miraculous power? Where was the messianic kingdom predicted by the prophets? Perplexed and despondent, John the Baptist eventually sent his disciples to inquire of Jesus:

> "Are you the one who is to come, or shall we look for another?" And Jesus answered them, "Go and tell John what you hear and see: the blind receive their sight and the lame walk, lepers are cleansed and the deaf hear, and the dead are raised up, and the poor have good news preached to them." (Matt. 11:3–5)

I am sure Jesus' answer was reassuring. But if he was the Messiah, then why didn't he exercise his authority and liberate John from prison? Instead, during Herod's birthday party, John was killed and his head presented to Herod's illegitimate wife on a platter. It was this kind of tyranny and gruesome evil that the Messiah was supposed to put an end to. All these prophecies seemed fulfilled in Jesus of Nazareth—except the part where he would bring forth justice to the nations, starting with "liberty to the captives." Both Rome's rule and King Herod's treatment of John were surely unjust. So where was the prophesied reign of justice?

The Disciples Were Also Confused

John the Baptist was not the only one confused by the missing messianic kingdom. The disciples were so convinced that Jesus was going to break the bonds of the Roman yoke, liberate Israel, and establish the messianic kingdom described by the prophets, that they made fools of themselves by jockeying for power in what they thought was the imminent reign of Christ. During the Last Supper, before his crucifixion, they even argued over who would have the most prestigious position in his impending reign: "A dispute also arose among them, as to which of them was to be regarded as the greatest" (Luke 22:24). But perhaps the most embarrassing episode illustrating their misunderstanding of the timing of Jesus' messianic reign is when the mother of James and John (known as the sons of Zebedee) asked Christ to appoint her two sons to leading positions of authority in his upcoming kingdom:

> Then the mother of the sons of Zebedee came up to him with her sons, and kneeling before him she asked him for something. And he said to her, "What do you want?" She said to him, "Say that these two sons of mine are to sit, one at your right hand and one at your left, in your kingdom." Jesus answered, "You do not know what you are asking. Are you able to drink the cup that I am to drink?" They said to him, "We are able." He said to them, "You will drink my cup, but to sit at my right hand and at my left is not mine to grant, but it is for those for whom it has been prepared by my Father." (Matt. 20:20–23)

The mother of James and John was looking forward to her sons ruling with Christ in his messianic kingdom—with all the implied power, prestige, and wealth that comes with positions of authority in a worldly empire. Ironically, little did she know that for her sons to be on his right and left sides in the circumstances at that time, would have placed them on the two crosses flanking Christ's cross in the impending crucifixion!

When these two disciples embarrassed themselves by sending their mother to secure high positions of authority in his anticipated reign, Christ gently rebuked them for their self-serving lust for power. But at the same time, he amazingly affirmed the legitimacy of the positions they were requesting. There will indeed be positions of authority and leadership when he establishes his kingdom and rules the world. But those positions will be decided by the Father: "To sit at my right hand and at my left is not mine to grant, but it is for those for whom it has been prepared by my Father" (Matt. 20:23).

In effect, rather than telling the mother and her sons that the request itself was wrong, Christ answered by saying that even though their motives were wrong and their timing was off, they were simply asking the wrong person for positions of authority in his messianic kingdom. God the Father makes those decisions.

Christ also promised the disciples that they would assist him in ruling over the twelve tribes of Israel when he does eventually rule the world. In fact, they will experience a real paradise on this earth as a reward for sacrificially following him:

> Jesus said to them, "Truly, I say to you, in the new world [the restored Edenic earth], when the Son of Man will sit on his glorious throne [and rule the world], you who have followed me will also sit on twelve thrones, judging the twelve tribes of Israel [assisting Christ in governing Israel]. And everyone who has left houses or brothers or sisters or father or mother or children or lands, for my name's sake, will receive a hundredfold [reward when the earth is renewed] and [in addition] will inherit eternal life [in the Father's heavenly kingdom in the age to come]." (Matt. 19:28–29)

When Christ, as the Son of God, rules over his restored creation, the disciples will then inherit a hundredfold reward and an abundant life on the restored Edenic earth. And they will have prominent positions of authority over Israel—before they inherit eternal life in the age to come.

After Jesus was resurrected, the disciples were still confused about when Christ was going to establish his kingdom and they would assist him in ruling over Israel. Maybe they had missed the part about the

Messiah being crucified for their sins, even though Isaiah had predicted as much. But with his resurrection, he was invincible to the Romans! So why not establish his glorious messianic kingdom now?

> So when they had come together, they asked him, "Lord, will you at this time restore the kingdom to Israel?" He said to them, "It is not for you to know times or seasons that the Father has fixed by his own authority." (Acts 1:6–7)

Notice that Jesus does not rebuke them for asking the question or for being slow to understand. He knew exactly what Philip and the disciples were asking him. He affirmed there would be a restoration of Israel, but it was not for them to know the time, for the Father has set the time when it will occur; just as the Father will determine who will have positions of authority in his kingdom. It is not a question of *whether* the restoration occurs when the Son of Man rules the world, but *when*.

In the meantime, Christ instructed them to be evangelists, preaching throughout the world that he was indeed the Messiah:

> "But you will receive power when the Holy Spirit has come upon you, and you will be my witnesses in Jerusalem and in all Judea and Samaria, and to the end of the earth." And when he had said these things, as they were looking on, he was lifted up, and a cloud took him out of their sight. (Acts 1:8–9)

The Messiah's sudden departure and ascension to heaven must have left the disciples utterly bewildered. The Messiah, born in the town of Bethlehem in Judea, was supposed to liberate Israel, restore the nation to glory, and even rule the world—and now he is gone! He was supposed to establish God's kingdom on this earth such that it would be characterized by peace, justice, righteousness, and prosperity. Instead, he left his followers in this fallen, demonic world. Indeed, as the apostles evangelized the world, it would take the Holy Spirit to convince people that Jesus was the Messiah, given his missing messianic kingdom.

Christ sent the Holy Spirit to comfort his people, but the world remains Satan's dominion of darkness, with evil prevalent throughout the affairs of man. It is definitely not paradise on earth, and the world remains heavily influenced by demons. As the apostle John teaches: "We know that we are children of God, and that the whole world is under the control of the evil one" (1 John 5:19 NIV). If Christ was currently sitting on his throne governing the world, then it would be under the control of the Holy One, and it would be paradise on earth.

Revelation

Finally, we consider the difficult book of Revelation written by the apostle John, who continued to experience Roman oppression as he was exiled on the island of Patmos for preaching the gospel. John not only affirms that one day Christ will rule the world when Satan is removed, but also that his reign will last for a thousand years. John teaches that the saints will inherit the Son's earthly kingdom, as promised by Christ:

> And they sang a new song, saying, "Worthy are you to take the scroll and to open its seals, for you were slain, and by your blood you ransomed people for God from every tribe and language and people and nation, and you have made them a kingdom and priests to our God, and *they shall reign on the earth*." (Rev. 5:9–10)

Notice John teaches that the ransomed people of God will inherit a messianic kingdom that will be "on the earth." In line with the prophets, John is distinctly referencing God's people from all nations inheriting a kingdom that is on the restored earth—before they inherit the eternal new heavens and new earth after this earth perishes.

But Philip, Peter, and the majority of the ransomed people of God have already died, so how on earth will they inherit Christ's millennial kingdom? John reveals that the solution to this dilemma is that there will be a resurrection of the departed saints at the beginning of the millennium. John specifically identifies those martyred during the Great Tribulation as experiencing this first resurrection. But one can easily conclude that all the departed ransomed people of God, including the disciples, will experience this resurrection so that they can "reign on the earth" during Christ's millennial kingdom. John revealed:

> They [the ransomed people of God from all nations] came to life and reigned with Christ for a thousand years [on the earth].... This is the first resurrection. Blessed and holy is the one who shares in the first resurrection! Over such the second death has no power, but they will be priests of God and of Christ, and they will reign with him for a thousand years [on the restored earth]. (Rev. 20:4–6)

This first resurrection will enable the departed saints to inherit Christ's 1,000-year messianic kingdom, which is described by the prophets as an Adamic paradise, with men and women getting married and continuing to fill an Edenic earth with their offspring. This would fulfill Christ's promise to the disciples that they would inherit the restored Edenic earth as a hundredfold reward in this Genesis age *before* they inherit eternal life in the age to come.

After the saints have experienced this Edenic paradise for a thousand years, John teaches that the Genesis creation perishes. This is the end of this creation, or the Omega, when Christ sits on his Great White Throne to judge all mankind. The sons of God will then experience the final resurrection of their immortal bodies so that they can inherit eternal life in the Father's kingdom, or the eternal new heavens and new earth. At the same time, unbelievers will inherit the lake of fire. John revealed that Christ taught:

> Behold, I am coming soon, bringing my recompense with me, to repay each one for what he has done [on Judgment Day]. I am the Alpha and the Omega, the first and the last, the beginning [of this Genesis creation] and the end [of this Genesis creation]. (Rev. 22:12–13)

> Then I saw a new heaven and a new earth, for the first heaven and the first earth had passed away,... And he who was seated on the throne said, "Behold, I am making all things new [Christ creates the new earth as the eternal habitat for the sons of God]." (Rev. 21:1–5)

When we believe in Christ, we become restored men or women of God *and* children of God. John reveals that as men and women of God, we are destined to experience the first resurrection so that we can inherit the Son's restored Edenic earth. He also taught that as children of God, we are destined to experience the final resurrection, so we can inherit the Father's eternal new earth.

Today's Confusion over Christ's Second Coming

But at this point in my presentation of the gospel to my non-Christian friend, I must admit that evangelical theologians today do not agree on God's plan of redemption. Evangelical theologians agree that the followers of Christ will inherit eternal life in heaven and will not experience the wrath of God on Judgment Day, but, unfortunately, they remain deeply divided as to whether there is a restoration of this Genesis creation to its Edenic condition for a thousand years before the eternal kingdom.

The current views on God's endgame can be extremely complicated and confusing because theologians have done a poor job of answering the following questions:

When does Christ return?
- Does he return to this earth at the beginning of the millennium to establish his messianic kingdom on this earth, as claimed by premillennialists?
- Or does he return on the last day to destroy this earth and take the immortal sons of God to heaven for eternity, as claimed by amillennialists and postmillennialists?

Where is Christ if, and when, he rules the world?
- Does he physically return to this earth to rule the world, as claimed by premillennialists?
- Or does he rule the Christianized world from his throne in heaven, as claimed by postmillennialists?

What is the nature of the first resurrection?
- Is it of the spirits of believers upon conversion and/or of their spirits to the celestial realm of heaven upon mortal death, as claimed by amillennialists and postmillennialists?
- Or is it of the raptured, immortal bodies of the sons of God, as claimed by premillennialists?
- Or is it of the natural, mortal bodies of the men and women of God, as claimed by the early millennialists?

When does the rapture of the saints occur?
- Does the rapture of the immortal sons of God occur *at the first resurrection* so that the glorified saints can inherit the restored earth, as claimed by premillennialists?
- Or does the rapture occur *at the final resurrection* so that the sons of God can inherit the eternal new earth, as claimed by amillennialists and postmillennialists?

Evangelical theologians have not been able to provide a coherent answer to these basic questions, which is a great disservice to people like my non-Christian friend. He is drawn to spending eternity as a child of God with a loving Father in heaven. But because he and his wife have not been able to have children, he is also drawn to living in a human paradise on this earth where all his aspirations for an abundant life as a husband, father, and grandfather would be fulfilled.

The disciples were befuddled by the fact that Christ did not establish his earthly kingdom during his first coming. And they may have embarrassed themselves by jockeying for power in what they thought was his imminent reign. But today, biblical scholars and theologians remain equally befuddled about what transpires at Christ's second coming. And they should be thoroughly embarrassed by their failure to provide simple, logical answers to these basic questions.

Many of these scholars and theologians have spent decades studying and teaching the Bible at prestigious seminaries. And many have written numerous articles and scholarly books on the subject. Yet, none can provide a rational and coherent understanding of God's plan of redemption to those who want to know more about God's plans for the future. Are we just going to heaven? Or do we first inherit a restored paradise on this earth for a thousand years? How can we have faith in God and share our faith with others if we do not know what to hope for?

During the Reformation, many of the Catholic Church's flawed doctrines on salvation were corrected by theologians who reexamined God's Word. But that was more than five hundred years ago, and since that time, little progress has been made in correcting the church's confusing doctrines of eschatology. The time has come for theologians to go back to the Scriptures and correct their flawed doctrines on God's endgame. When these theologians are right, they are right. But when their teachings plainly contradict the Scriptures, they are wrong.

Premillennialists claim that because Christ did not establish his messianic kingdom the first time he came to this earth, he must return to this earth once again at the beginning of the millennium to finally establish his earthly kingdom. He is the Messiah, after all. But as amillennialists point out, this is highly problematic, for Christ and the apostles teach that when Christ comes again, he destroys this earth, and the raptured sons of God are destined for the Father's imperishable kingdom of heaven—not the Son's restored Genesis earth. Numerous verses support this assertion.

But if premillennialism is biblically flawed, then so is amillennialism. Amillennialists claim that there is no messianic kingdom on this earth as described by the prophets. This present evil age continues right up until the last day, and there is never an age of righteous humanity on this earth. Our human aspirations for an abundant life on this earth as male and female human beings are never fulfilled. The saints only inherit the Father's eternal kingdom of heaven when Christ returns to rapture the immortal sons of God.

But Christ himself *confirmed* to his disciples on several occasions that there would indeed be a future restoration of Israel, as described by the prophets. He even promised the disciples that they would assist him in ruling over the twelve tribes of Israel. He also promised them that their human aspirations for an abundant life on this earth will be fulfilled a hundredfold when the earth is restored to its Edenic condition. Amillennialists have a Messiah without his *promised* messianic kingdom.

Postmillennialists, like amillennialists, also teach that Christ's second coming occurs on the last day. But they believe we can usher in a golden age of Christianity on this earth if we are faithful in evangelizing the nations. Yet, they admit that the curse on the earth is never removed, and Satan remains operational in this world until the last day. So even if we do disciple all nations, it still will not be paradise on this earth.

All the current versions of God's endgame have some merit. But they all have major flaws because they contradict some important Scriptures. This may explain why a consensus has never been reached on the subject and the debate rages on.

Postrestorationalism

I will present an alternative version of God's plan of redemption that can hopefully resolve the confusion about Christ's missing messianic kingdom. This approach affirms the assertion by amillennialists and postmillennialists that Christ's second coming is on the last day. It also affirms the assertion by premillennialists that there must be a literal 1,000-year restoration of this Genesis creation to its Edenic condition before the saints inherit the eternal new heavens and new earth. And it affirms the assertion by postmillennialists that Christ, as the Son of God, can rule the world from his throne in heaven without having to return to this earth.

The solution is elegantly simple, and I am surprised that modern theologians have never considered it. It is a view that the early church millennialists held for more than four hundred years, with a few important corrections and modifications. Like modern premillennialists, the early millennialists believed that Christ will return at the beginning of the millennium to establish his messianic kingdom. But unlike modern premillennialists, they believed that the *first resurrection will be of the natural bodies* of the departed saints, not of the raptured bodies. The resurrected saints will experience marriage and procreation as they fill an Edenic earth, as described by the prophets. That is because the ransomed people of God are destined to inherit the restored natural earth for a thousand years—a natural body for a restored natural earth.

They compare the first resurrection to the resurrection of the natural body of Lazarus by Jesus. Lazarus was regenerated into a natural body, and he could have gotten married and had children, for all we know. His second experience of life on this earth, however, was probably not any more pleasant than his first, for he came back to life on a cursed earth that was still under Satan's dominion. But when Lazarus and all the saints come back to life during the millennium, it will be paradise on earth because Satan will be removed, Christ will be ruling the world, the earth will be restored to its Edenic condition, and righteous men and women will be ruling the nations on Christ's behalf.

Furthermore, the early millennialists believed the *final resurrection* on the last day is when the saints are raptured into their eternal bodies not given in marriage. That is because the immortal sons of God are destined to inherit the eternal new heavens and new earth. To inherit eternal life in the Father's eternal kingdom, one needs an eternal body like Christ's resurrected body. According to the early millennialists, the rapture is not pre-trib, mid-trib, or even post-trib. Rather, they taught that it is post-millennial, or *after* the millennium *at the final resurrection on the last day.*

In their writings, they make a good biblical case for this understanding of the two resurrections. They also claim that these teachings on the nature of the two resurrections come directly from Jesus and John. Yet, no current view on God's endgame has even considered this understanding of the nature of the two resurrections. In fact, you will not find a single reference in any modern commentary on Revelation to the possibility that the first resurrection could be of the natural body. This is a glaring omission by biblical scholars, given that it was a view held by these early church millennialists for more than four hundred years. Moreover, it was a logical interpretation by these early church fathers, given how easily Christ resurrected Lazarus with a simple shout at his tomb. John seems to be describing a similar shout by Christ from heaven that is heard around the world that enables all the departed saints to come to life in their natural bodies to inherit his millennium kingdom. Chapters 21–24 are devoted to the very important teachings of the early church millennialists.

I agree with the early church millennialists' interpretation of these two resurrections because it is historical, logical, and conforms to the Scriptures. But I believe the Scriptures teach that instead of Christ returning to this earth to establish his millennial kingdom, Christ rules the world during the millennium from his throne in heaven at the right hand of the Father. As the Creator of this world, the Son of God does not need to return to this earth to rule over his own creation.

The ascended Son of God already has the authority and power to rule over his creation from his throne in heaven. But he is waiting on the Father to determine when his millennial reign will begin. During the millennium, he simply uses this divine authority and power to reclaim his creation and rule the world from his throne in heaven.

Summary

This version of God's endgame is called postrestorationalism and can be summarized as follows:

- When Satan is removed from this world, Christ, as the Son of God, rules over his restored Edenic earth during the millennium from his throne in heaven.
- The first resurrection at the beginning of the millennium will be of the Adamic bodies of the departed saints in order for the ransomed people of God to inherit the Son's kingdom—natural bodies for a restored natural earth.
- Christ returns *after* (post-) the 1,000-year restoration of this Genesis creation on the last day to rapture the saints and usher in the Father's eternal kingdom of heaven.
- The final resurrection will be of the immortal bodies of the sons of God so that they can inherit the Father's imperishable kingdom of heaven—eternal bodies for the eternal new earth.

This is a simple solution to understanding God's plan of redemption. It is a well-designed and well-constructed house of biblical ideas, for it has all the major biblical components of the house, and they are all properly arranged. The fact that it is similar to the eschatology of the early church millennialists, who had access to the oral teachings of the apostles, also gives it credibility. Most important, it conforms to all the relevant biblical data, as this book will demonstrate.

3

Method of Interpreting the Scriptures

Review

In the last chapter, I explored the confusion that John the Baptist and the disciples experienced when Christ did not set up his messianic kingdom while he was on this earth. The prophets had predicted that during the messianic kingdom, the world would be characterized by peace, justice, righteousness, and prosperity. The Messiah would usher in an age of righteous humanity for Israel and all nations. The disciples knew their Scriptures and were expecting Christ to overthrow the tyrannical Roman government and establish a Jewish-led kingdom in its place. They even made fools of themselves by jockeying for positions of power in what they thought was the imminent reign of Christ.

Instead, Jesus Christ allowed himself to be crucified by the Romans. And when he was resurrected, his disciples had hoped he would then overthrow the oppressive Roman Empire and establish his messianic kingdom. But he left this world and ascended into heaven, leaving his followers in this demonic, fallen world. As a result, the world remains characterized by strife and war instead of peace, injustice instead of justice, unrighteousness instead of righteousness, and systemic poverty instead of abundant prosperity. We continue to experience an age of unrighteous humanity on a cursed earth.

PART 1: Understanding the Adamic Order of Being

Before theologians make a biblical case for their respective eschatology, they often explain their methods of interpreting and analyzing the Scriptures to discern God's endgame. This field of study is known as "biblical hermeneutics." The objective is to properly read and interpret biblical data and develop it into a rational theology of the future.

When developing their eschatology, many theologians prefer to analyze the Scriptures based on which passages are literal and which are figurative. But this is not always helpful because they then argue about what is literal or figurative without advancing the discussion. For example, in Revelation 20 John has a vision of Satan bound by a great chain and locked up in a pit when Christ's reign begins:

> Then I saw an angel coming down from heaven, holding in his hand the key to the bottomless pit and a great chain. And he seized the dragon, that ancient serpent, who is the devil and Satan, and bound him for a thousand years, and threw him into the pit, and shut it and sealed it over him, so that he might not deceive the nations any longer, until the thousand years were ended. (Rev. 20:1–3)

I do not think any of these theologians believe that an evil spirit such as Satan would literally be bound with a steel chain. This is obviously a metaphor describing some event involving Satan. But what is John attempting to convey with this portrayal of Satan's imprisonment? Is the millennium that follows this event a literal earthly kingdom, or is it a metaphor for Christ's current reign over the saints in the celestial realm of heaven? The bottomless pit, or abyss, is depicted in the Scriptures as a kind of spiritual prison for demons. Like a criminal in his day, John described Satan being bound with a chain and thrown into a pit, which is then shut and sealed. Satan is a fallen angel, and he has been operational in this world ever since Adam and Eve rebelled against God, allowing Satan into the world. He is a powerful and clever evil spirit, and he influences every aspect of human activity. Humans are spiritual beings with sinful natures, so it does not take much for Satan to influence us to think and perform sinful acts that are contrary to God's will.

The question is not whether the binding of Satan with a great chain is metaphorical or literal, because both camps recognize it as metaphorical. Rather, does this elaborate metaphor describe a complete removal of Satan from this world in a future millennium, or a partial removal of Satan today for the purpose of salvation?

Premillennialists believe John is using the metaphor of the binding of Satan with a chain to convey the fact that, at some point in the future, Satan and all the demons are going to be completely removed from this world so that mankind can experience an age of righteous humanity during Christ's millennial reign.

Amillennialists interpret this metaphor to mean that Satan is only partially bound. They interpret the binding of Satan as a repetition of Christ's parable of the binding of the strong man. Satan is bound so that Christ can rob him of those held captive by demon possession (Luke 11:21–22). Once we are rescued from Satan's dominion, however, we remain in Satan's demonic world of temptation, influence, and control. Amillennialists believe John is describing a similar partial binding of Satan in the present millennial age. This enables Christ to rescue his chosen people from all nations from Satan's lies and deceptions to bring them into his righteous millennial kingdom today. Yet, Satan is still able to roam the world seeking to devour Christians and non-Christians alike.

I believe premillennialists have the better argument that this metaphor describes the complete removal of Satan from this world when Revelation portrays him as bound and thrown into a bottomless pit, which is sealed for a thousand years.

Today, when someone commits a heinous crime, people often say that the evildoer should be locked up in a maximum security prison and the key thrown away. This expression means that the criminal would be completely removed from society and prevented from ever harming anyone again. This punishment would not be a form of probation or community service, where he could still roam the world looking for victims. If he is released from prison in fifty years and commits another horrible crime, many would say to kill the evildoer.

John seems to be describing a similar series of events. Satan is locked up for a thousand years by an angel in a maximum security prison made just for demons, where he has no contact with unbelievers or believers. Since his place of imprisonment is completely sealed, he cannot escape and harm anyone. The angel that imprisoned him is the only one who holds the key to free him. After the thousand years have ended, he is let loose on the world once again to lead one last rebellion among unbelievers against God's people, who have recovered from war. Then he is recaptured by an angel and sent to the lake of fire for eternal destruction, never to be heard from again.

The book of Revelation is full of similar metaphors. They just need to be properly interpreted. For example, at the battle of Armageddon at the end of the Tribulation, Christ appears in heaven riding on a white horse. Premillennialists interpret this event to be the second coming of Christ on the clouds when he returns to this earth to establish his millennial kingdom. But in chapter 6, when I critique premillennialism, I will demonstrate that when one carefully reads this passage, it becomes clear that John never depicts Christ leaving the celestial realm on his white horse and descending to the earth. Rather, he is depicted as remaining in the celestial realm when he defeats the Antichrist and his armies and sends an angel to bind Satan. He then rules the world during the millennium from his throne in heaven.

God's Covenants

When developing a theology of the future, theologians also like to analyze the Scriptures based on God's covenants with Israel. Amillennialists believe God's covenant with Israel to restore them to an abundant promised land was conditional upon the Jews accepting their Messiah. Since the Jews largely rejected him, they consider this covenant null and void. And the nation has been permanently exiled. The temple's destruction in AD 70 is proof of this rejection.

Amillennialists claim that a new covenant with all God's people, regardless of race, has replaced this old, obsolete covenant. Repentant Jews simply join the body of Christ. And Christ and his church are the new Israel. There is no future restoration of the nation of Israel. The Jewish and Gentile believers who make up the church are all destined for the eternal kingdom of heaven, not a Jewish-led messianic kingdom on this earth.

Premillennialists argue that the hard-hearted first-century Jews do not have veto power over God's plans for Israel and this world. They believe there will indeed be a future dispensation when the Jewish people will repent en masse, which will lead to the restoration of Israel and all the nations in the messianic kingdom.

Again, I believe premillennialists have the better argument, for there is solid biblical evidence that the rejection of Israel is a temporary abandonment, and that repentant Israel will again be used by God to usher in the messianic kingdom. Or as Isaiah says:

> "For a brief moment I deserted you, but with great compassion I will gather you. In overflowing anger for a moment I hid my face from you [unfaithful Israel], but with everlasting love I will have compassion on you," says the LORD, your Redeemer. . . . "For the mountains may depart and the hills be removed, but my steadfast love shall not depart from you, and *my covenant of peace shall not be removed*," says the LORD, who has compassion on you. . . . "In righteousness you shall be established [as a righteous nation in the messianic kingdom]." (Isa. 54:7–14)

According to Isaiah, this future repentance by Israel is followed by the messianic kingdom being realized on this earth when the nation will experience a time of peace and righteousness. That is how Isaiah defines God's covenant with Israel based on God's unconditional love.

Paul also alludes to a future time when Israel will repent and believe in their own Messiah, which not only leads to the personal salvation of individual Jews, but also to the salvation of all of Israel, or the nation itself. Paul is probably referencing Isaiah's prophecy:

> Lest you be wise in your own sight, I do not want you to be unaware of this mystery, brothers: a partial hardening has come upon Israel ["I hid my face from you"], until the fullness of the Gentiles has come in [then "I will have compassion on you"]. And in this way all Israel will be saved, as it is written, "The Deliverer will come from Zion, he will banish ungodliness from Jacob; and this will be my covenant with them when I take away their sins [a "covenant of peace" with Israel when Christ establishes a righteous nation]." (Rom. 11:25–27)

This future repentance and conversion of the Jews described by Isaiah and Paul leads to the messianic kingdom for the whole nation. Despite this biblical evidence, many theologians continue to debate whether God's covenant with Israel was conditional or unconditional.

As such, this method of interpretation has not been able to resolve the debate over God's plan of redemption.

Already and Not Yet

When developing a theology of the future, many theologians adhere to the theme of God's inaugurated kingdom that "already is, in this present age, and is yet to come, in a future consummated kingdom" when Christ returns to usher in his kingdom. But these concepts clearly have some overlap. For example, John says:

> Beloved, we are God's children now [already, in the current covenant, dispensation, or inaugurated kingdom in this age], and what we will be [in the eternal age to come] has not yet appeared [yet to come in a future dispensation or age]; but we know that when he appears we shall be like him [transformed into an immortal, glorified body like his resurrected body], because we shall see him as he is [in his consummated kingdom]. (1 John 3:2)

John is teaching that even though we remain in mortal bodies on a perishable earth, we have already become God's children and are already in the inaugurated kingdom of God. He is also describing the rapture of the saints when Christ returns and our natural bodies are transformed into eternal bodies like his glorified body. We will then enter God's consummated kingdom in all its glory.

Theologians, however, then argue over what is yet to come when Christ returns to rapture the saints. Premillennialists would say he ushers in his messianic kingdom on this earth for the raptured saints. While amillennialists would say he ushers in his Father's eternal kingdom of heaven for the raptured saints. These are very different views on the future. As a result, the "already and not yet" approach has not helped resolve the debate over God's endgame.

Historical-Grammatical Method

The historical-grammatical method of interpreting the Scriptures is universally accepted by evangelical theologians. This method looks at the original intended message the author wanted to convey to his readers based on the original Hebrew or Greek words and their proper translation into English, Spanish, and so forth. It also considers the context of their overall writings and the historical context of when they wrote the book or letter. I have found it extremely rare that a poorly translated Hebrew or Greek word leads to a misinterpretation of the text. Today's modern translations are excellent, and the scholars who work on these translations should be commended. The historical context, however, always needs further exploration, for it is very important when determining what these biblical writers meant.

Consider the doctrine of pretribulation premillennialism as an illustration of this method of interpretation. These theologians believe the rapture can occur at any moment. This doctrine is based on the following verses in a letter from Paul to the young church at Thessalonica:

> For the Lord himself will descend from heaven with a cry of command, . . . And the dead in Christ will rise first. Then we who are alive, who are left, will be caught up [raptured] together with them in the clouds to meet the Lord in the air, and so we will always be with the Lord. . . . For you yourselves are fully aware that the day of the Lord will come like a thief in the night. (1 Thess. 4:16–17—5:2)

In the book *Evidence for the Rapture: A Biblical Case for Pretribulation*, the authors claim:
- "Paul's first letter to the Thessalonians contains the central Pauline teaching on the pretribulation rapture."
- "The return of Christ could be at any moment."
- "There are no signs or events that make it possible to predict when it will occur."
- "Paul believed the rapture was imminent (it could happen at any time)."[1]

In short, this view asserts that Paul taught that there are no prophetic events that must occur before Christ can return to rapture the saints.

Some seminaries, such as Dallas Theological Seminary, include this interpretation as part of their doctrinal statement that must be

---

1 John F. Hart, ed., *Evidence for the Rapture* (Chicago: Moody Publishers, 2015), 20, 82, 168.

adhered to by all their professors. The popular *Left Behind* fictional series of novels is also based on this premise.

The idea that an event will happen suddenly can mean it could occur at any moment. But it could also simply mean that it will occur very quickly. For example, when God saw how violent and depraved mankind had become during the days of Noah, he prophesied that a flood would soon destroy that generation. But the flood could not happen at that moment because Noah and his family had to first build the ark to be prepared for the flood. Until Noah finished the ark, the flood was not an imminent event. There were prophesied events that first had to take place. When the flood did come, it only came suddenly on those who were not prepared for God's judgment.

Let's now see what Paul meant to teach the Thessalonian Christians based on the historical-grammatical method of interpretation. For the rapture to be an imminent event for us today, it must have been able to occur at any moment for the Thessalonians, to whom the letter was originally addressed. Paul wrote this letter in AD 51. If he had meant to teach a pretribulation rapture as claimed by these theologians, then Christ could have returned in AD 51 or soon after that date to rapture the saints.

But Christ himself taught that there is a specific event that must take place before he returns. And that event had not yet occurred in AD 51 when the letter was written. Before Christ ascended to heaven, he informed Peter and the disciples that Peter would live to be an old man and would be martyred before he came again:

> Truly, truly, I say to you, when you were young, you used to dress yourself and walk wherever you wanted, but when you are old, you will stretch out your hands, and another will dress you and carry you where you do not want to go. (This he said to show by what kind of death he was to glorify God.) (John 21:18–19)

In other words, Christ taught that Peter would grow old and be martyred before Christ returned to rapture Peter and the saints. Therefore, Christ could not return until Peter was old and was martyred. Peter would be among the saints who were asleep when Christ returned.

Yet when Paul wrote this letter to the Thessalonians in AD 51 teaching them about the rapture, Peter was only middle-aged. He was not martyred in Rome until eighteen years later in AD 69, when he was an old man. If Christ had returned to rapture Peter and the saints in AD 51 when Paul wrote his letter, then Peter would have been middle-aged and very much alive. And Jesus would have been a false prophet!

Or if Paul had intended to teach that Christ could return at any moment in AD 51 while Peter was only middle-aged and still alive, then he would have been a false teacher! Of course, Christ was not a false prophet and Paul was not a false teacher.

Obviously, Paul did not intend to have his letter to the Thessalonians be understood as teaching an any-moment rapture. Therefore, based on the historical-grammatical method of interpretation, pre-tribulation premillennialism is the false teaching. Yet, one could fill a small library with books by theologians teaching this doctrine.

In fact, the book from which I previously quoted making the case for the any-moment rapture contains chapters from ten different scholars, and yet none of them wrestle with Christ's prophecy and this obvious contradiction to their interpretation of Paul's teachings.

Two Creations

I believe there is a method one can use to analyze the Scriptures that does have the potential to resolve the confusion over God's endgame. And it is a method theologians have not recognized or utilized in formulating their respective eschatology. This method of interpreting and organizing the Scriptures into a logical biblical theology of the future is based on two creations and two kingdoms of the triune God:

Two creations:
1. The Adamic creation
2. The new creation as sons of God

Two kingdoms of the triune God:
1. The Son's earthly kingdom for the restored Adamic creation in this Genesis age
2. The Father's heavenly kingdom for the new creation as sons of God in the eternal age to come

The Adamic Order of Being

The Bible describes different kinds of creatures, or what I refer to as "orders of being." For example, angels are a unique order of being. They are spiritual beings without bodies. Each angel represents an individual spirit or person, such as the angels Gabriel and Michael. They are immortal creatures because as spirits they do not need outside nourishment to sustain their lives. And without bodies they cannot experience marriage. The archangel Michael does not have an angelic wife nor newborn angels crawling around heaven.

Humans are a different kind of creature. We are spiritual creatures like angels, but our human spirits are contained within male or female bodies. And our natural bodies are mortal because we need outside air and food to sustain them. In addition, humans are creatures with sexual bodies who reproduce their kind, producing other embodied spiritual humans as sons and daughters. In the beginning, God created the Adamic order of being:

> Then God said, "Let us make man in our image, after our likeness." ... So God created man in his own image, in the image of God he created him; male and female he created them. ... And God said to them, "Be fruitful and multiply and fill the earth" ... Therefore, a man shall leave his father and mother and hold fast to his wife, and they shall become one flesh. (Gen. 1:26—2:24)

Man is defined as male and female individuals, who marry in sexual union as one flesh, become fathers and mothers, who reproduce more male and female human beings. These humans, in turn, fill and subdue the earth with their offspring.

Moreover, the Adamic order of being is defined as being made in the image of God. God is three persons in companionship but joined together as one God with one will. Mankind reflects this image as two persons joined together in a marriage companionship as one flesh. Further, God rules over and manages his dominion of heaven, and like God, man rules over and manages his dominion on this earth on God's behalf.

But unlike God, man is not omniscient. Adam and Eve could care for the garden in the region of Eden, but the world was way too big for them to subdue and manage by themselves. That is why they were to multiply, having sons and daughters who would fill the untamed earth, subdue and develop it, and then properly manage it. They would develop these wilderness areas into Edenic gardens, and create beautiful, sustainable human and animal habitats.

Genesis further reveals that God fashioned a male body of flesh and blood for Adam out of dust. God, who is Spirit and Life, then breathed spiritual life into his physical body and he became a living, embodied, spiritual creature. The person who would be known as Eve was then made from Adam's rib with a female human anatomy. They were sexual, spiritual creatures with natural bodies of flesh and blood designed for marriage and reproduction. Most important, as spiritual creatures, they were a man and woman of God in fellowship with their Creator.

In short, as defined in Genesis, we are sexual, spiritual creatures with natural bodies that are either male or female. We experience marriage, and through sexual union we reproduce sons and daughters as we fill and subdue the natural earth. In the Adamic order of being, marriage and reproduction are central operating functions of our nature as human beings on this Genesis earth. Even if we do not marry, we are products of the union of a man and a woman.

When we think of Adam and Eve before the fall, we consider them a righteous man and woman of God. In a way, they were also sons of God in that they were fathered by him and, as sons, they inherited certain character traits from him. But, technically, they were not "sons of God" in the New Testament sense. For example, as a man of God, Adam would not have addressed God as "Abba, Father" as Jesus did as the Son of God.

As human beings, they lived in an Edenic paradise and would have lived forever in fellowship with God if they had not disobeyed him by eating from the tree of the knowledge of good and evil. This did not, however, necessarily make them immortal beings by nature. Even before the fall, Adam and Eve were mortal beings who needed food and outside nourishment from the natural earth to sustain their natural bodies. Hypothetically, before the fall, if Adam and Eve had decided to stop eating food, they would have eventually starved to death. They were not immortal creatures, even in their sinless state.

When Adam and Eve broke God's commandment not to eat from the tree of the knowledge of good and evil, they became sinful creatures separated from the life of God. They were cursed by God; their natural bodies would now experience death. A curse was put on the Genesis earth as well, causing a change in its ecological system:

> Because you have listened to the voice of your wife and have eaten of the tree of which I commanded you, "You shall not eat of it," cursed is the ground because of you; in pain you shall eat of it all the days of your life; thorns and thistles it shall bring forth for you; and you shall eat the plants of the field. By the sweat of your face you shall eat bread, till you return to the ground, for out of it you were taken; for you are dust, and to dust you shall return. (Gen. 3:17–19)

As a result of their insubordination and disobedience, they were driven out of their Edenic paradise. And their existence outside the garden would involve some level of misery to produce sustainable food. Even with food, however, they would eventually die. Over time, their human bodies would age, weaken, die, and rot in the ground. Nature itself was now under a curse and became degenerate.

Before the fall, the world was God's dominion over mankind. But Adam and Eve's rebellion enabled Satan and his demonic host to enter this world, and it became his dominion. Satan became the de facto god of this fallen world. And he has a great deal of influence on sinful mankind, who became his spiritual children. Satan and his rebellious followers began to rule this world independent of God. With this regime change, the world has never been the same. The earth was God's kingdom before the fall, and it was a short age of righteous humanity on an Edenic earth. But after the fall, the world became Satan's kingdom or dominion, and it became an age of unrighteous humanity on a degenerate earth.

The world lost its glory as God's dominion when Adam and Eve rebelled against God, letting Satan into this world. Therefore, the world needs redemption if God's kingdom on earth is ever going to be restored. We need to be freed from Satan's dominion of darkness, freed from our sinful nature, freed from the curse of death, and freed from the curse on nature. Humanity is in desperate need of salvation from its current fallen condition.

The serpent, or Satan, was one of the key characters in the fall of humanity. Satan was a fallen angel, the leader among many fallen angels, or demons. At the end of the world, they will all be cast into hell. There is no record of any hope of salvation for Satan and the demons. Christ did not die on the cross for their sins. The fact that God did not establish a plan of redemption for fallen angels is very important to remember as we consider God's plans for humanity.

God's Response to Fallen Man

After the fall, God had several options for how he could deal with the tragic condition of fallen mankind. It is important to consider these options to understand his plan of redemption.

The first option is that God could have demonstrated his wrath against Adam and Eve and their sinful descendants by destroying this Genesis creation and letting mankind go the way of Satan and the demons, with no hope of salvation. After we died, our spirits would have been destined to hell. God did not have to save any of us.

A second option is that after he destroyed mankind and this Genesis creation, he could have created the children of God as a totally new creation. He could then have created a totally new kind of heavens and earth as the eternal home for his new creation. The children of God would not be like the Adamic creation, where male and female humans filled an Edenic earth with their sons and daughters. They would be embodied creatures, but like the angels, they would be nonsexual creatures who do not experience marriage and reproduction of their kind.

A third option is that he could have decided to have mercy on mankind and institute a plan of redemption whereby mankind would be forgiven of their sins and reconnected to their Creator. Then, through some process of resurrection and restoration, mankind could have returned to a restored Edenic earth. The human experience would have continued in a restored Genesis creation with mankind as male and female, experiencing marriage and reproduction. As we filled and subdued the earth, the world would have become an Edenic paradise. We would have operated properly as men and women of God under the renewed Lordship of the Creator.

But there is a fourth option revealed in the Scriptures. God will not only restore humanity for an extended period, but he will also take these same redeemed Adamic creatures and create a new order of being as children of God. After a long restoration of this creation, the human experience would come to an end on the last day, and the transformed sons of God would then inherit a new earth as their eternal home. In other words, rather than the children of God being created in heaven from nothing, God chose to create them from a preexisting human creation. God, by his own volition and wisdom, decided to institute a plan of redemption to accomplish both a restoration of this Genesis creation and a new creation for his people.

The Old Testament prophets portray the messianic kingdom as a restored paradise for a redeemed humanity. And the traditional Jewish understanding of resurrection in Jesus' day was of a resurrected human body of flesh and blood that would again marry and have children in God's restored kingdom on earth. That is why the liberal Sadducees, who did not believe in an afterlife or a resurrection of the body, thought they were asking a clever question when they asked Jesus whose wife the woman who had seven husbands would be in the messianic kingdom.

But the resurrection of the natural body is an essential part of the Old Testament vision. In Ezekiel's famous vision of the valley of dry bones coming to life, he foresees the departed Jewish saints being resurrected into male and female human bodies. Like the creation of Adam, they also have spiritual life breathed into their reconstituted natural bodies as they reenter a restored nation on this renewed earth:

> Thus, says the Lord God to these bones: Behold, I will cause breath to enter you, and you shall live. And I will lay sinews upon you, and will cause flesh to come upon you, and cover you with skin, and put breath in you, and you shall live [resurrection of the natural body], and you shall know that I am the Lord. . . . And I will bring you into the land of Israel. . . . They shall dwell in the land that I gave to my servant Jacob, where your fathers lived [an earthly kingdom]. They and their children and their children's children [marriage and reproduction] . . . (Ezek. 37:5–25)

> I will make the fruit of the tree and the increase of the field abundant, that you may never again suffer the disgrace of famine among the nations. . . . And they will say, "This land that was desolate has become like the garden of Eden [restored Edenic earth]." (Ezek. 36:30, 35)

Ezekiel's vision of the messianic kingdom is a graphic depiction of the restoration of the Adamic order of being. It foresees a resurrection of human beings into their natural bodies, who will marry and reproduce offspring on a Genesis earth that is restored to an Edenic paradise. The messianic kingdom is portrayed by the prophets as a restoration of the Adamic order of being to its original glory before the fall.

PART 2: Understanding the New Creation as Sons of God

The Old Testament vision of redemption is focused on the eventual restoration of this Genesis creation. But the New Testament reveals a new perspective on God's plan of redemption. Christ and the apostles shift their focus from the messianic kingdom on this Genesis earth to the new heavens and new earth in the eternal age to come. When we accept Christ and are born again, we not only become restored men and women of God, as defined in Genesis, but we also become sons of God in a new creation destined for the Father's eternal kingdom of heaven.

When responding to the Sadducees' question about the feasibility of a future resurrection of a natural body (such as the one described by Ezekiel), Jesus revealed that in heaven the sons of God will have non-sexual, immortal bodies instead of sexual human bodies like Adam's and Eve's. And, like the angels, we will not experience marriage and reproduction as we now do as descendants of Adam. In this remarkable and stunning revelation, Jesus is introducing a new order of being for his followers:

> The sons of this age marry and are given in marriage [the Adamic order of being in this Genesis age], but those who are considered worthy to attain to that age and to the resurrection from the dead [followers of Christ] neither marry nor are given in marriage [in the eternal age to come], for they cannot die anymore [immortal body], because they are equal to angels and are sons of God, being sons of the resurrection [a new order of being as eternal sons of God]. (Luke 20:34–36)

In Jesus' day, a son left his parents to marry, and a daughter was given in marriage by her parents. Jesus said that neither will occur in the eternal resurrection to make it very clear that the human experience of marriage will no longer exist when the sons of God are resurrected into new kinds of immortal bodies. Like angels, we will be eternal creatures that do not marry or reproduce. But unlike angels, our spirits will remain embodied.

Jesus revealed to us that on the last day, the Adamic order of being as male and female actually comes to an end. And in heaven, the immortal sons of God will live an embodied existence, but will not marry, reproduce, and fill the new heavens and new earth with their offspring.

Christ described the two creations, or orders of being:
1. The Adamic order of being as defined in Genesis
2. The new order of being as sons of God

Christ also described two ages:
1. The human experience in this Genesis age
2. The new creation in the eternal age to come

This is an extraordinary revelation about God's plan of redemption. And Jesus' description of the eternal resurrection of the sons of God must have dumbfounded his Jewish audience. In this Genesis age, humanity is by definition a sexual creation involving persons embodied in male and female natural bodies. We are designed for the union of marriage and reproduction. And the messianic kingdom was defined by the prophets as a restored human paradise on this Genesis earth.

Yet Jesus revealed that in the eternal age to come, the sons of God will be resurrected into immortal bodies that will not experience marriage. Our immortal bodies will be categorically different from the current Adamic bodies of flesh and blood that are designed for filling the natural earth with their offspring.

But heaven will not be some "spiritual bliss" in an ethereal realm that is devoid of real bodies. Rather, the eternal bodies will be real bodies in a real place. Nor will our individual spirits lose their identity as a person. We will each be the same person, but in a new kind of glorified body.

On this earth, Peter's spirit was in a male human body, and he was a husband, father, and likely a grandfather. When he became a Christian, however, he became a man of God. As a restored man of God, he learned how to be a loving husband to his wife and a loving father to his children. But when his spirit was regenerated by the Holy Spirit, he was also born again as a new creation as a son of God. When Peter is raptured to heaven, his regenerated spirit will then dwell in a new kind of nonsexual, immortal body. And he will be a son of God in a loving companionship with other eternal children of God.

The Scriptures define eternal life for believers as follows. Upon regeneration by the Holy Spirit, each believer receives an eternal living spirit as a son of God. When our bodies die, our regenerated spirits are taken to heaven, where we wait for a resurrection of our bodies, which sleep in the earth. At the final resurrection, our eternal spirits then enter into a new kind of eternal body like Christ's resurrected eternal body. And after this perishable earth is destroyed, the embodied sons of God then dwell on the imperishable new earth. In this eternal habitat, the eternal sons of God will enjoy eternal fellowship with the triune God, who is Life. When we tell non-Christians that they can inherit eternal life if they believe in Christ, we mean that life for the saints is an eternal embodied life on an eternal new earth in eternal fellowship with the living God in his eternal home.

In stark contrast, the Scriptures define eternal death for those who reject Christ as follows. Unbelievers are living, breathing people, but they are spiritually dead because as sinful creatures they are separated from the spiritual life of God. When their mortal bodies die, their unregenerate spirits are then held in hades until Judgment Day. At the general resurrection, they will be resurrected in souls and bodies, judged, and sent to the eternal lake of fire, which is defined as the second death. Eternal death is eternal separation from the life of God.

But let's get back to the life of a believer and God's plan of redemption. While we remain on this earth, we are experiencing the two orders of being concurrently. According to the Adamic order of being, I am one flesh with my wife, my female companion on this earth. But since my wife is a believer, she is also a fellow child of God in the new creation. When Christ comes again, our natural bodies will be transformed into eternal bodies adapted for heaven. At that time, my wife will no longer be my female partner in marriage. She will, however, be an eternal fellow child of God. Until then, the new creation as sons of God is temporarily superimposed onto this creation until we are taken to heaven.

Paul picked up on Christ's new perspective on redemption:

> You are all sons of God through faith in Christ Jesus, for all of you who were baptized into Christ have clothed yourselves with Christ. There is neither Jew nor Greek, slave nor free, male nor female, for you are all one in Christ Jesus. (Gal. 3:26–28 NIV)

In heaven, the sons of God will have no ethnic, class, or sexual distinctions. Paul taught that the new order of being as God's children is a distinctly "new creation" that begins now while we are still humans, but it is ultimately destined for heaven:

> For we know that if the tent that is our earthly home is destroyed [when our mortal human bodies die], we have a building from God, a house not made with hands, eternal in the heavens [an eternal body in the eternal kingdom] . . . From now on, therefore, we regard no one according to the flesh [the Adamic order of being] . . . Therefore, if anyone is in Christ, he is a new creation. (2 Cor. 5:1, 16–17)

As a new creation, we are waiting for a new kind of eternal body in a new kind of eternal home with God.

Adam and Eve were the first humans and the beginning of the human experience on this Genesis earth. But the resurrected and ascended Christ is the firstborn of the sons of God on the future new eternal earth. The Adamic order of being as male and female given in marriage is in the image of the triune God. But as sons of God the Father, we are in the image of his Son: "For those whom he foreknew he also predestined to be conformed to the image of his Son, so that he might be the firstborn among many brothers" (Rom. 8:29).

The Corinthian church was beginning to understand the concept of the new creation in which there is neither male nor female. But they seem to have attempted to implement the new order of being in the present age at the expense of the Adamic order of being. Some within the Corinthian church had begun to forbid sexual relations between husbands and wives, since we are now all brothers and sisters in Christ. They believed married couples should live as celibates as they waited for the eternal kingdom. Paul corrected them by teaching that even though we are a new creation destined for heaven where marriage will no longer exist, they should continue to function in the Adamic order of being as long as we are living on this earth:

> Now concerning the matters about which you wrote: "It is good for a man not to have sexual relations with a woman [the Corinthians writing to Paul]." . . . [then Paul's response] The husband should give to his wife her conjugal rights, and likewise the wife to her husband. For the wife does not have authority over her own body, but the husband does. Likewise the husband does not have authority over his own body, but the wife does. (1 Cor. 7:1–4)

The Corinthians were confusing the two orders of being. Paul taught them that while we remain on this earth living as both a man and woman of God *and* a child of God in the new creation, husbands and wives should continue to function as God intended.

Many evangelical feminists make the same kind of mistake the Corinthians made. They assume that because we are now a new creation in Christ with no distinction between male and female, then wives should no longer live in a submissive role to their husbands. The equality in the new creation trumps the hierarchy in the old creation. Rather than forbidding sex in the marriage relationship, these feminists forbid the submissive role of the wife now that we are a new creation in Christ with a fundamental equality between male and female. This is a popular teaching today.

But Paul was not confused by the two orders of being. He understood that they operated concurrently while we remain on this earth. Notice that Paul taught that a wife should submit to her husband even though they are now in Christ as a new creation that is neither male nor female: "Wives, submit to your husbands, as is fitting in the Lord [in the new creation]. Husbands, love your wives, and do not be harsh with them" (Col. 3:18–19). Even though we are now in the Lord as a new creation, it is still appropriate that a wife should submit to her loving husband.

In the new order of being, the wife will ultimately not be submissive to her husband because in heaven marriage between a man and a woman will no longer exist. In the meantime, while the children of

God are living in this Genesis creation, they should continue to function in the Adamic order of being. Husbands and wives should fulfill their marital duties to one another, and wives should continue to be submissive to loving husbands. Paul understood that the two creations operated concurrently while this creation continued to exist.

Paul also taught that the Genesis creation itself is longing for our transition to our eternal home, when our Adamic bodies will be transformed into bodies like Christ's:

> For all who are led by the Spirit of God are sons of God. . . . you have received the Spirit of adoption as sons, by whom we cry, "Abba! Father!" The Spirit himself bears witness with our [human] spirit that we are children of God [the new creation], and if children, then heirs—heirs of God and fellow heirs with Christ [of the eternal kingdom of heaven], . . . For the creation waits with eager longing for the revealing of the sons of God. For the creation was subjected to futility, . . . in hope, that the creation itself will be set free from its bondage to corruption and obtain the freedom of the glory of the children of God. For we know that the whole creation has been groaning together in the pains of childbirth until now. And not only the creation, but we ourselves, who have the firstfruits of the Spirit, groan inwardly as we wait eagerly for adoption as sons, the redemption of our bodies [into an eternal body in an eternal kingdom]. (Rom. 8:14–23)

The Holy Spirit within us informs our regenerated spirits that we are already sons of God. We can now call God "Abba! Father!" As God's children, we are eager to dwell with our Father in his eternal kingdom, where Christ has already ascended. The Genesis creation also longs for our transformation from Adamic creatures to our new creation as sons of God. And the Genesis creation itself will somehow be carried over into the eternal kingdom. Paul did not go into detail about which features of this Genesis creation will carry over into the eternal earth, probably because it remained a mystery to him.

The Corinthians must have been curious as to what kind of nonsexual bodies we will have in heaven. They could envision what a restored human body would be like, but what does an immortal and imperishable body look like? But in his first letter to the Corinthians,

Paul calls the Corinthians foolish for even asking about what kind of bodies we will have in heaven:

> But someone will ask, "How are the dead raised? With what kind of body do they come?" You foolish person! ... what you sow [the Adamic body] is not the body that is to be, ... Behold! I tell you a mystery. We shall not all sleep, but we shall all be changed [into a new kind body], ... and the dead will be raised imperishable, and we shall be changed [into a new kind of eternal body adapted for the eternal kingdom]. (1 Cor. 15:35–52)

Some popular books about heaven go into considerable detail about how we will continue to possess most of the features of our current natural bodies and how the eternal new earth will contain most of the features of this current Genesis earth. These authors claim that much of human civilization and culture will carry over to the new earth. We will continue to attend symphonies and even sporting events in heaven. These are all speculations that have no biblical basis.

These authors take the elaborate visions of the messianic kingdom found in the Old Testament and apply them to the eternal kingdom of heaven. All these visions, however, pertain to the restored earth during the millennium, not to the eternal new heavens and new earth. It is foolish to presume that we can know what heaven will be like, just as it is foolish to speculate about what our raptured bodies will be like.

Paul was given extraordinary revelations by the Holy Spirit and was once caught up into the third realm of heaven. But even then, he could not explain what he had seen and experienced (cf. 2 Cor. 12:1–4). If the nature of the paradise of heaven was a mystery to Paul, then it is surely a mystery to us. In fact, Paul warned us not to go beyond God's revelations: "I have applied all these things to myself and Apollos for your benefit, brothers, that you may learn by us *not to go beyond what is written*" (1 Cor. 4:6). Theologians who engage in this unwarranted speculation about the nature of the eternal earth would be wise to heed Paul's warning when writing about the nature of the eternal kingdom of heaven.

Christ in His Glorified Body

One of the reasons some theologians tend to impose features of the Adamic creation onto the new earth is because of how they understand the nature of Christ's resurrected body while he was still on this earth. Christ was raised into a body of flesh and blood that could be seen and touched. The disciples even ate breakfast with him. He was a male human being before he died, and he was a male human being after he was resurrected.

But after he ascended to heaven to the Father's right hand, his human body went through a process of transformation and glorification to adapt it to the glory he had with the Father before he came into this world. And Paul, who got a glimpse of the glorified Christ after he had already ascended to heaven, taught that the post-ascended Christ is in a glorified body that no man in his natural body has seen, or even can see. That is, until Christ returns and we, too, are transformed into glorified bodies like his resurrected body:

> To keep the commandment unstained and free from reproach until the appearing of our Lord Jesus Christ . . . who alone has immortality, who dwells in unapproachable light [in his glorified body], whom no one has ever seen or can see. (1 Tim. 6:14–16)

According to Paul, now that Christ has ascended to heaven and is in his glorified body, no one has seen the risen Christ. In fact, it is impossible for anyone in his natural body to approach and see Christ's immortal body. John also taught that we will not know what kind of resurrected bodies we will have until Christ comes again, and we are given glorified bodies like his eternal body:

> See what kind of love the Father has given to us, that we should be called children of God; and so we are . . . Beloved, we are God's children now, and what we will be has not yet appeared [unknown, glorified bodies]; but we know that when he appears we shall be like him, because we shall see him as he is [in his glorified body]. (1 John 3:1–2)

Before Christ ascended to heaven, John saw the resurrected body of Christ that appeared to him and the disciples in the Upper Room. He even watched him eat some broiled fish. But instead of referencing Christ's pre-ascended body that had appeared to him, John referenced the unknown, post-ascended, glorified body of Christ as a model for our future bodies.

Yet, many theologians ignore these teachings and incorrectly assume that our raptured bodies will be like Christ's nonglorified body of flesh and blood that the disciples saw in the Upper Room. They then extrapolate from this unbiblical assumption that our raptured bodies will be just like Christ's body while he was still on this earth—an immortal, natural body. And we will inherit a restored natural earth as our eternal habitat. But I cannot find a single verse in the New Testament that references the pre-ascended body of Christ as being representative of our future eternal bodies.

These theologians often set up a false dichotomy when discussing the nature of our eternal bodies and eternal home:
1. Our raptured, eternal bodies will be modified versions of Christ's pre-ascended body of flesh and blood, and we will dwell on a restored Genesis earth for eternity.
2. Or we will have immaterial spiritual bodies, and we will dwell in a boring ethereal realm of heaven with our spirits floating around like angels.

But the Scriptures plainly teach that our future bodies are neither modified Adamic bodies nor disembodied spirits. The correct view of our future eternal bodies and eternal home is that when Christ comes again, our natural bodies will be transformed into a real but presently unknown kind of immortal body like the unknown, glorified body of Christ. And the embodied eternal sons of God will dwell in a real but presently unknown kind of eternal habitat.

In other words, the nature of our eternal bodies *and* our eternal home remains a profound mystery. Theologians need to learn to live with this mystery. And they should stop imposing features of the Adamic body onto our future eternal bodies, and features of this Genesis creation onto the eternal new earth. Chapter 11, "The Final Resurrection," deals with the important topic of the nature of our future eternal bodies and why it should not be modeled on the pre-ascended Christ.

The New Creation as a Restored Genesis Creation

The trend today among amillennial theologians is to impose a version of the restored Edenic earth, as envisioned by the prophets, onto the eternal new earth. Heaven is essentially a restoration of our humanity as originally intended in the garden of Eden. Many amillennialists contend that the millennium is therefore not necessary because the eternal new earth is the restored earth as envisioned by the prophets. And the new creation is a renovated and renewed Genesis creation. We are not going to heaven; rather, we are going to experience heaven on this Genesis earth. The triune God in all his glory is coming to this Genesis earth to dwell with a restored humanity. This is a serious mistake, for it greatly distorts God's plan of redemption.

The following quote from J. Richard Middleton, an amillennial theologian, is a good example of this flawed theology:

> By attending to the basic thrust and movement of the [biblical] plot, we will discover that eschatological redemption consists in the renewal of human cultural life on earth rather than our removal from earth to heaven. . . . the dominant tenor of Scripture, which portrays the redemption of the entire created order and human redemption as the restoration of bodily life on earth—that is, the renewal of God's creational intent from the beginning.[2]

Middleton is attempting to make sense out of the Old Testament prophecies of a restored Edenic earth for a restored humanity by imposing these visions onto the eternal new heavens and new earth; the eternal kingdom essentially becomes a renovated and restored Genesis creation. There is no need, therefore, for a 1,000-year restoration of this earth before the eternal kingdom.

The amillennialist Anthony Hoekema also describes heaven as a renovated earth in his book *The Bible and the Future*:

---

[2] J. Richard Middleton, *A New Heaven and a New Earth* (Grand Rapids: Baker Academic, 2014), 58, 237.

> There will be a future fulfillment of these prophecies [of a restored Edenic earth], not in the millennium, but on the new earth. Whether they are all to be literally fulfilled is open to question; surely details about wolves and lambs, and about mountains dropping sweet wine, are to be understood not in a crassly literal way but as figurative descriptions of what the new earth will be like.[3]

According to Hoekema, there is no need for a 1,000-year messianic kingdom because the eternal new earth is the fulfillment of these messianic prophecies of a restored earth.

In contrast, premillennialists have traditionally taught that the millennium will be the restored earth as described by the prophets, and that after this Genesis earth perishes, it is replaced with a truly new earth. John F. Walvoord taught this view in his commentary on Revelation:

> The new heaven and new earth presented here are evidently not simply the old heaven and earth renovated, but an act of new creation. . . . There is remarkably little revealed in the Bible concerning the character of the new heaven and new earth, but it is evidently quite different from their present form of existence.[4]

Walvoord's interpretation is correct. The new earth is a truly new earth. Unfortunately, progressive premillennialists today have adopted the amillennial version of the eternal earth as a restored Genesis earth. The Genesis earth is not annihilated by fire on the last day but is only purged by a surface fire. The millennium simply becomes a dress rehearsal for the eternal earth. These theologians observe that during the millennium, people will still get old and some sinners will even experience death at the young age of one hundred (Isa. 65:20). But after the earth is purified by fire on the last day, there will be no sin and no death on the eternal restored earth.

They compare this process to how gold is purified by fire. When contaminated gold is refined by fire, it does not result in some unknown, new kind of mineral. Rather, the refining process produces a

---

3 Anthony A. Hoekema, *The Bible and the Future* (Grand Rapids: Eerdmans, 1979), 276.
4 John F. Walvoord, *The Revelation of Jesus Christ* (Chicago: Moody Press, 1966), 311.

pure form of gold. Likewise, after the millennium on the last day, the earth is purified by fire, which will produce a perfect Genesis creation with no sin and no death. In theological circles, this is referred to as a "new creationist" approach. This is a poor choice of words, however, because these new creationists do not believe the new earth is a truly new creation. Michael Vlach, a progressive premillennialist, advocates this position:

> A new creationist approach affirms that the coming new earth will be this present earth purged and restored. . . . All three relationships God placed man into at creation are fully restored [a restoration of humanity]. First, man is in proper relationship with his Creator [as a man and woman of God]. Second, man is in complete fellowship and harmony with other human beings [a restoration of human relationships]. And third, man's relationship with the creation is restored [on a purified earth]. All three relationships were marred at the fall, but now all three are complete.[5]

According to Vlach, the Genesis earth is only purged by fire, not destroyed by fire. And heaven is a complete restoration of our humanity on a restored Genesis earth. Darrell Bock, another well-known progressive premillennialist, also teaches the same doctrine:

> In sum, the kingdom and covenants are two of the key ways God reveals how He will execute His plan to restore creation to its intended goal for God's own glory. God's kingdom program is a reclamation project, taking humanity to where it was designed to be all along.[6]

According to Bock, the kingdom of heaven is really a restored Edenic earth where mankind picks back up where he left off.

---

[5] Michael J. Vlach, *He Will Reign Forever: A Biblical Theology of the Kingdom of God* (Silverton: Lampion Press, 2017), 14, 505.

[6] D. Jeffrey Bingham and Glenn R. Kreider, eds., *Dispensationalism and the History of Redemption* (Chicago: Moody Publishers, 2015), 154.

Craig A. Blaising, another progressive premillennialist, states:

> The consummation is viewed as a redemption and renewal of the present creation rather than its annihilation and replacement by a completely different, heavenly reality. . . . The holistic consummation of progressive dispensationalism can be described as a worldwide multinational kingdom order of redeemed peoples on a renewed earth.[7]

If Blaising were describing the millennium, I would agree with him. Redeemed humanity will indeed inhabit a renewed earth. But he is not describing the millennium; rather, he is describing the eternal new earth.

According to these amillennial and premillennial theologians, the sons of God will inherit a restored Genesis earth as the eternal kingdom, where we will experience the restoration of our humanity as "it was designed to be all along"; "the renewal of God's creational intent from the beginning"; and "the renewal of the present creation" where all the relationships Adam and Eve would have experienced in the garden "are fully restored." The "new creation" as sons of God is a restored humanity on a restored earth.

But Jesus informed us that in the kingdom of heaven, the sons of God will not experience marriage. And Paul told us that the new creation as sons of God is neither a male nor a female creature. These revelations represent a categorical change in our being. If the new creation does not include the most basic aspects of our humanity that began in Eden, how then can these theologians claim that the eternal kingdom will be "the renewal of God's creational intent from the beginning" if we will not marry, reproduce, fill, and subdue the new earth with our offspring? How can heaven be a restoration of our humanity if we will no longer experience the Adamic order of being as male and female?

These theologians are greatly confusing the Adamic order of being, as revealed in Genesis, with the new creation as sons of God. The human experience is designed and built around man created in the image of God as male and female. Living on this earth as a sexual human being as a man or woman with an anatomy designed for marriage and

---

7 Bingham and Kreider, *Dispensationalism*, 210.

reproduction gets to the very essence and core of what it means to be a human. And it is the most important organizing principle of our communal life on this earth.

In this Genesis age, we are each a man or woman with a natural, sexual, mortal body on this Genesis earth. As human companions on this earth, we are male or female, son or daughter, brother or sister, husband or wife, father or mother, grandfather or grandmother, uncle or aunt, and a male or female companion to our fellow human beings. These are very real human relationships, and they form the basis for our communal life on this earth. This is the community of man, and our current human society, culture, and civilization are built around these relationships.

Yet, in the eternal age to come as eternal children of God, none of these human relationships will exist on the eternal new earth. We are so accustomed to the human experience on this earth, it is hard to imagine a community and civilization in heaven without these kinds of relationships. But heaven will not be a restored humanity on a restored Genesis earth. Otherwise, all these relationships fundamental to the human experience would exist in heaven. Therefore, contrary to what these theologians erroneously assert, the eternal new earth will not be a restoration of our humanity on a restored Genesis earth.

Jesus' description of the eternal resurrection was not a minor or trivial detail about our eternal bodies in the new creation. It was quite profound, and his teachings should have a major impact on how we understand God's plan of redemption. But when I first read the theologians' books advocating these views, I was shocked to find that many of them do not even reference Jesus' description of the eternal resurrection of the sons of God, nor do they reference Paul's teaching in Galatians about the new creation that is neither male nor female. And when they do quote these Scriptures, they do not attempt to integrate these critically important teachings into a coherent biblical theology of the future. These theologians are simply not taking seriously the revelations about the new creation as sons of God.

The New Earth Is a Truly New Creation

From his celestial home, God created the current heavens and earth in space and time, and it had a presence before him. But on the last day, John describes the utter annihilation of this Genesis creation when he says: "From his presence earth and sky fled away and no place was found for them" (Rev. 20:11). John is teaching that on the last day, this creation will no longer have a "presence" before God, and this cosmos will have "no place" in space and time. Earth and sky cannot be "found" because they will no longer exist. Therefore, the children of God must be destined for a totally new cosmos and creation to replace this Genesis creation that perishes on the last day.

As Peter says, God created this Genesis creation by his word out of nothing (ex nihilo), and he will simply say the word again and it will cease to exist (2 Peter 3:10–13). Then by his word that can create, destroy, and create anew, he will create a new heavens and new earth (ex nihilo) adapted for God's children. A new order of being as eternal sons of God necessitates a totally new creation as its eternal habitat.

Within the Trinity, the Son of God is the Alpha, for he was the specific person of the Godhead who created this Genesis creation. And he is the Omega in that he brings it to an end. He is also tasked with creating the new heavens and new earth. When he brings this Genesis creation to an end on the last day, he will create a completely new creation for the children of God:

> And he who was seated on the throne said, "Behold, I am making all things new." Also he said, "Write this down, for these words are trustworthy and true." . . . "Behold, I am coming soon, bringing my recompense with me, to repay each one for what he has done. I am the Alpha and the Omega, the first and the last, the beginning and the end [of this creation]." (Rev. 21:5; 22:13)

As a new order of being, the children of God will inherit a new kind of body in a new kind of heavens and earth. The eternal earth will certainly have some continuity with this creation. But we are foolish to speculate what that continuity will be, and which features of this creation will carry over to the new earth.

As redeemed men and women of God, we are destined for a restored Genesis earth during the millennium, as envisioned by the prophets. When Christ returns after the 1,000-year restoration, the Adamic order of being and this Genesis creation will come to an end when it is destroyed by fire. The saints will then be raptured into indestructible glorified bodies like Christ's and will be taken to their eternal home on the eternal new earth. The followers of Christ will not only experience a restoration of their humanity for a thousand years, but they will also get to experience a new kind of eternal paradise as sons of God in an eternal new creation. Now that is an amazing plan of redemption!

I believe that when we are in heaven looking back on the human experience, we will forever remember God's mercy. We will always remember what it was like to be a sinful fallen human being before God saved us. And we will remember the incredible blessings he bestowed on us when we lived on the restored Edenic earth as a restored man or woman of God during Christ's millennial reign. Paul alludes to this truth:

> But God, being rich in mercy, because of the great love with which he loved us, even when we were dead in our trespasses [fallen human beings], made us alive together with Christ—by grace you have been saved—and raised us up with him and seated us with him in the heavenly places in Christ Jesus, so that *in the coming ages* he might show the immeasurable riches of his grace in kindness toward us in Christ Jesus. (Eph. 2:4–7)

In the eternal age to come, God's love and mercy toward fallen humanity will demonstrate something about the character of God himself.

Summary

When we accept Christ, we are reconciled to God and are born again. We then become children of God in the new order of being—a new creation that is neither male nor female. But we remain citizens of this Genesis earth and continue to experience the Adamic order of being. Therefore, we currently live a dual existence as two orders of being—as a man or woman of God *and* as a child of God. As a believer and a descendant of Adam, I am a restored man of God in the Adamic order of being. At the same time, I am a child of God and a citizen of heaven, which is my ultimate eternal destiny.

Marriage between a male and a female is the central design feature of the Adamic creation and is fundamental to communal life on this earth, whether it is the nuclear family or the extended family of male and female neighbors. But the eternal new earth will not be a restoration of our humanity on a restored natural earth. The new creation as sons of God is truly a new order of being, and its form and function are unknown until we experience the final resurrection.

This distinction between the Adamic order of being and the new creation as children of God may seem very simple and elementary. It is simple, but it has a profound impact on how we understand the nature of God's kingdom on earth and then in heaven. The next chapter explains how the two kingdoms of the triune God revolve around the two creations or orders of being.

God the Son's kingdom:
- The Son's 1,000-year messianic kingdom is a restoration of the Adamic order of being on a restored earth that occurs in this Genesis age.
- The departed saints inherit the Son's restored natural earth through a resurrection of their natural bodies at the first resurrection.

God the Father's kingdom:
- The Father's eternal kingdom (or the new heavens and new earth) is for the transformed eternal sons of God in the eternal age to come.
- The sons of God inherit the Father's eternal kingdom through a resurrection and rapture of their eternal bodies at the final resurrection.

4

The Two Kingdoms of God

Review

In the last chapter, I described my method of interpreting and organizing the Scriptures when developing a theology of the future. I described the two orders of being that Christians experience. The Adamic order of being represents humanity with natural bodies designed for marriage and procreation. The new order of being as children of God represents a new creation who, after being raptured, will have immortal bodies that will not experience marriage. To understand the kingdom of God on earth and then in heaven, it is very important to maintain the two distinct orders of being, their defining characteristics, and their corresponding kingdoms. There are two aspects to God's kingdom: one on the restored earth for a restored humanity, and another in heaven for the eternal sons of God.

Trinitarian Eschatology

The Scriptures teach that within the Trinity, this Genesis age and the corresponding Adamic order of being uniquely belong to God the Son. Whereas, in the eternal age to come and the corresponding eternal sons of God uniquely belong to God the Father. Paul taught:

For as in Adam all die, so also in Christ shall all be made alive. But each in his own order: Christ the firstfruits [the first to be raised into an immortal body], then at his coming those who belong to Christ [the raptured sons of God]. Then comes the end [of the world], *when he delivers the kingdom to God the Father* after destroying every rule and every authority and power [during his millennial reign]. (1 Cor. 15:23–24)

Throughout the New Testament, Christ and the apostles refer to the kingdom of heaven as the Father's imperishable kingdom and home.

The Son's Kingdom

Jesus Christ was the Jewish Messiah, but as John discovered, he was no ordinary human being. John taught:

In the beginning [of the Genesis creation] was the Word, and the Word was with God, and the Word was God. He was in the beginning with God. All things were made through him, . . . And the Word became flesh and dwelt among us. (John 1:1–14)

In a stunning revelation, John informs us that Jesus Christ is God the Son incarnate and the Creator who spoke this Genesis creation into existence. Hebrews also proclaims this truth:

In these last days he has spoken to us by his Son, whom he appointed the heir of all things, *through whom also he created the world*. . . . he upholds the universe by the word of his power. . . . You, Lord, laid the foundation of the earth in the beginning, and *the heavens are the work of your hands*. (Heb. 1:2–10)

This simple Jew from Nazareth is the Son of God who created the world, laid the foundation of the earth and crafted the heavens, and even sustains the universe today. Colossians repeats this remarkable truth about the Son of God:

For by him all things were created, in heaven and on earth, visible and invisible, whether thrones or dominions or rulers or authorities—*all things were created through him and for him.* (Col. 1:16)

Therefore, in the beginning before the fall, this Genesis creation was the Son of God's dominion. The world was the Son's kingdom on earth, and God's will was done on earth as it was in heaven. As the Son ruled over Adam and Eve, they were to rule over and manage his wonderful creation.

This is not to say that the Father is not involved with his Son's Genesis creation or that the Son will not be involved in the Father's kingdom of heaven. The triune God may be three persons, but they are one being and they have one will. When the Son's will is imposed on earth, it will primarily be his kingdom, but it will be the Father's kingdom as well. Likewise, Paul taught that on the very last day, the Son will hand over his kingdom to the Father, but the Son's reign will also continue. Once the Son's reign over this world begins, it is an everlasting kingdom even though the sons of God will transition to the Father's eternal kingdom on the last day.

But the Scriptures do reveal some important distinctions within the Trinity. The Son of God is described as the Creator of this Genesis creation, and he is described as the Omega of this creation when he brings it to an end on Judgment Day. Revelation also reveals that he is the unique person of the Trinity who will create the new heavens and new earth:

Behold, I [Christ] am coming soon, bringing my recompense with me, to repay each one for what he has done [on Judgment Day]. I am the Alpha and the Omega, the first and the last, the beginning [of this Genesis creation] and the end [of this Genesis creation]. (Rev. 22:12–13)

Then I [John] saw a new heaven and a new earth, for the first heaven and the first earth had passed away, . . . And he who was seated on the throne said, "Behold, I am making all things new [Christ creates the new earth]." (Rev. 21:1–5)

The Son of God created this Genesis creation, and it is the Son of God who will bring it to an end. Equally important, he is the specific person of the Trinity who creates the eternal new heavens and new earth. This is the eternal dwelling place for the bride of Christ and the Father's eternal sons.

The Holy Spirit

As a coequal member of the Trinity, the Holy Spirit also plays a central role throughout this age and the next. The Holy Spirit was essential to the creation of this world: "In the beginning, God created the heavens and the earth.... And the Spirit of God was hovering over the face of the waters" (Gen. 1:1–2). The Holy Spirit is also essential to our rebirth and regeneration as children of God:

> But when the goodness and loving kindness of God our Savior appeared, he saved us, not because of works done by us in righteousness, but according to his own mercy, by the washing of regeneration and renewal of the Holy Spirit. (Titus 3:4–5)

Jesus used the metaphor of the rivers of living water to describe the abundant life that flows into believers from the life of the Holy Spirit:

> Jesus stood up and cried out, "If anyone thirsts, let him come to me and drink. Whoever believes in me, as the Scripture has said, 'Out of his heart will flow rivers of living water.'" Now this he said about the Spirit. (John 7:37–39)

The same metaphor is used in Revelation to describe the flow of life from the Holy Spirit in the New Jerusalem in the Father's eternal kingdom:

> "To the thirsty I will give from the spring of the water of life without payment." ... Then the angel showed me the river of the water of life [from the Holy Spirit], bright as crystal, flowing from the throne of God [the Father] and of the Lamb [the Son]. (Rev. 21:6; 22:1)

Notice that the flow of eternal life on the eternal earth will emanate from all three persons of the Trinity.

It may seem that the Holy Spirit is not mentioned very often in this book. But that is because the Holy Spirit's work is to help us focus on God the Son and God the Father. Moreover, with every verse of Scripture that is quoted, I am creating a footnote that references the work of the Holy Spirit. So, in effect, the Holy Spirit is being referenced throughout this book. Yet, maintaining these important distinctions within the Trinity is critically important in developing a proper theology of the future.

Christ Is the God-Man

Theologians spend a great deal of time discussing Christ's dual nature as a both a human being and the Son of God. Christ is the God-man:

- As the son of David, Jesus is the promised human Messiah who according to the prophets would usher in the messianic kingdom of Israel.
- He is also God incarnate, or the eternal Son of God through whom this Genesis creation was made.

Thus, when the prophets describe the messianic kingdom on a restored Edenic earth, they are also describing the Son of God's reclaimed Genesis creation. In other words, because Jesus is the God-man, the millennium can be described as either the son of David's messianic kingdom on this earth or the Son of God's restored dominion over his Genesis creation. These are two ways of describing the same kingdom.

The prophet Isaiah even described the Messiah's kingdom on earth as synonymous with the Son of God's kingdom:

> For to us a child is born, to us a son is given [the human son of David]; and the government shall be upon his shoulder [he will rule Israel and the whole world], and his name shall be called Wonderful Counselor, Mighty God [God the Son], Everlasting Father, Prince of Peace. Of the increase of his government and of peace there will be no end, on the throne of David and over his kingdom, to establish it and to uphold it with justice and with

righteousness from this time forth and forevermore. The zeal of the LORD of hosts will do this. (Isa. 9:6–7)

Paul referenced this prophecy in Isaiah that describes the Messiah as both the son of David *and* the Son of God:

> ... the gospel of God, which he promised beforehand through his prophets in the holy Scriptures, concerning his Son, who was descended from David according to the flesh [human Messiah] and was declared to be the Son of God ["Mighty God"]. (Rom. 1:1–4)

Christ is both the son of David as a man and the Son of God. And as the Messiah-God, he will rule the world in an age of righteous humanity during his messianic kingdom. This understanding of the messianic kingdom has tremendous ramifications when evaluating the various views of God's endgame.

A Divine Covenant

For example, some amillennialists have argued that God's covenant with Israel to establish a messianic kingdom through their nation was conditional upon receiving their Messiah. That is debatable. But what is undeniable is that the Son of God has a divine right to remove Satan and reclaim his Genesis creation. And there is an unconditional covenant between the Father and the Son that one day the Father will indeed restore this Genesis creation to his Son. King David describes this covenant in one of his famous psalms: "The LORD [the Father] says to my Lord [the Son]: 'Sit at my right hand [in heaven], until I make your enemies [on this earth] your footstool'" (Ps. 110:1). God the Father is in heaven, and if his Son is seated at his right hand in heaven, then the Son would rule over his enemies on this earth from his throne in heaven when the Father determines it is time for his reign to begin.

Christ revealed this divine covenant between the Father and his Son when quoting from Psalm 110:

> Now while the Pharisees were gathered together, Jesus asked them a question, saying, "What do you think about the Christ? Whose son is he?" They said to him, "The son of David." He said to them,

"How is it then that David, in the Spirit, calls him Lord, saying, 'The Lord [God the Father] said to my Lord [God the Son], "Sit at my right hand [on his divine throne in heaven], until I [the Father] put your enemies under your feet"'? (Matt. 22:41–44)

The Pharisees were stumped and could not answer the question. The correct answer to Christ's question "Whose son is he?" is twofold: the Messiah will be the son of David as a man; but he will also be the almighty Son of God who created the heavens and earth.

Most important, notice that the Father has promised his Son that one day he will remove all his Son's enemies on this earth (including Satan and his tyrannical human rulers) and restore this Genesis creation to him. The Father's promise is not only to the son of David, but to his Son as well.

Christ's reference to his throne in heaven next to the Father is not an inferior position to the Father. Rather, it is a throne synonymous with the Father's own throne and deity. The ascended Christ has all the divine authority and power necessary to rule this world. He is just waiting on the Father to say when it's time to rule the world.

Amillennialists can argue as to whether the covenant with Israel was conditional or unconditional. But this is an intra-Trinitarian covenant within the Godhead itself between the Father and his Son. And this covenant is unconditional because Christ was always faithful to the Father, both as a man and certainly as the Son of God.

As the second Adam, Jesus withstood every temptation Satan could throw at him, and he lived a sinless life totally submissive to the Father. He was even obedient to the Father when he died on the cross for our sins, though he was not guilty of any sin. Therefore, Christ is the perfect Adam *and* the Son of God. And as promised by his Father, he will unquestionably rule this world when Satan is removed in the future millennium. As the Creator of this world, it was his creation before Satan invaded and took over his kingdom. This regime change is certain to occur because of his deity and his divine right to rule this world.

As the disciples wrestled with the fact that Christ ascended to heaven without establishing his messianic kingdom, they looked to Psalm 110 for an explanation. This psalm is either quoted or alluded to by Jesus and the New Testament writers more than twenty times, and it is the most quoted Old Testament text in the New Testament.

The disciples began to realize that the Jewish Messiah was also God incarnate, and one day, as the true God of this world, he would indeed rule over his creation from his throne in heaven at the Father's right hand.

They also learned from Psalm 110 that after Christ ascended to heaven, they must wait for some unknown period until the Father decides it is time for his Son to use his divine power to rule the world:

> But when Christ had offered for all time a single sacrifice for sins, he sat down at the right hand of God, *waiting* from that time until his enemies should be made a footstool for his feet. (Heb. 10:12–13)

Right before Christ ascended to heaven, the disciples asked if he would then restore Israel in the messianic kingdom. Jesus answered that the Father decides the times and seasons when his messianic kingdom will be established on this earth (Acts 1:6–7). In the meantime, as they followed Christ, preaching the gospel to all nations, they should expect hardship and persecution in this world. The disciples were keenly aware of the fact that although Christ was sovereign, Satan had not yet been removed and the Son's dominion had not yet been restored: "At present, we do not yet see everything in subjection to him" (Heb. 2:8). This explains why Christ's enemies continued to persecute them.

Using This Method

Below is a recap of this method of interpreting and organizing the Scriptures into a logical biblical theology of the future.

Discern the two orders of being:
- The Adamic order of being
- The new order of being as sons of God

Discern the two kingdoms of the triune God:
- The Son's earthly kingdom in this Genesis age for a restored humanity
- The Father's heavenly kingdom in the eternal age to come for the eternal sons of God

Let's put this method to a test. Consider Isaiah's famous description of the messianic kingdom, introduced as follows: "For behold, I create *new heavens and a new earth,* and the former things shall not be remembered" (65:17). In Revelation 20 and 21, John uses the same phrase to describe the eternal kingdom of heaven: "From his presence earth and sky fled away, and no place was found for them. . . . Then I saw a *new heaven and a new earth*" (20:11—21:1). Reconciling these two similar references has been a notorious problem for theologians. That is because they assume that since Isaiah and Revelation use the same terminology, they are describing the same kingdom. Isaiah, however, is describing the restored Genesis creation; whereas, Revelation is describing the eternal new earth after this creation perishes.

The use of the same figure of speech in Isaiah and Revelation is analogous to the way we use the word *transformed* as having two different meanings in different contexts. For example, whenever an especially sinful man becomes a Christian and dramatically changes his behavior, we might say, "He has been transformed into a new person." One day, however, when Christ returns in the clouds and he is raptured, he will be truly transformed when his natural body is changed into a new kind of immortal body adapted for heaven. The word *transformed* has two different meanings, depending on its context.

Likewise, Isaiah and Revelation are describing two different kingdoms of God. Isaiah is describing the Son's renewed or restored Genesis earth for a restored humanity. Humans marry, have children, and get old. Some sin exists and death can still be experienced. Revelation, however, is describing the Father's eternal paradise for the transformed sons of God that occurs after this earth perishes. It is described as a sinless kingdom for the immortal sons of God. Let's first examine Isaiah's prophecy:

> "For behold, I create new heavens and a new earth, and the former things shall not be remembered or come into mind [the hardships in this fallen world]. . . . No more shall there be in it an infant who lives but a few days, or an old man who does not fill out his days, for the young man shall die a hundred years old [mortality], and the sinner a hundred years old shall be accursed [some sin still exists]. They shall build houses and inhabit them [human habitats]; they shall plant vineyards and eat their fruit [agricultural fields]. . . . They shall not labor in vain or bear children for calamity [marriage and reproduction], for they shall

be the offspring of the blessed of the LORD, and their descendants with them [extended human families].... The wolf and the lamb shall graze together [nature restored]; ... They shall not hurt or destroy in all my holy mountain," says the LORD [peace and security]. (Isa. 65:17–25)

Isaiah describes the restoration of the Genesis creation in this Adamic age. This restoration involves mortal human beings. The people of God will marry, have children, build houses, and plant vineyards for their families. They will live extremely long lives of peace and prosperity. And they will live in an Edenic paradise, where "the wolf and the lamb shall graze together." According to the prophets, the messianic kingdom is by definition a restoration of the Adamic order of being, during an age of righteous humanity, when the world will experience peace and security on this restored earth. This restoration is not perfect, however, for there will still be some sinners who will continue to experience mortal death.

Revelation also uses the expression "new heaven and a new earth," which is created after the 1,000-year restoration of this Genesis earth. But John was not describing the restored earth with a restored Jerusalem as Isaiah described. Instead, he was referring to the eternal new earth and the New Jerusalem as the Father's eternal kingdom that replaces the Genesis heavens and earth after they perish. He described the children of God as being immortal and living in a sinless kingdom. As Jesus taught, it will be a place for the sons of God who, after being resurrected, "neither marry nor are given in marriage":

From his presence earth and sky fled away, and no place was found for them [the end of this Genesis creation].... Then I saw a new heaven and a new earth, ... And I saw the holy city, new Jerusalem, ... He will wipe away every tear from their eyes, and death shall be no more [immortality], ... And he who was seated on the throne said, "Behold, I am making all things new [the new eternal kingdom].... The one who conquers will have this heritage, and I will be his God and he will be my son [the children of God]." ... And I saw no temple in the city, for its temple is the Lord God the Almighty and the Lamb.... But nothing unclean will ever enter it, nor anyone who does what is detestable or false [sinless existence], but only those who are written in the Lamb's book of life [only believers]. (Rev. 20:11—21:27)

Isaiah envisioned the new heavens and new earth as a restored Genesis earth with a restored earthly Jerusalem in the restored land of Israel for a restored humanity—with some sinners. In contrast, John envisioned the new heavens and new earth as the eternal home of the sons of God who will live an immortal and sinless existence in the very presence of the triune God in all their glory.

Theologians have spent too much time trying to reconcile these two expressions of the new heavens and new earth. Isaiah and the apostle John were clearly describing two different kingdoms of the triune God:
1. The Son's restored earth—with marriage, reproduction, and an abundance of food from fruit-bearing trees, where some level of sin and mortality exists
2. The Father's eternal new heavens and new earth—a sinless kingdom for the immortal children of God

These are two very different kingdoms—one on earth and one in heaven—because they are adapted for two different orders of being.

The Reign of Christ

But where is Christ when he finally rules the world? Premillennialists claim that he must physically return to this earth to rule the world during his millennial kingdom. But amillennialists correctly note that the Scriptures teach that Christ destroys this world when he comes again to rapture the saints and take them to the eternal new earth. Logically, Christ cannot reign on the earth with his saints for a thousand years if the earth is destroyed when he comes again.

Isaiah gives us a clue as to where Christ is when he establishes his messianic kingdom on this earth. Immediately after describing "a new heaven and a new earth" as the restored Edenic earth, Isaiah reminds us that the Lord—who created this earth—continues to rule over his creation from his throne in heaven:

Thus says the Lord: "*Heaven is my throne*, and the earth is my footstool; what is the house that you would build for me, and what is the place of my rest? All these things my hand has made [the Genesis creation], and so all these things came to be, declares the Lord." (Isa. 66:1–2)

The "Lord" is a reference to the Son of God, who is the person of the Trinity who created this Genesis earth. Isaiah teaches that from his throne in heaven, the Lord "made" this earth when he just said the word, and it "came to be." And the earth continues to be his "footstool" (not his actual dwelling place). Isaiah teaches that the same Lord will also rule over his future renewed and restored Edenic earth from his throne in heaven, when he makes all his enemies a footstool.

Discerning where Christ will be when he finally rules the world during the millennium is rather simple. As the human son of David, one would expect the Messiah to rule over the world from a human throne on this earth. That is what the disciples initially expected. But as the Son of God and our Creator, one would expect our Lord to rule over his creation from his divine throne in heaven. The millennium is simply the Son's dominion over his Genesis creation restored.

Some theologians believe that when God spoke to Adam, God appeared physically on this earth. Others believe Adam and Eve only heard his voice in the garden. Either way, God primarily ruled over his creation from his throne in heaven. And he will do so once again when he rules the world during the millennium.

And what better person to properly manage the affairs of mankind than Jesus Christ? Not only does he know what it means to be a human on this earth, but from his exalted throne in heaven he also has the omniscience of God, with infinite awareness, infinite understanding, and infinite insight into the affairs of the world. As God, Christ certainly has the divine knowledge and ability to rule this world from heaven.

Throughout this book, I will make the biblical case that during the millennium, instead of Christ returning to this earth as the son of David to rule the world as claimed by premillennialists, the Son of God will remain on his throne in heaven at the right hand of God the Father after he removes Satan to rule over his restored Genesis creation. As God, he can surely rule over his creation from heaven—just as he would have ruled over Adam and Eve had they not rebelled against him. In fact, this is the only way Christ can rule the world and establish his messianic kingdom because the Scriptures teach that when Christ does return, it will be on Judgment Day, at the end of this Genesis age when he creates the new heavens and new earth and ushers in the eternal age to come.

The First and Final Resurrections

How are the saints going to physically inherit and inhabit the Son's restored earth, as described by Isaiah, if they have already died and their spirits have risen to heaven? And how are the saints going to then inherit the Father's eternal new earth, as described by John? The answers to these two questions are quite simple if we consider God's divine power of resurrection.

John identifies two resurrections:
- The *first resurrection* in order for the departed saints to inherit the Son's millennial kingdom
- The *second resurrection* in order for the saints to inherit the Father's eternal new heavens and new earth

Since the millennium is for the restored Adamic order of being, then we would expect the first resurrection to be of the natural bodies of the departed saints, as described in Ezekiel 37 (the valley of dry bones). The resurrected saints would marry and reproduce godly offspring in a restored Edenic paradise. This resurrection would be like the resurrection of Lazarus into his natural body. But instead of Lazarus and the saints coming back to life on a cursed earth under Satan's dominion, they would live again on a restored Edenic earth under Christ's dominion.

And since the subsequent new heavens and new earth are the eternal home for the Father's children, then we would expect the final resurrection to be of the raptured saints, when their natural bodies are transformed into eternal bodies like Christ's glorified body in order to inhabit the Father's eternal kingdom.

The Lord's Prayer

The Lord's Prayer begins to make more sense when one understands these two kingdoms of the triune God. We seek first God the Father's kingdom of heaven. But we also anticipate God the Son's kingdom on earth, when God's will is done on earth as it is in heaven. Note that Christ teaches us to address this prayer to God the Father.

> **Pray then like this:**
> **Our Father in heaven, hallowed be your name** [we start our prayers with worship of the Father].
> **Your kingdom come** [the Father's heavenly kingdom],
> **your will be done, on earth as it is in heaven** [during the Son's earthly kingdom when he establishes his righteous reign over this earth].
> **Give us this day our daily bread** [today, while waiting for these two kingdoms, we should live a life of dependence on God],
> **and forgive us our debts, as we also have forgiven our debtors** [and live a life of love and mercy],
> **And lead us not into temptation, but deliver us from evil** [deliver us from Satan now and during the Great Tribulation]. (Matt. 6:9–13)

Christ revealed a new perspective on God's plan of redemption. First, we seek the Father's kingdom of heaven and look forward to Christ's return to take us there. Next, we pray for the Son's kingdom, when Satan is removed and Christ sits on his throne in heaven and rules the world, establishing God's will on earth as it is in heaven.

Critiquing the Current Views on God's Endgame

This method of understanding the two kingdoms of the triune God is a simple but effective way to understand God's plan of redemption. It is also an effective way to analyze and critique the current views on God's endgame. For example, premillennialists believe the raptured saints will return to the restored Edenic earth with Christ during the millennium. But how are the glorified saints going to enjoy an Edenic paradise as restored human beings if they are immortal creatures and a new creation that no longer experiences marriage? The raptured saints clearly belong in the Father's kingdom of heaven, not on the Son's restored Edenic earth.

Amillennialists and postmillennialists assert that Satan is never totally removed from this evil world. We never experience a restoration of our humanity on a restored Edenic earth. The raptured saints only inherit the Father's kingdom. But doesn't Christ, as the Son of God, have a divine right to reclaim, restore, and rule over his own creation—before he returns and turns his kingdom over to the Father? It was the Son's kingdom to begin with, before Adam and Eve fell for Satan's temptation and Satan usurped his kingdom. Wouldn't a restoration of the Son's creation bring him great glory as he delights in his good creation once again? Isn't there an unconditional covenant between the Father and the Son that one day the Father will restore this Genesis creation to his Son?

God's plan of redemption includes an almost complete reversal of the curse and a restoration of the Adamic order of being on the Son's restored earth—before he returns and we are taken to the Father's home in heaven as his children.

Summary

Theologians use a variety of methods to evaluate the Scriptures to understand God's plan of redemption. I have found that the best method of interpreting the Scriptures to discern God's endgame is to understand the two different orders of being and the two kingdoms of the triune God. Postrestorationalism maintains the distinction between the two orders of being and their corresponding kingdoms:

- The Son's millennial kingdom is a restoration of the Adamic order of being on an Edenic earth—accessed through the first resurrection of the natural bodies of the departed saints.
- The Father's new heavens and new earth is a new creation and is the eternal home for the transformed sons of God—accessed through the final resurrection of their eternal bodies.

To establish his millennial kingdom, Christ simply removes Satan and rules over the restored Edenic earth during the millennium from his throne in heaven. He returns *after* (post-) this 1,000-year restoration of this Genesis creation on the last day to rapture the saints and usher in the Father's eternal kingdom of heaven.

5

A Chart of God's Endgame

Review

The last two chapters explained my method of interpreting and organizing the Scriptures to understand God's endgame. Theologians refer to these methods as "biblical hermeneutics." A popular expression among theologians today is that God's inaugurated kingdom "already is, and is yet to come" in a future consummation. But this does not answer the question about what is yet to come.

My method of interpreting and organizing the Scriptures into a biblical theology of the future is based on the two orders of being:

- The Adamic order of being
- The new order of being as sons of God

It is also based on the two corresponding kingdoms of the triune God:

- The Son's earthly kingdom for a restored Adamic order of being in this Genesis age
- The Father's heavenly kingdom for the immortal sons of God in the eternal age to come

When reading Scripture, I try to discern whether it is referring to the Son's messianic kingdom during this Genesis age for a restored humanity, or to the Father's eternal kingdom of heaven for the transformed sons of God. For example, the vivid description of Christ's messianic kingdom in Isaiah 65 describes the restored earth as a human paradise, with men and women having homes, vineyards, and large extended families.

Whereas in Christ's answer to the Sadducees, he taught that in the Father's eternal kingdom, the Adamic order of being as male and female given in marriage comes to an end when the sons of God are resurrected into immortal bodies. The eternal sons of God will have real bodies, but they will be very different from the current natural bodies that are adapted for marriage and the natural earth.

And the fact that we will not be given in marriage in heaven is not some incidental detail about our eternal existence. Christ was teaching that there will be a categorical change in our whole being. The sons of God will have a totally different kind of bodily experience than the one we now have in our sexual Adamic bodies. And we will experience a totally different kind of communal life on the new earth. I will no longer be a son, a brother, a husband, a father, a grandfather, or an uncle—I will simply be a fellow child of God to my companions in heaven.

In this chapter, I will create a chart by outlining the major events of the Bible—past, present, and future. Then, in the next two chapters, I will explain how the different views on God's endgame compare to this chart.

A CHART OF GOD'S ENDGAME | 91

PART 1: A Biblical Chart

Note: The following chart is best understood by watching a two-part video presentation online at www.godsendgame.net. It is also available on the website to download and print.

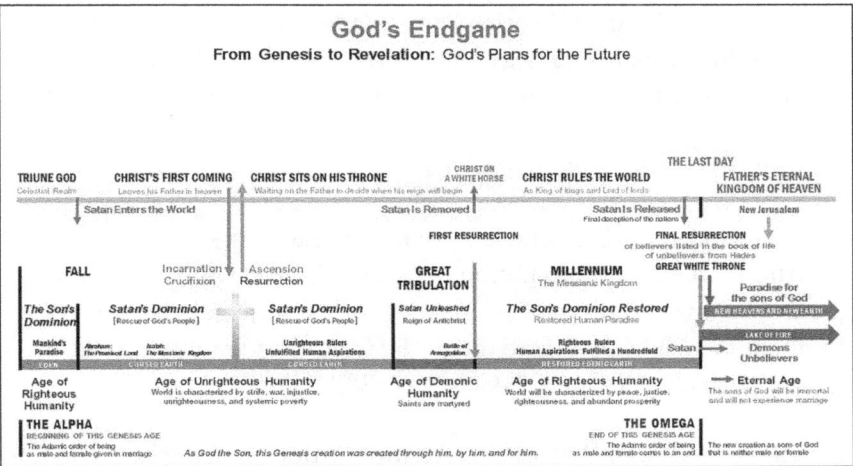

The Bible portrays God as living in his celestial home in heaven. From the celestial realm, God created this world: "In the beginning, God created the heavens and the earth" (Gen. 1:1). The heavens and the earth then had a presence before God in space and time.

God also created Adam: "Then the LORD God formed the man of dust from the ground and breathed into his nostrils the breath of life, and the man became a living creature" (Gen. 2:7). Adam became a spiritual creature contained in a physical body of flesh and blood. God then created an Edenic paradise for Adam:

> And the LORD God planted a garden in Eden, in the east, and there he put the man whom he had formed. And out of the ground the LORD God made to spring up every tree that is pleasant to the sight and good for food. . . . The LORD God took the man and put him in the garden of Eden to work it and keep it. (Gen. 2:8–15)

Adam was tasked with continuing to develop and manage the garden of Eden. But Adam was alone in this paradise and needed a helpmate, so God created Eve:

> Then the Lord God said, "It is not good that the man should be alone. I will make him a helper fit for him." . . . So the Lord God . . . took one of his ribs and . . . he made into a woman . . . Therefore a man shall leave his father and his mother and hold fast to his wife, and they shall become one flesh. (Gen. 2:18–24)

Genesis continues to define mankind:

> Then God said, "Let us make man in our image, after our likeness. And let them have dominion . . . over all the earth . . ." So God created man in his own image, . . . male and female he created them. . . . And God said to them, "Be fruitful and multiply and fill the earth and subdue it." (Gen. 1:26–28)

This is a description of the Adamic order of being as male and female given in marriage. Adam and Eve were to experience the union of one flesh and to multiply, filling the earth with their offspring. Their extended family would develop the untamed earth into an Edenic paradise, managing the earth on God's behalf. The garden of Eden was mankind's paradise and a short age of righteous humanity. From his celestial throne in heaven, God would rule over mankind as they properly managed the earth. God would be intimately involved in the affairs of man, and he would delight in watching mankind develop a civilization that would bring him great joy and glory.

We discover from the New Testament that the one God is a triune God as the Father, Son, and Holy Spirit. We also learn that this creation was uniquely created by the Son of God—through him, by him, and for him.

John revealed that Jesus Christ was God incarnate, the eternal Son of God through whom this creation was made (John 1:1–14). He was the Creator who spoke this Genesis creation into existence. Within the Trinity, the world was uniquely the Son's earthly kingdom. He was the Alpha and the beginning of this Genesis age. Hebrews also proclaims this truth:

In these last days, he has spoken to us by his Son, whom he appointed the heir of all things, through whom also he created the world. . . . He upholds the universe by the word of his power. . . . "You, Lord, laid the foundation of the earth in the beginning, and the heavens are the work of your hands." (Heb. 1:2–10)

Paul repeated this remarkable truth about the Son of God:

For by him all things were created, in heaven and on earth, visible and invisible, whether thrones or dominions or rulers or authorities—all things were created through him and for him. (Col. 1:16)

This Genesis creation was the Son's dominion over mankind. As he ruled over Adam and Eve, they were to rule over and manage his wonderful creation. The world would be the Son's kingdom on earth, and God's will would be done on earth as it was in heaven. The Son of God would visit Adam on this earth from time to time, but he primarily ruled over his creation from the celestial realm of heaven.

Then God tested Adam to see if he would remain under his Lordship:

The LORD God took the man and put him in the garden of Eden to work it and keep it. And the LORD God commanded the man, saying, "You may surely eat of every tree of the garden, but of the tree of the knowledge of good and evil you shall not eat, for in the day that you eat of it you shall surely die." (Gen. 2:15–17)

This restriction did not represent a deprivation, for Adam and Eve had everything they needed for a fruitful and abundant life.

Then Satan tempted Adam and Eve to reject God's dominion over them and set up their own autonomous kingdom of mankind: "But the serpent said to the woman, 'You will not surely die. For God knows that when you eat of it your eyes will be opened, and you will be like God, knowing good and evil'" (Gen. 3:4–5).

Adam and Eve succumbed to this temptation, which led to the tragic fall of mankind: "So when the woman saw . . . that the tree was to be desired to make one wise, she took of its fruit and ate, and she also gave some to her husband who was with her, and he ate" (Gen. 3:6).

Their flagrant disobedience led to their insubordination, insurrection, and rebellion against God's rule over them. With the knowledge of good and evil, they believed they no longer needed God to be their Lord. They could be the Lord of their own lives and of this world.

This infuriated God and brought down his wrath on mankind. Because of their rebellion, Adam and Eve were expelled from the garden of Eden, and God put a curse on the natural earth:

> To the woman he said, "I will surely multiply your pain in childbearing; in pain you shall bring forth children.". . . And to Adam he said, . . . "cursed is the ground because of you; in pain you shall eat of it all the days of your life; . . . By the sweat of your face you shall eat bread, till you return to the ground, for out of it you were taken; for you are dust, and to dust you shall return.". . . Therefore the Lord God sent him out from the garden of Eden. (Gen. 3:16–23)

Mankind became sinful creatures separated from the spiritual life of God. Now they would experience spiritual and mortal death. Paradise was lost, and the world became a hostile environment. Mankind would experience deprivation and misery on a degenerate earth until they died.

There was also a regime change when God allowed Satan and his horde of demons into their paradise, and the world became Satan's dominion. He became the god of sinful mankind, usurping the Son of God as true Lord of this world. As Paul taught, "And you were dead in the trespasses and sins in which you once walked, following the course of this world, following the prince of the power of the air" (Eph. 2:1–2). Sinful mankind was now under Satan's influence and control, and an age of unrighteous humanity began. The world became characterized by strife, war, injustice, unrighteousness, and systemic poverty. Mankind would now have to be rescued if they were ever going to escape from Satan's dominion.

Because of the fall, there are four fundamental problems with the world:
- It is a satanic world.
- Humans have a sinful nature.
- The world is ruled by unrighteous men and women.
- The creation is under a curse.

This explains why the world, even with its residual natural beauty and moments of joy, is such an inhospitable place with so much evil, misery, and death. It is definitely not paradise on earth. Some of us are fortunate enough to have fairly good lives that can be deeply fulfilling, but they are relatively short lives.

There are fundamental problems with humanity because the world is no longer the Son of God's kingdom on earth, even though this cursed earth was, and remains, his creation. God remains sovereign while he allows Satan and rebellious mankind to live ungodly lives, but he has not yet reimposed his righteous will on this earth.

Fallen mankind could have gone the way of Satan and the fallen angels, with no hope of salvation. There is no plan of redemption for fallen angels. They are purely evil creatures destined for wrath and hell. But God in his sovereignty decided to love mankind and save many of us from our fallen, sinful natures. After the fall, he introduced his plans for the future redemption of mankind and the eventual punishment of Satan and his removal from this world:

> The Lord God said to the serpent, … "I will put enmity between you and the woman, and between your offspring and her offspring; he shall bruise [or crush] your head, and you shall bruise [or strike] his heel." (Gen. 3:14–15)

God promised a Savior who will come from a descendant of Eve and who will eventually crush Satan. The process will bring some measure of suffering to the redeemer. This indicates that the redeemer will likely sacrifice his life to redeem mankind from Satan's dominion. But there is hope for the Son's earthly kingdom to be restored and for the restoration of mankind on a restored Edenic earth.

The Call of Abraham

God's plan of redemption is further developed with the call of Abraham, who was a descendant of Eve:

> Now the Lord said to Abram, "Go from your country and your kindred and your father's house to the land that I will show you. And I will make of you a great nation, and I will bless you and

make your name great, so that you will be a blessing.... In you all the families of the earth shall be blessed." (Gen. 12:1–3)

God's plan involves a nation formed from the heirs of Abraham, which will bring some form of salvation to all nations. His plan continued to develop with Moses and the nation of Israel. After the exodus from Egypt, God told Moses and the Jews: "Go in and take possession of the land that the Lord swore to your fathers, to Abraham, to Isaac, and to Jacob, to give to them and to their offspring after them" (Deut. 1:8).

As Israel became a nation, David became their king. Through the prophet Nathan, God informed David that one of his sons would usher in a restored dominion of God that would never be usurped by Satan again: "When your days are fulfilled and you lie down with your fathers, I will raise up your offspring after you, ... and I will establish the throne of his kingdom forever" (2 Sam. 7:12–13).

Isaiah also foretold of the promised son of David and the coming Messiah, who will govern Israel and the whole world:

> For to us a child is born, to us a son is given; and the government [of Israel and the world] shall be upon his shoulder, and his name shall be called Wonderful Counselor, Mighty God, Everlasting Father, Prince of Peace. Of the increase of his government and of *peace* there will be no end, on the throne of David and over his kingdom, to establish it and to uphold it with *justice* and with *righteousness* from this time forth and forevermore. The zeal of the Lord of hosts will do this. (Isa. 9:6–7)

The future Messiah would be a human being as a descendant of Eve, Abraham, and King David—as well as being "Mighty God." The Messiah would be the God-man who reestablishes the Son's kingdom on this earth. The world will be characterized by peace, justice, and righteousness. It will be an age of restored righteous humanity. The prophets described the messianic kingdom as an earthly kingdom in which the earth is restored to its Edenic condition. It will be a restoration of the Adamic order of being as originally intended in the garden of Eden.

Paul referenced this prophecy in Isaiah, which describes the Messiah as both the son of David and the Son of God:

> The gospel of God, which he promised beforehand through his prophets in the holy Scriptures, concerning his Son, who was descended from David according to the flesh ["a child is born"] and was declared to be the Son of God ["Mighty God"]. (Rom. 1:1–4)

Christ's First Coming

Christ's first coming was of the seed of the woman, born of Mary:

> And the angel said to her, . . . "behold, you will conceive in your womb and bear a son, . . . The Holy Spirit will come upon you, . . . therefore the child to be born will be called holy—the Son of God." (Luke 1:30–35)

The Son of God left his Father in heaven and entered the world through his incarnation as the human son of David: "In the beginning was the Word, and the Word was with God, and the Word was God. . . . And the Word became flesh and dwelt among us" (John 1:1, 14).

God the Father loved mankind. He sent his Son to become incarnate as a human being, which is a key part of his plan of redemption:

> For God so loved the world, that he gave his only Son, that whoever believes in him should not perish but have eternal life. For God did not send his Son into the world to condemn it, but in order that the world might be saved through him. (John 3:16–17)

However, only a remnant of faithful Jews in Jesus' day responded to Christ: "He was in the world, and the world was made through him, yet the world did not know him. He came to his own [creation and Jewish people], and his own people did not receive him" (John 1:10–11). That generation of Jews was hardhearted, blind, unregenerate, and unfaithful. And they had their own Messiah crucified by the Romans, even though Christ demonstrated many miraculous signs and wonders and numerous displays of love, compassion, and forgiveness.

But in God's divine plan, Jesus was crucified for our sins and resurrected to overcome Satan's power of sin and death over us. The cross was God's method of justifying the ungodly so that we could be reconciled with a holy God. Before we can enter his restored righteous kingdom on a restored Edenic earth, we first need to be made righteous through Christ's sacrificial death on the cross:

> And you, who once were alienated and hostile in mind, doing evil deeds, he has now reconciled in his body of flesh by his death, in order to present you holy and blameless and above reproach before him, . . . And you, who were dead in your trespasses . . . God made alive together with him, having forgiven us all our trespasses, by canceling the record of debt that stood against us with its legal demands. This he set aside, nailing it to the cross. (Col. 1:21–22; 2:13–14)

The disciples should have known from Isaiah that the Messiah must first die for our sins before we could enter his kingdom:

> He was despised and rejected by men; a man of sorrows, and acquainted with grief; . . . Surely he has borne our griefs and carried our sorrows; . . . Smitten by God, . . . he was pierced for our transgressions; he was crushed for our iniquities; upon him was the chastisement that brought us peace, . . . And the Lord has laid on him the iniquity of us all. . . . Although he had done no violence, and there was no deceit in his mouth. . . . By his knowledge shall the righteous one, my servant, make many to be accounted righteous. (Isa. 53:3–13)

After his resurrection, Christ appeared to two people walking home to the village of Emmaus. They did not understand why the Messiah had been crucified. He was supposed to overthrow the tyrannical Romans and set up his messianic kingdom on this earth. Christ rebuked them for their failure to understand the necessity of his crucifixion:

> Concerning Jesus of Nazareth, . . . our chief priests and rulers delivered him up to be condemned to death, and crucified him. But we had hoped that he was the one to redeem Israel. . . . And he

said to them, "O foolish ones, and slow of heart to believe all that the prophets have spoken! Was it not necessary that the Christ should suffer these things and enter into his glory [as the ruler of Israel and this world]?" And beginning with Moses and all the Prophets, he interpreted to them in all the Scriptures the things concerning himself. (Luke 24:19–27)

But the disciples still expected Jesus to set up his messianic kingdom. They probably thought that since the Romans could not kill him, he would overthrow their tyrannical regime and begin his reign over a restored Israel:

So when they had come together, they asked him, "Lord, will you at this time restore the kingdom to Israel?" He said to them, "It is not for you to know times or seasons that the Father has fixed by his own authority." . . . And when he had said these things, as they were looking on, he was lifted up, and a cloud took him out of their sight. (Acts 1:6–9)

Christ confirmed that there would be a messianic kingdom in the future but told them the Father decides when his reign will begin.

Christ then ascended in the clouds, when he entered the celestial realm of heaven to rejoin his Father. The prophet Daniel also foresaw the day when Christ would ascend in the clouds to heaven and would be given dominion over the world by the Father. The reference to the Ancient of Days is a reference to God the Father:

I saw in the night visions, and behold, with the clouds of heaven there came one like a son of man [Christ ascends in the clouds], and he came to the Ancient of Days and was presented before him. And to him was given dominion and glory and a kingdom, that all peoples, nations, and languages should serve him; his dominion is an everlasting dominion, which shall not pass away, and his kingdom one that shall not be destroyed. (Dan. 7:13–14)

After his resurrection, Christ ascended into the clouds to the right hand of God the Father in heaven, in fulfillment of Daniel's vision. He was given dominion over the whole world, not just over Israel.

The Jewish leaders were familiar with Daniel's vision and understood that the son of man was no ordinary man because he ascends into the very presence of God in heaven. They assumed that "the son of man" was a divine being. And when Christ applied the phrase to himself when he was being questioned by the chief priests and scribes, they accused him of blasphemy for claiming to be this divine being:

> Jesus said to him, "You have said so. But I tell you, from now on you will see the Son of Man seated at the right hand of Power and coming on the clouds of heaven." Then the high priest tore his robes and said, "He has uttered blasphemy [for claiming to be this divine being]." (Matt. 26:64–65)

Christ now sits on his throne in heaven, where he is waiting on the Father, or the Ancient of Days, to decide when his reign will begin. He now has all the divine power necessary to rule this world:

> And what is the immeasurable greatness of his power toward us who believe, according to the working of his great might that he worked in Christ when he raised him from the dead and seated him at his right hand in the heavenly places, far above all rule and authority and power and dominion, and above every name that is named, not only in this age [the Genesis age] but also in the one to come [the eternal age]. (Eph. 1:19–21)

As the book of Hebrews plainly teaches, however, he is not currently using his divine power and authority to remove Satan and the ungodly rulers of this world and reclaim his Genesis creation:

> "You made him [Christ] for a little while lower than the angels [during the incarnation]; you have crowned him with glory and honor [after his crucifixion, resurrection, and ascension], putting everything in subjection under his feet ["to him was given dominion"]." Now in putting everything in subjection to him, he left nothing outside his control [he is sovereign]. *At present, we do not yet see everything in subjection to him* [his enemies continue to operate]. (Heb. 2:7–8)

That is because Satan has not yet been removed, and the world remains his dominion. Christ is waiting on the Father to decide when Satan will be removed and when his reign will begin. As Hebrews further teaches:

> But when Christ had offered for all time a single sacrifice for sins, he sat down at the right hand of God, *waiting* from that time until his enemies should be made a footstool for his feet. (Heb. 10:12–13)

The disciples expected Christ to set up his messianic kingdom when he first came into this world. They were even jockeying for positions of authority and power in what they thought was his imminent reign. Instead, he left this world, leaving them in a hostile, demonic world where they were often unjustly persecuted. But they began to understand that the ascended Christ would have to wait on his Father to determine when his reign would begin.

In the meantime, Christ taught his disciples to shift their focus to the Father's eternal kingdom of heaven: "But seek first the kingdom of God and his righteousness, and all these things will be added to you" (Matt. 6:33). Soon after Pentecost, Peter initially focused on the restoration of Israel and the messianic kingdom:

> He may send . . . Jesus, whom heaven must receive until the time for restoring all the things about which God spoke by the mouth of his holy prophets long ago [the messianic kingdom on this earth]. (Acts 3:20–21)

But in his following letters, Peter shifts the focus to our inheritance of the Father's imperishable kingdom of heaven:

> Blessed be the God and Father of our Lord Jesus Christ! According to his [the Father's] great mercy, he has caused us to be born again [as sons of God] to a living hope through the resurrection of Jesus Christ from the dead [we hope for the same resurrection and ascension to heaven], to an inheritance that is imperishable, undefiled, and unfading, kept in heaven for you. (1 Peter 1:3–4)

The focus is clearly on the Father's eternal kingdom of heaven. Until then, Christ continues to gather his people chosen by the Father out of Satan's dominion of darkness and bring them into his kingdom:

> He has delivered us from the domain of darkness and transferred us to the kingdom of his beloved Son, in whom we have redemption, the forgiveness of sins." (Col. 1:13–14)

Now that Christ has died for our sins, he rescues his people who lived before his coming. And he rescues his people today and brings us into his righteous kingdom. But even after we are rescued from Satan's dominion, we remain in this fallen, demonic world ruled by Satan. Paul warns:

> Put on the whole armor of God, that you may be able to stand against the schemes of the devil. For we do not wrestle against flesh and blood, but against the rulers, against the authorities, against the cosmic powers over this present darkness, against the spiritual forces of evil in the heavenly places. (Eph. 6:11–12)

Demons are still very active in this world. And unrighteous men and women under their influence continue to rule over the nations. As a result, many of our human aspirations for a good life on this earth go unfulfilled. We may experience inner joy and peace through the indwelling of the Holy Spirit, but we continue to long for an abundant life that is free of Satan and the curse. Or as Paul taught, we continue to live on a cursed earth:

> For the creation waits with eager longing for the revealing of the sons of God. For the creation was subjected to futility, . . . For we know that the whole creation has been groaning together in the pains of childbirth until now. (Rom. 8:19–22)

During this interim period leading up to the time when Christ uses his divine power to set up his messianic kingdom, the rulers of this world will continue to cause wars between nations. Jesus said, "For nation will rise against nation, and kingdom against kingdom" (Matt. 24:7). The curse on the earth will remain in place as well. Jesus said,

"There will be famines and earthquakes in various places" (Matt. 24:7). That is because these events are leading up to even greater pain during the future Great Tribulation: "All these [wars and natural disasters] are but the beginning of the birth pains" (Matt. 24:8).

The disciples were expecting Christ to set up his messianic kingdom, but the nation of Israel rejected its Messiah when he came into this world during the first century. Therefore, Christ informed the unfaithful Jews that their temple would be destroyed as a sign that God had temporarily abandoned them:

> O Jerusalem, Jerusalem, the city that kills the prophets and stones those who are sent to it [unfaithful Israel]! How often would I have gathered your children together as a hen gathers her brood under her wings, and you were not willing [unrepentant Israel]! See, your house is left to you desolate [the temple will be destroyed]. For I tell you, you will not see me again, until you say, "Blessed is he who comes in the name of the Lord [repentant Israel]." (Matt. 23:37–38)

This occurred in AD 70 when the Romans sacked Jerusalem and the temple was destroyed. But Christ foresaw the day when they will indeed repent and believe in their Messiah.

Christ warned the disciples to flee Judea when they saw the Roman armies approaching to destroy the city and the temple:

> And he said, . . . "When you see Jerusalem surrounded by armies, then know that its desolation has come near. Then let those who are in Judea flee to the mountains, . . . for these are days of vengeance, . . . For there will be great distress upon the earth and wrath against this people [the unbelieving Jews]. They will fall by the edge of the sword and be led captive among all nations, and Jerusalem will be trampled underfoot by the Gentiles, until the times of the Gentiles are fulfilled." (Luke 21:8–24)

The Jewish Christians in Jerusalem heeded Christ's advice and escaped this judgment and tribulation against unrepentant Israel.

PART 2: The Great Tribulation

Many theologians believe the Great Tribulation took place in AD 70 and that it was directed against the generation of Jews who rejected Christ. For the purposes of this chart, however, I will assume that the Great Tribulation is a future event that affects all people living at that time. Before Christ's reign begins, there will be a period of unprecedented tribulation against the saints.

The prophet Daniel noted that the end of the Antichrist's reign of terror is the event that leads to the messianic kingdom. The Antichrist is described as a beast and also as a horn that appears on a beast:

> Then I desired to know the truth about the fourth beast [the Antichrist], which was different from all the rest [exceptionally evil], . . . As I looked, this horn made war with the saints and prevailed over them [during the Great Tribulation], until the Ancient of Days came, and judgment was given for the saints of the Most High, and the time came when the saints possessed the kingdom [the Son's dominion established]. (Dan. 7:19–22)

The tribulation experienced in AD 70 was directed at the unrepentant Jews. The saints could escape that tribulation by leaving Jerusalem when they saw the approaching Roman armies. But notice that when the Antichrist initiates the Great Tribulation, his persecution is specifically directed at the saints, and they will not be able to easily escape it. Also notice that the Ancient of Days will determine when the Messiah's reign will begin and the saints possess his Son's kingdom.

The world is currently Satan's dominion, and Christians are living in hostile territory: "Be sober-minded; be watchful. Your adversary the devil prowls around like a roaring lion, seeking someone to devour" (1 Peter 5:8). Satan is a powerful fallen angel with tremendous influence in the world. But the Scriptures teach that he is restricted in how much evil he can instigate. He must approach the throne of God in heaven to gain permission to attack us. Job's story illustrates this restraint.

The book of Daniel describes the archangel Michael as a powerful angel who can restrain Satan. When Michael is removed from restraining him, Satan will be unleashed on the world and the Great Tribulation will begin. This is the reign of the Antichrist:

At that time shall arise Michael, the great prince who has charge of your people [Michael, who protects Israel against Satan, is removed from restraining Satan]. And there shall be a time of trouble, such as never has been since there was a nation till that time [the unprecedented Great Tribulation begins]. (Dan. 12:1)

Once Michael is no longer restraining him, Satan can work through the Antichrist, who claims to be God incarnate on this earth:

And the king shall do as he wills. He shall exalt himself and magnify himself above every god [he makes himself out to be God], and shall speak astonishing things against the God of gods. (Dan. 11:36)

Satan and his Antichrist are unleashed on the world, which leads to an age of demonic humanity during which the saints are martyred in large numbers. Few will survive their reign of terror.

Revelation 12 also describes a cosmic battle in heaven between Michael and Satan, which culminates in Satan being unleashed on the world:

Now war arose in heaven, Michael and his angels fighting against the dragon [Satan]. . . . And the great dragon . . . was thrown down to the earth, . . . "But woe to you, O earth and sea, for the devil has come down to you in great wrath, because he knows that his time is short!" . . . And I saw a beast [the Antichrist] . . . And to it the dragon gave his power and his throne and great authority. . . . And the beast was . . . allowed to make war on the saints. . . . If anyone is to be slain with the sword, with the sword must he be slain. Here is a call for the endurance and faith of the saints. (12:7–12; 13:1–10)

Satan and the Antichrist go to war against the saints. Unbelievers will be deceived into believing the Antichrist is God incarnate and will become his followers. They will worship Satan and his Antichrist:

The whole earth marveled as they followed the beast. And they worshiped the dragon [Satan], for he had given his authority to the beast, and they worshiped the beast [the Antichrist], saying, "Who is like the beast, and who can fight against it?" (Rev. 13:3–4)

Paul warned us to be on the lookout for the Antichrist entering a rebuilt temple, making himself out to be God:

> Let no one deceive you in any way. For that day will not come [the second coming], unless the rebellion comes first, and the man of lawlessness is revealed, the son of destruction, who opposes and exalts himself against every so-called god or object of worship, so that he takes his seat in the temple of God, proclaiming himself to be God. . . . The coming of the lawless one is by the activity of Satan with all power and false signs and wonders. (2 Thess. 2:3–9)

Jesus, too, warned us to look for the Antichrist entering the temple:

> So when you see the abomination of desolation spoken of by the prophet Daniel, standing in the holy place (let the reader understand), . . . For then there will be great tribulation [against the saints], such as has not been from the beginning of the world. [As Daniel says, "This horn made war with the saints and prevailed over them."] (Matt. 24:15–21)

This outpouring of demonic wrath against God's people will last for three and a half years.

John taught that the Tribulation comes to an end at the battle of Armageddon. Christ will appear in the celestial realm of heaven riding on a white horse to engage the Antichrist and his armies. Like a sharp sword coming out of his mouth, the word destroys the Antichrist and his armies:

> Then I saw heaven opened [the celestial realm], and behold, a white horse! . . . From his mouth comes a sharp sword with which to strike down the nations, and he will rule them with a rod of iron. . . . On his robe and on his thigh he has a name written, King of kings and Lord of lords. . . . And I saw the beast and the kings of the earth with their armies gathered to make war against him who was sitting on the horse and against his army. And the beast was captured, and with it the false prophet. . . . These two were thrown alive into the lake of fire that burns with sulfur. And the rest were slain by the sword that came from the mouth of him who was sitting on the horse. (Rev. 19:11–21)

The Millennium

The next major eschatological event is the millennial reign of Christ, which occurs after Satan's removal from this world. In the next two chapters, I explain the various interpretations of the millennium, but for now let's continue to develop this chart based on the sequence of events found in Revelation.

Satan has been in this world ever since the fall. He will now be removed from this realm so that the Son's dominion can be restored. John taught that during the millennium, Satan will be locked up in a prison made for demons. This is a real game changer:

> Then I saw an angel coming down from heaven, holding in his hand the key to the bottomless pit and a great chain. And he seized the dragon, that ancient serpent, who is the devil and Satan, and bound him for a thousand years, and threw him into the pit, and shut it and sealed it over him, so that he might not deceive the nations any longer, until the thousand years were ended. After that he must be released for a little while. (Rev. 20:1–3)

This marks the beginning of the millennial reign of Christ, when he will rule the world as King of kings and Lord of lords. The prophet Isaiah also foretold this cosmic regime change:

> On that day the LORD will punish the host of heaven, in heaven [Satan and his demons], . . . They will be gathered together as prisoners in a pit; they will be shut up in a prison, . . . Then the moon will be confounded and the sun ashamed, for the LORD of hosts reigns on Mount Zion and in Jerusalem [the Messiah's reign begins]. (Isa. 24:21–23)

The cosmic changes in the moon and the sun metaphorically describe this regime change in the spiritual realm. Satan and his demons are gathered up and imprisoned so that the reign of Christ can begin. Jesus was probably referencing this verse and similar verses from the prophets when he described the cosmic regime change that takes place immediately after the Tribulation comes to an end:

> For then there will be great tribulation, such as has not been from the beginning of the world until now, no, and never will be. . . . Immediately after the tribulation of those days the sun will be darkened, and the moon will not give its light, and the stars will fall from heaven, and the powers of the heavens will be shaken [cosmic regime change when Satan is removed and Christ begins his reign]. (Matt. 24:21–29)

During the millennium, Christ, as the Son of God, will use his divine power and authority to rule the world, as he did before the fall. It was his creation to begin with before Satan came into this world, so he has a divine right to remove Satan and rule this world:

> Then the seventh angel blew his trumpet, and there were loud voices in heaven, saying, "The kingdom of the world has become the kingdom of our Lord and of his Christ," . . . And the twenty-four elders . . . worshiped God, saying, "We give thanks to you, Lord God Almighty, who is and who was [a divine, eternal being], for you have taken your great power and begun to reign [over his Genesis creation]." (Rev. 11:16–17)

Notice that John refers to Christ's deity when he foresaw the day when Christ will rule the world.

The prophets taught that the Messiah's reign will begin in Israel and then extend to all nations:

> "As for me, I have set my King on Zion, my holy hill." I will tell of the decree: The Lord [the Father] said to me, "You are my Son; today I have begotten you. Ask of me, and *I will make the nations your heritage, and the ends of the earth your possession.*" (Ps. 2:6–8)

When Christ rules the world, the whole earth will experience the messianic kingdom:

> The Lord has made known his salvation; he has revealed his righteousness in the sight of the nations. . . . All the ends of the earth have seen the salvation of our God. . . . He will judge the world with righteousness, and the peoples with equity. (Ps. 98:2–9)

The millennium will be an age of righteous humanity for all mankind. The whole world, not just the nation of Israel, will be characterized by peace, justice, righteousness, and abundant prosperity. The book of Micah describes this major transition from a world characterized by war to a world characterized by global peace:

> He [the Messiah] shall judge between many peoples, and shall decide for strong nations far away [he rules the world]; and they shall beat their swords into plowshares, and their spears into pruning hooks; nation shall not lift up sword against nation, neither shall they learn war anymore [global peace]. (4:3)

Many people equate the Great Commission with spreading the gospel. However, notice that Isaiah refers to the *realization* of the messianic kingdom as the good news of salvation for the world:

> How beautiful upon the mountains are the feet of him who brings good news, who publishes peace, who brings good news of happiness, who publishes salvation, who says to Zion, "Your God reigns" [the gospel realized when Christ rules the world]. . . . The Lord has bared his holy arm before the eyes of all the nations, and all the ends of the earth shall see [and experience] the salvation of our God. (Isa. 52:7–10)

Salvation involves more than just personal salvation from God's wrath on Judgment Day. It includes a salvation of humanity on this earth during Christ's reign, when all the ends of the earth shall see and experience the salvation of our God and Creator. Isaiah teaches that the realization of Christ's reign is a critical part of the good news.

In the following passage, I believe Christ was quoting from Psalm 98 when he affirmed that his messianic kingdom will be established on this earth before the end of the world. In effect, Christ was teaching that not only will the good news be preached throughout the world, but the prophetic vision of the messianic kingdom will be realized on this earth before the end of the world:

And this gospel of the kingdom ["Your God reigns"] will be proclaimed throughout the whole world [to "the ends of the earth"] as a testimony to all nations [when "all the ends of the earth shall see the salvation of our God"], and then the end [of the world] will come. (Matt. 24:14)

Notice how John describes his kingdom as being realized on this earth:

Then the seventh angel blew his trumpet, and there were loud voices in heaven, saying, "The kingdom of the world has become the kingdom of our Lord and of his Christ ["Your God reigns"]." ... And the twenty-four elders ... worshiped God, saying, "We give thanks to you, Lord God Almighty, who is and who was [a divine, eternal being], for you have taken your great power and begun to reign [over the world]." (Rev. 11:15–17)

The gospel of the kingdom is that the Son's dominion over his Genesis creation will be restored when he exercises his reign over this earth.

A Restored Humanity

The prophets described the messianic kingdom as a restoration of our humanity and as a human paradise on a restored Edenic earth. People will marry, build houses, and plant vineyards:

"They shall build houses and inhabit them; they shall plant vineyards and eat their fruit. . . . They shall not labor in vain or bear children for calamity [extended families]. . . . The wolf and the lamb shall graze together; the lion shall eat straw like the ox [restored Genesis creation], . . . They shall not hurt or destroy in all my holy mountain [peace and prosperity on earth]," says the LORD. (Isa. 65:21–25)

Ezekiel also described the abundant life that God's sheep will experience on the restored earth:

And the trees of the field shall yield their fruit, and the earth shall yield its increase [incredible abundance], and they shall be secure in their land. . . . And you are my sheep, human sheep of my pasture, and I am your God, declares the Lord God. . . . This land that was desolate has become like the garden of Eden [the restored earth]. (34:27–31; 36:35)

Many amillennial theologians point out that the only place the Bible references a 1,000-year reign of Christ is in the highly symbolic book of Revelation. But the millennium can easily be linked to numerous other Old Testament verses that vividly describe the Messiah's earthly kingdom.

An important New Testament passage that many theologians overlook is the story of a rich man asking Jesus how he can inherit eternal life. He walked away sad because Jesus asked him to give away his wealth and follow him in order to inherit eternal life. The disciples, who were willing to sacrificially follow Christ, then came to Jesus and asked what their reward would be for the deprivation they were experiencing by following him. He promised the disciples that in the future when he is ruling the world, they will experience an abundant life that will be a hundred times better than the rich man's life. They will live on a regenerated earth that is an Edenic paradise. In addition, after experiencing this human paradise on earth, they will inherit eternal life in the eternal age to come:

Jesus said to them, "Truly, I say to you, in the new world [regenerated earth], when the Son of Man will sit on his glorious throne [and rule the world], you who have followed me will also sit on twelve thrones, judging the twelve tribes of Israel [as ruling elders over Israel]. And everyone who has left houses or brothers or sisters or father or mother or children or lands, for my name's sake, will receive a hundredfold [in this Genesis age] and [in addition] will inherit eternal life [in the eternal age to come]." (Matt. 19:28–29; cf. Mark 10:28–30)

The "new world" is best translated "regenerated earth," which will happen when the curse is removed and the earth is restored to its Edenic condition. This is a reference to Christ's millennial reign when he sits on his glorious throne and rules the world as King of kings and Lord of lords. The disciples will even assist him in ruling over Israel. The disciples will inherit a restored human paradise, which Christ described as an Adamic paradise with homes, land, and extended human families. The disciples' human aspirations for an abundant life will be fulfilled a hundredfold.

But how are the disciples and all the departed saints going to inherit the restored earth if they have already died before Christ's reign has begun? John proposed that they will experience the first resurrection:

> Then I saw thrones, and seated on them were those to whom the authority to judge was committed [human rulers]. . . . They came to life and reigned with Christ for a thousand years. . . . This is the first resurrection. Blessed and holy is the one who shares in the first resurrection! . . . and they will reign with him for a thousand years. (Rev. 20:4–6)

The first resurrection enables all the departed saints that God has ransomed from all nations throughout the ages to inherit the restored earth during his messianic kingdom.

Theologians debate what kind of resurrection this represents. Let's assume that it is a resurrection of the bodies of the departed saints. That is the only form in which they can actually reside on the earth. John wrote:

> By your blood you ransomed people for God from every tribe and language and people and nation, and you have made them a kingdom and priests to our God, and *they shall reign on the earth.* (Rev. 5:9–10)

Notice that they reign on the earth, not in the celestial realm of heaven, which is why they must be resurrected into physical bodies. The fact that the messianic kingdom is made up of ransomed people "from every tribe and language and people and nation" correlates with the Great Commission: "Go therefore and make disciples of all nations, baptizing them in the name of the Father and of the Son and of the Holy Spirit, teaching them to observe all that I have commanded you" (Matt. 28:19–20). Ransomed people from all nations will experience the restoration.

At the end of the millennium, Satan will be released from his prison for one final deception of the nations. But this rebellion will not succeed. After this final deception, Satan will be sent to the eternal lake of fire, along with all the demons:

> And when the thousand years are ended, Satan will be released from his prison and will come out to deceive the nations that are at the four corners of the earth, Gog and Magog, to gather them for battle; their number is like the sand of the sea. And they marched up over the broad plain of the earth and surrounded the camp of the saints and the beloved city, but fire came down from heaven and consumed them, and the devil who had deceived them was thrown into the lake of fire and sulfur where the beast and the false prophet were, and they will be tormented day and night forever and ever. (Rev. 20:7–10)

During the millennium, Satan will be held in check, as in the game of chess. But this is now checkmate for Satan. Isaiah also foretold this day:

> They [the demonic host of heaven] will be gathered together as prisoners in a pit; they will be shut up in a prison [Satan and the demons are gathered up from around the world and imprisoned during Christ's reign], and after many days [one thousand years] they will be punished [thrown into the lake of fire]. (24:22)

The Last Day

This brings us to the last day, which is a multifaceted event. It is the final resurrection, or what is sometimes referred to as the "general" resurrection. It is the end of this Genesis age, literally the last day of this Genesis creation and the beginning of the eternal age. Christ will create the new heavens and new earth as the eternal habitat for the sons of God:

> From his presence earth and sky fled away, and no place was found for them.... Then I saw a new heaven and a new earth, ... And he who was seated on the throne said, "Behold, I am making all things new [the new habitat for the sons of God]."... And he said to me, "It is done! I am the Alpha and the Omega, the beginning and the end [of this Genesis creation]." (Rev. 20:11—21:1-6)

Christ is the Alpha of this Genesis creation in that it was created by him and for him, and he is the Omega of this creation when he brings it to an end. And just as it was the Son of God within the Trinity who created this Genesis creation, it will be the Son of God who creates the eternal new heavens and new earth.

Many theologians believe the Genesis earth will not be destroyed on the last day but will be only purified by a surface fire. They believe the eternal kingdom is a restored Genesis earth that exists in an eternal form. But John made it clear that the current heavens and earth perish on the last day, for they will no longer have a *presence* before God and will no longer have a *place* in the cosmos. The new heavens and new earth, therefore, are not a continuation of this Genesis creation. There will certainly be continuity with this creation, given that the eternal kingdom will be new versions of the current heavens and earth. It will be a real place for God's people who will have real resurrected bodies. Paul wrote that the current Genesis creation is groaning to transcend its current "bondage to corruption" for it to somehow become a part of the eternal kingdom:

> For the creation was subjected to futility, not willingly, but because of him who subjected it, in hope that the creation itself will be set free from its bondage to corruption and obtain the freedom of the glory of the children of God. (Rom. 8:20-21)

Just as our natural bodies will be transformed and taken to the new earth, so, too, this Genesis creation also transitions to the eternal new earth. How this transition works remains a mystery at this time.

A CHART OF GOD'S ENDGAME | 115

Judgment Day

The last day is also Judgment Day, when Christ sits on his Great White Throne and judges the world.

> Then I saw a great white throne and him who was seated on it. . . . And I saw the dead, great and small, standing before the throne, and books were opened. . . . And the dead were judged by what was written in the books, according to what they had done. . . . Death and Hades gave up the dead who were in them, . . . Then Death and Hades were thrown into the lake of fire. . . . And if anyone's name was not found written in the book of life, he was thrown into the lake of fire. (Rev. 20:11–15)

The final resurrection will be of believers who are listed in the book of life. They will be resurrected, judged, and rewarded for their good deeds and will then inherit eternal paradise in the eternal new heavens and new earth. At the same time, unbelievers will be resurrected from hades, judged for their evil deeds, and sent to the eternal lake of fire, along with Satan and the demons.

Jesus informed us about the final resurrection on Judgment Day:

> Do not marvel at this, for an hour is coming [on Judgment Day] when all who are in the tombs [believers and unbelievers] will hear his voice and come out [they are resurrected], those who have done good to the resurrection of life [believers], and those who have done evil to the resurrection of judgment [unbelievers who are held in hades]. (John 5:28–29)

On Judgment Day, the righteous will inherit the Father's eternal heavenly kingdom, while sinners will be sent to the lake of fire.

The sons of God will experience an immortal existence with God on the new earth.

> Behold, the dwelling place of God is with man. . . . and God himself will be with them as their God. . . . and death shall be no more [immortality], . . . The one who conquers will have this heritage, and I will be his God and he will be my son. (Rev. 21:3–7)

In heaven we will be immortal sons of God and will live in the very presence of God in all his glory. The Adamic order of being as male and female will come to an end, and we will be a new creation as sons of God that is neither male nor female. In the eternal age, the sons of God will be immortal and will not experience marriage.

John described the New Jerusalem as the eternal bride of Christ that comes down out of heaven to the new earth:

> And I saw the holy city, new Jerusalem, coming down out of heaven from God, . . . Then came one of the seven angels who . . . spoke to me, saying, "Come, I will show you the Bride, the wife of the Lamb." And he . . . showed me the holy city Jerusalem coming down out of heaven from God, having the glory of God, its radiance like a most rare jewel, like a jasper, clear as crystal. . . . The wall was built of jasper, while the city was pure gold, . . . And I saw no temple in the city, for its temple is the Lord God the Almighty [the Father] and the Lamb [the Son]. (Rev. 21:2–22)

John wrote that the triune God and the New Jerusalem will come down *from* heaven to what is also described as the kingdom of heaven *on* the eternal new earth. I am not sure how all this works, and any attempt to explain this dual description of heaven would be only speculation.

From Genesis to Revelation: God's Plans for the Future

Some theologians organize the flow of biblical events according to God's covenants or the various dispensations. But I prefer to view the flow of biblical history as a succession of ages of mankind:

- In the beginning, there was an age of righteous humanity on an Edenic earth.
- The fall took place, which ushered in an age of unrighteous humanity on a cursed earth.
- The Great Tribulation will occur, and an age of demonic humanity will begin.
- During the millennium, there will be a restored age of righteous humanity on a restored Edenic earth.

- On the last day, this creation and the human experience will come to an end. In the eternal age, the sons of God will inherit eternal life in the new heavens and new earth, and unbelievers will inherit eternal condemnation in the lake of fire.

This is the biblical data that theologians must integrate into a logical biblical theology of the future. When does Christ return? What is the nature of the millennium? What is the nature of the first resurrection? What is the nature of the final resurrection on Judgment Day? The next chapter explains how premillennialists answer these questions and interpret this chart of God's endgame.

6

A Critique of Premillennialism

Review

Note: This critique is best understood by watching a 45-minute video presentation online at www.godsendgame.net. The following chart is also available on the website to download and print.

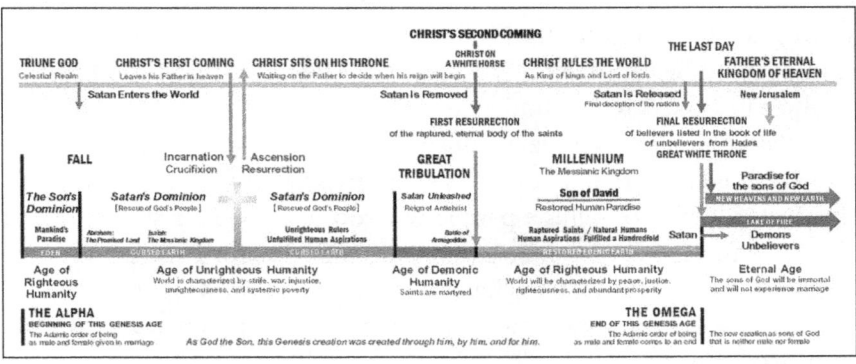

Premillennialists believe in a literal millennium. They insist that the Old Testament promises of a messianic kingdom centered in Israel are not null and void because the first-century Jews rejected their Messiah. They believe that since Christ did not establish his kingdom the first time he came to this earth, he must return a second time at the beginning of the millennium to accomplish this mission. Thus, the name *pre*millennialism. At the end of this 1,000-year messianic kingdom, Christ will take the saints to the eternal new heavens and new earth.

The following description by John Walvoord demonstrates how this view affirms the messianic kingdom:

> Premillennialism is founded principally on interpretation of the Old Testament. If interpreted literally, the Old Testament gives a clear picture of the prophetic expectation of Israel. They confidently anticipated the coming of a Savior and Deliverer, a Messiah who would be Prophet, Priest, and King. They expected that He would deliver them from their enemies and usher in a kingdom of righteousness, peace and prosperity upon a redeemed earth. . . . The Premillennial interpretation offers the only possible literal fulfillment for the hundreds of verses of prophetic testimony.[8]

The basic tenants of premillennialism are as follows. Christ returns at the beginning of the 1,000-year restoration of this Genesis creation to rule the world. Satan will be totally removed from the world, and Christ will return to the earth on his white horse. He will then sit on the throne of David and will physically reside in Israel when he establishes his reign.

For the departed saints to reinhabit the restored Edenic earth during the millennium, they will experience the resurrection of their immortal bodies at the first resurrection. The first resurrection will be of the raptured, eternal bodies of the saints. In their eternal bodies, they will no longer experience marriage and reproduction.

The final resurrection on the last day will be primarily for unbelievers. But it will also include people who do become Christians during the millennium. They will be given eternal bodies for the eternal kingdom. On the last day of this Genesis creation, the saints will inherit the eternal new heavens and new earth. This is the eternal paradise for the immortal sons of God.

Some premillennialists believe the Genesis earth perishes on the last day, will literally cease to exist, and will be replaced with a totally new earth. Others believe the earth will be purified by a surface fire on the last day and the eternal new earth will be a renewed and restored Genesis earth. These premillennialists are known as progressive premillennialists, for they see the millennium as the first phase

---

8 John F. Walvoord, *The Millennial Kingdom* (Grand Rapids: Zondervan, 1980), 114.

of the eternal earth. Regardless of how premillennialists understand the nature of the eternal new earth, premillennialism is defined by its belief that Christ returns to this earth with the raptured saints at the beginning of the millennium.

The rapture is when the sons of God are resurrected into eternal bodies like Christ's and caught up into the sky to meet the Lord. Paul taught:

> For the Lord himself will descend from heaven [the second coming] . . . And the dead in Christ will rise first. Then we who are alive, who are left, will be caught up together with them in the clouds to meet the Lord in the air [raptured], and so we will always be with the Lord. (1 Thess. 4:16–17)

Dispensational premillennialists believe the rapture can happen at any moment and the church will escape the Great Tribulation. Others believe the rapture will occur midway through the Tribulation, before God's wrath is poured out on the followers of the Antichrist. Historic premillennialists believe the rapture will occur simultaneously with Christ's return to this earth. The saints are caught up into the clouds, but then turn around and descend to this earth with Christ. Therefore, the church will endure the Great Tribulation.

All premillennialists believe the first resurrection represents the saints in their glorified bodies that reinhabit the restored earth. The world's population will be made up of the raptured saints *and* natural human beings who survive the Tribulation.

This comingling of billions of raptured saints in their glorified bodies with men and women in their natural bodies exposes a major problem with premillennialism. The prophets clearly describe the messianic kingdom as a restoration of the Adamic order of being. It is a restored human paradise where men and women marry, reproduce, and fill an Edenic earth. How are the raptured saints going to experience a restoration of their humanity if they are in their glorified bodies? Are these billions of celibate glorified children of God going to live next door to married couples with children or are they going to live in huge dormitories? The glorified sons of God belong in the eternal paradise in heaven, not on the restored earth.

Zechariah

Premillennialists quote several key verses to support their view of God's endgame. Some are found in Zechariah, in which the prophet describes the changes that will take place on this earth when the Messiah rules the world:

> On that day his feet shall stand on the Mount of Olives that lies before Jerusalem on the east, and the Mount of Olives shall be split in two from east to west by a very wide valley, so that one half of the Mount shall move northward, and the other half southward.... Then the LORD my God will come, and all the holy ones with him.... And the LORD will be king over all the earth. (Zech. 14:4–9)

This seems to indicate a literal and physical return of Christ to the Mount of Olives. That is one way this prophecy can be interpreted.

But Zechariah is full of similar symbolic language that should not be interpreted literally. For example, flying scrolls are sent out to enter the houses of thieves and destroy them (5:1–4). Women with wings fly around carrying baskets to gather up all the wickedness in the land of Israel (5:5–10). Angels riding on chariots with red and white horses are sent out to the four corners of the earth to establish peace (6:1–8). Although the messianic kingdom that the prophet depicts may be quite real, the description of Christ's feet standing on the Mount of Olives to initiate his reign can also be interpreted as a figurative description of his reign.

Psalm 110 teaches that Christ sits at the right hand of God waiting for the Father to put all his enemies under his feet. God does not literally have a right hand, and Christ will not literally have enemies sitting under his feet. The idea of subjecting one's enemies to one's feet is a common metaphor in the Old Testament that symbolizes the Lord as a warrior and conquering king with human rulers subject to him.

Even today we use the expression "put your foot down" figuratively to mean to bring an end to unruly conduct and to establish order. Changes in behavior take place because of this use of our authority, but the description of our foot being put down is obviously metaphorical.

In like manner, the prophets foresaw an actual reign of the Messiah, but these verses in Zechariah do not necessitate a literal return of Christ to the Mount of Olives so that he can put his foot down and restore his divine rule over this disobedient world. Zechariah further wrote:

> And I will pour out on the house of David and the inhabitants of Jerusalem a spirit of grace and pleas for mercy, so that, when they look on me, on him whom they have pierced, they shall mourn for him, as one mourns for an only child, and weep bitterly over him, as one weeps over a firstborn. . . . On that day there shall be a fountain opened for the house of David and the inhabitants of Jerusalem, to cleanse them from sin and uncleanness. (12:10; 13:1)

A water fountain will not literally cleanse the Jewish people from sin. Rather, it will be the Holy Spirit who will cleanse the repentant Jews. And unlike doubting Thomas, we can see the resurrected Christ through the eyes of faith without him physically appearing to us. So, too, when the Jews repent in the future, through the Holy Spirit they will see the Christ their people crucified, and they will be cleansed from their sin.

Some theologians hyper-spiritualize these verses when they interpret them as only having an internal spiritual meaning without any external ramifications in this world. Other theologians interpret them in a hyper-literal manner. When properly interpreted, however, these metaphors envision a real messianic kingdom when the Jewish Messiah rules the world through the power of the Holy Spirit.

This does not rule out any contact between Christ and this world at the beginning of the millennium. Christ appeared to Saul on the road to Damascus when Saul was converted, but that did not represent Christ's second coming. It may be that in a similar way, Christ will touch the Mount of Olives in a moment in time to regenerate this cursed earth into a restored Edenic earth as he begins his reign over this world from his throne in heaven. But this would not be his second coming.

Paul's Letter to the Thessalonians

To support their eschatology, premillennialists also reference Paul's second letter to the Thessalonians. This church was experiencing significant persecution by the Roman authorities. But Paul admonished them not to retaliate and to wait for God's vengeance on their persecutors on Judgment Day, which occurs when Christ returns to rapture the saints:

> When the Lord Jesus is revealed from heaven with his mighty angels in flaming fire, inflicting vengeance on those who do not know God [on Judgment Day] ... They will suffer the punishment of eternal destruction, away from the presence of the Lord [in the lake of fire] ... *when he comes on that day to be glorified in his saints* [a reference to the rapture], ... And then the lawless one [the Antichrist] will be revealed, whom the Lord Jesus will kill with the breath of his mouth and bring to nothing by the appearance of his coming [on Judgment Day]. (2 Thess. 1:7—2:8)

Paul connected Christ's second coming to the destruction of the Antichrist. This would conceivably put the second coming at the end of the Great Tribulation, when the Antichrist is destroyed at the battle of Armageddon. Premillennialists claim that Christ returns to this earth at that time to set up his millennial kingdom. But Paul also connected Christ's second coming and the rapture to Judgment Day at the end of the world, when these unbelievers persecuting the Thessalonians will experience eternal destruction in the lake of fire, which is described in Revelation as occurring *after* the millennium. Is the second coming on Judgment Day at the battle of Armageddon *or* at the end of the world? How do we resolve this apparent contradiction?

To solve this problem, premillennialists move Judgment Day to the end of the Great Tribulation. Instead of Judgment Day occurring at the Great White Throne judgment on the last day, it is at the beginning of the millennium. Unbelievers are resurrected from hades, judged, and sent to eternal destruction along with Satan and the demons. The saints are raptured, rewarded for their good deeds, and inherit the messianic kingdom for a thousand years. But this creates far more problems than it resolves, for John clearly places Judgment Day at the

Great White Throne judgment, which occurs at the end of the world—not at the beginning of the millennium. Attempts by premillennialists to circumvent these contradictions cause unnecessary confusion.

The book of Revelation contains a great deal of complicated recapitulation, but the events surrounding the millennium occur in a straightforward, linear progression. The Great Tribulation comes to an end at the battle of Armageddon. This is followed by the binding of Satan and the millennial reign of Christ. There is the first resurrection so that the saints can inherit the earth during the millennium. Toward the end of the millennium, Satan is released for one final deception of mankind that is referred to as the gathering of Gog and Magog. Afterward, Satan is sent to the lake of fire never to escape again. Then there is the final resurrection. The current Genesis earth perishes and is replaced with the eternal new heavens and new earth. Christ sits on his Great White Throne and judges the world. The end of the Tribulation is not Judgment Day.

There is a better solution to reconciling Paul's sequence of events to those in Revelation. Notice in Paul's two letters to the Thessalonians that he does not mention the earthly messianic kingdom whatsoever. Nor does Paul inform them about the two resurrections, one at the beginning of the millennium and another at the end of the millennium. Paul taught the Thessalonians about the coming Antichrist and the Great Tribulation, but it is likely that he had not taught them about Christ's 1,000-year messianic kingdom that would follow the defeat of the Antichrist.

The church was still very young, and the book of Revelation was not written until almost forty years later. At this embryonic stage of the church's growth, Paul had good reasons to keep the Jewish-led messianic kingdom under wraps. The Roman authorities would have surely seen Christ's earthly kingdom as a geopolitical threat. Paul kept the young church focused on inheriting eternal life in heaven when Christ returns on Judgment Day. Thus, in his letters to the Thessalonians, Paul gave them a highly condensed version of the future, omitting the first resurrection and the messianic kingdom altogether.

In fact, Paul associated the second coming and the rapture with the saints inheriting their citizenship in heaven, not with their inheriting Christ's earthly kingdom. In his letter to the Philippians, Paul wrote:

> But our citizenship is in heaven [where Christ has ascended]. And we eagerly await a Savior from there, the Lord Jesus Christ [to take us to join him in heaven], who, by the power that enables him to bring everything under his control, will transform our lowly bodies so that they will be like his glorious body [the rapture]. (3:20–21 NIV)

Paul taught that Christ has the power to control this world, but he did not expand on what that entails. But Paul was certainly referring to the second coming of Christ from heaven: "And we eagerly await a Savior from there." He was also referring to the rapture: "will transform our lowly bodies" to be like Christ's resurrected body. The raptured saints then inherit the Father's kingdom, or their "citizenship" in heaven.

According to Paul, when Christ comes again, the saints will be raptured and transformed into their eternal bodies and will inherit their citizenship on the eternal new earth. At the same time, unbelievers will be resurrected from hades, judged at the Great White Throne judgment, and sent to eternal destruction in the lake of fire. This would place the second coming, the rapture, and Judgment Day at the final resurrection on the last day—not at the first resurrection at the beginning of the millennium.

The Destiny of the Raptured Saints

When Christ approached his impending resurrection and ascension, he began telling his disciples that he was about to return to his Father in heaven. He said that someday he would return, resurrect them, and take them to join him and his Father in heaven for eternity:

> Let not your hearts be troubled. Believe in God; believe also in me. In my Father's house are many rooms.... And if I go and prepare a place for you [in heaven], I will come again and will take you to myself, that where I am you may be also [in heaven with his Father]. (John 14:1–3)

Christ ascended in the clouds to return to his Father in heaven. When he comes again in the clouds, he will take the raptured sons of

God to dwell with him in the Father's kingdom—not to dwell with him on this earth in his millennial kingdom.

This sequence can be outlined as follows:

> **Christ's second coming** ("I will come again")
> + rapture ("take you to myself")
> = ascend to heaven in our eternal bodies and join him in his "Father's house."

Peter never gave up hope for the messianic kingdom, but he also learned from Jesus that the destiny of the raptured saints on Judgment Day is the Father's eternal kingdom of heaven, not the restored earth during Christ's reign.

Peter and the disciples eventually understood what Christ meant by his resurrection and ascension to heaven to be with his Father. They began to hope for their own resurrection of immortal bodies like Christ's and their ascension to join him and his Father in heaven. Peter wrote:

> Blessed be the God and Father of our Lord Jesus Christ! According to his great mercy, he has caused us to be born again to a living hope through the resurrection of Jesus Christ from the dead [we hope for a resurrection of an immortal body like Christ's resurrected body], to an inheritance that is imperishable, undefiled, and unfading, kept in heaven for you, who by God's power are being guarded through faith for a salvation ready to be revealed in the last time [on the last day].... at the revelation of Jesus Christ. (1 Peter 1:3–7)

Peter's teaching can be outlined as follows:

> **"The revelation of Jesus Christ"**
> + "to be revealed in the last time" on the last day
> + "hope through the resurrection of Jesus Christ" (a reference to the resurrection of an eternal body like Christ's resurrected body)
> = inherit the imperishable kingdom "kept in heaven for you."

Premillennialists have overlooked this reference to the rapture in this section of Scripture. But when we hope for a resurrection like Christ's resurrection from the dead, we are looking forward to having raptured, eternal bodies like his. When this occurs, the raptured saints are clearly destined for the imperishable kingdom of heaven, not the perishable earth.

Let's compare Peter's teachings concerning the destiny of the raptured saints to Paul's and Christ's:

> **Peter**: "at the revelation of Jesus Christ" + "hope through the resurrection of Jesus Christ" of an eternal body = "an inheritance that is imperishable" in heaven.
> **Paul**: "we eagerly await a Savior" + "will transform our lowly bodies" into eternal bodies = our "citizenship is in heaven."
> **Christ**: "I will come again" + "will take you to myself" when raptured = the "Father's house" in heaven.

Christ's second coming and the rapture signal the beginning of the Father's eternal kingdom of heaven on the last day—not the beginning of the millennium. Again, these verses contradict the premillennial assertion that Christ returns to rapture the saints at the beginning of the millennium so that they can inherit the perishable earth for a thousand years. The raptured saints are destined for the Father's imperishable kingdom when Christ returns, not for the restored earth for a thousand years.

Christ on His White Horse

Probably the most important sections of Scripture used by premillennialists to make their case for God's endgame can be found in chapters 19 and 20 of Revelation. Premillennialists assume that the appearance of Christ on his white horse at the battle of Armageddon represents the second coming of Christ in the clouds. In his vision, John saw the celestial realm of heaven open and Christ riding on a white horse. If you read this passage closely, however, John never describes Christ as leaving the celestial realm of heaven and descending to this earth on his horse to destroy the Antichrist and his armies and establish his millennial reign. Instead, John portrays Christ as remaining in the celestial realm when he simply says the word and the Antichrist and his armies are destroyed and his reign over this earth begins:

> Then I saw heaven opened [a vision of the celestial realm], and behold, a white horse [in the celestial realm]! . . . From his mouth comes a sharp sword with which to strike down the nations [he merely says the word], and he will rule them with a rod of iron. . . . And I saw the beast and the kings of the earth with their armies gathered [on the earth] to make war against him who was sitting on the horse [still depicted as being in the celestial realm] . . . And the beast was captured, and with it the false prophet . . . These two were thrown alive into the lake of fire that burns with sulfur. And the rest [of his soldiers] were slain by the sword that came from the mouth of him who was sitting on the horse [spoken from the celestial realm]. (Rev. 19:11–21)

The Antichrist and his false prophet are so evil that they bypass hades and the Great White Throne judgment and are sent directly to the lake of fire. The soldiers killed by Christ's spoken word, however, remain in hades during the millennium until the final resurrection and Judgment Day, when they, too, will be sent to the lake of fire. Most important, notice that John made no reference whatsoever to Christ on his white horse coming down from the celestial realm to this earth to engage and destroy the Antichrist and his army. Rather, John consistently pictures Christ remaining in heaven when he says the word and destroys the Antichrist, bringing the Great Tribulation to an end. Therefore, contrary to what premillennialists assert, John is not describing the appearance of Christ on his white horse as the second coming of Christ in the clouds.

Let's compare John's vision of Christ in the celestial realm to Stephen's vision of Christ when Stephen was about to be stoned to death. Stephen had been preaching the gospel when he was arrested and brought before the high priest and the Sanhedrin for interrogation. In his defense, he delivered a convicting sermon, which infuriated the Jewish leaders. Stephen then saw the ascended Christ in the celestial realm at the right hand of the Father:

> Now when they heard these things they were enraged, and they ground their teeth at him. But he, full of the Holy Spirit, gazed into heaven and saw the glory of God, and Jesus standing at the right hand of God. And he said, "Behold, *I see the heavens opened*, and the Son of Man standing at the right hand of God." (Acts 7:54–56)

Stephen could see into the celestial realm, where he saw Christ in heaven at the Father's right hand. Stephen was then unjustly stoned to death. Christ, of course, had the authority and power to prevent this injustice. From his throne in heaven, Christ could have easily intervened to prevent Stephen's murder. He could have used his divine power and struck the unrepentant rulers with blindness the moment they picked up the first stone. But the time was not right for Christ to overthrow these unrighteous rulers and establish his reign of justice on the earth.

Notice the similarities between Stephen's vision of Christ in the celestial realm and John's vision:

> **Stephen said:** "Behold, I see the heavens opened, and the Son of Man standing at the right hand of God."
> **John said**: "Then I saw heaven opened, and behold, a white horse!"

Christ did not intervene to prevent Stephen's death. In John's vision, however, Christ does intervene against his enemies. But John portrays him as doing so from his celestial position in heaven at the right hand of God. He destroys the Antichrist and his armies by just saying the word. He also sends a powerful angel down to earth to lock up Satan for the next one thousand years. Stephen saw Christ waiting on the Father to decide when his reign of justice will begin, whereas John saw Christ when the time has come for Christ to rule the world as King of kings and Lord of lords.

Therefore, contrary to what premillennialists assert, John did not describe Christ leaving heaven on the clouds and descending to the earth on his white horse, dismounting, and walking on this earth again to establish his millennial kingdom.

John's vision was also similar to Elisha's and his frightened servant's vision when they were being threatened by a Syrian army:

Then Elisha prayed and said, "O LORD, please open his eyes that he may see." So the LORD opened the eyes of the young man, and he saw, and behold, the mountain was full of horses and chariots of fire all around Elisha [in the celestial realm]. And when the Syrians came down against him, Elisha prayed to the LORD and said, "Please strike this people with blindness." So he struck them with blindness in accordance with the prayer of Elisha. (2 Kings 6:17–18)

Elisha and his servant could see into the celestial realm of heaven, where they saw the angelic powers of God surrounding them. In this case, from his throne in heaven God chose to intervene with supernatural power to protect his people. But God did not have to come to the earth to accomplish this mission. Likewise, John saw Christ on his throne in heaven using his supernatural power against the Antichrist and his armies. Christ merely said the word, but instead of being blinded, they were killed.

John also portrayed the binding of Satan as the work of an angel sent by Christ from his throne in heaven:

Then I saw an angel *coming down from heaven*, holding in his hand the key to the bottomless pit and a great chain. And he seized the dragon, that ancient serpent, who is the devil and Satan, and bound him for a thousand years. (Rev. 20:1–2)

Again, Christ is not portrayed as coming down from heaven to the earth when Satan is bound by an angel. Only the angel comes down to this earth to bind Satan so that Christ's millennial reign can begin.

Human Thrones

When John saw thrones set up on the earth after the first resurrection, nowhere does he describe any of these thrones as being Christ's throne. They are all portrayed as human thrones:

Then I saw thrones, and seated on them were those to whom the authority to judge was committed.... They came to life [on the earth] and reigned with Christ for a thousand years.... This is the first resurrection. (Rev. 20:4–5)

These are all human thrones, and the resurrected saints seated on these thrones will reign with Christ while he remains in heaven, just as we walk with Christ today while he remains in heaven. Even John Walvoord, a pillar in the premillennial camp, admits in his commentary on Revelation that this section of Revelation does not specifically identify any of these thrones as being Christ's throne:

> The interpretation of verse 4 is complicated by a lack of specificity. ... Who are these sitting on the thrones and what is meant by the judgment given to them? One possibility is that the subject of the verb "sat" includes Christ.[9]

Since the text does not identify Christ as sitting on one of these thrones, premillennialists have to resort to mere speculation.

If Christ does come back to this earth as premillennialists claim, then one would be able to report that Christ was physically somewhere on this earth after his descent. He could be in Jerusalem one day and in New York City the next. In the Olivet Discourse, however, that is precisely what Christ said one would not be able to do when he comes again:

> Then if anyone says to you, "Look, here is the Christ!" or "There he is!" do not believe it. ... For as the lightning comes from the east and shines as far as the west, so will be the coming of the Son of Man. (Matt. 24:23–27)

Christ taught that he will not physically return to earth at his second coming so that one could find him over here or over there. Christ has already come in the flesh and dwelt among us. When he comes again, it will be to take us to his Father's heavenly kingdom. Therefore, any man who claims to be God operating physically on this earth is a false Christ, no matter how many signs and wonders he performs.

These verses in chapters 19 and 20 of Revelation are a critical section of Scripture for premillennialists, who are known for their literal interpretation of the text. But nowhere in these verses is Christ described as

---

9 John F. Walvoord, *The Revelation of Jesus Christ* (Chicago: Moody Bible Institute, 1966; Moody Paperback Edition, 1989), 296.

returning to this earth to establish his millennial kingdom. Rather, John portrayed Christ as remaining in the celestial realm of heaven when he says the word and destroys the Antichrist, has Satan bound by an angel, and rules the world as King of kings and Lord of lords.

The Wrath of God on Judgment Day

Judgment Day also presents a major problem for premillennialists. They recognize that there is a strong connection between the second coming of Christ and the wrath of God executed against mankind on Judgment Day. Paul wrote:

> For they themselves report concerning us the kind of reception we had among you, and how you turned to God from idols to serve the living and true God, and to wait for his Son from heaven, . . . *who delivers us from the wrath to come* [on Judgment Day]. (1 Thess. 1:9–10)

Premillennialists equate this wrath of God at Christ's second coming to the wrath of God poured out on the Antichrist and his armies described in Revelation: "He will tread the winepress of the fury of the *wrath of God* the Almighty [against the armies of the Antichrist]" (Rev. 19:15). But this wrath of God is not the wrath of God that Paul is referring to. Paul is alluding to the second death, when unbelievers are resurrected from hades on the last day, judged at the Great White Throne judgment, and sent to the lake of fire for eternity. Christians are delivered from this wrath because they are in Christ and clothed with his righteousness.

In contrast, the wrath of God poured out at the end of the Great Tribulation is like the wrath of God executed against Pharaoh and his armies during the Exodus. The Egyptian soldiers who were killed by the flooding of the Red Sea experienced the first death of their mortal bodies. Their souls or spirits were then sent to hades, where they remain until the final resurrection, when they will be resurrected in body and soul and will experience the second death in the lake of fire.

Likewise, at the battle of Armageddon, the armies of the Antichrist will simply be killed, and their departed spirits will remain in hades until the last day when they, too, will be resurrected and judged at the

Great White Throne and will experience the wrath of God when they are sent to the lake of fire. The wrath of God at the end of the Tribulation is temporal, whereas the wrath of God on Judgment Day is eternal. In short, the battle of Armageddon is not Judgment Day.

Revelation teaches that Judgment Day occurs on the very last day of this Genesis creation when the books are opened and every man is judged by what is recorded in the books. The saints will be judged by what is written in the Book of Life, and unbelievers will be judged by another unnamed book because their names are not in the Book of Life:

> Then I saw a great white throne and him who was seated on it. From his presence earth and sky fled away, and no place was found for them [the end of this Genesis creation]. And I saw the dead, great and small, standing before the throne, and books were opened [two sets]. . . . And the dead [believers and unbelievers] were judged by what was written in the books, according to what they had done [rewards and punishments]. . . . And if anyone's name was not found written in the book of life, he was thrown into the lake of fire. Then I saw a new heaven and a new earth, for the first heaven and the first earth had passed away, and the sea was no more. (Rev. 20:11—21:1)

John did not specifically state that this event is the second coming of Christ. But in a subsequent section of Revelation, John does connect Christ's second coming to the Great White Throne judgment on the last day of this creation, when the books are opened and mankind is judged:

> "Behold, I am coming soon, bringing my recompense with me [rewards and punishments], to repay each one for what he has done [believers and unbelievers]. I am the Alpha and the Omega, the first and the last, the beginning and the end." Blessed are those who wash their robes, so that they may have the right to the tree of life and that they may enter the city by the gates [New Jerusalem]. (Rev. 22:12–14)

These events in chapter 22 of Revelation describing Christ's second coming on Judgment Day correspond to the events surrounding the Great White Throne judgment described in chapter 20:

"Behold, I am coming soon"

- "I am the Alpha and the Omega, the first and the last, the beginning and the end [of this creation]" (Rev. 22) = "From his presence earth and sky fled away" (Rev. 20)
- "bringing my recompense with me, to repay each one *for what he has done*" (Rev. 22) = "And the dead were judged by what was written in the books, *according to what they had done*" (Rev. 20)
- "enter the city by the gates" (Rev. 22) = "Then I saw a new heaven and a new earth" (Rev. 20)

According to Revelation, the second coming and the rapture take place *after* the millennium when this Genesis earth is destroyed at the final resurrection of all mankind at the Great White Throne judgment.

Let's continue to let Scripture interpret Scripture. John wrote Revelation, but he wrote the gospel of John, too. In his gospel, he also records Christ teaching that his second coming occurs on Judgment Day, when believers and unbelievers are resurrected at the same time to inherit either eternal life or eternal death. Jesus taught:

> Do not marvel at this, for an hour is coming [on Judgment Day] when all who are in the tombs [believers and unbelievers] will hear his voice [at the second coming] and come out [they are resurrected], those who have done good to the resurrection of life [believers], and those who have done evil to the resurrection of judgment [unbelievers who are held in hades]. (John 5:28–29)

The "resurrection of life" of "those who have done good" occurs on Judgment Day, when they are resurrected into eternal bodies, judged according to their recorded good deeds, and sent to the eternal new earth. The "resurrection of judgment" of "those who have done evil" occurs at the same "hour," when they are resurrected from hades, judged according to their recorded evil deeds, and sent to the eternal lake of fire.

In the gospel of Matthew, Christ described believers as his sheep and unbelievers as goats. Notice the destiny of the sheep and the goats when he comes again on Judgment Day:

> When the Son of Man comes in his glory, and all the angels with him, then he will sit on his glorious throne [the Great White Throne]. Before him will be gathered all the nations [at the final resurrection], . . . And he will place the sheep on his right [the saints will be raptured into their eternal bodies], but the goats on the left [unbelievers will be resurrected from hades]. Then the King will say to those on his right, "Come, you who are blessed by my Father, inherit the kingdom prepared for you from the foundation of the world" [a reference to the Father's eternal kingdom]. . . . Then he will say to those on his left, "Depart from me, you cursed, into the eternal fire prepared for the devil and his angels." . . . And these will go away into eternal punishment [the lake of fire], but the righteous into eternal life. (Matt. 25:31–46)

These events can be outlined as follows:

"When the Son of Man comes in his glory"
+ the final resurrection of believers (the sheep) and unbelievers (the goats)
+ Judgment Day when Christ "will sit on his glorious throne"
= resurrected believers inherit "eternal life" in the Father's eternal kingdom of heaven
= resurrected unbelievers inherit "eternal punishment" in the "eternal fire prepared for the devil and his angels."

Christ's second coming and Judgment Day will occur at the end of the world when the sheep are raptured to inherit eternal life in the Father's eternal kingdom—not at the beginning of the Son's millennium kingdom, as claimed by premillennialists. The parable of sowing good seed among weeds, also in the gospel of Matthew, teaches this same concept:

> And his disciples came to him, saying, "Explain to us the parable of the weeds of the field." He answered, "The one who sows the good seed is the Son of Man. The field is the world, and the good seed is the sons of the kingdom. The weeds are the sons of the evil one, and the enemy who sowed them is the devil. The harvest is the end of the age [the Omega], and the reapers are angels. Just

as the weeds are gathered and burned with fire, so will it be at the end of the age [the Genesis age]. The Son of Man will send his angels, and they will gather out of his kingdom all causes of sin and all lawbreakers, and throw them into the fiery furnace [the lake of fire]. In that place there will be weeping and gnashing of teeth. Then the righteous will shine like the sun in the kingdom of their Father [in heaven]. He who has ears, let him hear." (Matt. 13:36–43)

Jesus taught in this parable that when he comes again on Judgment Day, the saints (the good seed) are resurrected to be taken to the Father's kingdom at the same time that unbelievers (the weeds) are raised to be judged and sent "into the fiery furnace." Note that this harvest is "at the end of the age," not at the beginning of another thousand years of the Genesis earth's existence.

Peter also placed the second coming and the rapture of the saints on the last day. He did not place the rapture at the beginning of the Tribulation, at the middle of the Tribulation, or at the end of the Tribulation. Rather, he connected the rapture to Judgment Day, when Christ comes again at the end of the world and the saints inherit the eternal new earth. Peter taught that this Genesis creation will be destroyed by fire and will pass away when the books are opened on Judgment Day. The raptured saints then inherit the eternal new heavens and new earth.

> Scoffers will come in the last days . . . They will say, "Where is the promise of his coming?" . . . But the day of the Lord will come like a thief, and then the heavens will pass away with a roar, and the heavenly bodies will be burned up and dissolved [the Omega], and the earth and the works that are done on it will be exposed [when the books are opened]. Since all these things are thus to be dissolved, what sort of people ought you to be in lives of holiness and godliness, waiting for and hastening the coming of the day of God, . . . But according to his promise [of an eternal body like Christ's ascended body in the Father's kingdom] we are waiting for new heavens and a new earth in which righteousness dwells. (2 Peter 3:3–13)

Notice that Peter places the second coming, the rapture, *and* Judgment Day at the end of the world when the saints inherit the eternal new earth, not at the beginning of the millennium. Christ cannot physically return to the earth with the raptured saints at the beginning of the millennium because the earth will be destroyed when he returns. It would be difficult to reign on the earth for a thousand years if it no longer existed! Peter plainly teaches that the resurrected saints are destined for the new earth when Christ returns on Judgment Day.

Peter's teaching can be outlined as follows:

> **"The promise of his coming . . . like a thief"**
> + the people of God, who are living holy and godly lives, are waiting for "the coming of the day of God"
> + the end of this Genesis creation: "will be burned up and dissolved"
> + Judgment Day: "the works that are done on it will be exposed"
> = the saints inherit the "new heavens and a new earth."

The book of Hebrews includes this same concept:

So Christ, having been offered once to bear the sins of many [the first coming], **will appear a second time**, not to deal with sin but to save those who are eagerly waiting for him [believers on Judgment Day]. . . . For if we go on sinning deliberately after receiving the knowledge of the truth, there no longer remains a sacrifice for sins, but a fearful expectation of judgment, and a fury of fire that will consume the adversaries [unbelievers on Judgment Day]. . . . But now he has promised, "Yet once more I will shake not only the earth but also the heavens [as John says, "earth and sky fled away"]." This phrase, "Yet once more," indicates the removal of things that are shaken—that is, things that have been made [the Genesis creation]—in order that the things that cannot be shaken may remain. Therefore let us be grateful for receiving a kingdom that cannot be shaken [an eternal heavenly kingdom], and thus let us offer to God acceptable worship, with reverence and awe, for our God is a consuming fire [when he returns on Judgment Day to save his people]. (Heb. 9:28; 10:26–27; 12:26–29)

This sequence of events can be outlined as follows:

"Will appear a second time"
+ Judgment Day for faithful believers: "to save those who are eagerly waiting for him"
+ Judgment Day for unbelievers: "a fearful expectation of judgment, and a fury of fire"
+ end of this Genesis creation: "the removal of things that are shaken—that is, things that have been made"
= the saints then inherit "a kingdom that cannot be shaken."

Like Peter, the writer to the Hebrews places the second coming on Judgment Day when the Genesis earth is destroyed, all mankind is judged, and the saints inherit the eternal kingdom of heaven.

This Age and the Eternal Age to Come

Another major problem with premillennialism is that the Scriptures portray Christ's second coming in terms of the end of this Genesis age and the beginning of the eternal age to come. After Christ warned the disciples about the temple's impending destruction, they asked him how they could recognize the signs leading up to its destruction as well as when his second coming would occur: "Tell us, when will these things be [the temple's destruction], and what will be the sign *of your coming and of the end of the age* [the Genesis age]?" (Matt. 24:3). Christ's second coming is linked to "the end of the age," or the Omega. Jesus also taught, "The harvest is *the end of the age*, and the reapers are angels" (Matt. 13:39). The harvest, or Judgment Day, is also linked to "the end of the age."

Jesus further taught:

> For this is the will of my Father, that everyone who looks on the Son and believes in him should have eternal life [in the Father's eternal kingdom], and I will raise him up [into an eternal body like his] *on the last day* [at the end of the age]. (John 6:40)

The rapture is linked to the final resurrection "on the last day." Christ's second coming, the rapture, and Judgment Day are all linked to the end of this age and the beginning of the eternal age to come. When Christ comes again on Judgment Day, unbelievers are gathered up by angels, judged by Christ, and sent to the lake of fire. The saints are raptured, judged for their good deeds, and inherit "eternal life" in the Father's kingdom. This places Christ's second coming at the Omega when he ushers in the eternal age.

But premillennialists believe the second coming and the rapture occur at the beginning of the millennium, which presents a dilemma. How can Christ's second coming usher in the eternal age to come if humanity and the Genesis earth last for another thousand years? Premillennialists attempt to make sense of this obvious contradiction by arguing that the millennium is a preliminary first phase of the eternal age to come. None of these attempts, however, make sense. If Christ's second coming ushers in the Father's eternal kingdom and the eternal age to come, then it ushers in the eternal age to come—*not* another thousand years of the earth's existence! Premillennialists are simply confusing events that will occur in this Genesis age with the events that will occur when Christ comes again to usher in the eternal age.

Paul taught the following order of events at Christ's second coming:

> But each in his own order: Christ the firstfruits [the first man to be resurrected into an eternal body and to ascend to heaven], *then at his coming those who belong to Christ* [the saints are raptured]. *Then comes the end* [of this age], *when he delivers the kingdom to God the Father* after destroying every rule and every authority and power. For he [Christ] must reign [over this world] until he has put all his enemies under his feet. The last enemy to be destroyed is death. (1 Cor. 15:23–26)

Paul's teaching can be outlined as follows:

    "Then at his coming"
    + "those who belong to Christ" [the saints are raptured]
    + "then comes the end" [of this age]
    = "when he delivers the kingdom to God the Father."

Throughout his letters to the Thessalonians, Paul connects the rapture to the second coming on Judgment Day:

For they themselves report concerning us the kind of reception we had among you, and how you turned to God from idols to serve the living and true God, and to wait for his Son from heaven, whom he raised from the dead, Jesus who delivers us from the wrath to come [the lake of fire on Judgment Day]. . . . For the Lord himself will descend from heaven [the second coming] . . . And the dead in Christ will rise first. Then we who are alive, who are left, will be caught up together with them in the clouds to meet the Lord in the air [the rapture], and so we will always be with the Lord [in his Father's eternal kingdom]. (1 Thess. 1:9–10; 4:16–17)

These verses can be outlined as follows:

"Wait for his Son from heaven"
+ the rapture: "caught up together with them in the clouds"
+ Judgment Day: "delivers us from the wrath to come"
= inherit the eternal kingdom: "so we will always be with the Lord."

Nowhere in these verses does it state that Christ is returning with the raptured saints to this earth on Judgment Day to reign on the earth for another thousand years, as claimed by premillennialists.

Coming on the Clouds

When Christ ascended in the clouds to heaven to return to his Father, angels appeared and said that his return would also be visible in the clouds:

And when he had said these things, as they were looking on, he was lifted up, and a cloud took him out of their sight. And while they were gazing into heaven as he went, behold, two men stood by them in white robes [angels], and said, "Men of Galilee, why do you stand looking into heaven? This Jesus, who was taken up from you into heaven, will come in the same way as you saw him go into heaven." (Acts 1:9–11)

142 | GOD'S ENDGAME

Premillennialists claim that when Christ returns in the clouds, he will return to this earth. But notice that the angels did not say Christ would return to this earth. Rather, Christ said he would return in the sky on Judgment Day to rapture his people into the clouds and take them to the Father's eternal kingdom:

> Then will appear in heaven the sign of the Son of Man, and then all the tribes of the earth will mourn [on Judgment Day], and they will see the Son of Man coming on the clouds of heaven with power and great glory. And he will send out his angels with a loud trumpet call, and they will gather his elect from the four winds, from one end of heaven to the other. (Matt. 24:30–31)

Christ's return on the clouds can be outlined as follows:
- At Christ's second coming on the last day of this age, he will visibly return in the clouds.
- Christ will send his angels to gather all unbelievers from the earth and from hades.
- The saints will be raptured into the sky to join Christ.
- The Genesis creation then perishes, and Christ will create the new heavens and new earth as the eternal habitat for the glorified sons of God.
- Christ will sit on his Great White Throne to judge all mankind.
- Unbelievers will be judged according to their sinful deeds and will be sent to the lake of fire.
- The saints will be purified by fire to burn off their bad deeds and will be rewarded for their good deeds that survive the fire.
- Christ and his glorified saints will descend to the eternal new earth to dwell with the triune God in all their glory.

Summary

Premillennialists have a noble objective. They are attempting to affirm the Son's messianic kingdom. They believe that because Christ ascended to heaven without establishing his messianic kingdom while he was on this earth, he must return to this earth a second time to accomplish this mission before he ushers in the Father's eternal kingdom. There is overwhelming biblical evidence, however, that Christ's second coming occurs *not* at the beginning of the millennium, but on the very last day of this creation to usher in the eternal age to come.

Christ's return occurs at the final resurrection of all mankind when he sits on his Great White Throne to judge the world. The saints, or the sheep, will be raptured into their eternal bodies and will inherit eternal life in the Father's eternal kingdom. Unbelievers, or the goats, will be resurrected from hades and will inherit the eternal lake of fire.

For those who want to affirm Christ's millennial kingdom, another solution other than premillennialism must be found. Postrestorationalism proposes that instead of Christ returning to this earth to establish his kingdom, he rules the world during the millennium from his throne in heaven. John never described Christ on his white horse returning to this earth to establish his kingdom. Christ is portrayed as remaining in the celestial realm of heaven when he rules the world.

And instead of the first resurrection being of the raptured saints, it will be a resurrection of the departed saints into their natural bodies—restored natural bodies for a restored natural earth. Therefore, Christ returns *after* (post-) his 1,000-year restoration of this Genesis creation at the final resurrection on Judgment Day to usher in the Father's eternal kingdom in the eternal age to come. The saints are raptured into their eternal bodies to inherit the new heavens and new earth, and unbelievers are resurrected from hades to inherit the lake of fire.

Amillennialists agree that the second coming is on the last day. They do not believe, however, in a future millennial age of righteous humanity before the eternal age. In the next chapter, we will examine amillennialism and postmillennialism.

7

A Critique of Amillennialism and Postmillennialism

Note: This critique is best understood by watching a 45-minute video presentation online at www.godsendgame.net. The following charts are also available on the website to download and print.

Review

In the last chapter, I critiqued premillennialism by using the chart of God's plans for the future. Premillennialists have a noble objective. They are attempting to affirm the Son's messianic kingdom. Since Christ did not establish his earthly kingdom the first time he came to this earth, they believe he must return to this world once again at the beginning of the millennium to establish his kingdom. At the end of the Great Tribulation when Satan is completely removed from this world, Christ will physically return to this earth to govern the world. The first resurrection represents the saints in their raptured, eternal bodies so that they can inherit the restored natural earth during Christ's reign.

There is overwhelming biblical evidence, however, that Christ's second coming occurs *not* at the beginning of the millennium but on the very last day of this Genesis creation at the final resurrection on Judgment Day to usher in the eternal age to come. The saints will be raptured and transformed into their eternal bodies and will inherit the eternal new heavens and new earth, and unbelievers will be resurrected from hades and will inherit the eternal lake of fire.

Amillennialism

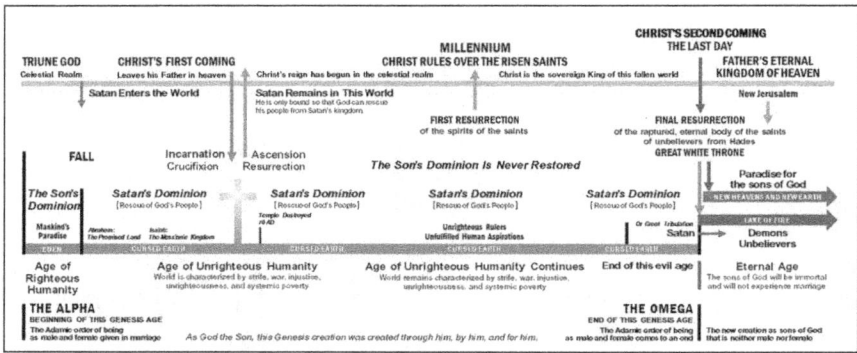

Amillennialists agree that Christ returns on the last day of this Genesis creation to usher in the eternal age to come. They ask premillennialists how Christ can return to this earth to rule over it for a thousand years if he destroys the earth when he returns. Amillennialists assert that there is never a millennial age of righteous humanity on this earth before the eternal kingdom. This present age remains an evil age until the last day.

In the Olivet Discourse we learn that Christ returns at the end of the Genesis age.

> As he sat on the Mount of Olives, the disciples came to him privately, saying, "Tell us, when will these things be [the temple's destruction], and what will be the sign of your coming and of the end of the age?" (Matt. 24:3)

Christ returns at the end of this Genesis age to usher in the eternal age. Amillennialists combine this teaching with the following teaching: "Grace to you and peace from God our Father and the Lord Jesus Christ, who gave himself for our sins to deliver us from *the present evil age*" (Gal. 1:3–4). According to amillennialists, "the present evil age" ends when Christ comes again at "the end of the age." Therefore, the world remains characterized by evil until Christ ushers in the eternal kingdom.

But in Galatians, Paul was simply describing the condition of the world at that time. His statement does not preclude a future age of righteous humanity. Just as Christ can deliver us from our sins today, he is more than capable of delivering mankind from this evil age someday in the future. Nonetheless, amillennialists believe the world will remain evil until Christ comes again at the end of the age.

God was supposed to use Israel to bring the Messiah into the world as the son of David who would restore the nation of Israel and usher in an age of righteous humanity on this earth. But the Jews rejected their Messiah. Therefore, according to amillennialists, the promises of a Jewish-led messianic kingdom on this earth are no longer valid. The mission of Israel has now shifted to Christ as the new Israel.

The promise of a paradise on this earth has also shifted to a paradise on the eternal new earth. Christ, as the new Israel, is now responsible for ushering in this eternal kingdom on the last day. The Jews are welcome to repent and believe in their Messiah, but that only means they are destined for the eternal kingdom of heaven, like all Gentile believers.

Amillennialists would interpret the chart of God's endgame as follows. God demonstrated his judgment and rejection of Israel by allowing the destruction of the temple by the Romans in AD 70. Many believe this was the predicted Great Tribulation. As such, there will be no future Great Tribulation. Christ is not waiting on the Father to establish his reign over this earth. And Christ will never rule this current fallen world as King of kings and Lord of lords. The Son's dominion over this Genesis creation will never be restored. The earth will never be restored to its Edenic condition. There will never be a restored human paradise on this earth for a thousand years. Unrighteous rulers will remain in power until the last day. Our human aspirations for an abundant life on the earth as men and women of God will never be fulfilled. There will never be an age of righteous humanity on this current earth. The curse on this earth will remain until the last day, when Christ returns and the Genesis earth is replaced with the eternal new heavens and new earth.

While on the cross, Jesus proclaimed that his death and resurrection would remove Satan: "Now is the judgment of this world; now will *the ruler of this world be cast out*" (John 12:31). Jesus also said, "How can someone enter a strong man's house and plunder his goods, unless he first *binds the strong man* [Satan]? Then indeed he may plunder his house" (Matt. 12:29). Amillennialists equate these teachings to John's reference to Satan being bound at the beginning of Christ's millennial reign:

> Then I saw an angel coming down from heaven, holding in his hand the key to the bottomless pit and a great chain. And he seized the dragon, that ancient serpent, who is the devil and Satan, and bound him for a thousand years. (Rev. 20:1–2)

Since Satan is now bound and cast out, he is somehow removed from this world, and Christ's millennial reign over his people has already begun.

But amillennialists recognize that Satan continues to rule this fallen world. He is only bound so that God can rescue his people from Satan's kingdom. Once converted, Christians remain in a demonic world until Christ returns and sends Satan to the lake of fire.

Amillennialists believe the first resurrection is not of a physical body but is of the spirits of the saints when they are born again and their spirits are raised from spiritual death to newness of life. Their fallen spirits are rescued from Satan's dominion and brought into Christ's millennial kingdom. Or it is when their spirits are raised to be with the Lord when they physically die. The spirits of the departed saints are in heaven as a cloud of witnesses watching God's plan of redemption unfold on this earth. Amillennialists claim that Christ's millennial reign currently exists in the celestial realm of heaven, where he rules over the risen spirits of the saints (believers on earth and the departed spirits already in heaven).

Christ is the sovereign King of this fallen world, even though the world remains Satan's dominion until the last day. He allows unrighteous rulers to continue to govern the nations. But the Son's dominion is never truly restored. The world remains characterized by strife, war, injustice, unrighteousness, and systemic poverty until Christ returns on the last day and takes us to the Father's eternal kingdom. There is no messianic kingdom of peace, justice, righteousness, and prosperity on this earth as described by the prophets. Anthony Hoekema explains this view in his book *The Bible and the Future*:

Amillennialists interpret the millennium mentioned in Revelation 20:4–6 as describing the present reign of the souls of deceased believers with Christ in heaven. They understood the binding of Satan mentioned in the first three verses of this chapter as being in effect during the entire period between the first and second comings of Christ, though ending shortly before Christ's return. They teach that Christ will return after this heavenly millennial reign.[10]

Some amillennialists believe there could very well be a future Great Tribulation at the end of the world. This evil age could get much worse in the last days leading up to Christ's second coming. John's description of Satan's final deception of mankind involving Gog and Magog at the end of the millennium is a recapitulation of Christ's second coming on Judgment Day at the battle of Armageddon when Christ appears on his white horse. When Christ comes again on the last day, it will be to send Satan to the lake of fire and bring this evil age to an end. He will destroy this Genesis creation and take us to the Father's eternal kingdom of heaven.

Many amillennialists believe the Genesis earth is not destroyed on the last day but is only purified by a surface fire. The eternal kingdom is a restored Genesis earth. The New Jerusalem comes down to this earth. God the Father and Christ come down to the renewed earth to dwell with mankind. Therefore, the millennium is not necessary because the age of righteous humanity described by the prophets will be realized on the eternal new earth.

Yet, John teaches that the Genesis creation comes to an end on the last day: "From his presence earth and sky fled away, and no place was found for them" (Rev. 20:11). After the termination of this planet and the universe, the Genesis creation ceases to have a presence before God. It will have "no place" in space and time.

Christ, as the Son of God, then creates the new heavens and earth as the eternal home for the sons of God.

> Then I saw a new heaven and a new earth, for the first heaven and first earth had passed away [no longer had a presence before God], . . . And I saw the holy city, new Jerusalem, coming down out of

---

10 Anthony A. Hoekema, *The Bible and the Future* (Grand Rapids: Eerdmans, 1979), 174.

heaven from God [to the new earth], ... And he [Christ] who was seated on the throne said, "Behold, I am making all things new [the new eternal habitat for the sons of God]." (Rev. 21:1–5)

Notice that the New Jerusalem comes down to the new earth and *not* to the old earth, which had passed away. Therefore, the sons of God are destined for a totally new creation on the last day.

Most important, the eternal kingdom cannot be a fulfillment of the prophecies of the messianic kingdom because Isaiah and the prophets described the Messiah's earthly kingdom as a restored Adamic paradise. The messianic kingdom will be an age of righteous humanity with men and women experiencing marriage and procreation. The prophets are not describing the eternal home for the immortal sons of God, who will no longer experience marriage. Isaiah described this Adamic paradise:

I will rejoice in Jerusalem and be glad in my people; no more shall be heard in it the sound of weeping and the cry of distress. ... They shall build houses and inhabit them [human habitats]; they shall plant vineyards and eat their fruit [agricultural fields]. ... They shall not labor in vain or bear children for calamity, for they shall be the offspring of the blessed of the Lord, and their descendants with them [marriage and reproduction]. (Isa. 65:19–23)

Isaiah is not describing the New Jerusalem on the eternal new earth; rather, he is describing the restored earthly Jerusalem on the restored Genesis earth. The eternal new earth will not be a joyful restoration of our humanity as described by Isaiah; otherwise, the immortal sons of God would experience marriage and reproduction in heaven. Therefore, the eternal kingdom cannot be a fulfillment of the messianic prophecies of a restored Genesis earth. Thus, without a millennial reign of Christ, amillennialists are simply missing the messianic kingdom altogether.

According to amillennialists, Christ returns after this present evil age comes to an end, which occurs on the last day of this cursed Genesis creation. Christ's millennial reign over the resurrected spirits of his people exists only in the celestial realm of heaven. The first resurrection is of the spirits of the saints. Christ's second coming occurs at the final resurrection on Judgment Day. The saints are raptured into eternal bodies in order to inherit the eternal new heavens and new earth, while unbelievers are resurrected, judged, and sent to the lake of fire.

Amillennialism means no literal millennial reign of Christ. Some amillennialists object to this name because they claim that Christ's kingdom does exist, even if it is in the celestial realm. But the name *is* appropriate because they assert that there is no period in human history when Satan is completely removed from this world before the eternal kingdom is ushered in. The curse on this earth is never removed, and the earth is never restored to an Edenic paradise for a thousand years.

Amillennialists are correct when they assert that Christ returns at the end of this Genesis age to usher in the eternal age to come. But the amillennial version of God's endgame has some serious flaws. For example, amillennialists are inconsistent in their interpretation of the two resurrections identified in Revelation. On one hand, they believe the final resurrection represents a literal bodily resurrection of unbelievers and believers. Yet, they assert that the first resurrection represents only a resurrection of the spirits of the saints, even though John uses the same Greek word for bodily resurrection as he does for the final resurrection. Of the first resurrection, he wrote:

> They came to life [the departed saints are bodily resurrected] and reigned with Christ for a thousand years [physically on the earth]. The rest of the dead [the departed spirits of unbelievers held in hades] did not come to life [are not bodily resurrected at that time] until the thousand years were ended [when they are resurrected at the final resurrection]. (Rev. 20:4–5)

John treats both resurrections as of a real body. Moreover, throughout Revelation, John is well aware that the martyred saints killed during the reign of the Antichrist have already experienced a resurrection of their spirits to the celestial realm of heaven. John refers to them as singing and worshiping in heaven after they are martyred (Rev. 7:9–14; 19:1–2). So if the first resurrection is only of the spirits of the saints, as claimed by amillennialists, and John already knows their spirits have been raised to heaven, then why would John teach that the spirits of the martyred saints needed to be resurrected again at the first resurrection in order to inherit Christ's millennial kingdom? Do their spirits need to be resurrected twice in order to be with the Lord in heaven?

John is obviously referring to a bodily resurrection of the departed saints, which would enable them to reinhabit the earth during Christ's millennial reign. The book of Revelation is complex, but it is not illogical. John specifically states that the departed people of God whose spirits are in heaven will one day physically reside on the earth again:

> By your blood you ransomed people for God from every tribe and language and people and nation [throughout history], and you have made them a kingdom and priests to our God, and *they shall reign on the earth*. (Rev. 5:9–10)

The ransomed people will reign "on the earth"—not in the celestial realm of heaven. And to reside on the earth, God's people will need a real resurrected body. John's vision of the earthly kingdom of Christ is not some form of mysticism. He is describing a real kingdom on this earth.

Amillennialists are inconsistent in their interpretation of the first and final resurrections. If the eternal new earth is a real place accessed through a real resurrection of the raptured, immortal body, then John's vision of the millennium would be a real kingdom on this earth accessed through a resurrection of a real body.

Furthermore, as premillennialists point out, amillennialists have a Messiah with a missing messianic kingdom. A great deal of Old Testament prophecy about a restored earth during an age of righteous humanity will go unfulfilled. Isaiah described the messianic kingdom as a kingdom *on this earth*:

> For to us a child is born, to us a son is given; and the government [of Israel and the world] shall be upon his shoulder, . . . Of the increase of his government and of *peace* there will be no end, on the throne of David and *over his kingdom*, to establish it [on this earth] and to uphold it with *justice* and with *righteousness* from this time forth and forevermore. (Isa. 9:6–7)

According to Isaiah, one day this present evil age will indeed come to an end, and the Messiah will rule the world such that it will be characterized by peace, justice, and righteousness.

Even though Jesus did not establish his messianic kingdom while he was on this earth, he informed the disciples that after he ascended to the right hand of God, on a day set by the Father, Israel would surely experience the messianic kingdom:

> So when they had come together, they asked him, "Lord, will you at this time restore the kingdom to Israel [establish the messianic kingdom]?" He said to them, "It is not for you to know times or seasons that the Father has fixed by his own authority." (Acts 1:6–7)

Jesus knew exactly what the disciples were asking. They knew their Old Testament Scriptures and were rightly expecting the messianic kingdom. Jesus' answer indicates that it is not a question of *if* there will be a restoration, but *when* it will occur. Jesus informed them that only the Father has the authority to determine when his kingdom will be established on this earth. Yet, amillennialists continue to insist that the nation of Israel has been cut off from God's plan of redemption and that the Jews will never experience a restoration of their nation when their Messiah rules the world.

This reveals an even greater flaw with amillennialism. The Scriptures teach that as God the Son, this Genesis creation was created through him, by him, and for him. Christ is the Alpha and the Omega of this creation. In the beginning, the world was the Son's dominion. If Adam and Eve had not sinned, the world would have remained his dominion. This creation would have been the Son's earthly kingdom, and he would have ruled over his kingdom from his throne in heaven. He would have delighted in his good creation as he watched man, as male and female, experience the union of marriage and reproduce godly children. Their children's children would have subdued and filled the earth, developing the untamed earth into an Edenic paradise. The human experience on this earth would have brought him great joy. Most important, as this creation fulfilled its original purpose, it would have brought him great glory as the Creator of this wonderful creation!

But when Adam and Eve rebelled against God, mankind and this creation lost its glory. Satan was allowed into our world, negatively influencing all aspects of human thought and behavior. The world became his dominion, thereby robbing the Son of God of the joy of his rightful reign over his "good" creation. The Son lost the delight of his wonderful creation. He takes no pleasure in the evil that exists in this age of unrighteous humanity. Rather, this fallen world brings him grief and anger. It does not bring him the glory he deserves.

According to amillennialists, Satan is never completely removed from this world. There will never be an age of righteous humanity on a restored Edenic earth. The world will remain evil until the very last day of this Genesis age. The Son's dominion over his own creation will never be restored. Christ may be sovereign, but he will never get his good Genesis creation back, free of demonic evil and human depravity. Satan will be destroyed in the end, but the world will remain Satan's dominion throughout human history. Christ will return on the last day of this evil age to take us to heaven and will then turn his kingdom over to his Father.

In this version of God's endgame, Christ loses his battle with Satan for he never truly removes Satan and becomes the absolute king of this world, reestablishing God's will on earth as it was in the garden of Eden before the fall. This would not only be a tragedy for humanity, but it would also be a divine tragedy for the Son of God.

That is something God the Father will not allow, however, for he has promised his Son that one day he will restore his creation to him. Quoting from Psalm 110, Jesus said, "For David himself says in the Book of Psalms, 'The Lord [the Father] said to my Lord [the Son], 'Sit at my right hand [in heaven], until I make your enemies your footstool [human and demonic]'" (Luke 20:42–43). This is an *unconditional* covenant within the Trinity itself between the Father and his Son, who was always faithful, both as a man and certainly as the Son of God.

The Father has promised his Son that one day he will remove all his enemies, including Satan, and give his Son's Genesis kingdom back to him. Since this creation was created for the Son of God, he has a divine right to rule this world without the influence of Satan. And we have yet to see the regime change that would usher in his restored kingdom over a restored humanity. Christ has ascended to the right hand of God and may be the declared King of this world, with all power and authority at his disposal, but it is obvious that he is not currently exercising that power and authority to establish his kingdom of righteousness on this earth. Hebrews proclaims this truth:

> "You made him [the Son] for a little while lower than the angels [during his incarnation]; you have crowned him with glory and honor [after his crucifixion, resurrection, and ascension], putting everything in subjection under his feet [he is Lord of this world]." Now in putting everything in subjection to him, he left nothing outside his control. *At present, we do not yet see everything in subjection to him* [his enemies, demonic and human, continue to operate]. (Heb. 2:7–8)

The ascended Christ may be King-elect or Lord-elect of this world, having been elected by the Father as the absolute ruler of this world, but he has yet to take office and subject all his enemies to his will. In the meantime, Satan remains the god of this world, and unrighteous men and women under his influence continue to rule it. We are still waiting on the Father to say it is time for Christ to remove Satan and rule this world with absolute justice as the true God of this creation.

Despite this covenant between the Father and his Son, amillennialists boldly claim that the Son's dominion is never restored to him. If that is true, then one would have to conclude that God the Father misled his Son when he promised him that his Genesis creation would one day be restored to him. But Christ has a divine right to rule this world without any demonic influence whatsoever because this is his creation! Notice how John described Christ's reign over this earth as the reign of God Almighty:

> Then the seventh angel blew his trumpet, and there were loud voices in heaven, saying, "The kingdom of the world has become the kingdom of our Lord and of his Christ," . . . And the twenty-four elders . . . worshiped God, saying, "We give thanks to you, *Lord God Almighty*, who is and who was [a divine, eternal being], for *you have taken your great power* [his divine power] *and begun to reign* [over the world]." (Rev. 11:15–17)

John foresaw the day when Christ, as "Lord God Almighty," will use his divine power and authority to rule over his creation. The world will become the kingdom of Christ with "everything in subjection to him"—just as the Father has promised his Son. These verses in Revelation plainly contradict the amillennial assertion that there is no period in human history when Christ, as Lord God Almighty, rules over his own creation.

The Promised Restoration in This Genesis Age

Amillennialists often point out that the only place in the Bible a millennial reign of Christ is even mentioned is in the obscure book of Revelation, which should not be taken too literally. In an often overlooked passage, however, Jesus himself promises that one day he will sit on his throne in heaven and will rule over a restored Genesis creation in this age *before* he comes again to usher in eternal life for the sons of God in the age to come. This promised restoration can easily be linked to the millennium described in Revelation, which further informs us that this reign and restoration will last for a thousand years and is accessed by the first resurrection.

Jesus made this promise when a rich man approached him, asking how he could inherit eternal life. Jesus recognized that the man's wealth had become an idol, so he told the man to sell all that he had and then follow him and he would be rewarded with eternal life.

Sadly, the man refused to part with his wealth and follow Christ. The disciples then asked Christ what their reward would be for sacrificially following him. Mark recorded Christ's answer:

> "I tell you the truth," Jesus replied, "no one who has left home or brothers or sisters or mother or father or children or fields for me and the gospel will fail to receive a hundred times as much *in this present age* (homes, brothers, sisters, mothers, children and fields—and with them, persecutions) *and in the age to come, eternal life.*" (Mark 10:29–30 NIV; cf. Luke 18:29–30)

Notice that the hundredfold reward occurs "in this present age," which means that it will occur on this Genesis earth before it comes to an end. And the reward of eternal life occurs "in the age to come," or

A CRITIQUE OF AMILLENNIALISM AND POSTMILLENNIALISM | 157

in the eternal kingdom. Jesus taught that this occurs when he comes again on the last day of this Genesis age: "As he sat on the Mount of Olives, the disciples came to him privately, saying, . . . 'what will be the sign of your coming and of the end of the age [the Genesis age]?'" (Matt. 24:3).

Matthew also recorded Jesus telling the disciples of their rewards:

> Truly, I say to you, *in the new world* [the regenerated Genesis earth], *when the Son of Man will sit on his glorious throne,* you who have followed me will also sit on twelve thrones [on the regenerated earth], judging the twelve tribes of Israel. And everyone who has left houses or brothers or sisters or father or mother or children or lands, for my name's sake, will receive a hundredfold ["in this present age"] and ["in the age to come"] will inherit eternal life [eternal embodied life in the eternal kingdom of heaven]. (Matt. 19:28–29)

The Greek word for "the new world" is more accurately translated "in the regeneration" (ASV).[11] The curse on this earth will be removed, and the natural world will experience a radical regeneration, restoring it to its Edenic condition. Christ promised his disciples that when he rules the world, they will inherit this restored Edenic earth.

He also promised them that they would inherit eternal life. This will occur when Christ comes again on the last day to usher in the Father's kingdom. The followers of Christ will experience the final resurrection when they are raptured and transformed into eternal bodies to inherit eternal life on the eternal new earth.

Christ's promises to his followers can be summarized as follows. On a day determined by his Father, the Son's dominion will be restored. This present evil age will come to an end when Satan is removed from this world and the millennium begins. Christ will sit on his throne in heaven and rule the world. Through the first resurrection, his followers will inherit his kingdom on a regenerated earth during an age of righteous humanity. This occurs in this Genesis age when this creation is restored to its Edenic condition. Our human aspirations will be fulfilled a hundredfold during his reign. Revelation informs us that his

---

11 American Standard Version

reign will last for a thousand years. And when Christ comes again, we will inherit eternal life in the age to come, which occurs on the last day when Christ ushers in the eternal age.

These verses in Mark and Matthew provide critically important information about Christ's kingdom on this earth—information that is as important as the teachings on the millennium in Revelation 20. Whenever I have brought these verses to the attention of amillennial theologians, however, they have not been able to provide a logical interpretation of these teachings of Christ.

To circumvent these verses, amillennialists often claim that the hundredfold reward is a reference to Christ sending the Holy Spirit to the disciples. They experienced an abundant inner life of the Holy Spirit as they walked through this troubled world suffering persecution, imprisonment, and even martyrdom. But notice that Christ ties the hundredfold reward to a period of human history when the curse will be removed from this earth and the earth is regenerated and restored to its Edenic condition. That did not occur in the first century, and the curse has remained in place for the last two thousand years!

Other amillennialists claim that the reference to the regenerated earth is a reference to the eternal new earth, not to this present cursed earth. Christ makes it quite clear, however, that their hundredfold reward on a regenerated earth occurs in this present Genesis age, not in the eternal age to come. They will receive "a hundred times as much *in this present age.*"

Christ's promise is twofold. When Christ sits "on his glorious throne" and rules the world, the disciples will inherit a life on the regenerated earth during this Genesis age that is a hundred times better than the rich man's life. And in addition, when he comes again at the end of the age, they will inherit eternal life in the age to come. They will inherit God the Son's kingdom on this restored earth—as well as God the Father's eternal kingdom of heaven on the imperishable new earth.

Yet, amillennialists continue to insist that the Genesis age remains an evil age until the last day. Paradise was lost at the fall and will never be restored. There is no hope for a redemption of the Adamic order of being. The human experience on this earth has a tragic ending. The saints will experience only one resurrection—on the last day when Christ returns to take us to the eternal paradise in heaven.

Amillennialism may be correct in that Christ's second coming occurs on the last day. And amillennialists are correct to reject premillennialism. But when they assert that this Genesis age will remain an evil age until it comes to an end on the last day, they are making many serious biblical mistakes. Amillennialism contradicts the following biblical doctrines:

- The prophets' predictions of an age of righteous humanity when the Messiah, as God Almighty, rules the world.
- Jesus' promise to his followers that one day when he rules the world, they will inherit a restored humanity on the regenerated earth in this Genesis age.
- The Father's unconditional promise to his Son that one day he will remove his enemies and restore this creation to his Son.

Even though Christ has a divine right to reclaim his Genesis creation and rule this world, amillennialists contend that the Son's dominion over his creation is never restored. The world will remain Satan's dominion until this Genesis creation comes to an end. The Son of God will never get to enjoy his creation free from the demonic influence of Satan and the corruption of sinful mankind.

Reformed theologians often say the chief purpose of mankind is to bring glory to Christ. Yet, without the Son's thousand-year restoration of this Genesis creation, they are missing one of the most important ways the ransomed people of God will bring glory to the Son of God. Amillennialists omit the Son's millennial kingdom altogether.

Most amillennialists probably do not realize how deficient their view of God's endgame is. But as the amillennial chart graphically demonstrates, the elimination of the Son's restored Genesis earth is quite shocking. This view of God's endgame dismisses major components of God's plan of redemption. We will inherit the kingdom of heaven, but we will never experience a rich and abundant life on this earth as restored human beings. Most important, the Son of God, as the creator of this world, will never receive the glory he would have received had this creation been restored to its Edenic condition under his Lordship. Amillennialism is flawed because it does not correspond to the biblical data.

Postmillennialism

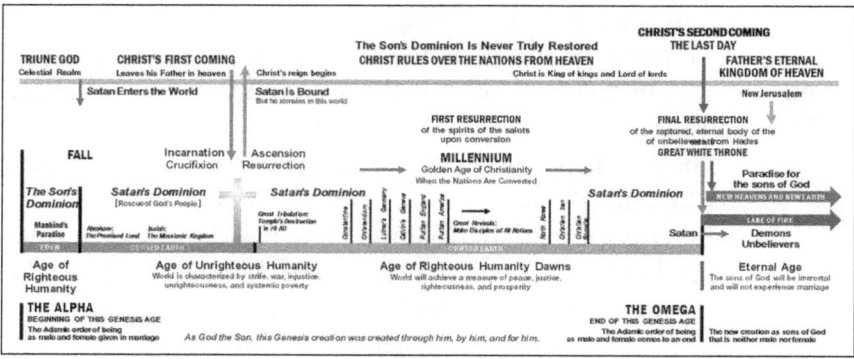

Postmillennialism is like amillennialism in that it also asserts that Christ returns on the last day to usher in the eternal kingdom. But postmillennialists believe that before Christ returns to usher in the eternal kingdom, there will be a golden age of Christianity on this earth.

Satan is now bound so that we can complete the Great Commission to disciple all nations. They claim that if we are faithful in evangelism, the Holy Spirit will Christianize the nations and usher in an age of righteous humanity. Instead of the millennium being in the celestial realm of heaven, as amillennialists assert, postmillennialists believe it will be experienced on this earth when the nations are converted. But the millennium will not necessarily last for a literal thousand years.

They claim that Christ's reign as the Messiah began after his ascension and that he presently rules over the nations from his throne in heaven. He does not need to return to this earth to establish his earthly kingdom. Christ is already King of kings and Lord of lords. Once the nations have become Christianized, an age of righteous humanity will dawn. The world will achieve a measure of peace, justice, righteousness, and prosperity. With advances in technology and human civilization, much of the misery we experience on this earth will be greatly reduced. We can experience a better life on this earth before we go to heaven.

But they acknowledge that Satan remains in this world until the very last day of this Genesis creation, and the curse on this earth remains in place. The millennium will essentially be the world we know today, but Christianized. Once this golden age on this cursed earth comes to an end, Christ will return on the last day to take us to heaven. Thus, the name *post*millennialism.

This Christianization began in Europe when Emperor Constantine converted from paganism to Christianity in AD 312 and began the process of transforming pagan Rome into a theocratic Christian nation. Israel had rejected their Messiah, but with the conversion of the Gentile kings and nations, the reign of Christ was gradually being implemented.

This view was later popularized by Saint Augustine and became the predominate view of the Catholic Church. This form of theocracy became known as Christendom in Europe. Civil rulers, in cooperation with Catholic religious rulers, had a God-ordained duty to sit on powerful thrones and reign over Christ's kingdom on his behalf. Those deemed to be heretics were punished or killed.

Martin Luther helped usher in a Protestant version of Christendom in Germany in the early 1500s. And John Calvin set up a Christian theocracy in Geneva as a model for other cities and nations. Then the Puritan movement took place in England, Scotland, and America, spearheaded by the Protestant Reformers. These great revivals were fulfilling the Great Commission by making disciples of all nations. Today, however, many evil nations remain in this world. Countries such as North Korea, Iran, and Somalia have a long way to go in becoming Christian nations. And many former Christian nations have digressed and will have to be Christianized again.

Postmillennialism can be summarized as follows. Satan is partially bound, and Christ will establish his millennial reign when the nations are converted to Christianity. But the Son's dominion is never truly restored, for the world will remain Satan's dominion until the last day. The Genesis earth is never restored to its Edenic condition. The first resurrection is of the spirits of the saints upon conversion. Christ's second coming will occur at the final resurrection on Judgment Day, when the saints are raptured into eternal bodies to inherit the eternal new heavens and new earth and unbelievers are resurrected, judged, and sent to the lake of fire.

This view of God's endgame is also flawed. As long as sinful men and women are ruling this world, Christian theocracies often lead to the loss of religious liberty and civil liberties. These imperfect rulers can still be easily influenced by Satan. This has led to a great deal of religious tyranny and persecution of those who disagreed with the religious authorities in power. Catholic rulers persecuted Protestant Reformers, and Protestant rulers persecuted Catholics. This battle between Catholic and Protestant versions of a Christian theocracy on this earth also led to long and brutal religious wars. Today, many Christians believe the church best fulfills the Great Commission when there is religious liberty, even if this allows false religions and heresies to coexist within the church.

While Satan is operational in this world, it is highly unlikely that we will be able to Christianize the nations and set up the messianic kingdom on this earth. Satan's influence is the reason the world continues to be characterized by strife, war, injustice, unrighteousness, and systemic poverty. The modern world has made great progress, and the spread of Christianity has truly had a tremendous civilizing effect on many nations. But there is as much evil in the world today as there was in Christ's day, if not more. Peace and prosperity have proven to be elusive goals, even with the best efforts of missionaries. Poverty remains entrenched throughout the world. After two world wars and brutal communist revolutions in Russia and China, postmillennialism became largely discredited. As a result, it is not popular today.

Moreover, the earth remains under a curse until the end of the world. So even if we do evangelize and Christianize the nations, people will continue to experience short lives with a great deal of sickness and misery on a degenerate earth.

And without the first resurrection, the departed saints will never experience this golden age of Christianity. Peter and the disciples have all died. According to the postmillennial view, the disciples will never inherit the hundredfold reward on a restored earth as promised by Christ *before* he comes again to take them to heaven. They will only inherit eternal life when Christ returns to rapture their bodies into eternal bodies.

The Son of God will never get to enjoy a restored humanity free of Satan and the curse, even though the Father has promised his Son that one day he will remove his enemies and restore this Genesis creation to him. Despite what the name implies, postmillennialists do not really believe in a literal millennium. Paradise will only be partially restored, because Christ's kingdom remains on a degenerate earth. We will only inherit the Father's eternal kingdom when Christ comes again and turns his kingdom over to the Father. When compared to God's plans for the future, it is evident that postmillennialism does not correspond to the biblical data.

Summary

Each of the three current views of God's endgame—premillennialism, amillennialism, and postmillennialism—are remarkably different. And as the critique of each view has demonstrated, not one accurately corresponds to all the biblical data.

Premillennialists make a good case that there must be a messianic kingdom on this earth before the eternal kingdom. Jesus Christ, as the Son of God, has a divine right to restore this earth, remove Satan, and reclaim his creation. But they have Christ's second coming in the wrong place. They claim that Christ returns to this earth at the beginning of the millennium to establish his kingdom. The Scriptures reveal, however, that when he comes again, he will destroy this Genesis creation and usher in the eternal age to come—not another one thousand years of the earth's existence. Furthermore, it makes no sense for the raptured, glorified saints to return to this earth to live alongside natural human beings who survive the Great Tribulation. The prophets describe the messianic kingdom as an Adamic paradise for restored human beings—not for the immortal sons of God, who belong in heaven.

Amillennialists claim that there is no millennium. They have Christ's second coming in the right place, but they have a Messiah without his messianic kingdom. The world remains an evil age until the last day, even though Christ teaches that there will be an age of righteous humanity on a restored Edenic earth *before* the saints inherit eternal life on the new earth.

Postmillennialists have the second coming in the right place, but they have a watered-down messianic kingdom, which is of no value to any of the departed saints. Peter and the disciples will only inherit the eternal kingdom of heaven at the final resurrection, even though Jesus promised them that they would inherit the regenerated earth and an Edenic paradise in this age *before* he comes again to take them to heaven.

Each camp rightly accuses the other of major scriptural contradictions by pointing out how some Scriptures are misinterpreted, mishandled, misapplied, distorted, and even ignored. None of them organize the biblical data into a rational and coherent theology of the future. This may explain why the current state of eschatology is full of so much confusion.

Maybe it is time to revisit the Bible and allow the Holy Spirit to guide us into a better understanding of God's plans for the future, one that theologians have yet to consider. In the next chapter, I will make the biblical case for postrestorationalism.

8

A Case for Postrestorationalism

Review

In chapter 5, I developed a chart of God's endgame outlining the major events of the Bible—past, present, and future. Unfortunately, theologians do not agree on how to interpret and understand this biblical data. Premillennialists place Christ's second coming at the beginning of the millennium. They believe Christ returns to this earth, ushering in the first phase of the eternal age to come. The first resurrection will be of the raptured saints to reinhabit the regenerated earth. But as demonstrated in the critique of this view in chapter 6, the Scriptures plainly teach that Christ's second coming to rapture the saints occurs at the final resurrection on Judgment Day, when the glorified sons of God inherit the Father's eternal paradise in heaven—not the Son's restored earth.

Amillennialists assert that there is no millennial reign of Christ on this earth before the eternal age and that the millennium only exists in the celestial realm. They believe the Son of God's earthly paradise was lost at the fall and is never restored. We will remain on a demonic and degenerate earth until the end of this evil age on the last day. There is never an age of righteous humanity. The second coming occurs on Judgment Day and ushers in eternal paradise on the new earth for believers and eternal punishment in the lake of fire for unbelievers.

But the Son has a divine right to remove Satan and rule this world that was created through him and for him. Amillennialists also ignore the unconditional covenant between the Father and the Son in which the Father promised his Son that one day he would remove all his enemies and restore this Genesis creation to him.

Postmillennialists, like amillennialists, believe the second coming and the rapture of the saints occur on the last day. They believe paradise will be partially restored on this earth when the nations are Christianized through effective evangelism. But postmillennialists also acknowledge that the earth remains under a curse until the last day. And without a first resurrection of the actual bodies of the departed saints, there is no way these saints can inherit a golden age of Christianity. They will only inherit eternal life, even though Christ promised his followers that they would inherit a hundredfold reward on the restored Edenic earth for sacrificially following him *before* they inherit eternal life in the age to come.

It is evident that none of the current views on God's endgame correspond well with all the biblical data, which may explain why evangelical theologians have never reached a consensus on eschatology. The subject of God's endgame needs a fresh analysis and reformulation. Maybe it is time that we continue in the tradition of the Reformers and reexamine God's Word concerning his plans for the future. Let's see if there is a better way to interpret and organize the biblical data.

There are two basic questions that need to be answered to correctly understand God's endgame:
1. Where is Christ when he rules the world?
2. What is the nature of the first and final resurrections?

Postrestorationalism

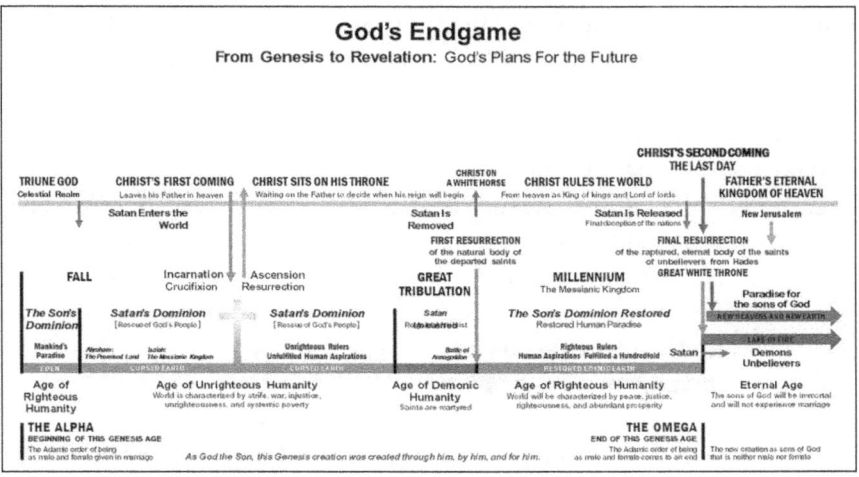

Postrestorationalism proposes that when Satan is completely removed from this realm, Christ will rule the world from his throne in heaven. As the Son of God, he does not need to return to this earth to rule over his own creation. As our Creator, he will regenerate the earth to an Edenic paradise. And in order for the departed saints to inherit this paradise on earth, they will experience the first resurrection of their natural, Adamic bodies. Christ will come again *after* this 1,000-year restoration at the final resurrection on Judgment Day. The sons of God will then be raptured into their eternal bodies so they can inherit the eternal paradise in heaven. Thus, the name *post*restorationalism.

In chapters 3 and 4, I explained my method of interpreting and organizing the Scriptures into a logical biblical theology of the future. God's plan of redemption is structured around two orders of being: the Adamic order of being that began in Genesis, and the new order of being as sons of God that began with Christ. In the Adamic order of being, we are male and female with natural bodies designed for marriage and reproduction. In the new order of being as sons of God, however, we will have immortal bodies that are neither male nor female. When we are resurrected and taken to heaven in our immortal bodies, we will no longer experience marriage and reproduction. My wife will no longer be my female partner in marriage. The Adamic order of being comes to an end, and we will all be fellow children of God.

I further explained how the Scriptures reveal a Trinitarian eschatology that revolves around these two orders of being. There are two kingdoms of the triune God: one on the earth during the millennium for a restored humanity and the other in heaven on the eternal new earth for the eternal sons of God.

Postrestorationalism is based on the two orders of being and the two corresponding kingdoms of the triune God:

- **The Adamic order of being** corresponds to the Son's thousand-year restoration of the human experience on the restored Genesis earth.
- **The new creation as sons of God** corresponds to the Father's new heavens and new earth as the eternal home for the glorified sons of God.

The triune God is one being with one will and at the same time three persons, each with a distinctive role in God's plan of redemption. For example, sometimes the Son is described as ruling this world. But his reign would also include the Father's will and rule. Likewise, heaven is sometimes described as being the Father's reign over his heavenly kingdom. This would also include the Son's everlasting reign. Both the Son's kingdom on this earth and the Father's kingdom in heaven compose the triune God's kingdom. But the Scriptures do differentiate between the Father's kingdom and the Son's kingdom.

The Scriptures also emphasize the fact that this creation was uniquely created through, by, and for the Son of God. Thus, before the fall, the world was the Son's kingdom on earth. After the fall, his kingdom was usurped when Satan entered the world. When Satan is removed from this world during the millennium, one would logically expect this earthly kingdom to be identified as the Son's kingdom restored.

Another important consideration in discerning God's endgame is Christ's dual nature as both the son of man and the Son of God. As the son of man, he was the son of David and was the Jewish Messiah. As the son of David, one would expect him to rule the world *from this earth* through Israel after he establishes his messianic kingdom. But he was also the Son of God incarnate, and he is often referred to by theologians as the God-man. As the Son of God, however, one would expect him to rule over his Genesis creation from his throne in heaven. Now risen to heaven where he sits at the right hand of God, he is the infinite Son of God who somehow remains in a glorified body as the Christ. As Paul taught, "He who descended is the one who also ascended far above all the heavens, that he might fill all things" (Eph. 4:10).

Seated at the Right Hand of God

During his first coming, the eternal Son of God left his Father in heaven and became incarnate as a human being to dwell with mankind on this earth. During his trial before the high priest, Jesus taught that after his crucifixion and resurrection, he would return to his Father in heaven: "But *from now on* the Son of Man shall be seated at the right hand of the power of God" (Luke 22:69). Being seated at the right hand of God the Father is not an inferior position of power. Rather, it is a position that is coequal with the Father. The Jewish rulers understood this was a claim of deity, and they accused him of blasphemy and sent him to Pontius Pilate to be crucified.

Most important, Christ taught that after his ascension to heaven, he would from then on relate to this world from his exalted position in heaven. He would *"from now on"* be seated at the right hand of God. Therefore, God's endgame will unfold while Christ remains in heaven.

In this chapter, I will make the biblical case that Christ *remains seated on his throne in heaven*:

- As he **waits** on the Father to say when it is time for him to remove Satan and reclaim his Genesis creation
- When he **governs** the world during his messianic kingdom
- When he comes again to **judge** mankind at the Great White Throne judgment
- When he **creates** the new heavens and new earth as the eternal home for the sons of God

These four forms of sitting on his throne in heaven can be defined as follows.

1. Sitting and Waiting

Since he has ascended to the right hand of God, Christ, as the God-man, now has all the authority and power necessary to rule this world:

And what is the immeasurable greatness of his power toward us who believe, according to the working of his great might that he worked in Christ when he [the Father] raised him from the dead and *seated him at his right hand in the heavenly places*, far above all rule and authority and power and dominion, and above every name that is named, *not only in this age but also in the one to come* [the eternal age]. (Eph. 1:19–21)

According to Paul, after Christ ascended to heaven, he remains seated at the Father's right hand in heaven throughout this Genesis age and the eternal age to come. If we combined Christ's teaching with Paul's, it would read as follows:

But *from now on* ["not only in this age but also in the one to come"] the Son of Man shall be seated at the right hand of the power of God ["far above all rule and authority and power and dominion"]. (Luke 22:69)

But when will Satan be removed and Christ use his authority and power to govern the world? This is where the relationship within the Trinity between the Father and his Son plays an important role in determining when this regime change will take place. Christ is waiting on the Father to decide the time when he will use his divine power to rule the world:

But when Christ had offered for all time a single sacrifice for sins, *he sat down* at the right hand of God, **waiting** [on the Father] from that time until his enemies should be made a footstool for his feet. (Heb. 10:12–13)

Christ informed the disciples right before his ascension:

So when they had come together, they asked him, "Lord, will you at this time restore the kingdom to Israel [establish the messianic kingdom]?" He said to them, "It is not for you to know times or seasons *that the Father has fixed by his own authority.*" (Acts 1:6–7)

Christ also taught, "The Lord [the Father] said to my Lord [the Son], 'Sit at my right hand [in heaven], *until I* [the Father] put your enemies under your feet'" (Matt. 22:44). Within the Trinity, the Son is waiting on the Father to determine when his reign over this world will begin.

Paul taught that until then, despite Christ's sovereignty and the divine power available to him, the world will remain Satan's dominion:

> Put on the whole armor of God, that you may be able to stand against the schemes of the devil. For we do not wrestle against flesh and blood, but against the rulers, against the authorities, *against the cosmic powers over this present darkness*, against the *spiritual forces of evil in the heavenly places*. (Eph. 6:11–12)

Christ's reign over this world will not begin until Satan and these demonic forces of evil are removed from this realm.

In the book of Daniel, God the Father is referred to as the Ancient of Days. The son of man, or Christ, is portrayed as ascending into the clouds to the Ancient of Days, where he is given dominion over this world. But he must wait on the Ancient of Days to say when it is time to bring the Great Tribulation to an end, to remove Satan, and to begin his reign:

> I saw in the night visions, and behold, with the clouds of heaven there came one like a son of man [Christ ascends in the clouds], and he came to the Ancient of Days and was presented before him. And to him was given dominion and glory and a kingdom, that all peoples, nations, and languages should serve him; his dominion is . . . everlasting . . . and his kingdom one that shall not be destroyed. (Dan. 7:13–14)

Daniel further taught:

> Until the Ancient of Days came [God the Father], . . . *and the time came* when the saints possessed the kingdom [as determined by the Father]. . . . But the court shall sit in judgment, and his dominion [Satan and the Antichrist's] shall be taken away, to be consumed and destroyed to the end. And the kingdom and the

dominion and the greatness of the kingdoms under the whole heaven shall be given to the people of the saints of the Most High [his reign begins]. (Dan. 7:22, 26–27)

The son of man was given dominion over this world after he ascended in the clouds to the Father. But the saints will not experience his righteous kingdom until the Father decides it is time for Satan's dominion to be taken away.

As the letter to the Hebrews reveals, Christ does not currently fully exercise the authority and power at his disposal:

> "You made him [the Son] for a little while lower than the angels [during the incarnation]; you have crowned him with glory and honor, *putting everything in subjection under his feet*" [after his ascension to the right hand of God]. Now in putting everything in subjection to him [as Paul says, he is "above all rule and authority and power and dominion"], he left nothing outside his control [he is the sovereign Lord of the world]. *At present, we do not yet see everything in subjection to him.* (Heb. 2:7–8)

These verses can be summarized as follows. After his ascension, Christ was given dominion over this world by the Father. He now reigns supreme by his position of authority at the right hand of God. He has all the divine power necessary to rule the world and subject this world to his righteous will. At present, however, he does not fully use his authority and power to establish his messianic kingdom. That is why the world remains a demonic realm filled with spiritual forces of evil. In his sovereignty, he allows evil to operate on this earth against his righteous will, but the evil deeds practiced by sinful mankind are not his will for mankind. He allows evil, but he is not the author of evil.

Some theologians claim that Christ is already the ruling King of this world. Christ is the declared sovereign King of this world by the Father, but there is a big difference between Christ *having* the power to rule this world and Christ *using* that power to establish his righteous will on this earth. We daily see the activities of Satan and depraved humanity. Mankind remains in a state of rebellion against God, with evil prevalent throughout human affairs.

Christ did not use his authority and power to prevent his arrest and crucifixion, and he does not prevent Satan from harassing and persecuting his followers today. In fact, when we suffer he also suffers. When Paul terrorized Christians before his conversion, Christ asked him, "Saul, Saul, why are you persecuting me?" (Acts 9:4). We remain in hostile territory, and every day we battle Satan, who attacks us with what Paul calls flaming arrows. That is why we must continually pray to the Father, asking him to deliver us from evil and that his will be done on earth as it is in heaven.

When Stephen was about to be unjustly stoned to death, he saw the ascended Christ at the Father's right hand:

> Now when they heard these things they were enraged, and they ground their teeth at him. But he, full of the Holy Spirit, gazed into heaven and saw the glory of God, and Jesus standing at the right hand of God. And he said, "Behold, I see the heavens opened, and the Son of Man standing at the right hand of God [with all the authority and power of God]." (Acts 7:54–56)

If Christ had wanted to prevent Stephen's death, he could have easily intervened with supernatural power from heaven. He could have just said the word, or sent an angel, and these unrighteous men would have been killed the moment they picked up the first stone. Christ chose not to intervene, and he allowed Stephen to be murdered.

David and Saul

The story of David and King Saul is a good illustration of this concept of Christ waiting on the Father to remove Satan so that his reign can begin. When King Saul disobeyed God, the kingdom of Israel was given to David, a man after God's own heart. Subsequently, the prophet Samuel found young David as a shepherd and anointed him as the king of Israel.

There was one problem, however. Saul was still ruling as king at the time David was anointed king. David did not rule Israel at that time; he had to wait until God removed Saul as king. In the meantime, Saul persecuted, hounded, and harassed David for years.

One day as Saul was pursuing him, David and his small army caught Saul and his men off guard and asleep. One of David's men wanted to take the opportunity to kill Saul so David could begin his reign. But David said:

> "Do not destroy him, for who can put out his hand against the Lord's anointed and be guiltless?" And David said, "As the Lord lives, the Lord will strike him, or his day will come to die, or he will go down into battle and perish." (1 Sam. 26:9–10)

Even though David knew God had anointed him to rule over Israel, he refused to set the time and season of his reign by killing Saul when he had the opportunity. Eventually, the Lord decided it was time for Saul's reign to come to an end, and he was killed in battle. David, the anointed one, then began his reign as king.

The prophets foretold a day when out of Bethlehem will come a son of David, whose origins are from eternity, who will sit on the throne of David. He will establish a kingdom in Israel and rule the world with justice and righteousness. The word *Messiah* means "anointed one." But there is one problem. Satan remains the current ruler of this world, and he continues to persecute Christ and his followers, just as Saul harassed David and his followers. Christ has been anointed king, but his reign has not yet begun.

The day will come, however, when the Father will determine it is time for Satan to be removed. Then the anointed Christ, the son of David, will use his great power to begin his rightful reign over this world. Just as David, the anointed king of Israel, waited on God to remove Saul so his reign could begin, so, too, Christ, the anointed king of the world, is waiting on God the Father to remove Satan so his reign can begin.

The difference, of course, is that David was a human king who ruled over Israel from this earth; whereas the son of David is also the Son of God who ascended to heaven, and he will rule the whole world as God from his throne in heaven. As Daniel revealed, Christ's dominion and kingdom will include "all peoples, nations, and languages."

2. Sitting to Govern

For the true God of this world to reclaim and rule over his creation, Satan must be removed. Toward the end of the Tribulation, Christ will appear in the celestial realm on a white horse, and he will say the word and the Antichrist and his army will be destroyed. Satan will then be completely removed from this world by an angel, and his tyranny of evil will come to an end. From his throne in heaven, Christ will fully exercise his authority and use his divine power to reign over this world. He will bring everything on this rebellious earth under his control and establish an age of righteous humanity.

After the battle of Armageddon, the Son of God's dominion over this earth will be restored:

> Then I saw an angel coming down from heaven, holding in his hand the key to the bottomless pit and a great chain. And he seized the dragon, that ancient serpent, who is the devil and Satan, and bound him for a thousand years, and threw him into the pit, and shut it and sealed it over him, so that he might not deceive the nations any longer, until the thousand years were ended. After that he must be released for a little while. (Rev. 20:1–3)

The "bottomless pit" is also translated "abyss" (NIV) and is described in the Gospels as a special prison for fallen angels or demons. Satan is bound and thrown into this prison, which is securely sealed for a thousand years. In our world, when a particularly bad criminal is arrested, we lock him up in a maximum security prison. This makes it impossible for him to escape back into the world to harm anyone during his confinement. John is quite graphic in his description of Satan's imprisonment and removal from this world. He wants to make it very clear that during Christ's reign, Satan and his demons will not be able to have any contact with mankind whatsoever. Satan will no longer be able to deceive the nations. This is the regime change we have been waiting for.

As a result of Satan's removal, there will be monumental changes in every conceivable aspect of life on this earth. All the cosmic powers of darkness and spiritual forces of evil that Paul described will be totally removed from this world. Satan will not even be around to tempt mankind, as he was in the garden. The Father's righteous will can finally be established on earth as it is in heaven. Christ's long-promised messianic kingdom will at last be implemented on this earth. He will rule the world as King of kings and Lord of lords, and the government of this world will finally be on his shoulders.

But most important, Christ does not need to return to this earth to rule over his creation. As the Son of God, he can simply rule the world from heaven. John foresaw the day when Christ, *as God Almighty*, would *use* his immeasurable power to rule this world:

> And the twenty-four elders who sit on their thrones before God fell on their faces and worshiped God, saying, "We give thanks to you, *Lord God Almighty*, who is and who was, *for you have taken your great power and begun to reign* [over the earth from his throne in heaven at the right hand of God]." (Rev. 11:16–17)

The prophet Isaiah, too, alluded to the fact that the physical son of David is also God, who will one day rule over his kingdom:

> For to us a child is born, to us a son is given; and the government shall be upon his shoulder, and his name shall be called Wonderful Counselor, *Mighty God*, Everlasting Father, Prince of Peace. Of the increase of his government and of peace there will be no end, on the throne of David and over his kingdom, to establish it and to uphold it with justice and with righteousness from this time forth and forevermore. (Isa. 9:6–7)

When Christ as God rules the world, it will no longer be characterized by evil. Instead, the world will experience peace, justice, and righteousness.

Christ described the day when he would use his power as God to govern the world from heaven:

> Truly, I say to you, in the new world [the restored Edenic earth], when the Son of Man *will sit on his glorious throne* [in heaven at the Father's right hand], you who have followed me will also sit on twelve thrones, judging the twelve tribes of Israel. (Matt. 19:28)

The disciples will even assist him in governing the affairs of Israel.

This concept of sitting on a throne to govern is like the way an emperor in the Roman Empire ruled over his people. The emperor would enter a large government hall and might casually interact with government officials until he sat down on his throne to begin the process of ruling over the affairs of state. The issue could be a new construction project such as a new aqueduct to bring spring water to a city like Antioch, or it could be to settle a dispute between two Roman cities. Once the emperor sat on his throne, he governed the affairs of his kingdom. Likewise, when Christ sits on his throne in heaven, he will begin to govern the affairs of this world.

In fact, if Christ did physically return to this earth to rule over the nations, it would be logistically difficult and inefficient. If he ruled from Jerusalem, one could only imagine the long line of diplomats and leaders from around the world seeking his assistance to settle longstanding border disputes and other sources of friction between nations. Even when Christ was on this earth, the crowds were often oppressive and overwhelming.

But ruling from heaven as "Mighty God," Christ will use his divine omniscience to communicate directly with his appointed leaders from around the world. Communicating through the Holy Spirit, he can assist them in settling disputes anywhere in the world. And what better person to properly manage the affairs of mankind than Jesus Christ? Not only does he know what it means to be a human on this earth, but from his exalted throne in heaven as God, he has infinite awareness, understanding, and insight into the affairs of the whole world.

John described Christ ruling the world with authority and power during his millennial reign: "From his mouth comes a sharp sword with which to strike down the nations, and he will rule them with a rod of iron" (Rev. 19:15). In Christ's day, shepherds used a rod as a staff to protect their sheep from predators. To rule "with a rod of iron" refers to the destruction of the armies that attack Christ at the end of the Great Tribulation, and Christ ruling the world with complete authority and power to protect mankind from evil behavior.

It is important to realize that only the armies of the Antichrist are killed at the battle of Armageddon. Many civilian unbelievers not engaged in the battle will survive the Tribulation and will enter the millennium. These unbelievers will still have sinful natures, and even without Satan in the world to tempt them, they can have evil thoughts that left unchecked may lead to sinful actions. Although unbelievers may have evil thoughts, I do not believe Christ will allow any resulting evil actions to occur. I believe he will use his supernatural powers, or his rod of iron, to prevent evil thoughts from turning into evil actions. He will prevent violence between nations as well as violence within households. No longer will a greedy dictator terrorize a nation, or an ill-tempered husband abuse his family. Christ will intervene from heaven before anyone can commit a crime or act of violence. Without the tyranny of evil, we will be able to enjoy life on the earth to the fullest.

Christ's Inaugurated Kingdom

Many theologians like to say that Christ's kingdom has already been inaugurated, but they believe his actual reign over his kingdom will not occur until it is consummated when he comes again. The concept of an "inaugurated kingdom" is misleading, however, because it implies that his reign as Lord over this world has already begun. And the word "consummated" is a poor choice of words because it means "to bring to a completion or an end." The start of the millennium represents the beginning of his kingdom reign, not its conclusion. His second coming *after* the millennium represents the conclusion of his reign. This, in turn, will be the inauguration of the Father's eternal kingdom for the sons of God, which has no end.

A better way to describe his future reign would be to say that today, he is Lord-elect of this world. His inauguration as Lord of this world will begin when Satan is removed and he takes office. His Lordship over this world will be consummated after his one thousand years in office are completed, when he comes again, destroys this Genesis creation, and turns his kingdom over to the Father.

Paul alluded to this extraordinary sequence of events in his letter to the Corinthians. Christ comes again after he has destroyed all his enemies during his reign over this world. We learn from Revelation's expanded view on God's endgame that his enemies include the false prophet, the Antichrist and his armies, the group of sinful mankind who rebel at Gog and Magog, and, of course, Satan himself, who is finally sent to the lake of fire for eternity. The very last enemy to be destroyed is mortal death itself, which is overcome when Christ comes again and the saints are given immortal bodies like his. The sequence of events in this passage is somewhat jumbled, so I will outline the sequence immediately following the passage:

> But each in his own order: Christ the firstfruits, then at his coming [the consummation] those who belong to Christ [the raptured sons of God]. Then comes the end [of his reign *and* the world], when he delivers the kingdom to God the Father [the inauguration of the Father's eternal kingdom] *after* destroying every rule and every authority and power [accomplished during his millennial reign]. For he must reign [over this world as the Messiah] until he [the Father] has put all his enemies under his feet. The last enemy to be destroyed is death [when the saints are raptured into immortal bodies and taken to heaven]. (1 Cor. 15:23–26)

This sequence of events that Paul describes can be outlined as follows:
- Christ is currently Lord-elect of this fallen world.
- He will be inaugurated into office when the Father puts "all his enemies under his feet."
- During his reign, he will destroy "every rule and every authority and power" that stand against God's will.
- When he comes again, the saints will be raptured: "then at his coming those who belong to Christ."
- Then the consummation will take place: "Then comes the end, when he delivers the kingdom to God the Father."

President-Elect

Christ's dominion and reign as King over his people has begun, but the implementation of his reign over this evil dominion of darkness has not. By way of another illustration, consider the way in which a president of the United States is elected. We elect our president every four years on Election Day in November. The winner of the election is referred to as "president-elect." The president-elect does not take office until he is inaugurated in January of the following year. In the meantime, the sitting president remains in office and continues presiding over the nation.

But the president-elect is not idle while waiting to take office. During this interim period, he is busy selecting people to join his administration. He selects key advisors such as the fifteen members of his Cabinet and thousands of other government officials to assist him in ruling the nation. On Inauguration Day, the sitting president steps down, and the president-elect takes office and begins governing the nation with his Cabinet and other members of his administration.

Likewise, Satan's term of office will one day come to an end when he is removed as the false god of this world. Christ will then be inaugurated into office to begin his millennial reign and will govern mankind as the true God of this world. John revealed that he will be dressed for the occasion: "On his robe and on his thigh he has a name written, King of kings and Lord of lords" (Rev. 19:16). Instead of Satan's sinful men and women ruling the nations, men and women of God from around the world will be appointed by Christ to rule over their respective nations. The twelve disciples also will be a part of his administration, and they will be raised at the first resurrection to assist him in governing Israel. John described this future administration: "Then I saw thrones, and seated on them were those to whom the authority to judge was committed" (Rev. 20:4). Nations such as Russia, North Korea, Iran, and Somalia will be ruled by godly leaders who will serve their people as Christ served us.

3. Sitting to Judge

Upon completion of his millennial reign, the next major eschatological event will be Christ's second coming on Judgment Day. This Genesis creation will come to an end, and the final resurrection will take place. Christ will sit on his throne and judge all mankind at the Great White Throne judgment. This form of sitting on his throne on Judgment Day also occurs from heaven, where he said he would be "from now on":

> When the Son of Man comes in his glory, and all the angels with him [his second coming], *then he will sit on his glorious throne* [in heaven]. Before him will be gathered all the nations [the final resurrection—all rise], and he will separate people one

from another as a shepherd separates the sheep from the goats [on Judgment Day]. And he will place the sheep on his right [to inherit the Father's eternal kingdom of heaven], but the goats on the left [to go to the eternal lake of fire]. (Matt. 25:31–33)

Christ taught that "when the Son of Man comes in his glory" on Judgment Day, "all the nations" will be resurrected at the final resurrection. He will separate the believers from the unbelievers. His people will inherit the Father's kingdom, and unbelievers will inherit the lake of fire. This description of his second coming to "*sit on his glorious throne*" to judge mankind corresponds to the *Great White Throne* judgment, which occurs after the millennium on the last day:

> Then I saw *a great white throne and him who was seated on it.* From his presence earth and sky fled away, and no place was found for them [the end of this Genesis creation]. And I saw the dead, great and small, standing before the throne, and books were opened. Then another book was opened, which is the book of life. And the dead [the sheep and the goats] were judged by what was written in the books, according to what they had done. (Rev. 20:11–12)

Or as Jesus revealed:

> Behold, I am coming soon, bringing my recompense with me [rewards and punishments], to repay each one for what he has done [believers and unbelievers]. I am the Alpha and the Omega, the first and the last, the beginning and the end [of this creation]. (Rev. 22:12–13)

The Scriptures plainly teach that Christ's second coming is on Judgment Day at the end of the world. After Christ ascended to heaven, he never leaves his throne in heaven.

4. Sitting to Create

The final form of Christ "sitting" on his throne in heaven is when he creates the new heavens and new earth as the eternal home for the immortal sons of God. John wrote:

> Then I saw a new heaven and a new earth, for the first heaven and the first earth had passed away, . . . *And he who was seated on the throne said,* "Behold, I am making all things new." (Rev. 21:1–5)

The Son of God is the unique person of the Trinity who created this Genesis heavens and earth. And the Son of God is also the person of the Trinity tasked with creating the new heavens and new earth as the eternal home for the sons of God. But he accomplishes this task while seated on his throne in heaven!

There will certainly be continuity with this Genesis creation given that the eternal kingdom will be new versions of the current heavens and earth. Paul taught that the current creation is groaning to transcend its current "bondage to corruption" and become a part of the eternal kingdom:

> For the creation was subjected to futility, not willingly, but because of him who subjected it, in hope that the creation itself will be set free from its bondage to corruption and obtain the freedom of the glory of the children of God [in the eternal kingdom]. (Rom. 8:20–21)

This earth may perish on the last day, but just as our natural bodies will be transformed and taken to the new earth as immortal children of God, so, too, this Genesis creation will also transition to the eternal new earth. How this will all play out in the end remains a mystery. But John does make it clear that the new earth will not be a continuation of the current natural earth inhabited by natural human beings.

In short, all four forms of Christ sitting on his throne occur from heaven at the right hand of God:

- He sits on his throne in heaven while he **waits** on the Father to say when it is time for him to rule the world.
- He sits on his throne in heaven when he **governs** this world during the millennium.
- He sits on his throne in heaven when he **judges** mankind at the Great White Throne judgment.
- He sits on his throne in heaven when he **creates** the new heavens and new earth as the eternal home for the sons of God.

As Jesus taught, after his departure from this world, "But *from now on* the Son of Man shall be seated at the right hand of the power of God" (Luke 22:69).

The First Resurrection

Now that it has been established that Christ rules the world during the millennium from his throne in heaven, the next major question that must be answered is, what is the nature of the first resurrection at the beginning of the millennium? John taught that one day all the ransomed people of God will inherit Christ's earthly kingdom:

> And by your blood you ransomed people for God from every tribe and language and people and nation, and you have made them a kingdom and priests to our God, and *they shall reign on the earth.* (Rev. 5:9–10)

But how are the ransomed people of God going to reinhabit the restored earth if they have died before his reign begins? How are the departed disciples going to inherit their hundredfold reward on the regenerated earth in this Genesis age that Jesus promised?

John taught that they would experience the first resurrection:

> I saw the souls of those who had been beheaded for the testimony of Jesus and for the word of God, and those who had not worshiped the beast or its image and had not received its mark on their foreheads or their hands. They came to life [on the earth] and reigned with Christ for a thousand years. . . . This is the first resurrection. . . . Over such the second death has no power, but they will be priests of God and of Christ, and they will reign with him for a thousand years. (Rev. 20:4–6)

John specifically identifies those saints martyred during the Great Tribulation as experiencing this resurrection. But it is a fair extrapolation that all the ransomed people of God from all nations throughout history will be included in this resurrection so that they can reside on the earth when Christ rules the world.

This doctrine can be outlined as follows:

The "ransomed people for God" = "you have made them a kingdom" = "they shall reign on the earth" = "they will reign with him for a thousand years" through the first resurrection.

But what is the nature of this first resurrection? Premillennialists claim that the first resurrection represents the rapture of the saints into their eternal bodies not given in marriage. But the Scriptures link the rapture directly to Christ's second coming, which occurs *after* the millennium at the *final* resurrection when Christ takes the transformed sons of God to their citizenship in heaven.

Amillennialists claim that the first resurrection is of the souls of the saints upon conversion, or of their spirits when their mortal bodies die and their spirits are raised to the celestial realm of heaven. But how can a person's spirit reside on the earth without a body? Furthermore, John is aware that the departed spirits of the saints have already risen to heaven after they died, for he often described them in heaven as singing and praying while they wait for justice and Christ's reign.

Instead of the spirits of the saints rising to heaven, John specifically stated that it is the souls of the saints that come to life on the earth through the first resurrection so that they can physically reside on this earth during Christ's millennial reign: "I saw the souls of those who had been beheaded for the testimony of Jesus . . . They came to life [on the earth]." John was describing a real bodily resurrection, just as he described the final resurrection as a real resurrection of the bodies of believers and unbelievers.

But what is the nature of the first resurrection if it is not of the raptured, eternal body? The answer is simple. If the millennium is a restored human paradise when our human aspirations are fulfilled a hundredfold on a restored Edenic earth during an age of righteous humanity, then it logically follows that the ransomed people of God would come back to life on this earth in human bodies of flesh and blood. Therefore, the first resurrection would be of the natural bodies of the departed saints, who could then marry and reproduce.

This will be a resurrection like the resurrection of Lazarus's natural body. It will not matter if the saints have been dead for four days like Lazarus or for four years, four hundred years, or four thousand years.

And it will not matter how many saints are resurrected. It could be four million saints, four billion saints, or all the departed saints since Abel. With the divine power of resurrection, Christ can reward the whole cloud of witnesses in heaven by having their spirits come back to the restored Edenic paradise on this earth in regenerated human bodies in order to live out the human experience as it was originally intended before the fall. The millennium is the Son's dominion over his Genesis creation restored, so it only makes sense that the saints would return to this earth as restored human beings in the image of God as male and female.

When trying to understand John's vision, it is critical to remember the following prophecy in Isaiah 65 in which the messianic kingdom is described as an Edenic paradise with humans experiencing marriage and reproduction:

> I will rejoice in Jerusalem and be glad in my people; no more shall be heard in it the sound of weeping and the cry of distress.... They shall build houses and inhabit them [human habitats]; they shall plant vineyards and eat their fruit [agricultural fields].... They shall not labor in vain or bear children for calamity, for they shall be the offspring of the blessed of the LORD, and their descendants with them [marriage and reproduction]. (Isa. 65:19–23)

Isaiah is describing the messianic kingdom as a restored humanity on a restored Edenic earth. The joyous people of God will live in houses, grow abundant crops, and have large extended families.

The first resurrection described by John can also be linked to the type of resurrection described by the prophet Ezekiel. Through Ezekiel, God promised the Jews that one day they would be restored to a glorious promised land during the messianic kingdom. But the Jews in Ezekiel's day knew they were going to die in captivity, so how could this promise be fulfilled? When describing the restored nation of Israel in the messianic kingdom, Ezekiel taught that for the departed Jewish saints to inherit this kingdom, they would be resurrected into their natural bodies:

> Thus, says the Lord God to these bones: Behold, I will cause breath to enter you, and you shall live. And I will lay sinews upon you, and will cause flesh to come upon you, and cover you with skin, and put breath in you, and you shall live [resurrection of the natural body], . . . And I will bring you into the land of Israel. . . . They shall dwell in the land that I gave to my servant Jacob, where your fathers lived. They and their children and their children's children . . . And I will set them in their land and multiply them [marriage and reproduction]. (Ezek. 37:5–12; 25–26)

Ezekiel is clearly describing a resurrection of the natural bodies of the departed Jewish saints because he states that their families will multiply after they are resurrected. Ezekiel and Isaiah are describing the messianic kingdom as an Adamic paradise on this restored Genesis earth with God's people experiencing marriage and reproduction. They are not describing heaven, when the immortal sons of God will no longer experience marriage and reproduction.

The Resurrection of Lazarus

To better understand the first resurrection, it would be helpful to examine Christ's resurrection of Lazarus. After the resurrection of his mortal body, Lazarus could have married, had children, and lived for another twenty years. But the problem with his return to this earth in his natural body was that the world was still under a curse, and the world remained Satan's dominion. Lazarus was also still living under the tyranny of the pagan Romans and the unrighteous Jewish leaders, who were trying to kill him. His second experience of life on this earth was probably not any more pleasant than his first one.

During Christ's millennial reign, however, life for Lazarus and all the resurrected saints will be vastly different. Satan will be removed, and righteous men and women will be ruling the nations on Christ's behalf. The curse will be removed, and the Genesis earth will be restored to its Edenic condition. It will be a human paradise on earth, as it was in the beginning. When Lazarus and the saints come back to life in the millennium, they will be able to marry and have all the children and grandchildren they desire. Our human aspirations for an abundant life on this earth will be fulfilled a hundredfold—just as Jesus promised.

Leaving the Paradise of Heaven

One issue that often comes up when I am describing the return of the departed saints at the beginning of the millennium is why we would want to return to this earth if we have gone to heaven and tasted of the heavenly paradise. It is important to remember that the departed saints are only spirits made perfect in heaven. As perfected spirits, they experience the joy and peace of God's presence, but they have not yet received their immortal bodies. Nor have they received their final inheritance in the new heavens and new earth because our eternal home has not yet been created.

Moreover, John emphatically says it is a real blessing for the saints who have tasted of heaven to come back to the restored earth through the first resurrection: "Blessed and holy is the one who shares in the first resurrection!" (Rev. 20:6). If John teaches that it is a blessing for the holy saints to leave heaven and return to this earth to experience the Son's kingdom, then it would not be retrogressive. Our departed spirits may experience paradise in heaven, but when we return to this earth in resurrected natural bodies, we will experience a paradise on earth as restored human beings. We were always meant to be embodied creatures, not just perfected spirits in heaven.

It is also important to remember that the millennium will not be only for our joy and pleasure. It will also be for the glory of the Son of God, who will get to enjoy his good Genesis creation as it was intended in the beginning before the fall. Sinful humanity has fallen far short of the glory of God. But when we live godly lives on this earth during the millennium, we will bring him the glory and joy he deserves as the Creator of this wonderful creation.

Another interesting question I am often asked when I present this view of the first resurrection is, will we have the same spouse in the millennium as we have today? In Paul's first letter to the Corinthians, he taught that if a spouse dies, the marriage bond is broken and the surviving spouse is free to marry again. Likewise, when the departed saints come back to life in their natural bodies, they will be free to marry whomever they wish. Some may want to marry the same person they deeply loved, while others may welcome the opportunity to find a more suitable spouse.

Another frequent question is, since the resurrected saints are in their mortal bodies, can they die again during the millennium? The reason we experience death is because we have sinful natures and continue to sin. But the Scriptures teach that when we die, our spirits in heaven are described as an assembly of "spirits of the righteous made perfect" (Heb. 12:23). Notice that John describes the returning saints at the first resurrection as having a nature that is holy: "Blessed and *holy* is the one who shares in the first resurrection!" (Rev. 20:6). In other words, when we return to this earth, we will no longer have sinful natures that cause us to sin. If we do not sin, then there is no reason we would die again.

John also indicates that the holy saints who experience the first resurrection will live for the entire millennium: "They came to life and reigned with Christ for a thousand years" (Rev. 20:4). We would therefore be alive when Christ returns at the final resurrection to transform our mortal bodies into eternal bodies.

Unbelievers who survive the Great Tribulation and who become Christians during the millennium, however, will continue to have sinful natures. Therefore, they can still sin and die, even though Isaiah says that a sinner who dies at a hundred years old will be considered a mere youth. These believers will be asleep when Christ returns on the last day.

Two Resurrections and Two Kingdoms of God

Because God's people are destined to inherit two kingdoms of the triune God, there are two resurrections. As men and women of God, we will inherit the Son's restored earth through a resurrection of natural, Adamic bodies—natural bodies for a restored natural earth. After the millennium, we will experience the final resurrection. As sons of God the Father, we will inherit the Father's eternal kingdom of heaven through a resurrection of eternal bodies like Christ's glorified body—eternal bodies for an eternal new earth. God's divine power of resurrection is the key to understanding how he will fulfill his promises.

Abraham understood this power. God had promised Abraham that through his son Isaac, all the nations of the world would be blessed. Yet God tested Abraham and told him to sacrifice Isaac. But if Isaac was killed as a young man before he had produced any heirs, then how could God possibly fulfill this promise? Abraham's faith in God to fulfill his promise led him to trust in God's divine power of resurrection as the solution to this dilemma:

> By faith Abraham, when he was tested, offered up Isaac, and he who had received the promises was in the act of offering up his only son, of whom it was said, "Through Isaac shall your offspring be named." He considered that God was able even to raise him from the dead, from which, figuratively speaking, he did receive him back. (Heb. 11:17–19)

In Abraham's mind, if God was going to keep his promise, then it was essential that he raise Isaac from the dead. Likewise, when Christ promises his people that one day they will inherit the restored earth when he is ruling the world, then it is imperative that they somehow be resurrected.

Christ also promised that one day his followers will inherit eternal life in his Father's house. Paul described how Christ will use his divine power to bring this sinful world under his control and then use this same power to transform our natural bodies into eternal bodies adapted for heaven:

> But our citizenship is in heaven. And we eagerly await a Savior from there, the Lord Jesus Christ, who, *by the power that enables him to bring everything under his control* [during his reign as God], will transform our lowly bodies so that they will be like his glorious body [into glorified eternal bodies adapted for the eternal kingdom in heaven]. (Phil. 3:20–21 NIV)

The Scriptures portray God's divine power as fundamental to his plan of redemption:
- As the Son of God, he used his divine power to create this Genesis creation.
- During his incarnation, he manifested his divine power when he demonstrated a complete mastery over nature, sickness, physical death, and demons.
- During the millennium, he will use his divine power to regenerate this earth to its Edenic condition.

- He will use his divine power to regenerate our natural bodies at the first resurrection.
- When he comes again at the final resurrection, he will use his divine power to transform our natural bodies into eternal bodies.
- He will also use his divine power to destroy this Genesis creation.
- And he will use his divine power to create the new heavens and new earth, which will be the eternal home for the sons of God.

Now that is the divine power of God!

Summary

Jesus Christ was the Jewish Messiah. But he was also God incarnate. As God the Son, this creation was created through him, by him, and for him. Before the fall the world was the Son's kingdom, or his dominion. When Adam and Eve sinned, however, God allowed Satan to enter the world, and it became Satan's dominion. God also put a curse on this earth.

The Father sent his Son into this world as the human Messiah. Through the cross, he instituted a way to justify the ungodly and reconnect sinful man to his Creator. When we believe in Christ, we become restored men and women of God. But we remain in a demonic and cursed creation.

After his resurrection and ascension to heaven, the next phase of Christ's mission is to restore redeemed mankind for a thousand years. On a day set by the Father, he will use his divine power and authority to rule the world from his throne in heaven. For the departed saints to inherit the restored Edenic earth during the millennium, we will experience the first resurrection of our natural Adamic bodies. As we marry, reproduce, and fill an abundant earth, we will experience our full humanity as originally intended in the garden of Eden before the fall.

As the true God of this world, the ascended Christ has a divine right to restore this earth, remove Satan, and reclaim his creation. The Father promised his Son that one day Satan and all his enemies will be removed and his kingdom and creation will be restored to him. This is an unconditional covenant between the Father and the Son.

Once this mission of redemption and restoration is complete, Christ's mission as the Messiah will be complete. It will be time for the Son to return, bring this Genesis creation to an end, and inaugurate a new eternal kingdom of the Father for the sons of God. After the millennium, Christ will come again on the last day of this creation at the final resurrection on Judgment Day. The saints will be raptured into eternal bodies to inherit the Father's eternal new heavens and new earth, and unbelievers will be resurrected from hades, judged, and sent to the lake of fire.

The key to understanding God's endgame is understanding the two kingdoms of the triune God as they revolve around these two orders of being. The Son's millennial kingdom is a restoration of this creation for the Adamic order of being. The Father's eternal kingdom of heaven is for the sons of God who are new creations that have no sexual distinctions.

9

A Hundredfold Reward on a Restored Earth

Review

Chapter 8 presented the biblical case for postrestorationalism. I demonstrated that since Christ ascended to heaven and sat down at the right hand of God the Father, God's plans for the future will unfold while Christ remains seated on his throne in heaven. Jesus taught that after his ascension, "*from now on* the Son of Man shall be seated at the right hand of the power of God" (Luke 22:69). From his throne in heaven, Christ has all the divine authority and power necessary to execute and complete God's plan of redemption.

To understand God's endgame, it is critical to understand the following forms of Christ sitting on his throne in heaven:

- He sits on his throne in heaven and **waits on the Father** to say when it is time for him to rule the world.
- He sits on his throne in heaven **to govern this world** during his messianic kingdom when Satan is removed.
- He sits on his throne in heaven **to judge mankind** when he comes again, rewarding his people with eternal life and punishing unbelievers with eternal condemnation.
- He sits on his throne in heaven **to create the eternal new heavens and new earth** as our eternal home.

Christ's Struggles in This World

While Christ was on this earth, he was filled with the joy and peace of the Holy Spirit without measure. But he did not live what we would consider an abundant life. He experienced considerable unhappiness in this fallen world. He agonized over the physical condition of the multitudes that came to him to be healed. He was often exasperated by the disciples' slowness of understanding. He was sad when his hometown rejected him. He was deeply disturbed by the people's hard hearts. He was indignant when the temple was turned into a center of commerce and profit. He was infuriated by the unwarranted hostility he received from the Pharisees and religious leaders. He was appalled at their hypocrisy and their refusal to show compassion for the people. He lamented the failure of the Jews to recognize the coming of their own Messiah. His public ministry was often exhausting, and he thought foxes and birds had better homes and places of rest than he did. His death was not pleasant either.

As his followers, we should expect to experience some of the same anguish that he experienced. Many of us live comfortable lives and are too content with this materialistic world. We have become insensitive to the evil around us, unlike Lot who was considered righteous because he was distressed by the sexual depravity around him in Sodom (2 Peter 2:7).

The disciples experienced great deprivation as they followed Christ even though they, too, were filled with inner joy and peace from the indwelling Holy Spirit. They faced significant opposition from unrighteous Roman and Jewish rulers. Their houses and land were sometimes confiscated. They were abandoned by family members. They were jailed, and most of them were martyred. The first century was not paradise on earth. The apostle Paul experienced both internal and external suffering because he sacrificially followed Christ:

> Are they servants of Christ? I am a better one . . . with far greater labors, far more imprisonments, with countless beatings, and often near death. Five times I received at the hands of the Jews the forty lashes less one. Three times I was beaten with rods. Once I was stoned. Three times I was shipwrecked; a night and a day I was adrift at sea; on frequent journeys, in danger from rivers,

danger from robbers, danger from my own people, danger from Gentiles, danger in the city, danger in the wilderness, danger at sea, danger from false brothers; in toil and hardship, through many a sleepless night, in hunger and thirst, often without food, in cold and exposure. (2 Cor. 11:23–27)

For someone who experienced an abundant internal life of the Spirit, Paul lived a pretty miserable physical and emotional life.

Throughout history, some saints may have lived pleasant, albeit short, lives. But all have lived with some level of misery, sickness, and death. Some lived miserably as a result of their faith:

Some were tortured, refusing to accept release, so that they might rise again to a better life. Others suffered mocking and flogging, and even chains and imprisonment. They were stoned, they were sawn in two, they were killed with the sword. They went about in skins of sheep and goats, destitute, afflicted, mistreated—of whom the world was not worthy—wandering about in deserts and mountains, and in dens and caves of the earth. (Heb. 11:35–38)

Christ promised, however, that during his millennial reign he will make it up to his followers when they inherit the restored Edenic earth for a thousand years before they are taken to heaven, where they will experience a new kind of eternal paradise.

Amillennialists like to note that the Bible only references a millennial reign of Christ in the complex and symbolic book of Revelation. But God knows that we can link the millennium described in Revelation to other scriptures to make sense of John's vision. When developing a theology of the future, theologians must be able to synthesize these scriptures into a coherent eschatology.

Hundredfold Reward for Following Christ

Christ made an important reference to his earthly kingdom that can easily be linked to his 1,000-year reign described by John. This passage has been referenced in preceding chapters, but in this chapter it will be explored in greater detail. Christ was approached by a rich man who wanted to know how he could inherit eternal life. Christ asked him to sacrificially follow him by giving up his riches, which had become his idol. But the rich man walked away sad because his heart had become too attached to the temporal things of this world. He was living what he had thought was the good life and did not want to give it up to follow Christ.

Afterward, the disciples asked Christ a question regarding what they would inherit, since they *were* willing to leave everything to follow him. Christ's extraordinary answer is packed with meaning:

> Then Peter said in reply, "See, we have left everything and followed you. What then will we have?" Jesus said to them, "Truly, I say to you, in the new world [the restored earth], when the Son of Man will sit on his glorious throne [to rule the world], you who have followed me will also sit on twelve thrones, judging the twelve tribes of Israel. And everyone who has left houses or brothers or sisters or father or mother or children or lands, for my name's sake, will receive a hundredfold [when the earth is renewed] and [in addition] will inherit eternal life [in the heavenly kingdom in the age to come]." (Matt. 19:27–29)

Mark recorded the same conversation:

> "I tell you the truth," Jesus replied, "no one who has left home or brothers or sisters or mother or father or children or fields for me and the gospel [those willing to experience deprivation following Christ] will fail to receive a hundred times as much ***in this present age*** (homes, brothers, sisters, mothers, children and fields—and with them, persecutions) and ***in the age to come***, eternal life." (Mark 10:29–30 NIV; cf. Luke 18:29–30)

The reference to "persecutions" in Mark's account is parenthetical. For followers of Christ, persecution often comes with the territory. That is because Satan remains the ruler of this present evil age. And sinful rulers under his influence continue to govern the world. In their day, Caesar, Pontius Pilate, Herod, and the high priest ruled their world.

But in the future, when Christ is ruling the world in this Genesis age, the earth will experience an age of righteous humanity. The disciples will inherit a hundredfold reward of houses, lands, and extended human families. And they will assist Christ in ruling over Israel. Then, in the age to come, they will inherit eternal life. This occurs when Christ comes again to usher in the Father's eternal kingdom. Paul taught:

> But each in his own order: Christ the firstfruits [the first man to be resurrected into an eternal body], then at his coming those who belong to Christ [the saints are raptured into eternal bodies like his]. Then comes the end [of this Adamic age], when he delivers the kingdom to God the Father [in the eternal age to come]. (1 Cor. 15:23–24)

Jesus taught that when he is ruling the world in this Adamic age, the disciples will experience the "new world." This word is translated from the Greek word *palingenesia*. It means the rebirth of this Genesis creation or the "regeneration" of the earth, as translated by the American Standard Version. One could describe God's curse on the Genesis earth as a form of *degeneration* such that the current natural world is in a fallen, degenerate state. This explains why there are earthquakes, floods, droughts, famines, diseases, and other natural calamities.

Conversely, in the future when Christ rules the world, he will remove the curse of degeneration. Then, through a process of regeneration, he will restore this creation to its pre-fallen state of paradise. The curse will be removed, and the natural world will be restored to its Edenic condition.

Christ performed many miracles while he was on this earth, such as healing the blind, the deaf, and the paralyzed. These miracles required a regeneration of major body parts to their original functions. He also regenerated the natural body of Lazarus, even though it had experienced significant decay after four days. And from a few fish and loaves of bread, he generated enough food to feed a crowd of five thousand people. These regenerative powers over nature and the human body that Christ demonstrated while he was on this earth should give us a sense of what he was referring to when he spoke about the future regeneration of this Genesis creation.

Notice that Christ characterized the hundredfold reward as an Adamic existence with "houses" as human habitats, with "lands" for food production, and with human companionships that are derived from marriage, such as "father or mother or children." In this Genesis age, the human experience as men and women is structured around marriage and procreation. In fact, Jesus was probably alluding to Isaiah 65, which describes the messianic kingdom as a human paradise. Read the following verses carefully with Christ's promise in mind:

> "They shall build houses and inhabit them ["houses"]; they shall plant vineyards and eat their fruit ["lands"]. . . . They shall not labor in vain or bear children for calamity ["father or mother or children"]. . . . The wolf and the lamb shall graze together; the lion shall eat straw like the ox [when the earth is regenerated to its Edenic condition], . . . They shall not hurt or destroy in all my holy mountain," says the Lord [peace and prosperity on earth when the Messiah is ruling the world]. (65:21–25)

Christ was clearly referencing his messianic kingdom as described by Isaiah when he informed the disciples that they would inherit a hundredfold reward on this earth as restored human beings.

Christ's promises can be summarized as follows. When the Son of Man sits "on his glorious throne" in heaven and rules the world, the Genesis creation will be renewed, restored, or regenerated to its Edenic condition. The disciples will inherit a life that is a hundred times better than the rich man's life, with houses, lands, and extended human families. They will also assist Christ by ruling over Israel. After experiencing this restoration, when he comes again they will inherit eternal life in the age to come.

But the disciples lived out their lives in the first century on a cursed earth with Satan still ruling the world. Since they all died in the first century before Christ's reign began, how is Christ going to fulfill his promise to them of a wonderful life on a restored earth before he returns to take them to heaven? With Revelation as a guide, we can begin to understand Christ's endgame and how he will fulfill these promises.

The Two Resurrections

The book of Revelation may at times seem obscure, but it is important because it is a continuation of Christ's teachings. As John revealed in the very first verse: "The revelation of Jesus Christ, which God gave him [the apostle John] to show to his servants the things that must soon take place" (Rev. 1:1). A critical part of this revelation of God's endgame are the two resurrections described in chapter 20. John taught that the way the disciples and all the departed ransomed people of God will inherit the regenerated earth will be through the first resurrection:

> *They came to life* and reigned with Christ for a thousand years. . . . This is the first resurrection. . . . they will be priests of God and of Christ, and they will reign with him for a thousand years [on the regenerated earth when Christ sits on his throne to rule the world]. (Rev. 20:4–6)

John did not specify what kind of bodies the resurrected saints will have. Will they be natural bodies or immortal bodies? In the previous chapter, I made the case that the first resurrection can be linked to the resurrection that Ezekiel portrayed in his vision of the valley of dry bones coming to life. Ezekiel described the departed Jewish saints as being resurrected into reconstituted human bodies of flesh and blood that would experience marriage and reproduction when they entered the restored promised land in the messianic kingdom. It is a vivid portrayal of the resurrection of natural, Adamic bodies.

In the millennium, the saints throughout the ages will come back to life free of any infirmities and handicaps they may have had. Isaiah foresaw this restoration of our health during the messianic kingdom:

> And no inhabitant will say, "I am sick"; the people who dwell there will be forgiven their iniquity. . . . Say to those who have an anxious heart, . . . "He will come and save you." Then the eyes of the blind shall be opened, and the ears of the deaf unstopped; then shall the lame man leap like a deer, and the tongue of the mute sing for joy. (Isa. 33:24; 35:4–6)

With this in mind, Christ's promise of a hundredfold reward begins to make sense. When Christ rules the world during the millennium, our departed Adamic bodies will be regenerated into natural bodies at the first resurrection so that we can inherit the regenerated natural earth. We will marry and live abundant lives on a restored earth during a time of peace and prosperity. To fulfill the promise of eternal life, Christ will return after the millennium on the last day of this Genesis age at the final resurrection to resurrect and transform our natural bodies into immortal bodies so that we can inherit eternal life in the Father's kingdom in the age to come.

The rich man who wanted eternal life did not understand what he was walking away from. He traded his brief, wealthy life in a frail human body on a cursed earth for what could have been a life of abundance on a restored Genesis earth as a healthy human being for a thousand years. And then in the age to come, he could have inherited eternal life as an immortal child of God in an eternal paradise! Jesus taught us that wealthy people tend to be complacent and to think that their lives in this world are as good as it gets; whereas, poor people are more likely to realize that something is wrong with this world. The poor tend to long for and search for a better life.

The Restoration

The word *restoration* is an accurate way to portray the millennium. During Christ's millennial reign, our bodies will be *restored* to healthy human bodies. The Genesis creation will be *restored* to its Edenic condition. The nation of Israel will be *restored* to the land promised to Abraham. And with Satan removed, Christ will be *restored* to his rightful place as the true God of this world. The millennium will be a *restoration* of this Genesis creation to its original function and purpose.

We tend to think that this future paradise will be for *our* pleasure. It will be for our pleasure, but the most important aspect of the millennial kingdom is that it will be for the Son of God's pleasure and glory. Before Adam and Eve rebelled against him, he delighted in his good creation. He enjoyed fellowshiping with righteous humanity in the garden of Eden and looked forward to mankind reproducing godly offspring and expanding this Edenic paradise throughout the earth.

But the Son of God was robbed of this pleasure when Adam and Eve disobeyed him, letting Satan into this world. His magnificent creation became demonized and cursed. An age of unrighteous and depraved humanity dawned. This fallen world has surely brought him great anguish and disappointment. At one point before the flood in Noah's day, when mankind had become exceptionally corrupt and evil, he expressed regret that he had even created this world. The world has lost its glory as God's kingdom on earth. As sinful human beings living in an age of unrighteous humanity, we all fall short of the glory of a holy and righteous God.

Reformed theologians believe that the chief purpose of mankind is to glorify God. This is true, yet the future restoration is also for the glory of God. For one thousand years, he will once again delight in his creation when it is restored to its original glory. Notice that the word *glorious* is used to describe Christ's reign: "when the Son of Man will sit on his *glorious* throne." It is not that the throne itself is glorious; rather, his reign over the restored earth and a restored humanity will reflect his glory as our God and Creator and Savior.

As Christians, we are supposed to bring him glory in all aspects of our lives. Yet in this current evil age, we remain sinful humans and rarely bring him the glory he deserves. During the future restoration, however, an age of righteous humanity will dawn, and we will once again bring him great honor and glory.

I have discussed these verses about Christ's future reign over the restored earth with numerous amillennial theologians. Many insist that the promised "hundredfold" reward is *metaphorical*. They claim that it represents the internal joy and peace the disciples experienced as they walked with God through this troubled world. Paul experienced the joy of the Holy Spirit throughout all his various forms of misery.

But I point out that this *cannot* be what Christ is referring to because Christ links the hundredfold reward the disciples will experience *directly* to the removal of the curse and the regeneration of this earth to its Edenic condition. The curse on this Genesis earth was obviously not removed in the first century. Christ had even predicted that earthquakes and famines would continue to occur in the disciples' lifetimes. Therefore, Christ must be referring to a *future* period of human history when the disciples and all followers of Christ will receive a hundredfold reward on *a regenerated earth*—before they inherit eternal life when he returns.

Other amillennialists assert that the regenerated earth is a reference to *the eternal new heavens and new earth*. But Christ states that the hundredfold reward associated with the regenerated earth will occur "in this present age" and that the reward of eternal life in the eternal kingdom will occur "in the age to come." Consequently, the regenerated earth refers to this Genesis earth when Christ rules the world—not to the future new heavens and new earth when he delivers his kingdom over to his Father.

Premillennialists, too, have an odd interpretation of these teachings. They have the departed disciples coming back to this earth at the first resurrection in their raptured, eternal bodies which are not given in marriage. Yet, Christ plainly describes the saints as experiencing a human paradise on this earth in their natural bodies, with marriage and extended human families as described by Isaiah and Ezekiel. We will inherit the regenerated earth through the regeneration of our natural human bodies, and when Christ returns, we will inherit the kingdom of heaven through the rapture and transformation of our natural bodies into immortal bodies. The rapture occurs at the final resurrection.

The Delay of His Kingdom

I have often wondered why the Father has waited so long to establish his Son's kingdom on this earth. He could have done so in the first century, soon after Christ's ascension. Instead, for the last two thousand years his followers have experienced all kinds of misery, sickness, and death in this fallen world. Living on a cursed earth can be challenging, to say the least. The idea of a delayed messianic kingdom is something we should all stop and think about.

It is important to realize that this delay is part of God's wisdom and divine plan. He first wants to demonstrate his mercy on sinful mankind while we are held captive in Satan's dominion of darkness. And then when we are saved by grace, he wants to know if we will trust in his character and promises while we remain in this evil world where many of our human aspirations go unfulfilled. It does not matter if we experience his messianic kingdom in our current lifetimes because, with the power of resurrection, Christ can bring us back to life when he does eventually remove Satan and establish his kingdom.

Consider an abused slave living in the Deep South before the Civil War. When he heard the gospel for the first time, he would have had to overcome Satan's lies about God's love and character. *If God really loves me, then why am I enslaved by such an abusive master? Why am I a slave in the first place? Why am I poor and having to work long hours in unbearably hot, humid conditions, day in and day out? Why do my wife and children have to suffer under these same horrid condi-*

tions? And whenever he objected to the way his wife or children were being treated, he likely would have been subjected to the indignity of being whipped as if he were an unruly animal. His dignity as a man, a husband, and a father had been stolen, with no hope for the future.

If he and his family miraculously became Christians through the power of the Holy Spirit, how would he have reacted to his continued unjust situation? Would he have become bitter toward God? How would he have reacted if his master had resented his conversion and, out of spite, sold his beloved wife and children to another abusive master? Would he have had the maturity to wait patiently for God's justice and plan of redemption to unfold?

If this man had been born during the millennium, he would be living a prosperous life in ideal circumstances when he was first introduced to the gospel. God obviously wants to demonstrate his power of redemption while we remain under Satan's dominion, blinded by his lies about God's love and character. Once we are saved by his grace, we can count on experiencing trials and tribulations to test our character to see if we will continue to trust in his love for us. God wants to see what we are made of. Apparently, that must mean a lot to him because through the ages his people have had to endure all kinds of hardship.

But Christ promised his followers that he would reward them in the future. With the divine power of resurrection, he can richly reward all his people, including this poor Christian slave. When this slave is resurrected into his regenerated natural body at the first resurrection, he will live a peaceful, abundant, and fulfilling life in an Edenic paradise with his beloved wife and children. He will no longer be enslaved to anyone. And when Christ comes again for the sons of God, the former slave will inherit eternal life in a heavenly paradise. Now that is poetic justice!

It is sad that these truths of the millennial kingdom are not being taught in churches today. We may not experience the deprivations of a slave, but many Christians experience disappointing lives with many unfulfilled aspirations. It would certainly help them in their walk with Christ if they knew that their deepest longings would be fulfilled a hundredfold during the millennium.

For example, some women are unable to have children, but they deeply long to be mothers. It may be comforting to remind them that they are going to heaven when Christ returns. But as Jesus taught, their desire for motherhood is not going to be fulfilled in heaven, for the children of God will no longer experience marriage and reproduction in the eternal kingdom. If they had been taught these truths about the first resurrection of the natural body in a restored Genesis creation, however, they could look forward to all their unfulfilled aspirations of motherhood being fulfilled during Christ's millennial kingdom.

This expectation of the future restoration of humanity gives us a spiritual immunity to protect us from becoming bitter toward God when circumstances in life do not go as we had hoped and prayed they would.

An Abundant Life on the Edenic Earth

There are other prophecies that can be linked to this hundredfold reward on the restored earth. The prophets describe the Messiah as a good shepherd who leads his sheep to an abundant life on this earth. Jesus claimed to be a fulfillment of this prophecy:

> The thief comes only to steal and kill and destroy. I came that they may have life and have it abundantly. . . . I am the good shepherd. I know my own and my own know me. (John 10:10, 14)

Notice in the following prophecy in Ezekiel that the Lord will one day shepherd his sheep to an abundant life on a restored earth:

> I will make with them a covenant of peace and banish wild beasts from the land, so that they may dwell securely in the wilderness and sleep in the woods. And I will make them and the places all around my hill a blessing, and I will send down the showers in their season; they shall be showers of blessing. And the trees of the field shall yield their fruit, and the earth shall yield its increase [incredible abundance], and they shall be secure in their land [peace]. . . . And you are my sheep, human sheep of my pasture, and I am your God, declares the Lord God. . . . And they will say, "This land that was desolate has become like the garden of Eden [the regenerated earth]." (Ezek. 34:25–31; 36:35)

Christ is claiming to be the good shepherd who will one day usher in paradise on earth for his sheep. These prophecies are not merely a metaphor for the internal life of a Christian, as amillennialists assert. They are a description of a human paradise on an Edenic earth. Christ was not exaggerating when he promised his sheep an abundant life on this earth before he takes them to heaven.

Yet the disciples, like Jesus, did not experience an abundant life on this earth. But during his future millennial reign, the Good Shepherd will bind Satan and will remove the curse on this earth. Then, through the first resurrection, he will bring his sheep back to this earth in regenerated natural bodies to experience prosperous lives without anguish and suffering in a creation that has been restored to its Edenic condition.

Those who advocate a prosperity gospel apparently do not understand the current fallen world. Presently, we experience deprivation and all the other ill effects of living in a demonic world under God's curse. Christians often feel entitled and expect to be exempt from the things that plague mankind. But we should expect to experience some level of misery in this world. And becoming a child of God can even intensify Satan's attacks. Try convincing a Muslim living in a conservative Muslim nation that his life will be more pleasant on this earth after he becomes a Christian.

Do not misunderstand me. There is nothing wrong with hard work, resourcefulness, and taking advantage of opportunities to experience material success and comfort. We should strive for the well-being of our families and neighbors. We should attempt to restore human dignity on this earth whenever possible. But inevitably, we and our neighbors will suffer, to one degree or another, particularly as we age.

The prosperity gospel is simply misplaced. Jesus did not "promise us a rose garden" in this life. Only in the restoration will there be true prosperity for those who believe in Christ. At that time, he indeed does promise his sheep an abundant and prosperous life on this earth, as described by the prophets.

Paul understood this. He did not live in a palatial villa on the Mediterranean. Nor did he become wealthy from his income as a pastor or from selling his letters. He earned a living as a tentmaker so that no one could accuse him of marketing the gospel for profit.

Nature Restored

Before the fall, the trees and plants produced food for humans and the other living creatures. Apparently, all the earth's vegetation was edible. There were no poisonous plants, berries, fruit, or mushrooms. The creation account suggests that humans and other living creatures were vegetarians. In the garden of Eden, abundant vegetation provided food for man and animals:

> And God said, "Behold, I have given you every plant yielding seed that is on the face of all the earth, and every tree with seed in its fruit. You shall have them for food. And to every beast of the earth and to every bird of the heavens and to everything that creeps on the earth, everything that has the breath of life, I have given every green plant for food." (Gen. 1:29–30)

After the fall, the curse, and the flood, the eating habits of man and the other creatures changed. It was after the catastrophic flood that God introduced the eating of meat: "Every moving thing that lives shall be food for you" (Gen. 9:3). Animals in the wild are fearful, and rightfully so. Lions, leopards, wolves, and bears feed on sheep, goats, and various cattle. Their newborns are particularly vulnerable and must be protected by shepherds. This predator-based ecological system is a tragic one.

In Isaiah 11, the prophet foresees the day when the original "good" creation will be restored, affecting both mankind and the animal kingdom. Rather than quote this long prophecy, I will outline the vast changes in the animal kingdom that will take place when the natural earth is restored to its Edenic condition.

During Christ's reign:
- Wolves will live with lambs.
- Leopards will lie down with goats.
- Lions and calves will eat together.
- A little child will play with a lion.
- Bears and cows (and their young) will graze together.
- Lions will eat straw like oxen.
- A nursing child will play over the hole of a cobra.

Isaiah is describing an extraordinary change in the ecological system of this creation. All animals will live peacefully together with mankind as they are restored to the vegetarian-based ecology that existed before the fall. We can truly enjoy their company without being afraid.

The Holy Spirit in the Restoration

The Holy Spirit will play a crucial role in establishing righteousness during the restoration. While Christ remains in heaven with the Father, he in effect comes to the world through the person of the Holy Spirit, just as he came to the disciples through the Holy Spirit at Pentecost. Ezekiel seems to foreshadow yet another type of Pentecost occurring during the restoration. I label this "Pentecost Phase 2." It is through the Holy Spirit that we shall see the face of Christ in the restoration:

> And I will give you a new heart, and a new spirit I will put within you. And I will remove the heart of stone from your flesh and give you a heart of flesh. *And I will put my Spirit within you*, and cause you to walk in my statutes and be careful to obey my rules. You shall dwell in the land that I gave to your fathers, and you shall be my people, and I will be your God. . . . And I will not hide my face anymore from them, when I pour out my Spirit upon the house of Israel, declares the Lord God. (Ezek. 36:26–28; 39:29)

Christ does not need to physically return to this earth for us to see his face. All he must do is pour out his Spirit, and we will sense his presence.

Because of the outpouring of the Holy Spirit and the regeneration of this creation, the restoration will be a time of tremendous joy and thanksgiving. Isaiah poetically described this joy that the world would experience during Christ's reign:

> Oh sing to the Lord a new song,
> > for he has done marvelous things!
> His right hand and his holy arm
> > have worked salvation for him.
> The Lord has made known his salvation;
> > he has revealed his righteousness in the sight of the nations.

> He has remembered his steadfast love and faithfulness
>> to the house of Israel.
> All the ends of the earth have seen
>> the salvation of our God.
> Make a joyful noise to the Lord, all the earth;
>> break forth into joyous song and sing praises!
> Sing praises to the Lord with the lyre,
>> with the lyre and the sound of melody!
>
> With trumpets and the sound of the horn
>> make a joyful noise before the King, the Lord!
> Let the sea roar, and all that fills it;
>> the world and those who dwell in it!
> Let the rivers clap their hands;
>> let the hills sing for joy together
> before the Lord, for he comes
>> to judge the earth.
> He will judge the world with righteousness,
>> and the peoples with equity. (Ps. 98:1–9)

Today Satan orchestrates the affairs of sinful man on this cursed earth. The result is many sour and discordant sounds in a world that is full of selfishness, greed, and strife—even war. Sometimes we hear the echo of the garden of Eden, but the world is badly out of tune. One day, however, the mighty God who orchestrated the creation of this world will remove this alien conductor and reclaim his creation. Through the Holy Spirit, the Prince of Peace will then orchestrate the affairs of man, and the sounds in this world will be harmonious and joyful once more. The regenerated earth will be in tune again.

The world will be so thrilled by Christ's conducting such magnificent works that even the rivers will "clap their hands" and the hills will "sing for joy." When our deepest human aspirations are fulfilled during the restoration, we will sing and rejoice every day for hundreds of years. The Old Testament is full of remarkable descriptions of the Messiah's coming earthly kingdom. And when Christ comes again on the last day to take us to heaven, we will sing a totally new song of joy and thanksgiving.

To demonstrate how well postrestorationalism harmonizes with the Old Testament vision of the messianic kingdom, I have paraphrased and combined Christ's teaching of a hundredfold reward with John's teaching on the millennium in Revelation:

> Truly, I say to you, in the future when Satan is removed and I sit on my glorious throne in heaven and govern the world, I will remove the curse and restore this Genesis creation to its Edenic condition. And you who have sacrificially followed me will experience a regeneration of your natural bodies through the first resurrection so that you can inherit this paradise on earth. You will also sit on earthly thrones and assist me in governing the twelve tribes of Israel, along with other righteous men and women who will sit on thrones that will be set up around the world to govern their people. Everyone who has been willing to leave houses or lands or their families for my name's sake will receive a life on this regenerated earth that is a hundred times better than the rich man's life.
>
> After you experience my earthly kingdom for a thousand years, I will come again on Judgment Day and rapture you into eternal bodies as sons of God so that you can inherit eternal life when you join me in my Father's kingdom. As the Alpha, I created this Genesis creation, but as the Omega, I will destroy this creation and send Satan, his demons, and all unbelievers to the lake of fire. I will then create the new heavens and new earth as our eternal home, where you will see me and my Father in all our glory. There you will experience rivers of life and joy from the Holy Spirit. I have revealed my plans for the future to you through John's vision. Be careful not to distort or deny any of these truths. Be vigilant and remain faithful until I come again to take you to an eternal paradise in heaven.

Summary

The rich man in Jesus' day thought he was living the good life. When Christ told him that he would have to give up his temporal wealth to inherit eternal life, he walked away sad. The disciples, who were experiencing a great deal of deprivation as they followed Christ, wanted to know what their reward would be for devoting their lives to him.

Christ's answer was remarkable. He promised the disciples that when he sits on his throne in heaven and rules the world as the Messiah, they will inherit an Edenic paradise on a regenerated earth that is a hundred times better than the rich man's life. A hundredfold reward indicates that our deepest human aspirations that have not been fulfilled in this current fallen world will be abundantly fulfilled during his reign. In addition, he promised that they would inherit eternal life in the age to come. They would inherit God's kingdom on earth *and* in heaven. God's divine power of resurrection will enable these promises to be fulfilled.

10

The Gospel of the Kingdom

Review

Chapter 9 explored how our deepest human aspirations will be fulfilled when we are resurrected to live again during Christ's reign over the restored earth. Christ's promise of an abundant life is not just a metaphor for our life in the Spirit today. As the Good Shepherd, he will lead us to an abundant life on this earth. The prophets described the messianic kingdom as an Edenic paradise for the restored human beings. Nature will be restored, and human health will be restored. The Holy Spirit will play a key role in implementing this age of joyful humanity.

The Olivet Discourse

The Olivet Discourse found in the Gospels is a lecture by Jesus to the disciples on the signs leading up to his second coming on the last day. Jesus insisted that the "gospel of the kingdom" be preached and realized on this earth *before* the end of the world and the beginning of the eternal kingdom of heaven:

> But the one who endures to the end will be saved. And this **gospel of the kingdom** will be proclaimed throughout the whole world **as a testimony to all nations**, and then the end will come [of the Genesis age]. (Matt. 24:13–14)

Many theologians interpret these verses to mean we must complete the Great Commission before Christ comes again. But that is not what Christ was referring to. Christ was likely quoting from Isaiah when he referenced the "gospel of the kingdom." Isaiah equated the gospel or the good news not only with the preaching of the gospel, but also with the full realization and implementation of the Messiah's kingdom. Isaiah described the messianic kingdom that the whole world will experience on this earth:

> How beautiful upon the mountains are the feet of him who brings good news, who publishes peace, who brings good news of happiness, who publishes salvation, who says to Zion, ***"Your God reigns"*** [the gospel realized when Christ exercises his reign as Lord]. The voice of your watchmen—they lift up their voice; together they sing for joy; for eye to eye they see the return of the Lord to Zion. Break forth together into singing, you waste places of Jerusalem, for the Lord has comforted his people; he has redeemed Jerusalem. The Lord has bared his holy arm before the eyes of all the nations, and ***all the ends of the earth shall see the salvation of our God.*** (Isa. 52:7–10)

The following psalm also envisions the reign of the Messiah:

> The Lord has made known his salvation; he has revealed his righteousness in the sight of the nations. . . . All the ends of the earth have seen the salvation of our God. . . . let the hills sing for joy together before the Lord, for he comes to judge the earth. He will judge the world with righteousness, and the peoples with equity. (Ps. 98:2–9)

The "good news" is not only the preaching of peace and salvation for sinners, but also the messianic kingdom being realized on this earth when the Messiah rules the world, establishing his righteous reign over redeemed sinners. There will be peace, joy, and comfort in the world. The messianic kingdom will begin in Israel, but it will extend throughout the world as "all the ends of the earth . . . see the salvation of our God."

Notice the striking similarities between Christ's prophecy in the Olivet Discourse and Isaiah's prophecy:

> **And this gospel of the kingdom** ["Your God reigns"] **will be proclaimed throughout the whole world** [to "the ends of the earth"] **as a testimony to all nations** [when "The Lord has bared his holy arm before the eyes of all the nations, and all the ends of the earth shall see the salvation of our God"], **and then the end will come.** (Matt. 24:14)

All the earth shall see and experience God's salvation of this Genesis creation. His reign of peace, justice, and prosperity will indeed serve as a testimony that Christ is the true loving God of this world.

If part of the good news is the reign of Christ fully implemented before the eyes of all the nations, then the messianic kingdom that the prophets describe is indeed the "gospel of the kingdom" that Jesus alluded to. It will be realized on this earth after the Great Tribulation during the millennium when the Son sits on his throne in heaven and finally establishes his earthly kingdom. After the world has experienced Christ's 1,000-year messianic kingdom, he will come again at the end of the world.

We may not see his reign today because of Satan's continuous rule. But when this regime change takes place, his Lordship will be fully revealed during the restoration. As Christ told the disciples, these extraordinary prophecies of the messianic kingdom being seen and experienced all over the world must be fulfilled on this Genesis earth *before* he comes again to take us to heaven.

Some of Paul's subtle and sometimes vague references to Christ's messianic kingdom begin to make sense in light of these teachings of Isaiah and Christ. Paul portrayed the heavenly kingdom as the Father's kingdom. Christ is responsible for coming again to take us to his Father's kingdom *after* he has completed his mission of restoring this Genesis creation to himself through the messianic kingdom. Paul taught:

> But each in his own order: Christ the firstfruits [the first man to be resurrected into an eternal body and to ascend to heaven], then at his coming those who belong to Christ [the rapture of the succeeding sons of God]. *Then comes the end*, when he delivers the

kingdom to God the Father *after* destroying every rule and every authority and power. For he must reign ["Your God reigns"] until he has put all his enemies under his feet [during his messianic kingdom]. The last enemy to be destroyed is death [through the resurrection of an eternal body when he comes again]. (1 Cor. 15:23–26)

Let's compare the teachings of Isaiah, Jesus, and Paul:

Isaiah: "How beautiful upon the mountains are the feet of him who brings good news, . . . 'Your God reigns.' . . . all the ends of the earth shall see the salvation of our God."
Jesus: "And this gospel of the kingdom will be proclaimed throughout the whole world as a testimony to all nations, and *then the end will come.*"
Paul: "For he must reign until he has put all his enemies under his feet." And, "*Then comes the end*, when he delivers the kingdom to God the Father."

Paul does not provide specific details about the earthly kingdom of Christ in his letters to the Corinthians. He alludes to it, but he seems to avoid the subject. The messianic kingdom is rather stealthy in the New Testament. After carefully reading the book of Revelation, one realizes that God may have wanted to keep the truth about Christ's future reign over the nations obscure. This topic will be addressed in chapter 20, "The Stealthy Restoration."

Once we understand these two kingdoms of the triune God, many other teachings of Christ begin to make more sense. In the Sermon on the Mount, Jesus promised that his meek followers will inherit the earth *and* the kingdom of heaven:

Blessed are the meek, for they shall inherit the earth [the Son's earthly kingdom]. . . . Blessed are those who are persecuted for righteousness' sake, for theirs is the kingdom of heaven [the Father's eternal kingdom]. (Matt. 5:5–10)

It is amazing how many of the Scriptures come alive with meaning after we understand God's endgame.

Summary

Jesus Christ is the Lord of this creation, even if we do not see it today and the world does not receive him. In the restoration, however, this creation will be restored to him. The "good news" includes the preaching of the gospel that Jesus is the Savior and true Lord of this world, and that one day he will exercise his reign over this world. At that time, there will be a regime change from Satan to Christ. This creation will be regenerated to its Edenic condition, and an age of righteous humanity will dawn as God's will is done on earth as it is in heaven. This is the redemption of humanity that the prophets envisioned. As Isaiah proclaimed:

> How beautiful upon the mountains are the feet of him who brings good news, . . . "Your God reigns." . . . all the ends of the earth shall see the salvation of our God. (52:7–10)

This is the "gospel of the kingdom" that must be realized on this earth as a testimony to all nations that Christ is the true God of this creation. After he has put "all his enemies under his feet" during his messianic kingdom "as a testimony to all nations," "*then comes the end*, when he delivers the kingdom to God the Father."

11

The Final Resurrection

Review

In the last chapter, I demonstrated that Christ's reference to the gospel of the kingdom being preached on this earth before he comes again is a reference to the "good news" described by Isaiah. Isaiah taught that the good news is the messianic kingdom being fully realized on this earth when God reigns over this world. Christ's reign will serve as a testimony to all nations that he is the true Lord of this world. These extraordinary prophecies of the messianic kingdom must be fulfilled on this earth *before* he comes again to rapture the saints and take us to heaven.

The Transformed Body

Revelation reveals that the followers of Christ are destined to experience two resurrections. As men and women of God, we are destined to experience the first resurrection of our natural bodies so that we can inherit the Son's restored earth for a thousand years. And as children or sons of God, we are destined to experience the final resurrection of our eternal bodies so we can inherit the Father's eternal new earth. Paul taught:

But our citizenship is in heaven. And we eagerly await a Savior from there, the Lord Jesus Christ [who ascended to heaven and promised to return and take us to join him in his Father's house], who, by the power that enables him to bring everything under his control, will transform our lowly bodies so that they will be like his glorious body [adapted for heaven]. (Phil. 3:20–21 NIV)

Christ ascended to heaven to the Father, and we eagerly await his return from heaven. When Christ returns, he will transform our bodies to be like his glorious body. We will then inherit "our citizenship" in heaven to be with Christ and the Father in their eternal kingdom. Paul taught that our transformed Adamic bodies will be patterned on Christ's glorified body—an eternal body that will ascend to an eternal kingdom. But what will our raptured, glorified bodies be like?

Like the Pre-Ascended Christ's Body?

Many theologians speculate that our future resurrected bodies will be like Christ's resurrected body that had appeared to the disciples while he was still on this earth. After his resurrection, Jesus approached the disciples:

Jesus himself stood among them, and said to them, "Peace to you!" But they were startled and frightened and thought they saw a spirit. And he said to them, "Why are you troubled, and why do doubts arise in your hearts? See my hands and my feet, that it is I myself. Touch me, and see. *For a spirit does not have flesh and bones as you see that I have.*" . . . He said to them, "Have you anything here to eat?" They gave him a piece of broiled fish, and he took it and ate before them. (Luke 24:36–43)

Christ had a resurrected body of flesh and blood and could even eat food. But his natural body was also immortal, so he did not have to eat to sustain his life. In contrast, Adam and Eve were mortal creatures in natural bodies of flesh and blood who did have to eat to sustain their bodies. Christ could walk through walls and could suddenly disappear or appear, but those events could simply be considered supernatural and not how he normally operated in a real body in space and time.

THE FINAL RESURRECTION | 219

After appearing to many more believers, Christ physically ascended in the clouds to join his Father in heaven. When he comes again in the clouds, he will give us resurrected bodies like his glorified body. Many theologians conclude that since Christ had a real body of flesh and blood while he was on this earth, then we, too, will have similar immortal, natural bodies in the eternal kingdom. Our resurrection and ascension will be patterned on Christ's resurrection and ascension. We will not be disembodied spirits in heaven experiencing some form of spiritual bliss.

Many theologians also believe that we are not going to heaven. Rather, Christ and the Father are coming to dwell with us on this renewed earth for eternity, after it has been purged and purified by fire. This doctrine assumes that after Christ ascended to heaven, he remains in the same kind of resurrected body that he had while he was on this earth. In other words, the ***post-ascended*** Christ is just like the ***pre-ascended*** Christ who appeared to the disciples. When he comes again in his immortal body of flesh and blood, we will be given immortal natural bodies like his pre-ascended body. We will then dwell on a restored Genesis earth.

But is this doctrine biblically correct? I believe the Scriptures teach that when Christ ascended to heaven, his resurrected body of flesh and blood was transformed into a very different kind of glorified body adapted for the future new heavens and new earth that are created after this Genesis creation is destroyed. Our raptured bodies will be patterned on his glorified body, not on the natural body he manifested while he was still on this earth.

In fact, we will not know what Christ's glorified body is like until he appears again and gives us glorified bodies like his. Since no one has seen Christ in his post-ascended, glorified body, no one really knows what his eternal body is like. Therefore, when Christ returns, our transformed bodies will be like the unknown ***post-ascended*** body of Christ—not like the known pre-ascended body of Christ.

Consider the teachings of the apostle John. He saw the pre-ascended Christ when Christ appeared to him and the disciples. But notice that John does not reference this version of Christ's resurrected body as the model, or prototype, of what our future bodies will be like. Rather, he references the ***unknown*** post-ascended body that has not yet appeared as the model for our future raptured bodies:

See what kind of love the Father has given to us, that we should be called children of God; and so we are [a new creation as sons of God that is neither male nor female]. . . . Beloved, we are God's children now, and what we will be **has not yet appeared**; but we know that when he appears [in his glorified body] we shall be like him [like the post-ascended body of Christ], because we shall see him as he is [in his glorified, eternal body]. (1 John 3:1–2)

John knew what Christ's resurrected body was like because he had seen the resurrected Christ. If our future bodies are going to be like the pre-ascended body of Christ that had appeared to John and the other disciples, then John could have simply said they are going to be like the resurrected body that he had seen, touched, and eaten with. But instead, John referenced the unknown glorified body of Christ that will be revealed from heaven on the last day—that is, the post-ascended body of Christ. When John said, "What we will be has not yet appeared," he admits that he does not know what the children of God's raptured bodies will be like. Unless we know more about the nature of Christ's glorified body than John, it remains a mystery to us as well.

The Transfiguration

The transfiguration foreshadows Christ in his glorified body when he returns, and it must have had a profound impact on John. Jesus taught:

"For the Son of Man is going to come with his angels in the glory of his Father, and then he will repay each person according to what he has done. Truly, I say to you, there are some standing here who will not taste death until they see the Son of Man coming in his kingdom." And after six days Jesus took with him Peter and James, and John his brother, and led them up a high mountain by themselves. And he was transfigured before them, and his face shone like the sun, and his clothes became white as light. (Matt. 16:27—17:2)

Natural human beings do not shine like the sun. The transfiguration that John witnessed gives us some idea as to what Christ's glorified body will be like when he comes again. It will obviously be very different from the body that appeared to John and the disciples in the Upper Room.

Now that Christ has ascended to heaven, no one knows what his glorified body is like. Yet, many theologians continue to assert that our future raptured bodies will be modeled on the pre-ascended Christ, and they treat this belief almost as an orthodox tenant of the faith. If anyone teaches otherwise, he is branded as a heretic. Yet, I cannot find a single New Testament reference to the pre-ascended body of Christ as being representative of the kind of bodies we will have in the eternal kingdom! Again, none of the apostles reference the pre-ascended body of Christ that the disciples saw and touched as being a model of what our future raptured bodies will be like.

Paul's Vision of the Post-Ascended Christ

The resurrected Christ had also appeared to the apostle Paul. But Paul was not converted until *after* Christ had already returned to heaven. Consequently, Paul saw the *post-ascended* body of Christ. And Christ was in a glorified body very different from the kind of body that the disciples saw and touched in the Upper Room. Paul's vision of the glorified Christ was so bright that it blinded him, and he had to be miraculously healed. Paul describes this event when he was being interrogated by King Agrippa:

> At midday, O king, I saw on the way a light from heaven, **brighter than the sun**, that shone around me and those who journeyed with me. And when we had all fallen to the ground, I heard a voice saying to me in the Hebrew language, "Saul, Saul, why are you persecuting me?" ... And I said, "Who are you, Lord?" And the Lord said, "I am Jesus whom you are persecuting." (Acts 26:13–15)

When Paul saw the resurrected Christ on the road to Damascus, he did not sit down with him and eat lunch with him. That is because Paul saw the resurrected Christ *after* his ascension and *after* he was in his glorified body. He got a glimpse of the glorified Christ, who appeared brighter than the sun. The post-ascended Christ who blinded

Paul is distinctly different from the pre-ascended Christ who appeared to the disciples. Because of this experience, Paul declared that since Christ has ascended to heaven and is in his glorified immortal body, no one in a natural body on this earth has seen, or even can see, the post-ascended Lord:

> To keep the commandment unstained and free from reproach until the appearing of our Lord Jesus Christ, . . . who alone has immortality, who dwells in unapproachable light, whom **no one has ever seen or can see**. (1 Tim. 6:14–16)

Christ is the only person to have received an immortal body. Since he entered the eternal kingdom, no one has seen him. And according to Paul, no one in his natural body *can see* the post-ascended, glorified Christ. Paul knew from firsthand experience that the post-ascended Christ was an unapproachable light to anyone in his natural body. Therefore, no one has ever seen or touched the glorified Christ.

Again, John and the disciples saw and touched the *pre-ascended* resurrected body of Christ. But Paul taught that the ascended Christ is in a transformed, immortal, and glorified body that no one in his natural Adamic body *"has seen or even can see."* That is, until Christ comes again to transform our bodies to be like his glorified body. Then, we will be able to not only see him, but also to dwell with him and his Father in all their glory on the eternal new earth. To be in the very presence of the triune God in all his glory, we will need glorified bodies.

Despite claims to the contrary, no one knows what Christ's glorified body is like. The apostles taught us that when Christ returns, we shall be like the **unknown**, post-ascended, glorified Christ. No one knows what our future eternal habitat on the eternal new earth will be like, either. That is because it has not yet been created as the eternal home for the glorified sons of God. As such, we should not speculate as to what our future raptured bodies will be like or what the new earth will be like.

Yet, I imagine that if a young Christian asked his pastor what our future bodies will be like, the vast majority would say that our resurrected bodies will be like the pre-ascended body of Christ that the disciples saw, touched, and ate and drank with. I hear it all the time. I suppose that some people are uncomfortable with the mysteries of not knowing what kind of glorified bodies we will have and what heaven will be like.

Theologians are making a serious mistake, however, when they insist that our resurrected bodies will be like the body of Christ that appeared to the disciples in the Upper Room. They are claiming to know more about our future bodies than John or Paul. Paul specifically warns against this kind of unbiblical speculation:

> This is how one should regard us, as servants of Christ and stewards of the mysteries of God. . . . I have applied all these things to myself and Apollos for your benefit, brothers, that you may learn by us *not to go beyond what is written*. (1 Cor. 4:1–6)

When theologians claim that our raptured bodies will be like the pre-ascended body of Christ, they are clearly going beyond what is written, for there is no scripture to support this assertion.

A New Kind of Body

One of the best discussions about our future eternal bodies can be found in Paul's first letter to the Corinthians. The pagan Roman religions did not believe in an afterlife that included a resurrected body. If there was an afterlife, only the human spirit survived to experience it. They viewed a resurrection of a body as a resuscitation of a corpse and thought of it as repugnant.

After the Roman Gentiles in Corinth accepted Paul's gospel and listened to his unusual teachings about our being a new creation as sons of God destined for an embodied existence in heaven, they must have been curious about what kind of bodies we will have after they are transformed and taken to heaven. They could imagine what a restored Adamic body would be like on a restored natural earth, but what would a transformed body be like? Paul called them "foolish" for even thinking they could know what kind of resurrected bodies they will have in the eternal kingdom. Paul's response was a strong rebuke for even asking about something that is fundamentally unknowable now.

Paul compared the way the natural body will be changed into a new kind of body to the way a seed or nut is transformed into something different when it is planted into the ground and germinates. One cannot examine the seed or nut and determine in advance what the resulting plant will be like. Likewise, one cannot examine the current natural human body and determine in advance what the future immortal body will be like:

> But someone will ask, "How are the dead raised? With what kind of body do they come?" ***You foolish person!*** . . . what you sow [the Adamic body] is not the body that is to be, but a bare kernel, perhaps of wheat or of some other grain. But God gives it a body as he has chosen, and to each kind of seed its own body. . . . So is it with the resurrection of the dead. What is sown is perishable; what is raised is imperishable. . . . It is sown a natural body; it is raised a spiritual body. . . . The first man was from the earth, a man of dust; the second man is from heaven. As was the man of dust, so also are those who are of the dust, and as is the man of heaven, so also are those who are of heaven. Just as we have borne the image of the man of dust [a natural Adamic body], we shall also bear the image of the man of heaven [an eternal body]. I tell you this, brothers: flesh and blood [the Adamic body] cannot inherit the kingdom of God, . . . Behold! I tell you a mystery. We shall not all sleep, but we shall all be changed, in a moment, in the twinkling of an eye, at the last trumpet [at the rapture]. For the trumpet will sound, and the dead will be raised imperishable, and we shall be changed [into an eternal body adapted for the Father's eternal kingdom]. For this perishable body must put on the imperishable, and this mortal body must put on immortality. (1 Cor. 15:35–53)

Paul is quite emphatic that the current natural Adamic body adapted for this earth does not represent the kind of body we will have after the final resurrection. That is because a perishable body of flesh and blood "cannot inherit the kingdom of God."

Rather, the future bodies of God's children will be patterned on the unknown, glorified Christ and will be adapted for the Father's imperishable kingdom of heaven. Until we get to heaven, Paul admonishes us not to foolishly speculate as to the kind of bodies God will provide us so that we can dwell with him in his eternal kingdom.

In other words, Paul is teaching us that we cannot examine the current human body and have any idea what our future bodies will be like. Nor can we study the pre-ascended, non-glorified Christ as a model for our future raptured bodies. We will have real bodies, but the nature of those bodies remains a complete mystery. All we *do* know is that they will be immortal, imperishable, and incorruptible.

Paul compares this transformation process of the Adamic body that dies and returns to the dust of the earth to a variety of kernels or seeds that are sown into the ground and experience germination. When the outer shell or coat of the seed dies and falls away, the inner seed comes alive when it sprouts into a plant. This may seem obvious, but when a seed is planted and germinates, the result is not another seed exactly like the one planted. Rather, the seed is transformed into an entity that is very different from the original seed. It is sown as a seed, but it comes up out of the ground as a plant!

To further illustrate what Paul is teaching, consider a pecan and a pecan tree. When a pecan is planted, it does not come up out of the ground as another pecan. Rather, upon germination, the pecan is transformed into a pecan tree, which is vastly different in design and structure from the pecan that was planted in the ground. The mature tree represents a profound transformation of the small pecan. Most important, we cannot determine what the pecan tree will look like by examining the nut's exterior or by cracking it open and analyzing its interior. The pecan itself does not prefigure what the resulting pecan tree will be like. The pecan is transformed into a new entity with a totally different form, structure, and function.

Likewise, the Adamic body of flesh and blood that dies and is sown into the ground does not come up out of the ground when it is resurrected as the same kind of sexual Adamic human body. Rather, it is going to be transformed into a presently unknown kind of eternal body with a totally different form, structure, and function adapted for the new eternal habitat. One cannot discern what this new body will be like by analyzing the Adamic body any more than one can discern what a pecan tree will look like by analyzing the pecan. Paul is not stressing continuity with our current human bodies when we are resurrected; rather, he is emphasizing the incredible discontinuity.

Paul continued with another analogy to demonstrate God's immense creative ability to design and form different kinds of living creatures in this current creation:

> But God gives it a body as he has chosen, and to each kind of seed its own body. For not all flesh is the same, but there is one kind for humans, another for animals, another for birds, and another for fish. (1 Cor. 15:38–39)

Some bodies are created and designed to function on the ground, while others are created to operate in the air or in water. A human cannot live in the air or the ocean. A deer would have difficulty navigating the clouds. An eagle would not survive for long in the ocean. And a dolphin could not live on the land. Each unique *kind* of body that God created is adapted to its own environment, or habitat. Likewise, God will create a new kind of eternal body for the sons of God. It will be uniquely adapted for its new habitat that he will create in the new heavens and new earth.

Paul continues, "There is one glory of the sun, and another glory of the moon, and another glory of the stars" (1 Cor. 15:41). Even the planets and the stars are very different kinds of heavenly bodies. The illumination of the sun is different from that of the moon, which is different from that of the various stars.

With this elaborate illustration, Paul is making a simple, yet profound point about God's proven ability to create unique kinds of bodies adapted for different settings. Paul is reminding us that we have an awesome God! We do not need to know what kind of eternal bodies we will have in heaven, for we can trust our Creator to use this same incredible creativity once again when he creates our new kind of eternal bodies adapted for the new heavens and new earth. Being a child of God destined for a new creation necessitates a new kind of body adapted for that creation.

There will certainly be some continuity with our current bodies and this current creation. Paul taught that this Genesis creation will somehow be carried over into the eternal kingdom. But he did not identify any of the features of our current existence that will carry over. It all remains a mystery to us until the last day.

Yet, many theologians ignore these teachings of John and Paul and incorrectly assume that our transformed natural bodies will be like Christ's non-glorified body of flesh and blood that appeared to the disciples in the Upper Room. And from this false assumption, they extrapolate that we will inherit a restored natural earth as our eternal habitat.

Some of these theologians have set up a false dichotomy of the nature of our eternal bodies and eternal home. They claim:

- Our bodies will be patterned on Christ's pre-ascended body of flesh and blood, and we will dwell on a restored Genesis earth for eternity.
- Or our bodies will be immaterial and spiritual in nature, and we will dwell in a boring ethereal realm of heaven with our spirits floating around like angels.

The Scriptures plainly teach, however, that the future eternal body is neither a modified natural body of flesh and blood nor a disembodied spirit. The correct view of the future eternal body and eternal home is that when Christ comes again, the natural body will be transformed into a real but presently unknown kind of glorified eternal body like the unknown, glorified body of Christ. And the embodied eternal sons of God will dwell in a real but presently unknown kind of eternal habitat. In other words, as John and Paul taught, the natures of our eternal bodies and our eternal home remain a profound mystery for now! Theologians should learn to live with this mystery. And they should stop imposing features of the Adamic body and this Genesis creation onto our eternal existence on the eternal new earth.

Adam's body was made from the dust of the earth and was a natural body adapted for the garden of Eden. Adam and Eve were the first human creatures fashioned into natural bodies and were the beginning of the human experience on this Genesis earth—natural bodies for a natural habitat. The human body is mortal because it needs outside sustenance from the produce of the earth to sustain itself. Adam and Eve were to multiply and fill the Edenic earth with their sons and daughters. The anatomy of the male and female human body is specifically designed around the functions of marriage and reproduction. All our communal relationships are a derivative of marriage.

The first resurrection will indeed be of the natural bodies of the departed saints so that we can inherit the restored natural earth during the millennium. That is because the 1,000-year messianic kingdom will be a restoration of our humanity. The curse will be removed, and mankind will experience a restored human paradise on this earth.

The ascended Christ, however, is the firstborn of the new order of being as sons of God. He has led the way to the heavenly kingdom—the future home of the succeeding sons of God. The transformed body will have neither a male nor a female anatomy and will no longer experience marriage and reproduction. The eternal body will be immortal and will not need food, water, and air to sustain itself. It will be imperishable and will not decay and die. It will be incorruptible, unable to disintegrate into its many parts. Our glorified bodies will be immortal, imperishable, and incorruptible—adapted for a new eternal habitat.

Faulty Views of God's Endgame

I believe the primary reason many of the current views on God's endgame are flawed is because many theologians have wrongly assumed that the raptured body will be like the body of the pre-ascended Christ. This incorrect assumption has led these theologians to make grave mistakes when developing biblical theologies of the future. For example, premillennialists believe the first resurrection will be of the *raptured* saints so that they can reinhabit the restored earth when Christ returns to this earth. During the millennium, the glorified saints will comingle with natural human beings who survive the Tribulation.

After his resurrection, Christ comingled with the disciples and others while he was still on this earth. Because premillennialists believe our raptured bodies will be like Christ's pre-ascended immortal natural body, they have no problem envisioning the glorified saints comingling with natural human beings during the millennium. If Christ's resurrected body can eat and drink, then it would logically follow that the raptured saints can return to this restored earth in their immortal natural bodies to comingle with mortal human beings. They contend that we will have a different kind of body after we are raptured, but not that different.

Theologians are making a critical mistake when they build their view of God's endgame on these premises. The apostles never compared our future eternal bodies to the pre-ascended Christ. Instead, they taught that our raptured bodies will be like the unknown, post-ascended, glorified Christ that has not yet appeared. And they taught that the nature of this new kind of body is such a mystery that Paul calls us "foolish" to even suppose that we can know what our raptured bodies will be like.

In fact, Paul specifically teaches that the Adamic body of "flesh and blood **cannot** inherit the kingdom of God," even if it is an "immortal" natural body. Therefore, the raptured body will be very different from the current Adamic body of flesh and blood—and its eternal habitat will also be very different from the current Genesis earth!

Summary

As children of God, we are a new order of being that is neither male nor female. In heaven, we will no longer experience the Adamic functions of marriage and reproduction. That is a major change in the very nature of our being that necessitates a new kind of body and a new kind of habitat. At the final resurrection after the millennium, our Adamic bodies will be transformed to be like Christ's glorified body so they can be taken to the new heavens and new earth—a new kind of body for a new order of being on a new kind of earth. Our spiritual bodies will be real bodies, but they will be in the image of the resurrected Christ from heaven—not in the image of Adam and not in the image of the pre-ascended Christ.

God already demonstrated his remarkable creativity when he created the many different kinds of bodies suitable for different habitats on this Genesis earth. Paul taught us that we can trust our Creator to use this same infinite creativity when he creates a new version of our current bodies and a new version of the heavens and earth.

12

The Second Coming on Judgment Day

Review

Chapter 11 explored the nature of the future raptured body. Paul taught that the Adamic body of flesh and blood cannot inherit the kingdom of heaven. The natural human body that is male or female will need to be transformed into a presently unknown kind of immortal body so that God's people can inherit the eternal kingdom of heaven.

Paul compared this transformation process to seeds or nuts planted into the ground. A planted pecan does not germinate into another pecan. Rather, it is transformed into a magnificent tree. We cannot examine the exterior of the pecan, or crack it open and examine its interior, and determine what kind of plant will emerge when it germinates. Likewise, we cannot examine our natural bodies to determine what our future bodies will be like. The current natural body is adapted for the Genesis earth, but the transformed eternal body of the sons of God will be adapted for the eternal new heavens and new earth.

I also made the case that our glorified bodies will be like the post-ascended body of Christ—not like the known pre-ascended body of Christ. Paul taught that we need not worry about heaven being a boring existence, for God has already demonstrated his remarkable creativity when he created many kinds of bodies in this

Genesis creation. We can trust him to use this same creativity again when he creates our new kind of bodies that are adapted for the new heavens and new earth.

The Second Coming Occurs on Judgment Day

Throughout the preceding chapters, I made the case that Christ comes again on the last day to:
- Destroy this Genesis creation
- Create the new heavens and new earth
- Sit on his Great White Throne and judge all mankind
- Rapture the sons of God—asleep or alive—into immortal bodies like his glorified body and take them to the Father's eternal kingdom of heaven
- Resurrect and send unbelievers to the eternal lake of fire

There will be two sets of books opened on Judgment Day. One is the Book of Life, which records the good deeds of all believers. Believers will be judged to determine their rewards in heaven for their faithful good works as they followed Christ. Another unnamed book records the evil deeds of unbelievers. Unbelievers will be judged to determine their level of punishment in hell based on the extent of their evil deeds. John described Christ's return when he sits on his Great White Throne and judges all mankind:

> **Behold, I am coming soon** [the second coming], bringing my recompense with me [rewards and punishments], to repay each one [the believer and unbeliever alike] for what he has done [based on what is recorded in the books]. I am the Alpha and the Omega, the first and the last, the beginning [of this Genesis creation] and the end [of this Genesis creation]. Blessed are those who wash their robes [believers], so that they may have the right to the tree of life and that they may enter the city by the gates [the New Jerusalem in the new heavens and new earth]. (Rev. 22:12–14)

The second coming can be outlined as follows:

"Behold, I am coming soon"
+ Judgment Day: "bringing my recompense with me, to repay each one for what he has done"
+ The end of this Genesis creation: "I am the Alpha and the Omega, the first and the last, the beginning and the end"
= Believers "enter" the eternal city, or the New Jerusalem, and have "the right to the tree of life"

In the Days of Noah and Sodom

Postrestorationalism proposes that when Christ returns to rapture the saints after the millennium, the world will still be experiencing an age of peace and righteous humanity. There is a final deception of the nations at Gog and Magog, but this short-lived rebellion does not succeed, and the world remains at peace under Christ's governance.

Some theologians, however, believe the earth will be characterized by evil when Christ returns. They arrive at this conclusion because Christ referenced the days of Noah and Sodom, times of great evil, in relation to his second coming. Jesus told the disciples: "Just as it was in the days of Noah, so will it be in the days of the Son of Man [at his second coming]" (Luke 17:26). The days of Noah were indeed a time of corrupt and violent humanity:

> The LORD saw that the wickedness of man was great in the earth, and that every intention of the thoughts of his heart was only evil continually.... Now the earth was corrupt in God's sight, and the earth was filled with violence. (Gen. 6:5, 11)

At first glance, the evil conditions at the time of Noah seem to present a problem for the postrestorationalism. But we should be careful not to read too much into Christ's analogy. Christ was merely describing the unexpected nature of his coming to unbelievers, like the flood was unexpected. He was not describing the evil conditions of the world when he returns. Rather, unbelievers will be experiencing normal everyday activities. Because of the apparent tranquility of everyday life, Christ's return on Judgment Day will be an unexpected event for these unbelievers. But for believers, like Noah and Lot, his coming will be expected, because they know him and have believed his forewarning. Jesus taught:

> Just as it was in the days of Noah, so will it be in the days of the Son of Man. They were eating and drinking and marrying and being given in marriage [normal everyday life], until the day when Noah entered the ark, and the flood came and destroyed them all [sudden judgment and destruction]. Likewise, just as it was in the days of Lot—they were eating and drinking, buying and selling, planting and building [normal everyday life], but on the day when Lot went out from Sodom, fire and sulfur rained from heaven and destroyed them all—so will it be on the day when the Son of Man is revealed. . . . There will be two women grinding together. One will be taken and the other left. (Luke 17:26–35)

Christ made no mention of a grossly immoral people, such as those at the time of Noah or Sodom. He was simply describing the goings-on of ordinary life:
- People are "eating and drinking and marrying and being given in marriage."
- They are "buying and selling, planting and building."
- Women are "grinding together."

Christ did not make this analogy to communicate the depravity of the world at the time of his coming; rather, he made it to reveal how ordinary life will be at his sudden appearance on Judgment Day.

The purpose of this comparison to the judgments poured out in the past is to teach that Christ's second coming will be unexpected by *unbelievers*—just as the flood was a surprise to unbelievers living normal lives in Noah's day, and the fire and sulfur were a surprise to unbelievers living normal lives in the days of Sodom. Both Noah and Lot believed the Lord's warning about his impending wrath, and they were prepared for it. As a result, they escaped God's judgment. Likewise, believers expect that Christ will one day come back to destroy the world with fire and to judge all mankind, and they will be prepared. When Judgment Day arrives, believers will not be surprised and will escape his wrath.

Christ Is Coming Soon

The Scriptures have a unique way of approaching time. Toward the end of Revelation, Jesus said, "I am coming soon. Blessed is the one who keeps the words of the prophecy of this book" (Rev. 22:7). Of course, Jesus said this right after he had sent an angel to inform John that there would be at least a thousand more years of the earth's existence before he comes again on Judgment Day to destroy this earth! The New Testament authors often depicted their world as being in the last days—and that was two thousand years ago.

Numerous examples throughout the Bible express the idea of long periods of time condensed into but a brief moment. King David said that "in just a little while" the meek would inherit the land in the messianic kingdom, even though he wrote this psalm more than three thousand years ago:

> Be still before the Lord and *wait patiently for him*;
>> fret not yourself over the one who prospers in his way,
>> over the man who carries out evil devices!
>
> Refrain from anger, and forsake wrath!
>> Fret not yourself; it tends only to evil.
>
> For the evildoers shall be cut off,
>> but those who wait for the Lord shall inherit the land.
>
> *In just a little while*, the wicked will be no more;
>> though you look carefully at his place, he will not be there.
>
> *But the meek shall inherit the land*
>> and delight themselves in abundant peace. (Ps. 37:7–11)

The millennial reign of Christ might not occur for another two thousand years, but from David's perspective, time collapsed for the departed meek who would "shortly" inherit the land. The departed saints whose spirits are in heaven probably experience time differently than we do. They do not have natural bodies with biological clocks that relate to the twenty-four-hour rotation of the earth. In effect, David only had to wait for the end of his lifetime to be ready for the restoration to take place. His body is now asleep in the Lord, and his spirit waits in heaven for the messianic kingdom to take place "in just a little while."

The prophet Isaiah offered another example of condensing many years into a brief moment. Like Paul, he prophesied that the Jews would be hardened but someday would be grafted back in:

> "For a brief moment I deserted you, but with great compassion I will gather you. In overflowing anger for a moment I hid my face from you, but with everlasting love I will have compassion on you," says the Lord, your Redeemer. (Isa. 54:7–8)

This "brief moment" has lasted more than two thousand years, and the Jews have yet to repent and be grafted back in. Because of the way time collapses for believers when they die, the Bible can speak of events happening to believers "in just a little while" or "for a brief moment." Christ can say he is "coming soon."

The world has entered a period of history characterized as the last days. Christ's first coming represents the pivot point in human history. All history that follows his first coming, including the restoration, is part of the last days. These last days will continue until Christ returns a second time on the very last day, when the earth is destroyed and the saints inherit the kingdom of heaven.

John Could Have Been Alive When Christ Returned

Jesus informed Peter in the presence of the other disciples that Peter would not be alive when he returned:

> Truly, truly, I say to you, when you were young, you used to dress yourself and walk wherever you wanted, but when you are old, you will stretch out your hands, and another will dress you and carry you where you do not want to go. (This he said to show by what kind of death he was to glorify God.) (John 21:18–19)

In response, Peter asked Jesus if John would be alive to see his second coming:

> When Peter saw him [the apostle John], he said to Jesus, "Lord, what about this man?" Jesus said to him, *"If it is my will that he remain until I come, what is that to you? You follow me!"* So the

saying spread abroad among the brothers that this disciple was not to die; yet Jesus did not say to him that he was not to die, but, "If it is my will that he remain until I come, what is that to you?" (John 21:21–23)

Christ left the disciples with the impression that all prophetic events yet to come, including the millennium, *could* take place in John's lifetime and that John could still be alive when Christ returned at the end of the world! But Jesus only said that John *could* be alive when he returned—not that he *would* be alive on the last day.

In what scenario could John have possibly been alive at Christ's second coming? There must be a logical sequence of all prophetic events that *could* transpire for John to potentially be living when Christ returned. Following is a hypothetical scenario that could have occurred to allow for the possibility of John being alive to witness Christ's second coming.

John was a young man during this conversation between Christ and Peter. Let us assume that he was eighteen years old when Christ ascended into heaven. Forty years later, the Jews initiated a rebellion, causing the Roman emperor to declare war against them, destroying their temple in the process. The temple was destroyed in AD 70, so John would have been about fifty-eight years old at the time. Having been forewarned by Jesus of the temple's destruction, John would have headed for the mountains to escape the destruction of Jerusalem.

Then, assume ten years go by and an influential Jewish person, such as the Jewish historian Josephus, was able to meet with the emperor in Rome and convince him that restoring both Jerusalem and the temple would be beneficial for the empire. The Jews had learned their lesson, and the empire would not be at risk for another revolt. Assume the emperor heeded Josephus's counsel. The Romans were exceptional builders and could have rebuilt the temple in perhaps ten years. John would now be seventy-eight years old.

Assume another ten years go by and Paul's prayers for the Jews are answered—their hearts are no longer hardened, and they are grafted back into the natural olive tree. John is now eighty-eight years old.

Next, the gears of the seven-year Great Tribulation start to turn. The Antichrist enters the rebuilt temple proclaiming to be God, and he pursues John and the saints with a vengeance. But when John sees the abomination of desolation enter the temple, he would heed Christ's advice again and head for the mountains to hide from the Antichrist.

Having safely hidden in some remote cave in the wilderness, John would be ninety-five years old when the Tribulation ends. Satan is then bound, and Christ begins his 1,000-year reign from his throne in heaven. Nature is regenerated to an Edenic state. In this restored habitat, people can live for hundreds of years.

John survives the Tribulation and enters the millennium in a restored human body. As a result, he could possibly live for a thousand more years. At the end of the millennium, John would be 1,095 years old.

Next, Satan is released one final time to deceive the world. But before he can harm anyone, he and his army are destroyed. Ezekiel informs us that after the destruction of Gog and Magog, it takes seven years to clean up and burn their weapons for fuel (Ezek. 39:9–10). After this clean-up period, all the prophetic events have been fulfilled and Christ can come at any moment. John is a healthy 1,102 years old. He lives longer than Adam (930 years), Seth (912 years), and Noah (950 years). Perhaps ten more years go by, and Christ suddenly returns and finds John has reached the ripe old age of 1,112!

The early church operated upon the premise that all the prophetic events could take place within their lifetimes, so they could still be alive when Christ returned. Theoretically, as illustrated above, all those events could have taken place in the disciples' lifetimes (with the exception of Peter), with Christ returning while they were still alive.

The Sequence of Events on the Last Day

Many events take place at the second coming of Christ on the last day. Determining the exact chronological order of these events is not an easy task. For example, Christ comes again at the final resurrection of all mankind on the last day. But which comes first, the rapture of believers or the resurrection of unbelievers to face judgment? The answer is more complex than one might expect, because Christ used numerous parables to describe these events and each parable depicts a slightly different sequence. The point of the parable might not be to teach the exact sequence of the events that take place, but simply to teach that all these events take place on the last day.

Consider the parable of the weeds in Matthew 13:27–30. Jesus taught that the angels will first gather and remove the weeds (unbelievers) and then gather the wheat (believers) into his barn (heaven). In contrast, when the second coming is compared to the days of Noah and Lot in Luke 17:26–37, one could conclude that the righteous are removed first and the unrighteous are left behind to be destroyed along with the earth. On the other hand, when Christ described two women grinding grain together at the end of the passage, he said that one is taken to where "the vultures will gather," which would represent unbelievers. Thus, believers are left behind. Even within the same illustration of his second coming, one can come up with two seemingly opposite scenarios as to the exact sequence of events at the final resurrection of all mankind.

The parable of the ten virgins in Matthew 25:1–13 provides yet another version of the sequence of events of the final resurrection. Those prepared for Christ's return enter into heaven to meet the coming bridegroom, *leaving behind* those who are unprepared and shut out of the kingdom of heaven.

In the final analysis, it is difficult to determine the exact sequence of the events on the last day. I am not sure that determining their exact sequence is even an important issue, for they all happen suddenly, "in the twinkling of an eye." I have taken the position that unbelievers are removed first and then believers are raptured and transformed. *Then*, the current heavens and earth are destroyed by fire, and the books are opened with everyone being judged at the Great White Throne judgment.

Summary

In conclusion, the last day can be outlined as follows:
1. People will be leading normal lives; they will be eating, drinking, marrying, buying, selling, planting, building, and grinding grain when Christ comes again (Luke 17:22–36).
2. Christ suddenly appears in the clouds like a bolt of lightning that is seen all over the world: "For as the lightning flashes and lights up the sky from one side to the other, so will the Son of Man be in his day" (Luke 17:24).

3. Christ sends angels to gather all unbelievers, alive and dead, for judgment and destruction (Matt. 13:41–42).
4. Deceased unbelievers are resurrected into bodily form from hades, where their fallen spirits have been held until the day of judgment (Rev. 20:13).
5. Christ sends angels to gather all the saints (Matt. 24:31). Those whose bodies are asleep are resurrected first to rejoin their spirits descending from heaven, and those who are still alive on this earth "will be caught up together with them in the clouds to meet the Lord in the air" (1 Thess. 4:15–17).
6. Christ then transforms their natural bodies into glorified bodies that are immortal, incorruptible, imperishable, and adapted for heaven (1 Cor. 15:52–53).
7. The Genesis heavens and earth are completely destroyed by fire—they flee from his presence (2 Peter 3:10–13 and Rev. 20:11; 21:1).
8. Christ then sits on the Great White Throne in heaven to judge all mankind, because all judgment has been given to him (John 5:22).
9. All the saints whose names are in the Book of Life are judged first and given their rewards (1 Peter 4:17). They are judged by fire to test the quality of their works. The good works that survive affect their eternal existence in heaven (1 Cor. 3:11–15).
10. Unbelievers are judged according to their evil deeds and are sent to the lake of fire to experience the second death (Rev. 20:12–15).
11. Christ then creates the new heavens and new earth as the eternal home for the children of God: "Behold, I am making all things new" (Rev. 21:1–5).
12. The Adamic order of being comes to an end. What we will be like as children of God remains a mystery, "but we know that when he appears we shall be like him" (1 John 3:2).
13. Christ announces, "It is done! I am the Alpha and the Omega, the beginning and the end" (Rev. 21:6). He has finished the work the Father has given him.
14. Now that Christ has destroyed every rule and every authority and power including the last enemy, death, he delivers the kingdom over to the Father (1 Cor. 15:24–28).

15. In the Father's kingdom of heaven, we will dwell with the triune God in all his glory. And we shall reign in his heavenly kingdom "forever and ever" (Rev. 22:4–5).

13

The New Heavens and New Earth

Review

In chapter 12, I described many of the events that will occur when Christ comes again on Judgment Day. For unbelievers who do not know him, his return will be unexpected and sudden. It will be like a thief in the night—just as it was to unbelievers in the days of Noah and Sodom. They were living ordinary lives when judgment suddenly came upon them. On the other hand, for believers who know and are expecting him, his return will not be a surprise.

The Glory of Heaven

As a human being, Jesus of Nazareth was the Jewish Messiah. But he was also the eternal Son of God. Before his incarnation, he dwelled with God the Father in a loving relationship. When he was on this earth and about to be crucified, he looked forward to returning to the glory he had experienced in heaven with his Father. One could say he was a bit homesick. He also looked forward to his second coming, when he would take his people to be with him in heaven to see his glory with the Father. While praying to his Father, Jesus taught:

> I glorified you on earth, having accomplished the work that you gave me to do. And now, Father, glorify me in your own presence with the glory that I had with you before the world existed. . . .

> Father, I desire that they also, whom you have given me, may be with me where I am [in heaven], *to see my glory* that you have given me because you loved me before the foundation of the world. (John 17:4–5, 24)

When we join Christ in heaven, we will see the glory he had with the Father before the creation of the world. We will also be in the very presence of God the Father. In fact, the new heavens and new earth can be referred to as the Father's heavenly home, or dwelling place.

Biblical scholars disagree as to whether or not the Genesis earth will be purged by a surface fire on the last day and the new earth is to be a restored earth, or if the current earth will be totally annihilated and replaced with a truly new earth. The trend among evangelical theologians today is to envision the eternal kingdom of heaven as a restored earth. When Christ returns, both the Son of God and God the Father come down to our restored planet to dwell with the children of God. We will see the glory of the triune God on this restored Genesis earth.

But Jesus taught that we are destined to dwell with the Father in his *heavenly* home, not that he and his Father are coming to dwell with us in our home on this restored planet. It is hard to imagine that God in all his glory could dwell on this Genesis earth—even if it were a restored earth.

The first verse of the Bible teaches that "in the beginning, God created the heavens and the earth" (Gen. 1:1). The Genesis creation then existed as a real place for mankind in space and time. It had a real presence before God. But God remained in his dwelling place in heaven as mankind dwelled on this earth. In Revelation, John described the utter annihilation of this Genesis creation: "From his presence earth and sky fled away, and no place was found for them" (20:11). After the termination of this planet and the universe, the Genesis creation ceases to have a "presence" before God. It has "no place" in space and time. God then makes all things new when he creates the new heavens and earth as the eternal home for his children. Only this time, the children of God will dwell with God himself on the new earth. Therefore, the children of God must be destined for a totally new cosmos that will replace the one completely destroyed.

In the garden of Eden, one finds the Son of God walking and conversing in fellowship with Adam. The Son of God even appeared to

Abraham, Jacob, and Moses. Theologians refer to these appearances as theophanies. And, of course, through the incarnation, the Son of God dwelt among us as a fully incarnate human being. But notice that throughout the Scriptures, God the Father is never depicted as setting aside his glory and dwelling on the Genesis earth with mankind. When he does communicate with man, it is usually through a voice heard from the heavens. The Father always remains in his dwelling in heaven.

As transformed sons of God in glorified bodies, however, we will be able to actually dwell with the Father in all his glory. The apostle John revealed an extraordinary change in habitat, explaining that when we enter the new heavens and new earth, we will be dwelling in the very presence of God the Father, as well as the glorified Christ. Immediately after describing the end of this Genesis creation and the creation of the new heavens and the new earth, Revelation proceeds with a description of the New Jerusalem and our being in the presence of God the Father and Christ. Notice that the New Jerusalem comes down to the new earth, not to a restored Genesis earth:

> Then I saw a new heaven and a new earth, for the first heaven and the first earth had passed away, . . . And I saw the holy city, new Jerusalem, coming down out of heaven from God, . . . And I heard a loud voice from the throne saying, "Behold, the dwelling place of God is with man. . . . they will be his people, and God himself will be with them as their God." . . . And he who was seated on the throne said, "Behold, I am making all things new [the new habitat for the sons of God]." . . . The one who conquers will have this heritage, and I will be his God and he will be my son. . . . And I saw no temple in the city, for its temple is the Lord God the Almighty [the Father] and the Lamb [the Son]. (Rev. 21:1–7, 22)

The new earth will be a categorical change in type of dwelling place because we will be in the presence of God the Father in his full glory. We must receive a glorified body like Christ's in order to dwell with the Father. The new earth must be an entirely new creation made suitable for both God the Father and his transformed children, where we will dwell together as never before.

Therefore, whenever we are described in the Scriptures as actually dwelling in the presence of God the Father, we can legitimately say we are destined to dwell in heaven, the Father's heavenly home. We will still be embodied creatures in a real place. But we just do not know what kind of bodies we will have and what that place is going to be like because the eternal dwelling place for the sons of God has not yet been created.

The Son of God Creates the New Earth

Christ, as the eternal Son of God, claims to be the "Alpha" of this Genesis creation whereby he was the specific person of the Godhead that brought the heavens and the earth into existence. He also claims to be the "Omega" of this Genesis creation when he says the word and brings it to an end. And he is responsible for making all things new when he creates the new heavens and new earth as the eternal dwelling place for the transformed sons of God:

> Then I saw a new heaven and a new earth, for the first heaven and the first earth had passed away, and the sea was no more.... And he [the Son] who was seated on the throne said, "Behold, I am making all things new [the Son creates the new earth]." ... And he said to me, "It is done! [The Genesis earth and the human experience come to an end.] I am the Alpha and the Omega, the beginning [of this Genesis creation] and the end [of this Genesis creation]." (Rev. 21:1–6)

As Peter says, God created this Genesis creation *by his word* (*ex nihilo*), and one day he will simply say the word again and it will cease to exist:

> For they deliberately overlook this fact, that the heavens existed long ago, and the earth was formed out of water and through water by the word of God [the Alpha], ... But by the same word the heavens and earth that now exist are stored up for fire [the Omega], being kept until the day of judgment and destruction of the ungodly [on Judgment Day]. ... But according to his promise we are waiting for new heavens and a new earth in which righteousness dwells. (2 Peter 3:5–13)

By the Son's word that can create, destroy, and create anew, Christ will create a totally new heavens and new earth adapted for God's children. A new order of being in a new kind of eternal body necessitates a totally new creation. The sequence of events can be outlined as follows:

- The Son of God creates this Genesis creation out of nothing for his delight and glory.
- The Son of God restores this Genesis creation during the millennium for his glory.
- The Son of God annihilates this Genesis creation.
- The Son of God raptures the children of God into glorified bodies so that they can dwell with the Father.
- The Son of God then creates a totally new eternal habitat and dwelling place for the eternal sons of God.

There will certainly be some continuity with this Genesis creation, given that the eternal kingdom will be a new version of the current heavens and earth. And it will be a real place for real resurrected beings in real bodies. In Romans 8, Paul says that the current Genesis creation is groaning to transcend its current bondage to decay and somehow become a part of the eternal kingdom. How this all plays out in the end remains a mystery.

As Paul taught, we cannot examine the current natural body to determine what kind of immortal bodies we will have. So, too, we cannot examine the current planet to determine what kind of eternal habitat we will inherit. I am not sure that a verbal description of our future home would be helpful at this time anyway, which is why Revelation 21 and 22 relate an almost indescribable New Jerusalem that defies the laws of gravity and physics.

The New Jerusalem

John described a magnificent New Jerusalem that comes down to the new earth after the current heavens and earth are destroyed:

> Then I saw a new heaven and a new earth, for the first heaven and the first earth had passed away, and the sea was no more. And I saw the holy city, new Jerusalem, coming down out of heaven from God [to the new earth], *prepared as a bride adorned for her husband.* (Rev. 21:1–2)

John then described a vision of a cubed city with streets of gold and with foundations, walls, and gates made of a vast array of precious stones and minerals. The nature of this eternal city of God is another subject that has puzzled biblical scholars over the years. Is it a physical city with real streets of gold, or is John's vision a figurative description of a celestial city that is essentially indescribable at this time without the use of metaphors?

Some theologians believe that John was depicting a literal cubed city with actual streets of gold and gates of pearls. But the fact that John depicted the New Jerusalem as the bride of Christ should make us cautious not to interpret this description too literally. In fact, there are other indications in John's description of this city that tend toward a more figurative representation of this future heavenly dwelling place. For example, unbelievers outside the city gates are described as dogs:

> Blessed are those who wash their robes, so that they may have the right to the tree of life and that they may enter the city by the gates. Outside are the dogs and sorcerers and the sexually immoral and murderers and idolaters, and everyone who loves and practices falsehood. (Rev. 22:14–15)

If the streets and gates are to be interpreted literally, will there also be real dogs outside the gates? I don't think so. The dogs are a metaphorical representation of evil people who are excluded from entering the city of God. In fact, at this point in Revelation, the unrighteous will be in the lake of fire—not outside the gates of the eternal city. If the dogs are a metaphor for unrighteous unbelievers kept outside of heaven, then the gates and streets, as well as the cube-shaped city itself, are most likely metaphors as well. But that does not mean the city described is not an actual place.

What makes this analysis so difficult is that John also referred to objects in the New Jerusalem, such as the tree of life, that we recognize from other scriptures as real. For example, we know from Genesis that in the garden of Eden there was a real tree of life with real fruit. Let's read the Genesis account:

THE NEW HEAVENS AND NEW EARTH | 249

And the LORD God planted a garden in Eden, in the east, and there he put the man whom he had formed. And out of the ground the LORD God made to spring up every tree that is pleasant to the sight and good for food [common trees]. The tree of life was in the midst of the garden, and the tree of the knowledge of good and evil. A river flowed out of Eden to water the garden. (Gen. 2:8–10)

These two trees were real trees with real fruit in a real place. But they imparted more than mere food for the body. Presumably, the fruit from the tree of life has something to do with Adam and Eve being able to live immortal lives. The fruit from the tree of knowledge of good and evil also imparted spiritual qualities that went far beyond nutritional food for the body. These two trees were not metaphorical, even though they had transcendent qualities.

If the tree of life is real in some sense, then the New Jerusalem would also be a real place. Just as our spiritual bodies are going to be real bodies or containment vessels of some unknown kind, our eternal home will also be a real dwelling place for our resurrected eternal bodies.

The River of Life

John also described a river of life coming from the throne of God in the New Jerusalem, with the tree of life along its banks. Is this a real river, like the tree of life, or is this a metaphor for the flow of life from the Holy Spirit? John wrote:

> "It is done! I am the Alpha and the Omega, the beginning and the end. To the thirsty I will give from the spring of the water of life without payment." . . . Then the angel showed me the river of the water of life, bright as crystal, flowing from the throne of God and of the Lamb through the middle of the street of the city; also, on either side of the river, the tree of life with its twelve kinds of fruit, yielding its fruit each month. The leaves of the tree were for the healing of the nations. (Rev. 21:6; 22:1–2)

So how do we interpret the meaning of this river flowing from the throne of God? Is it a real river of some kind, or is it simply a metaphor for the spiritual life that flows from God? Or is it both, in the same way that the tree of life in the garden of Eden was a real tree that also had a spiritual dimension to it? There is definitely a metaphorical aspect to the river of life, for Christ used the same expression to describe the flow of spiritual life from the Holy Spirit into our hearts. This living water, however, does not flow from an actual river:

> On the last day of the feast, . . . Jesus stood up and cried out, "If anyone thirsts, let him come to me and drink. Whoever believes in me, as the Scripture has said, 'Out of his heart will flow rivers of living water.'" Now this he said about the Spirit, whom those who believed in him were to receive, for as yet the Spirit had not been given, because Jesus was not yet glorified. (John 7:37–39)

In his gospel, John interprets the expression "rivers of living water" as the flow of spiritual life from the Holy Spirit, which began at Pentecost. Applying this interpretation to Revelation, "the river of the water of life, . . . flowing from the throne of God" corresponds to a phenomenal flow of spiritual life from the Holy Spirit. If we interpret the river of life in the New Jerusalem as an actual river with real trees along its banks, we could be seriously underestimating its meaning as a symbol of the flow of spiritual life from the Spirit of God. On the other hand, this river and the tree of life bearing fruit along its banks could be real in some unknown sense and may represent a supernatural phenomenon that cannot be comprehended until we inherit the eternal city. Again, from the Genesis account, we know that the tree of life was a real tree with real fruit, even though it had a profound spiritual dimension to it.

In fact, there are some other very interesting parallels between the garden of Eden and the New Jerusalem. A river flowed out of Eden that was essential to the natural life of the garden. Likewise, a river flows from God himself into the New Jerusalem that will be essential to our eternal life on the new earth. The New Jerusalem will be a new kind of eternal paradise for the sons of God, patterned in some fashion on this Genesis creation. Perhaps metaphorical comparisons to this creation are the best way for God to communicate to earthlings whose only frame of reference is this earth.

The New Jerusalem as the Bride of Christ

John used another important biblical metaphor when he described the New Jerusalem as the bride of Christ. Human marriage is a typology of the church as the bride of Christ and is one of the most interesting typologies in the Scriptures. A wife is joined to her husband in the most loving and intimate form of companionship. So, too, our relationship with Christ is an intimate companionship. Obviously, our oneness with Christ is of the spirit, not of the flesh: "Do you not know that your bodies are members of Christ? . . . But he who is joined to the Lord becomes *one spirit with him*" (1 Cor. 6:15–17).

John described the New Jerusalem as the bride coming down out of heaven to consummate the wedding of Christ and his bride. But since Christ is holy and perfect, and we remain blemished by sin in this life, the wedding cannot be consummated until the church has been perfected and purified. This occurs on Judgment Day when Christ judges our works, burning off our bad works through a process of purification and then rewarding us for our good works. With these rewards, we are then properly clothed and adorned for the wedding, prepared as the pure and radiant bride of Christ. The wedding procession between Christ and his body can now begin:

> "Let us rejoice and exult and give him the glory, for the marriage of the Lamb has come, and his Bride has made herself ready; it was granted her to clothe herself with fine linen, bright and pure"—*for the fine linen is the righteous deeds of the saints.* (Rev. 19:7–8)

In effect, today we remain engaged to Christ, with the wedding to be consummated only after we are made holy—like Christ—on the last day. This is the final wedding procession, as the holy and pure bride made suitable for Christ comes from God the Father, who gives the bride away:

And I saw the holy city, new Jerusalem, coming down out of heaven from God, prepared as a bride adorned for her husband. . . . "Come, I [an angel] will show you the Bride, the wife of the Lamb." And he carried me away in the Spirit to a great, high mountain, and showed me the holy city Jerusalem coming down out of heaven from God, having the glory of God, its radiance like a most rare jewel, like a jasper, clear as crystal. (Rev. 21:2, 9–11)

John described a wedding procession, as the bride comes down out of heaven from God the Father. The Father chose the members of the bride for his Son, and now he gives away the bride to his Son. The radiant jewels represent the rewards for the saints as they enter into an eternal relationship with Christ. Like a bride on her wedding day, the bride of Christ is as radiant as precious jewels.

In Roman times, the women were known for wearing extravagant clothing and jewelry, particularly on their wedding days. They would be adorned with gold and jewels from head to toe. Some Gentile converts were so obsessed with extravagant clothing and jewelry that they presented a problem for the early church, which was made up of converts from all social-economic strata, including slaves. Paul addressed this issue: "Women should adorn themselves in respectable apparel, with modesty and self-control, not with braided hair and gold or pearls or costly attire" (1 Tim. 2:9).

In the ruins of Pompeii, an ancient Roman city buried under volcanic ash in AD 79, archaeologists have found an unusually large amount of gold jewelry, which helps us understand the problems Paul was confronting. Excavated jewelry includes gold hair braids, earrings, necklaces, upper armbands, forearm bands, wristbands, rings, belts, anklets, and even toe rings. Many of these gold adornments were encrusted with pearls, emeralds, and other precious stones. One can only imagine what a Roman bride might have looked like on her wedding day, dressed in her finest clothing and wearing her finest jewels.

John also compared the bride of Christ to a magnificent city. Many Roman cities had areas of slums, but compared to the rest of the ancient world the Romans were known for their beautiful cities of great architecture and streets paved with stones. They built magnificent aqueducts and paved canals to carry fresh spring water from surrounding mountains into the city. This spring water supplied baths, public fountains, and private households throughout the city.

John merged the image of a lavishly adorned bride of the Roman world with a magnificent ancient city, with its foundations, walls, gates, and streets made of the purest gold and every kind of precious stone one can think of. Like a bride, this jeweled city is decked out from head to toe—from its foundations to its walls, gates, and streets:

> The foundations of the wall of the city were adorned with every kind of jewel. The first was jasper, the second sapphire, the third agate, the fourth emerald, the fifth onyx, the sixth carnelian, the seventh chrysolite, the eighth beryl, the ninth topaz, the tenth chrysoprase, the eleventh jacinth, the twelfth amethyst. And the twelve gates were twelve pearls, each of the gates made of a single pearl, and the street of the city was pure gold, like transparent glass. (Rev. 21:19–21)

John's vision draws upon the magnificent Roman architecture and city planning of his day, as well as the beauty of a Roman bride adorned in splendor on her wedding day. Understanding the Roman setting in which John was writing is the key to understanding his vision of the New Jerusalem as a bride on her wedding day. The New Jerusalem in her magnificent jewels is arrayed like a beautiful bride, representing the consummation of the wedding of Christ and his bride, the church.

Summary

God the Father has been planning the wedding of Christ and his bride since before the foundation of the world. The 1,000-year restoration will be the rehearsal dinner. Our experience of the magnificent city of the restored earthly Jerusalem on the restored earth during the millennium will enable us to better foresee the incomparable beauty and joy of the future New Jerusalem on the new eternal earth.

The New Jerusalem on the new earth represents the consummation of the marriage between Christ and his bride. Today we remain betrothed, or engaged, to Christ. On the last day, we are judged and made pure; our righteous deeds will be rewarded like jewels. We can then experience the consummation of the wedding with Christ, "for the marriage of the Lamb has come, and his Bride has made herself ready."

14

The Great Tribulation

Review

In chapter 13, I examined the nature of the new heavens and the new earth as well as the New Jerusalem that comes down to the new earth after the Genesis earth is destroyed. The eternal city represents a real place for the glorified saints who will have real resurrected bodies. We just do not know what the New Jerusalem will be like, any more than we can know what kind of bodies we will have after they are transformed to be like Christ's ascended body.

I also discussed the way in which John portrayed the New Jerusalem as the bride of Christ that has been purified and rewarded for her good deeds. We are engaged to Christ today, but on the last day, the wedding is consummated as the New Jerusalem comes down out of heaven from the Father, who gives the bride away to be joined to Christ. John used two aspects of the Roman world as metaphors to describe the eternal city: a magnificent Roman city and a Roman bride dressed in fine linen, decked out from head to toe in gold and precious stones.

Satan's Control over Mankind

This book has followed a general flow of successive events. In this chapter, I will backtrack and readdress the Tribulation that occurs before the millennium. The Scriptures reveal a great deal about this period of unparalleled persecution against the saints. Currently,

Satan is operational in this world, instigating all sorts of evil schemes to keep fallen man alienated from God. Because of their sinful nature, unbelievers are naturally responsive to Satan. As John taught, "We know that we are children of God, and that the whole world is under the control of the evil one" (1 John 5:19 NIV). Satan's control over the minds of unbelievers takes many forms. It could be convincing unbelievers to ignore God completely as they live in a materialistic world. Or it could be leading them to accept any number of false beliefs about the supernatural realm.

But God does rescue people from Satan's control when we respond to the gospel and are reconciled to him. God then begins a long process of educating his people, progressively bringing them under his righteous influence through the indwelling power of the Holy Spirit. In the mean-time, Satan remains in this world and continues his assault on believers. He tempts us to sin and be unfaithful. And when we succumb to his temptations, he appears in heaven before God to accuse the saints of moral or spiritual failures.

But God restricts Satan's attempts to exercise control over the saints. He must approach God in heaven to gain permission for many of the evil things he does to the saints. For example, he appeared before God to question the sincerity of Job's faith in God, and he had to ask God for permission to test and persecute Job. God granted him permission to test Job, and Job's life became like hell on earth. In the end, Job's faith survived the test, and his life was restored to health and prosperity.

Satan can be compared to a rabid dog, driven mad with evil. This dog, however, is on a leash; God restrains how much evil Satan can accomplish. But one day this rabid dog will be unleashed on the world and an age of demonic humanity will begin. All the saints living at that time will experience a period of great persecution, similar to Job's testing.

But why would God allow an unrestrained Satan to have so much influence and power over the world? That is a very good question. It is important to remember that when Adam and Eve rebelled against God, they inadvertently let Satan into this world and it has never been the same. It is also important to realize that God did not have to intervene with a gracious plan of redemption for mankind. He did not have to show love and mercy to fallen man. He could have let mankind go the way of demons that have no hope of salvation. Perhaps God wants heaven and earth to witness what would have happened to fallen humanity if he had not intervened with a plan of redemption. What would the world be like if sinful man, under the unrestrained influence of Satan, was given free rein to act out a godless existence? During the Tribulation, we will find out.

The book of Daniel contains a wealth of information about the Great Tribulation. We learn that the Tribulation period will last about seven years and that it revolves around Israel and its temple. The Great Tribulation begins when a highly skilled and influential man negotiates a peace treaty between Israel and her surrounding enemies. At this point, Satan is still restrained by God, although God allows a great delusion to come upon unbelievers. They will begin to believe this leader is the Messiah who will bring peace and prosperity to the world. This period of peace only lasts for three and a half years before Satan deludes this leader into believing he is the Messiah. As the Antichrist, this leader enters a rebuilt Jewish temple and claims to be God incarnate. Satan is then released from heaven, and he is given unrestrained influence over unbelievers who are under his control. Satan will convince people that this leader really is God incarnate. The saints will reject these claims and refuse to worship him, and a period of intense persecution will break out against God's people, which lasts for three and a half years.

In his letters to the Thessalonians, Paul discusses the coming of the Antichrist. It is likely that Paul had been teaching the Thessalonians about Daniel's prophecies of the future Tribulation, for he assumes that they already know certain details about these future events. For example, Paul taught that one day the Antichrist will arrive on the scene, enter the temple, claim he is God, and demand to be worshiped. But Paul taught that Satan is currently restrained from initiating this phase of the Great Tribulation. Theologians have debated about who restrains Satan. Is it the Holy Spirit or is it the church?

Daniel clearly identified the restrainer as Michael the archangel. And Paul assumed that his readers already knew this detail, so he did not bother to reference him by name. Michael is an archangel, as was Satan before he fell. As such, Michael is just as powerful as Satan, if not more so. God tasked Michael with restraining Satan and protecting Israel against his attacks. Let's first read Daniel's prophecy, and then read Paul's exposition of it in his letter to the Thessalonians. Daniel revealed that the removal of Michael's restraint of Satan marks the emergence of the Antichrist:

> At that time *shall arise Michael*, the great prince who has charge of your people [Michael, who protects Israel against Satan, is removed from restraining Satan]. And there shall be a time of trouble, such as never has been since there was a nation till that time [the unprecedented Great Tribulation begins]. (Dan. 12:1)

Once Satan is no longer restrained by Michael, he works through a king who claims to be God incarnate:

> And the king shall do as he wills. He shall exalt himself and magnify himself above every god [he makes himself out to be God], and shall speak astonishing things against the God of gods. (Dan. 11:36)

When the Antichrist enters the temple and discontinues the regular burnt offering by the high priest, he sets himself up as the Messiah and demands to be worshiped. The temple sacrifices are then no longer necessary because God himself has supposedly come to the earth through the Messiah. This false messiah also sets up an idol of himself in the temple and demands that people worship this idol. This idol in the temple and the false Christ are an abomination to God.

Christians will refuse to worship the idol and the false messiah, and they will be attacked with a vengeance. After learning about this horrible future period of persecution against his people, Daniel asked the angel Gabriel how long this period of great tribulation will last:

> "How long shall it be till the end of these wonders?" And I heard the man clothed in linen, . . . "And from the time that the regular burnt offering is taken away and the abomination that makes desolate is set up [the Antichrist enters the temple and exalts himself as God], there shall be 1,290 days [three years and seven months]." (Dan. 12:6–11)

In his exposition of Daniel, Paul taught that when the restrainer is removed, the Antichrist will be revealed when he enters the temple:

> Let no one deceive you in any way. For that day will not come [the second coming and the end of the world], unless the rebellion comes first, and the man of lawlessness is revealed [the Antichrist], the son of destruction, who opposes and exalts himself against every so-called god or object of worship, so that he takes his seat in the temple of God, proclaiming himself to be God ["the abomination that makes desolate"]. Do you not remember that when I was still with you I told you these things? And you know [from the teachings of Daniel] what is restraining him now so that he may be revealed in his time. For the mystery of lawlessness is already at work [Satan is already instigating persecution against the saints]. Only he who now restrains it will do so until he is out of the way [when Michael the archangel is removed]. And then the lawless one will be revealed, . . . The coming of the lawless one is by the activity of Satan with all power and false signs and wonders. (2 Thess. 2:3–9)

Because they were already experiencing significant persecution, the Thessalonians were well aware that Satan was at work in this world. Yet, Paul informed them that Michael still limits Satan, preventing him from having full rein over the world through the Antichrist. When Michael arises, or is removed from restraining Satan, the Antichrist will be revealed. He will then enter the temple, make himself out to be God, and a time of trouble unlike any other in the history of the world will begin.

In Revelation, John also pictures Satan in heaven accusing the saints. But notice what happens when Michael is involved in a battle with Satan, and Satan is released from heaven and sent down to the earth with permission to persecute the saints during the Great Tribulation:

> Now war arose in heaven, Michael and his angels fighting against the dragon. And the dragon and his angels fought back, but he was defeated, and there was no longer any place for them in heaven. And the great dragon was thrown down, that ancient serpent, who is called the devil and Satan, the deceiver of the

whole world—he was thrown down to the earth, and his angels were thrown down with him [Satan is unleashed on the world]. And I heard a loud voice in heaven, saying, . . . "the accuser of our brothers has been thrown down, who accuses them day and night before our God. . . . Therefore, rejoice, O heavens and you who dwell in them! But woe to you, O earth and sea, for the devil has come down to you in great wrath, because he knows that his time is short [the Great Tribulation begins]!" (Rev. 12:7–12)

Michael is involved in this celestial battle with Satan that results in Satan being cast out of heaven. Satan comes down to the earth in great wrath against God's people because he knows that the days before he ends up in the lake of fire are numbered. Satan has been instigating periods of terrible evil throughout human history, but the severity of evil that will take place after Michael is removed from restraining Satan has no rival.

The Antichrist and the Rebuilt Temple

For the Tribulation to begin, a Jewish temple must be in place for the Antichrist to enter and make himself out to be God. However, the Jewish temple was torn down by the Romans in AD 70 and an Islamic mosque, the Dome of the Rock, currently occupies what is known as the ancient temple mount. As long as a rebuilt temple is not in place for the Antichrist to enter, we know that the Tribulation is not at hand. Someday, however, according to Daniel's prophecy and Paul's teachings, there must be another temple in existence for the Antichrist to enter.

Some historians believe that the current temple mount is really the old Roman fort or garrison used when the Romans occupied Jerusalem. They believe that the actual location of the Second Temple is below this site in the old city of David. In other words, the temple could be rebuilt without the Dome of the Rock being demolished. Regardless of where the temple is to be rebuilt, a Jewish organization in Israel presently has detailed plans for a rebuilt temple, once there is political will to construct one.

The future construction of a temple will undoubtedly cause another major conflict in the region. This war over the temple's construction could be the event that leads up to the beginning of the Tribulation. The book of Daniel informs us that the seven-year tribulation period begins with a peace treaty between Israel and her many enemies, which means there is probably a major war that precedes this treaty:

> And he [the Antichrist] shall make a strong covenant with many [a covenant of peace] for one week [seven years], and for half of the week [after three and a half years] he shall put an end to sacrifice and offering [when the Antichrist enters the temple claiming to be God]. And on the wing of abominations shall come one who makes desolate [the Great Tribulation begins], until the decreed end is poured out on the desolator [when the Antichrist is destroyed after seven years]. (Dan. 9:27)

The Antichrist will have to be a very gifted leader if he is to negotiate a covenant of peace between Israel and her many enemies. How the Antichrist will accomplish this stunning act of diplomacy, we do not know. But one thing is certain: he will be universally admired for the accomplishment. Perhaps he allows this admiration to go to his head and begins to delude himself into believing that he is the savior of the world. Then, with God allowing Satan to use his powers of deception to create a delusion among unbelievers, the world will rapidly begin to believe this lie as well.

According to Revelation, the Antichrist will be assassinated and then resurrected, leading to an even greater deception. Satan will likely use this supernatural event to increasingly delude the world into believing that the Antichrist is the true Messiah. John described his vision:

> And the beast [the Antichrist] that I saw was like a leopard; its feet were like a bear's, and its mouth was like a lion's mouth. And to it the dragon [Satan] gave his power and his throne and great authority. One of its heads seemed to have a mortal wound [he is killed], but its mortal wound was healed [he is resurrected], and the whole earth marveled as they followed the beast [as the savior of the world]. And they worshiped the dragon [Satan], for he had given his authority to the beast, and they worshiped the beast [the Antichrist], saying, "Who is like the beast, and who can fight against it?" (Rev. 13:2–4)

The beast imitates Christ when he receives a mortal wound but is resurrected and healed. When the beast dies, however, he will find himself in hades and will know with absolute certainty that he is destined for hell in a few short years. The Scriptures teach, "And just as it is appointed for man to die once, and after that comes judgment" (Heb. 9:27). When a man dies, God immediately judges him to determine whether his spirit goes to heaven to be with the Lord or whether his spirit goes to hades. Hades is a temporary form of hell, where the spirits of unbelievers are kept away from God's presence until Judgment Day.

When the Antichrist is mortally wounded, he will find himself in hades, where he will be confronted with the finality of his ultimate destiny of hell. When his human spirit is resurrected from hades, after getting a taste of hell, he will know with absolute certainty that he is like a demon, with no hope of redemption and destined for the lake of fire for all eternity. He will realize that he has only a few years to experience any carnal pleasures on this earth before being sent to the lake of fire.

As a result, he will direct his wrath against God and his saints. His rule over this world will be one of madness, vengeance, and rage. He will be possessed by Satan himself and will be an incredibly powerful and evil human being, with legions of other demons at his disposal. Satan will also know that his time is short before he, too, is sent to the lake of fire. When Satan is thrown down to earth from heaven, a loud voice in heaven warned, "Woe to you, O earth and sea, for the devil has come down to you in great wrath, because he knows that his time is short!" (Rev. 12:12). Jesus also warned that this outpouring of demonic wrath is unprecedented in the history of the world: "For then there will be great tribulation, such as has not been from the beginning of the world until now, no, and never will be" (Matt. 24:21).

A false prophet, who will imitate the prophet Elijah, will accompany the Antichrist. The false prophet will perform many signs and wonders that will further deceive unbelievers into believing the Antichrist is the true Christ. In a showdown with the prophets of Baal, Elijah called fire down from heaven (1 Kings 18:37–39). Malachi prophesied that Elijah will be sent before the coming of the Lord to "turn the hearts of the fathers to their children, and the hearts of the children to their fathers" (Mal. 4:5–6).

John taught that the first beast is the Antichrist and the second beast is the false prophet:

> Then I saw another beast rising out of the earth [the false Elijah].... It exercises all the authority of the first beast in its presence, and makes the earth and its inhabitants worship the first beast, whose mortal wound was healed. It performs great signs, even making *fire come down from heaven to earth* in front of people, and by the signs that it is allowed to work in the presence of the beast it deceives those who dwell on earth. (Rev. 13:11–14)

Because of his ability to perform such miracles, people will be deceived into believing this beast is Elijah, who is to return to earth as a forerunner of the Christ. During the Tribulation, there will be a great deception and distortion of many other Old Testament prophecies concerning the coming of the Messiah and the messianic kingdom.

Most of the early church councils were formed to refute heretical teachings that denied that Jesus was fully God and fully human or to refute false teachings about the Trinity such that the only begotten Son did not eternally coexist with the Father. The Antichrist will probably espouse other heresies about the Trinity. He might teach that there are two Sons of the Father: the first Son (Jesus of Nazareth) was sent as an atoning sacrifice for our sins, and the second Son (the Antichrist) is being sent to establish the Messianic kingdom, or world empire. And since we are followers of the sacrificial Son, we, too, should be sacrificed. He might also distort the following teachings of Paul to convince the followers of the Antichrist into believing that tracking down and sacrificing the followers of Jesus completes the mission of the first Son: "that I may know him and the power of his resurrection, and may share his sufferings, *becoming like him in his death*" (Phil. 3:10). Or, "Now I rejoice in my sufferings for your sake, *and in my flesh I am filling up what is lacking in Christ's afflictions* for the sake of his body, that is, the church" (Col. 1:24).

Many pagan religions throughout the ancient world included human sacrifice. John alluded to a similar sacrifice during the reign of the Antichrist: "And I saw the woman, drunk with the blood of the saints, the blood of the martyrs of Jesus" (Rev. 17:6).

Believers in the Tribulation

What happens to the saints who do not believe the deceptions of Satan and the Antichrist? Many premillennialists are also pretribulationists, meaning that they believe the church is raptured, or removed from this earth, before the persecution phase of the Great Tribulation begins. They claim that we are saved from God's wrath and therefore do not have to experience God's anger poured out on the earth during the Tribulation.

But God's wrath during the Tribulation is very different from God's wrath on Judgment Day. It is at the Great White Throne judgment that we are saved from the eternal wrath of God because as believers in Christ, we escape the lake of fire. This is the wrath of God we are saved from because we are covered in the blood of Christ.

Those who believe in the any-moment rapture of the saints also point out that John only refers to the word *church* in the beginning of the book of Revelation when he is addressing specific congregations. And as the Great Tribulation unfolds in Revelation, John uses only the word "saints." They interpret this lack of reference to the word "church" to indicate that the church has been raptured before the Tribulation begins.

But there is a much simpler reason that John no longer refers to the church. The church is an assembly of saints who worship and fellowship together. Once the Tribulation unfolds, these saints will no longer be meeting as congregations in public. Rather, they will have headed for wilderness areas and will be hiding from the Antichrist and his followers. If they appear in public without the mark of the beast, they will immediately be recognized, imprisoned, and tortured.

This would be similar to what the Jews experienced in Nazi Germany. Before Hitler began rounding up the Jews, many of them continued to meet and worship in their synagogues. But after the Final Solution to exterminate them was implemented and the Nazis began arresting them, they went into hiding and no longer met together in their synagogues.

Moreover, the case has already been made that the rapture of the saints occurs at the final resurrection, which is *after* the millennium on the last day of this Genesis creation. Therefore, believers will surely experience the Tribulation. Revelation is quite clear on the matter. In fact, the evidence in Revelation indicates that Satan will attack with a vengeance believers living at that time:

> And the beast was given a mouth uttering haughty and blasphemous words, and it was allowed to exercise authority for forty-two months [three and a half years]. . . . Also *it was allowed to make war on the saints* and to conquer them. . . . If anyone has an ear, let him hear: If anyone is to be taken captive, to captivity he goes; if anyone is to be slain with the sword, with the sword must he be slain. Here is a call for the endurance and faith of the saints. (Rev. 13:5–10)

But how can the saints endure such persecution and martyrdom? By looking forward to the joy set before them when they will experience the first resurrection and a thousand years of paradise on this earth. Satan will be bound as Christ exercises his reign from his throne in heaven. This is how Christ endured his suffering on the cross—he looked forward to his resurrection, his ascension to heaven, and his glorious kingdom:

> Let us run with endurance the race that is set before us, looking to Jesus, the founder and perfecter of our faith, who *for the joy that was set before him* endured the cross, despising the shame, and is seated at the right hand of the throne of God. (Heb. 12:1–2)

During the Tribulation, the days for nominal Christianity will be over. As the Tribulation unfolds, the tares in the church will receive the mark of the beast, whereas the wheat, or God's elect, will not. The tares will no longer believe it beneficial to be part of a persecuted group of believers. Jesus warned us that Satan will delude the social Christians and they will become hostile to committed Christians:

> Then they will deliver you up to tribulation and put you to death, and you will be hated by all nations for my name's sake. And then many will fall away and betray one another and hate one another. . . . the love of many will grow cold. But the one who endures to the end will be saved. (Matt. 24:9–13)

Because the demonic tyranny of the Tribulation is worldwide, it will be difficult for Christians to escape capture or death. Satan's universal system of personal identification will make survival almost impossible without allegiance to the false Christ:

> Also it [the second beast] causes all, both small and great, both rich and poor, both free and slave, to be marked on the right hand or the forehead, so that no one can buy or sell unless he has the mark, that is, the name of the beast or the number of its name. (Rev. 13:16–17)

The saints who refuse to accept this mark of the beast will surely stand out, and unbelievers will report any Christian they find, considering it an act of service to their god, the Antichrist.

Today there is a large underground church in China despite periodic persecution from the communist government. When these Chinese believers are in public, they look like every other citizen. As long as they are careful about sharing their faith in public, they can carry on normally. In contrast, the unmarked believers during the Tribulation will be easily identifiable in any public setting as the enemies of the Antichrist. As a result, believers will have to remain in seclusion, hiding from everyone except fellow believers.

God's Wrath During the Tribulation

Revelation describes the Tribulation as a period when God will pour out his great wrath on the earth as a result of the extreme evil perpetrated against his saints. Much of Revelation is devoted to describing God's fury during the Tribulation. As the blood of hundreds of millions of innocent Christians flows, it is little wonder that God begins to visit such intense wrath on the world.

As the world becomes unbearably evil in his sight, God displays his anger by creating a variety of plagues. Revelation 16 describes some of the forms of God's wrath: "harmful and painful sores came upon the people who bear the mark of the beast and worshiped its image"; another bowl causes the sun "to scorch people with fire"; another angel sent from heaven "poured out his bowl on the throne of the beast, and its kingdom was plunged into darkness. People gnawed their tongues in anguish and cursed the God of heaven for their pain and sores" (16:2–11). And many more plagues follow.

Revelation informs us that the saints are exempt from God's acts of vengeance on those with the mark of the beast, in much the same way that the Jews in Egypt were passed over by the angels of wrath sent by God. The angels of wrath will only direct their vengeful anger at those with the mark of the beast, and they will pass over the saints, who do not bear this mark:

> So the first angel went and poured out his bowl on the earth, and harmful and painful sores came upon *the people who bore the mark of the beast* and worshiped its image [unbelievers]. (Rev. 16:2)

Believers will also have a special seal of God on their foreheads that will allow the angels of wrath to identify and pass over them:

> They were told not to harm the grass of the earth or any green plant or any tree, but only those people who do not have *the seal of God on their foreheads*. (Rev. 9:4)

Revelation further reveals that it will be a blessing for the saints to be killed rather than continue to endure satanic torture during the Tribulation:

> Here is a call for the endurance of the saints, those who keep the commandments of God and their faith in Jesus. And I heard a voice from heaven saying, "Write this: Blessed are the dead who die in the Lord from now on." "Blessed indeed," says the Spirit, "that they may rest from their labors [from enduring torture], for their deeds follow them!" (Rev. 14:12–13)

From the letter to the Hebrews, we learn that the departed saints are a cloud of witnesses in heaven, watching the events on the earth unfold (Heb. 12:1). With so many Christians slain during the Tribulation, John has a vision of the multitude of departed saints in heaven praising God:

> After this I looked, and behold, a great multitude that no one could number, from every nation, from all tribes and peoples and languages, standing before the throne and before the Lamb, clothed in white robes, . . . and crying out with a loud voice, "Salvation belongs to our God who sits on the throne, and to the Lamb!" . . . Then one of the elders addressed me, saying, "Who are these, clothed in white robes, and from where have they come?" . . . And he said to me, "These are the ones coming out of the great tribulation. They have washed their robes and made them white in the blood of the Lamb." (Rev. 7:9–14)

By the end of the Tribulation, the world will be a wreck. Virtually all the saints will have been slain during the Antichrist's reign of terror. Only a small number of them will have successfully hidden in wilderness areas. Many unbelievers will also have been killed. Earthquakes and plagues will have devastated the planet.

But a significant number of unbelievers will have survived. There will be enough to send an army to join the Antichrist in one final battle against Christ. During the battle of Armageddon, Christ will demonstrate the full measure of his anger over the evil perpetrated against his people during this terrible period of human history.

As the armies of the Antichrist gather, Christ will appear in the celestial realm of heaven on a white horse. By his word, described as a sword, he then destroys these armies. He sends the Antichrist and his false Elijah directly to the lake of fire, bypassing the Great White Throne judgment. Satan is then bound, and the millennial reign of Christ begins when Christ sits on his throne in heaven and governs the world.

Summary

When Adam and Eve sinned, mankind became spiritual children of Satan and he entered our world. That is why mankind remains hostile to God and the world remains an unrighteous place. God's chosen people have been rescued from Satan's dominion of darkness, but we remain in this fallen, demonic world. And Satan continues to instigate all kinds of evil against us.

But God, through his archangel Michael, currently restrains Satan in how much harm he can inflict on us. When God removes Michael, Satan will be unleashed on the world, and an unprecedented period of tribulation against the saints will begin.

Why does God allow Satan to delude mankind and create the Great Tribulation? Perhaps God wants to reveal to heaven and earth the full extent of the fallen nature of mankind as spiritual children of Satan. He wants to reveal what a truly godless humanity under the direct influence of Satan is capable of. The Tribulation will also reveal the righteous indignation of a holy God who will vent "the fury of the wrath of God the Almighty" against demonic humanity.

In contrast, the 1,000-year messianic kingdom that follows the Great Tribulation will demonstrate what the human experience would have been like had Adam and Eve not rebelled and allowed Satan into our world. Through the power of resurrection, God will restore all his ransomed people to an Edenic paradise on this earth to demonstrate what redeemed humanity will be like without Satan. The millennium will be an age of righteous humanity when it is ruled by its divine Creator.

15

The Battle of Armageddon

Review

In chapter 14, Satan is described as a rabid dog who is out to destroy God's people. But Satan is on a leash. Michael is described as a powerful angel who restrains Satan, limiting the extent of evil he can instigate against God's people.

According to the books of Daniel and Revelation, when Michael is removed from restraining Satan, this powerful fallen angel will be cast down to the earth. Knowing that his time is short, Satan will direct his demonic wrath against God's people. The Antichrist will be revealed, and the Great Tribulation will begin. The Great Tribulation will demonstrate what the fallen human race would have become under Satan's rule if God had not intervened with his plan of redemption.

Much of Revelation is devoted to describing God's anger toward this unprecedented evil against his people. There will be all kinds of plagues and other examples of God's wrath, culminating in his wrath at the battle of Armageddon.

The Battle of Armageddon

During this climactic battle, Christ will demonstrate the full measure of his anger against unbelievers for their worship of the Antichrist and their horrible persecution of the saints. In Revelation 19, Christ is depicted as coming out of heaven riding on a white horse to destroy the Antichrist and his army and put an end to the Great Tribulation:

> Then I saw heaven opened, and behold, a white horse! . . . in righteousness he judges and makes war. . . . From his mouth comes a sharp sword with which to strike down the nations. (Rev 19:11–15)

This battle takes place between Christ in the celestial realm of heaven and a real army on the plane of this earth. Christ just says the word and the armies on the earth that are gathered against him are destroyed. He also sends the Antichrist and the false prophet directly to the lake of fire, bypassing the Great White Throne judgment altogether. Satan is then bound, and the millennial reign of Christ begins.

Premillennialists believe that the appearance of Christ on his white horse represents Christ's second coming. But as was demonstrated in chapter 6, "A Critique of Premillennialism," Christ is never depicted as leaving the celestial realm of heaven on his white horse and descending to this earth to engage the Antichrist and his armies. He remains in heaven when the Antichrist is destroyed and Satan is bound by an angel. He then rules the world during the millennium from his throne in heaven.

This battle is reminiscent of an event in the Old Testament when the prophet Elisha is with his servant. An earthly army with horses and chariots surrounded their city, and Elisha's servant became concerned:

> "Alas, my master! What shall we do?" He said, "Do not be afraid, for those who are with us are more than those who are with them." Then Elisha prayed and said, "O LORD, please open his eyes that he may see." So the LORD opened the eyes of the young man, and he saw, and behold, *the mountain was full of horses and chariots of fire* all around Elisha. (2 Kings 6:15–17)

While there was a real army on earth threatening Israel, there was also a real army of God's powerful angels in the celestial realm of heaven. When the army advanced against Israel, Elisha prayed and God struck the soldiers with blindness.

Later in 2 Kings 19, we learn that when Hezekiah was king of Judah, and Jerusalem was surrounded by an Assyrian army, a single angel of the Lord struck down 185,000 soldiers in one night. Jesus referred to this angelic power when he was being arrested and Peter wanted to use his sword to prevent the arrest: "Do you think that I cannot appeal to my Father, and he will at once send me more than twelve legions of angels?" (Matt. 26:53).

Twelve legions of angels is more than 72,000. If a single angel of the Lord could strike down 185,000 Assyrians, then that is enough angelic power to kill more than 13 billion soldiers! Jesus claimed to have enormous angelic power at his immediate disposal in the celestial realm. Jesus, like Elisha, knew what powers existed around him in the celestial realm of heaven.

Yet Jesus chose not to have angels intervene at that time, and he suffered greatly during his trial and crucifixion. At the battle of Armageddon, however, the ascended Christ will indeed intervene. The spirits of the departed saints will be involved in this celestial battle as well, for they are described as "the armies of heaven, arrayed in fine linen, white and pure, . . . *following him* on white horses" (Rev. 19:14).

In Hebrews, the departed saints are described as a cloud of witnesses in heaven. During this battle, the departed saints go from being mere spectators to being participants. There is no evidence, however, that they fight in this battle. Satan's army is swiftly destroyed when Christ merely says the word. The spirits of the saints following Christ are then depicted as continuing their descent and reinhabiting the earth through the first resurrection. They will dwell on the earth once again through a resurrection of their natural bodies.

Although the spoken word of Christ destroys the large armies gathered at Armageddon, many civilians not engaged in this battle will survive and enter the millennium. Many of these survivors will surely become believers when they witness the reign of Christ and the earth being restored to its Edenic condition. But not all of them will be converted.

Gog and Magog

Proof that some unbelievers will remain in the world during the millennium is that at the end of that period, when Satan is released one final time, he leads them into one last rebellion against God. Satan's power of deception is remarkable, for the world will have just experienced a thousand years of an earthly paradise under the reign of Christ. Yet for one last time, Satan exposes fallen mankind's susceptibility to deception and greed. John taught that these armies of Satan come from Gog and Magog. They surround Jerusalem, but they are destroyed before they can do any harm to God's people:

> And when the thousand years are ended, Satan will be released from his prison and will come out to deceive the nations that are at the four corners of the earth, Gog and Magog, to gather them for battle; their number is like the sand of the sea. And they marched up over the broad plain of the earth and surrounded the camp of the saints and the beloved city, but fire came down from heaven and consumed them. (Rev. 20:7–9)

Some theologians believe the reference to Gog and Magog after the millennium is actually a recapitulation of the battle of Armageddon that occurs *before* the millennium. John, however, clearly described these events surrounding Gog and Magog as occurring *after* the millennium:

> *And when the thousand years are ended*, Satan will be released from his prison and will come out to deceive the nations that are at the four corners of the earth, Gog and Magog. (Rev. 20:7–8)

Revelation contains a great deal of recapitulation and connecting many of these various texts can be difficult. But chapters 19, 20, and 21 proceed in a very clear linear progression.

A more detailed description of the battle involving Gog and Magog can be found in Ezekiel. In chapter 37, Ezekiel first tells of the dry bones of Israel coming to life as the departed Jewish saints inherit the messianic kingdom. During the restoration, wars will not take place because Christ will be ruling the world. Villages and cities will have no need for walls to defend themselves against hostile invasions. After many years of peace and prosperity, Israel will have accumulated great wealth from gifts from other nations in gratitude for the joy and blessings brought about by the reign of the Jewish Messiah. Ezekiel then describes the people of Gog and Magog inspired by Satan seeking to plunder this wealth by attacking a land of "unwalled" villages that have recovered from war:

> The word of the Lord came to me: "Son of man, set your face toward Gog, of the land of Magog, . . . After many days you will be mustered ["when the thousand years are ended"]. In the latter years you will go against the land that is restored from war [during the restoration], . . . You will be like a cloud covering the land, you and all your hordes, and many peoples with you [a huge army]. On that day, thoughts will come into your mind, and you will devise an evil scheme and say, 'I will go up against the land of unwalled villages. I will fall upon the quiet people who dwell securely, all of them dwelling without walls, and having no bars or gates,' to seize spoil and carry off plunder." (Ezek. 38:1–12)

But with Christ continuing his reign over this world from his throne in heaven, they will not succeed:

> I will enter into judgment with him [Gog], and I will rain upon him and his hordes and the many peoples who are with him torrential rains and hailstones, fire and sulfur. (Ezek. 38:22)

John also revealed that they will be destroyed by fire, but he further informed us of Satan's demise:

> But fire came down from heaven and consumed them, and the devil who had deceived them was thrown into the lake of fire and sulfur where the beast and the false prophet were, and they will be tormented day and night forever and ever. (Rev. 20:9–10)

After Gog and Magog are destroyed by fire and Satan is permanently sent to hell, the earth remains in its restored state, with Christ still reigning from heaven. After these events, however, all the prophecies that must occur on this earth before Christ comes again have been fulfilled. The fig tree will be ripe, and Christ's second coming in the clouds on Judgment Day could happen at any moment: "So also, when you see all these things, you know that he is near, at the very gates" (Matt. 24:33).

Summary

During the Tribulation, when Satan is given unrestrained control over unbelievers, the world will experience an age of unparalleled demonic humanity. This will demonstrate what this world would be like if God had not intervened with a plan of redemption. This terrible period of human history comes to an end at the climactic battle of Armageddon.

Like Old Testament prophets, John had a vision of the celestial realm in which he saw heaven opened and Christ riding on a white horse. From the celestial realm, Christ merely says the word and the Antichrist and his false prophet are destroyed. Satan is then bound by an angel sent from heaven, and the millennial reign of Christ begins.

There is one final revolt by sinful man inspired by Satan, but Christ's reign is everlasting because this revolt does not succeed. Christ's kingdom then transitions to the Father's eternal kingdom of heaven or the new heavens and new earth.

16

Daniel and the Olivet Discourse

Review

In chapter 15, I examined the events surrounding the battle of Armageddon that bring the Great Tribulation to an end. Christ appears on a white horse in the celestial realm, merely says the word, and the Antichrist and the armies following him are destroyed. Christ then sends an angel to bind Satan for a thousand years so that Christ's reign over this world can begin. After the millennium, Satan is released and leads one final rebellion of fallen man against God. But this short-lived revolt fails, and Satan is sent to the eternal lake of fire, never to be heard from again.

The Destruction of the Temple

Any book that deals with the subject of eschatology should wrestle with Christ's Olivet Discourse, a sermon on the end times. In Jerusalem, much of Christ's preaching took place at the temple. Christ and his disciples would retire at night to the Mount of Olives, where the disciples would ask him to further explain his teachings of that day. One day, after leaving the temple with his disciples, Jesus predicted that the temple itself would be destroyed:

> Jesus left the temple and was going away, when his disciples came to point out to him the buildings of the temple. But he answered them, . . . "Truly, I say to you, there will not be left here one stone upon another that will not be thrown down." (Matt. 24:1–2)

The temple was of immense importance to the Jewish people, and the disciples were shocked by this prediction of its destruction.

In Jewish history, the temple represented God's spiritual presence on this earth—his house, so to speak. It was a place where people could approach God to worship him. The temple also set Israel apart from pagan nations, which often set up their own temples to worship idols or demons.

The temple had been in existence for more than five hundred years when Jesus predicted its destruction. The last time the temple had been destroyed was during the Babylonian Empire in 586 BC. The Jews had been persistently unfaithful in their covenant with God, despite the repeated warnings of Jeremiah and other prophets. As judgment against Israel for their idol worship, God allowed the Babylonian rulers to destroy the temple and take the Jews into exile.

The prophet Daniel was a young man among these exiles who rose to prominence in the Babylonian government. He was not only a brilliant administrator in their government but also a prophet God used extensively to reveal his endgame for Israel and its temple. When the Jews came out of captivity and returned to Jerusalem, the temple was rebuilt. It is referred to as the "Second Temple." But Israel was never truly restored.

There are two ways in which the temple could be desecrated, and each is a form of abomination to God:

- When a pagan nation invades Israel and physically destroys the temple
- When a pagan nation in control of Israel imposes a pagan form of worship and sacrifice within the temple itself

The destruction by the Babylonians represents the first form of desolation, and the second form of desecration occurred when the Greek Empire controlled Israel. The Second Temple was not destroyed by an invading army, but it was desecrated when the Greek ruler of that region, Antiochus IV Epiphanes, forced the Jewish high priest to sacrifice a pig to the pagan god Zeus in the temple. This inspired an insurrection and a war against the Greek Empire, known as the Maccabean Revolt, which succeeded in liberating Jerusalem.

When the Romans conquered Israel, they were mainly interested in gaining material wealth from the country, rather than in spreading their pagan religion. To avoid an insurrection, they wisely did not destroy the temple. They also let the Jewish temple practices remain in place, rather than attempt to impose their pagan forms of worship on the Jewish nation.

A Sermon on Daniel

In his Olivet Discourse, Christ referenced the book of Daniel when he preached about the temple's desolation: "So when you see the abomination of desolation *spoken of by the prophet Daniel*, standing in the holy place (let the reader understand)" (Matt. 24:15). Thus, to properly "understand" the future events surrounding Israel's temple, the reader of his discourse needs to *read and understand* Daniel's visions that revolve around Israel and its temple.

I will make the case that Daniel's visions and Jesus' Olivet Discourse foresaw two distinct desolations of the temple: one by the Romans, when the temple is destroyed in AD 70 (similar to the Babylonian destruction), and another by the Antichrist, when he enters a rebuilt temple claiming to be God and sets up an idol of himself to be worshiped (similar to the Greek desolation). The book of Daniel teaches that this last desolation leads to the Great Tribulation, followed by a restored temple in the messianic kingdom when Israel becomes a truly righteous nation.

The Temple in the Messianic Kingdom

Daniel, like several other Jewish prophets, taught that a restored Jewish temple would be at the center of the messianic kingdom. This is problematic because we know that Christ is the ultimate sacrifice for our sins and that the temple sacrifices by the high priest are no longer necessary. It helps to remember, however, that the temple was more than a place for sacrifices to be made for sins. In many cases, the offerings made by the priests on behalf of the people were a form of thanksgiving to God for a good harvest. It should be noted that James, Peter, and the Jewish believers in Jerusalem continued to gather and worship at the temple for decades until the temple was destroyed. They were not being legalistic or hypocritical. Regardless of the theological difficulty of reconciling another temple with Christ's sacrifice for our sins, the rebuilt temple is an inseparable part of the messianic kingdom.

Ezekiel, a contemporary of Daniel, also foretold a temple during the messianic kingdom. He taught that the Jewish temple will serve the world as a center of worship and prayer, a center of learning and dissemination of truth, and the judicial center for Israel and the world. Chapters 40 through 48 of Ezekiel go into considerable detail about the temple during the messianic kingdom.

The restored temple shows up repeatedly in other messianic prophecies as well. Isaiah referenced a restored Jerusalem with a restored temple in his famous vision of the messianic kingdom:

> "I will rejoice in Jerusalem and be glad in my people; no more shall be heard in it the sound of weeping and the cry of distress." . . . For thus says the Lord: "Behold, I will extend peace to her like a river, and the glory of the nations like an overflowing stream; . . . And they shall bring all your brothers from all the nations . . . to my holy mountain Jerusalem, says the Lord, just as the Israelites bring their grain offering in a clean vessel to the house of the Lord [an offering of thanksgiving in the restored temple]. And some of them also I will take for priests and for Levites, says the Lord [restored priestly services]." (Isa. 65:19; 66:12–21)

During the messianic kingdom of peace and prosperity, believing Jews will be brought back to a restored Israel and a restored Jerusalem. And the temple will be restored with priestly services. According to Isaiah, the temple is an inseparable part of the messianic kingdom.

The book of Micah also envisions Jerusalem and its temple as the center of the Messiah's earthly kingdom:

> It shall come to pass in the latter days that the mountain of the house of the Lord shall be established as the highest of the mountains [Jerusalem and its temple], . . . and many nations shall come, and say: "Come, let us go up to the mountain of the Lord,

to the house of the God of Jacob, that he may teach us his ways and that we may walk in his paths [a center of learning]." . . . He [the Messiah] shall judge between many peoples, and shall decide for strong nations far away [the Messiah rules the world]; and they shall beat their swords into plowshares, and their spears into pruning hooks; nation shall not lift up sword against nation, neither shall they learn war anymore [global peace]. (Mic. 4:1–3)

One day, the Messiah will restore Jerusalem *and its temple* in an age of righteousness, justice, and peace. These prophecies are clearly describing the messianic kingdom, and the restored temple is an essential component of these prophecies.

The condition of the temple throughout the Scriptures reflects the spiritual condition of Israel. God's covenant with Israel to protect Jerusalem and its temple from hostile nations was contingent upon the Jews remaining faithful to God's commandments. When they were repeatedly unfaithful and unrepentant, as they were during the time of Jeremiah and Daniel, God allowed the Babylonians to conquer them, destroy their temple, and take them into exile.

The temple was eventually rebuilt. But there would be another period when the Jews would be unfaithful—when the Messiah came into the world. Yet, even while predicting the temple's destruction as a form of judgment against the unfaithful Jews, Christ predicted a time in the future when they will repent and be faithful:

> O Jerusalem, Jerusalem, the city that kills the prophets and stones those who are sent to it [unfaithful Israel]! How often would I have gathered your children together as a hen gathers her brood under her wings, and you were not willing [unrepentant Israel]! See, your house is left to you desolate [the temple will be destroyed again]. For I tell you, you will not see me again, until you say, "Blessed is he who comes in the name of the Lord [repentant Israel, which leads to the messianic kingdom and the restoration of the temple]." (Matt. 23:37–39)

This covenant with Israel can be outlined as follows:
- Faithful Israel: temple protected and Israel flourishes
- Unfaithful Israel worships pagan idols: temple destroyed by the Babylonians
- Unfaithful Israel rejects their Messiah: temple destroyed by the Romans
- Repentant Israel accepts their Messiah: temple restored during the messianic kingdom

Jesus predicted the temple would be destroyed during the unrepentant generation of those who heard his message. About forty years later, around AD 70, Jewish Zealots started a war against Rome in an attempt to liberate Israel. Rome responded by sending three legions of soldiers to put down this rebellion. They ruthlessly put down the revolt, sacked Jerusalem, and destroyed the temple. The temple walls were made of large cut stones, and its roof contained wooden rafters. Gold was used throughout the temple to adorn its architecture, furnishings, and utensils. When the temple caught fire during the chaos of war, the extensive gold within the temple melted. The molten gold then seeped into the crevices between the stones of the temple walls. After the fire stopped and the molten gold hardened, the Roman soldiers overturned every stone to gain access to the solidified gold sandwiched between the stones. As Jesus predicted, not one stone would be left upon another (Matt. 24:1–2)!

The Jews' rejection of their Messiah led to the destruction of the Second Temple by the pagan Romans. But according to Daniel's visions, this is not the last time the temple will be desecrated by unbelievers. There is a future desolation of a rebuilt temple. It will be perpetrated by the Antichrist when he enters the temple claiming to be God. Daniel refers to this as the final "abomination and desolation." This will be followed by the restoration of the temple in the messianic kingdom when the Jews repent and believe in their Messiah.

Nebuchadnezzar's Dream

Nebuchadnezzar was the ruler of the Babylonian Empire when God began to give Daniel visions of the future. Daniel had one main vision, which was an interpretation of a dream of Nebuchadnezzar's.

The dream was of a human figure divided into five sections. Each section represents one of five great empires and its impact on Israel, its temple, and the world.

All these kingdoms are led by sinful men influenced in one way or another by Satan, the god of this world. They are greedy and ambitious leaders, often going on rampages to conquer other nations in order to create extravagant wealth for themselves and their people. In the process, thousands of men, women, and children are killed or enslaved.

Almost all these leaders become deluded into thinking they are gods and demand to be worshiped. Daniel himself faced such a leader, refused to worship the Babylonian rulers, and was thrown into the lions' den.

The last section of the human figure in Daniel's vision represents the kingdom of the Antichrist, when Satan is unleashed on the world. When this last kingdom is destroyed, all these evil kingdoms led by sinful humans come to an end, and the messianic kingdom becomes a reality.

Many theologians do not believe in a future messianic kingdom revolving around Israel. They understand this vision to represent only four kingdoms, with the last one being the Roman Empire, which was in power when Christ came into the world. Christ defeats Satan at the cross and then sets up his kingdom. Christ's kingdom may have begun during the Roman Empire, but it is obvious that his reign of peace and prosperity has not yet begun.

As I quote Daniel's interpretation of Nebuchadnezzar's dream, I will enumerate the five sinful human kingdoms inspired by Satan. The stone in the vision represents the Messiah. When he destroys the fifth kingdom, all these kingdoms will come to an end and the messianic kingdom will begin. Christ's empire will be a kingdom that will never be destroyed:

> You saw, . . . a great image. . . . The head of this image was of fine gold [one], its chest and arms of silver [two], its middle and thighs of bronze [three], its legs of iron [four], its feet partly of iron and partly of clay [five]. As you looked, a stone was cut out by no human hand, and it struck the image on its feet of iron and clay, and broke them in pieces [during the fifth kingdom]. Then the iron, the clay, the bronze, the silver, and the gold, all together

were broken in pieces, and became like the chaff of the summer threshing floors [all sinful human empires come to an end]; . . . But the stone that struck the image became a great mountain and filled the whole earth [the messianic kingdom]. . . . the God of heaven will set up a kingdom that shall never be destroyed, nor shall the kingdom be left to another people. (Dan. 2:31–44)

These kingdoms can be identified as follows:
- The head of "fine gold" represents the Babylonian Empire.
- The "chest and arms of silver" represent the Medo-Persian Empire.
- The "middle and thighs of bronze" represent the Greek Empire.
- The "legs of iron" represent the Roman Empire.
- And the "feet partly of iron and partly of clay" represent the reign of the Antichrist during the seven-year Tribulation.

When this last kingdom is crushed by the Messiah, the messianic kingdom will begin, which is a kingdom "that shall never be destroyed."

Like many theologians today, the rabbinic teaching in Jesus' day misinterpreted Daniel's vision to represent only four great kingdoms. They believed the "legs of iron" and its "feet of iron and clay," together represented the Roman Empire. As a result, they expected the stone, or the Messiah, to arrive on the scene at any time to crush the fourth-kingdom Roman Empire and set up the messianic kingdom. The Messiah would set up a worldwide empire centered in Israel that would never be invaded or destroyed again.

Consequently, expectations among first-century Jews (including the disciples) for the Messiah to overthrow the Roman Empire and set up his own Jewish-led, worldwide empire were quite enlivened. The Romans were keenly aware of these messianic rumblings, which explains their sensitivity toward any possible insurrection led by a Jewish Messiah.

But, as the Jews discovered, much to their disappointment, Jesus of Nazareth did not overthrow the Roman Empire and set up his messianic kingdom on this earth. Instead, he was crucified by the Romans. Pontius Pilate even mocked this feeble "stone," or powerless Jewish Messiah, when his soldiers placed a purple robe on him and put a crown of thorns on his head. He further mocked him with an inscription on his cross that read "Jesus of Nazareth, the King of the Jews" (John 19:19). A dead Jewish Messiah was hardly a threat to their powerful empire.

Instead of the "legs of iron" being crushed by the supernatural stone, Christ was crushed by the legs of iron. Furthermore, through its efficient war machine, the Roman Empire continued to extend itself throughout the Mediterranean world, reaching as far into Europe as England. Rome's military of iron kept them in power for centuries. The messianic kingdom surely did not begin with the defeat of the Roman Empire. Since Christ left this earth and ascended to his Father in heaven, wars and rumors of war have continued unabated, just as he predicted.

The first-century Jews failed to consider an important detail in Daniel's interpretation of Nebuchadnezzar's dream. The stone does not crush Rome's legs of iron; rather, it crushes the feet of iron and clay that belong to the fifth kingdom. When the fifth part of the image is destroyed by the supernatural stone, the image of satanic warring kingdoms—from head to toe—comes to an end and the Messiah sets up his kingdom:

> As you looked, a stone was cut out by no human hand, and it struck the image on its *feet of iron and clay*, and broke them in pieces. Then the iron, the clay, the bronze, the silver, and the gold, all together were broken in pieces. (Dan. 2:34–35)

Once the "stone" destroys the fifth kingdom, "the God of heaven will set up a kingdom that shall never be destroyed." This corresponds to the teachings of Revelation. The Christ, or the stone, will crush the beasts of Satan at the battle of Armageddon, bind Satan, and rule the world as King of kings and Lord of lords.

The Messiah came into this world during the fourth-kingdom Roman Empire, but he was crushed by the legs of iron. His reign of peace and righteousness over this earth did not begin at that time. Instead, after making atonement for the sins of his people, Christ left this world and ascended to the Ancient of Days in heaven, where he remains today waiting on the Father to determine when his reign will begin.

Inauguration Day

But when does Christ's inauguration as the Lord of this world begin? According to Daniel, the Ancient of Days inaugurates the Messiah's reign immediately after a particular ruler during the fifth kingdom is destroyed. The fifth kingdom is the short reign of the Antichrist over the world. Daniel refers to him as a horn of a fourth beast:

> Then I desired to know the truth about the fourth beast, which was different from all the rest [exceptionally evil], . . . the horn that had eyes and a mouth that spoke great things, and that seemed greater than its companions. As I looked, this horn made war with the saints and prevailed over them [during the Great Tribulation], until the Ancient of Days came, and judgment was given for the saints of the Most High, and the time came when the saints possessed the kingdom [inauguration day]. (Dan. 7:19–22)

Notice that the messianic kingdom begins immediately after the Antichrist's reign of terror comes to an end. Daniel repeats this pattern of the messianic kingdom following the Antichrist's reign several times to stress its importance:

> He shall speak words against the Most High, and shall wear out the saints of the Most High, and shall think to change the times and the law; and they shall be given into his hand for a time, times, and half a time [three and a half years of the Great Tribulation]. But the court shall sit in judgment, and his dominion shall be taken away, to be consumed and destroyed to the end [the Antichrist's fifth kingdom is crushed]. And the kingdom and the dominion and the greatness of the kingdoms under the whole heaven shall be given to the people of the saints of the Most High; his kingdom shall be an everlasting kingdom, and all dominions shall serve and obey him. (Dan. 7:25–27)

According to Daniel's visions, the promised messianic kingdom starts immediately after the reign of the Antichrist comes to an end. This pattern is so prevalent in Daniel's visions that it becomes an axiom, or self-evident truth. This axiom can be outlined as follows:

Michael is removed + Satan is unrestrained + Antichrist is revealed + Great Tribulation is endured + Antichrist is destroyed = the messianic kingdom is inaugurated

This is the same pattern found in Revelation. After Satan's kingdom of the Antichrist is destroyed at the battle of Armageddon, Christ's 1,000-year messianic kingdom begins.

17

The Seventy Weeks in Daniel

Review

In the last chapter, I made the case that Daniel's interpretation of Nebuchadnezzar's dream consists of five unrighteous empires occurring before a supernatural stone crushes the last empire with "feet of iron and clay." When this last empire is destroyed, the messianic kingdom is inaugurated. I discussed Daniel's axiom, which teaches that Christ's actual reign over this world begins immediately after the fifth kingdom of the Antichrist is destroyed and the Great Tribulation comes to an end. This is the same sequence of events found in Revelation.

I also described the central role that the restored temple of Israel plays in the messianic kingdom. The existence of a temple with priestly services during Christ's reign is difficult to reconcile with the teachings of the New Testament. But one really cannot have the messianic kingdom without the restored temple, for the temple is an inseparable feature of numerous Old Testament prophecies.

The Seventy Weeks of Years

Daniel's famous vision of the "seventy weeks" recorded in Daniel 9 provides an excellent outline of the events surrounding the temple that lead up to the restoration of Israel, Jerusalem, and its temple in the messianic kingdom. The vision is somewhat complex and requires a great deal of concentration, so bear with me as I work my way through an analysis of it.

Much ink has been spilled on the interpretation of this vision, with many analyses driven by the interpreter's view of God's endgame. I will offer an interpretation from the perspective of postrestorationalism, which teaches that there will be a literal seven-year Tribulation that is followed by the millennial reign of Christ, when Christ removes Satan and rules the world from his throne in heaven. The second coming occurs on the last day, when Christ ushers in the eternal age to come.

Daniel's visions occurred after the Babylonians had conquered Jerusalem, destroyed the temple, and taken the Jews into exile. Daniel knew from the prophet Jeremiah that God had brought these judgments on Israel because of their sin of idolatry. As a man of God and a man of prayer, Daniel had been praying for the nation to repent and for God to restore Jerusalem and its temple. In response to his prayer, God sent the angel Gabriel to Daniel to give him understanding as to how this restoration would come about. Daniel reported:

> While I was speaking in prayer, the man Gabriel, . . . came to me . . . "Oh Daniel, I have now come out to give you insight and understanding. . . . Seventy weeks are decreed about your people and your holy city." (Dan. 9:21–24)

In the Olivet Discourse, Christ refers to Daniel's vision of the seventy weeks when he discusses the temple's future:

> So when you see the abomination of desolation spoken of by the prophet Daniel, standing in the holy place (let the reader understand) [Daniel's vision]. (Matt. 24:15)

Christ is telling us to read Daniel's vision of the seventy weeks in conjunction with his discourse in order to understand what must take place on this earth before he comes again at the end of the age. In effect, he is preaching a sermon that includes an exposition of Daniel's vision, particularly as it relates to the temple's future desolations. Therefore, it is imperative that we understand the vision of the seventy weeks to properly understand the Olivet Discourse and God's endgame.

The prophet Jeremiah had been with the Jews in Israel before and during the exile. He correctly predicted their exile for unfaithfulness. But he also foretold a day when the Jews would repent, be given new hearts, and return to the promised land during an age of righteousness. Daniel was aware of the following prophecy by Jeremiah:

> There is hope for your future, declares the Lord, and your children shall come back to their own country. . . . Behold, the days are coming, declares the Lord, when I will make a new covenant with the house of Israel . . . For this is the covenant that I will make with the house of Israel after those days [after judgment], . . . I will put my law within them, and I will write it on their hearts. And I will be their God, and they shall be my people. (Jer. 31:17–33)

From this prophecy, Daniel knew that one day the Jews would be given new hearts under a new covenant. They would then be restored to the promised land during the messianic kingdom.

Daniel was also aware of another prophecy by Jeremiah as to how long they would be in exile: "This whole land shall become a ruin and a waste, and these nations [Israel and Judah] shall serve the king of Babylon seventy years" (Jer. 25:11). Daniel most likely linked these two prophecies together. The desolation of Jerusalem and its temple by the Babylonians would last about seventy years, at which time the Jews would be given new hearts under a new covenant, ushering in the messianic kingdom. Daniel began to pray earnestly for this restoration and the rebuilt temple, which he believed would occur after seventy years of captivity.

Much to his disappointment, Gabriel appeared to Daniel in response to his prayer and informed him that it may take seventy years before the Jews return to Jerusalem to begin rebuilding the temple, but it will take much longer than seventy years for Israel to truly repent in preparation for God to fully restore Israel and its temple in the messianic kingdom. In fact, Gabriel informed Daniel that it would take *seventy times seven years* to usher in an age of righteousness for Israel. And there will be even more occasions when Israel is unfaithful and the temple desecrated yet again as punishment for their transgressions.

Introductory Overview

The vision from Gabriel begins with an introductory overview, which culminates with the restoration of Israel and its restored temple in the messianic kingdom. Following the overview is an amplification of this vision. This section includes a sequential breakdown of the seventy weeks. The restoration of Israel and its temple occurs at the end of this period of seventy weeks of years.

A careful analysis of the vision of the seventy weeks reveals that it includes two future desolations of the temple. The first desolation can be linked to the destruction of the temple in AD 70 during the fourth-kingdom Roman Empire, when a large majority of the Jews rejected their Messiah. The second desolation will occur during the Great Tribulation of the fifth kingdom, when the Antichrist enters the temple to be worshiped as God. This is followed by the restoration of Jerusalem and the temple in the messianic kingdom, which completes the vision. Let's begin with the overview:

> Seventy weeks are decreed about your people [Israel, or the Jews] and your holy city [Jerusalem], to finish the transgression, to put an end to sin, and to atone for iniquity, to bring in everlasting righteousness [the messianic kingdom], to seal both vision and prophet, and to anoint a most holy place [restore the temple in an age of righteousness]. (Dan. 9:24)

The phrase "to finish the transgression" means that the Jews in exile are still being disciplined for their unfaithfulness. But there will be additional forms of transgression in the future (such as when they reject their Messiah). The phrase "to atone for iniquity" is most likely a reference to Christ's atoning sacrifice on the cross.

The phrase "to bring in everlasting righteousness" means to bring in a continuous "age of righteousness" during the messianic kingdom. The phrase "to seal both vision and prophet" means that the prophets' predictions of the messianic kingdom will be fulfilled after the seventy weeks are complete. The phrase "to anoint a most holy place" is a reference to the Holy of Holies and the temple that are to be consecrated for religious services during the messianic kingdom.

THE SEVENTY WEEKS IN DANIEL | 293

Daniel knows the prophecies of Isaiah, Jeremiah, Ezekiel, and Micah that reference the restoration of Israel and its temple in the messianic kingdom. Within this grammatical-historical context, there are sound reasons to conclude that the phrase "to anoint a most holy place" refers to the reestablishment of religious services at the restored Ezekiel temple in the messianic kingdom during an age of continuous righteousness after the renewal and restoration of Israel.

In the amplified section that follows this overview, Gabriel lays out a pattern of events that will occur over seventy weeks of years before the restoration is complete and the messianic kingdom is realized on this earth. This is when the Ancient of Days establishes the Son of Man's dominion over this earth.

The concept of weeks can be understood as sabbatical years based on the way Jewish jubilees were computed. One week would be seven years instead of seven days. Seventy weeks would be 70 x 7 = 490 years. After the completion of seventy weeks of years, the Anointed One, or the Messiah, will restore Jerusalem and its temple in an age of righteousness.

In this vision, the word *prince*, which means ruler, is used in two ways. "An anointed one, a prince" refers to the Messiah as the ruler of Israel and the world. The Messiah will initially be cut off after making atonement for our sins, but after the Antichrist is destroyed, he will set up his messianic kingdom. And "the prince who is to come" refers to Satan as the ruler of this world of unbelieving Jews and Gentiles. Satan will incite his people to cause two future desolations of the temple before the Messiah rules the world.

Let's read the vision and then do the math to determine the timeline for the restoration of Israel, Jerusalem, and its temple, when Christ establishes his kingdom on this earth:

> Know therefore and understand that from the going out of the word to restore and build Jerusalem to the coming of an anointed one, a prince [Christ], there shall be seven weeks. Then for sixty-two weeks it shall be built again with squares and moat, but in a troubled time [the temple's rebuilding begins]. And after the sixty-two weeks, an anointed one shall be cut off and shall have nothing [Christ is crucified]. And the people of the prince [Satan] who is to come [in the final week] shall destroy the city and the

sanctuary [Jerusalem and the rebuilt temple]. Its end shall come with a flood, and to the end there shall be war. Desolations are decreed. And he [the Antichrist] shall make a strong covenant with many for one week, and for half of the week he shall put an end to sacrifice and offering [in another temple]. And on the wing of abominations shall come one who makes desolate [during the Great Tribulation], until the decreed end is poured out on the desolator [the Antichrist is destroyed]. (Dan. 9:25–27)

Once the desolator is destroyed, the seventy weeks are complete and the reign of the Messiah over this world begins. The Jews are given new hearts and Jerusalem and its temple are restored during an age of righteous humanity.

Gabriel describes seventy weeks of years (7 + 62 + 1) until the Ancient of Days establishes the Anointed One's messianic kingdom. And we would multiply the particular number of sevens times the number seven to compute the sequence of events until Christ's reign begins.

Let's do the math. The first seven weeks would be 7 x 7 years = 49 years. Many scholars date the call to restore the temple to its full priestly services to the decree of Artaxerxes I in 457 BC, based on Ezra 7:11–16. Daniel was writing in 457 BC. Thus, it would be 49 years after the decree that the temple functions would be restored: 457- 49 = 408 BC, which is historically accurate. Daniel said that "it shall be built again with squares and moat, *but in a troubled time*" (9:25). We know from Ezra and Nehemiah that the returning Jews faced significant opposition when they rebuilt the temple (Ezra 4 and Neh. 4—6).

It is another 62 weeks (62 x 7 = 434 years) until the "anointed one" arrives on the scene (408 BC - 434 = AD 26). This places Christ's arrival around AD 26—or about the time of Christ's public ministry. His coming to this earth was also the time of his rejection and crucifixion, when he is "cut off" after atoning for our sins. This means that his age of everlasting righteousness on this earth was not inaugurated at that time.

After atoning for our sins and being cut off, the Anointed One ascends to the Ancient of Days in the clouds. As Lord-elect, sitting at the right hand of God, he waits until the end of the seventy weeks for the inauguration of his dominion over this earth.

Gabriel tells Daniel that after the Anointed One is cut off, yet another destruction of Jerusalem and its temple like the Babylonian destruction will follow: "And the people of the prince who is to come shall destroy the city and the sanctuary" (9:26). This occurred in AD 70 when the Romans sacked the city and destroyed the temple. As Jesus said, not one stone will be left on another.

Daniel says the following about Satan and his people:

> And after the sixty-two weeks, an anointed one shall be cut off and shall have nothing. And the people of the prince [Satan] who is to come [again in the final week] shall destroy the city and the sanctuary. Its end shall come with a flood. (9:26)

The "prince" is a reference to Satan, who inspired unbelievers (his people) to act against Jerusalem and its temple. In AD 70 the Romans poured into Jerusalem and swiftly destroyed the temple. Satan's "people" include the unbelieving Jewish Zealots whom he inspired to start a revolt against Rome as well as the unbelieving pagan Romans whom he inspired to crush the revolt. Even though Christ had ordained the destruction of the temple, it was Satan's people (unbelieving Jews and pagan Romans) who would "destroy the city and the sanctuary."

During Jeremiah's day, it was Satan who influenced his people, the unbelieving Jews, to rebel against God's covenant and worship idols. And it was Satan's people, the pagan Babylonians, whom he used to destroy Jerusalem and the temple as a God-ordained form of judgment against the unfaithful Jews. And it is Satan "who is to come" in the final week who influences his people in that day.

At this point, we have sixty-nine out of seventy "sevens" accounted for. That leaves only one seven-year period remaining before the restoration of Israel and the inauguration of the Messiah's kingdom of everlasting righteousness on this earth. The "anointed one" has been cut off and has ascended to heaven. In the meantime, over the centuries, Christ has continued to gather repentant sinners into his kingdom. But he is waiting on the Father to determine when the last week will unfold and come to an end so that his reign over this world can begin. Therefore, we do not know how many years go by until the last seven-year period occurs and Christ's inauguration day arrives. Jesus taught the disciples that only the Father knows when the last seven-year period will unfold and the messianic kingdom will be established:

> So when they had come together, they asked him, "Lord, will you at this time restore the kingdom to Israel?" He said to them, "It is not for you to know times or seasons that *the Father has fixed by his own authority*." (Acts 1:6–7)

The Father has the authority to determine the "times and seasons" when this final week will occur. At its conclusion, it leads to Christ's reign and the restoration of Israel.

During this interim period leading up to the Tribulation during the seventieth week, the world will remain Satan's dominion. Unrighteous rulers under his influence will continue to cause wars between nations: "To the end there shall be war." As Jesus said, "For nation will rise against nation, and kingdom against kingdom" (Matt. 24:7). The curse on the earth will remain in place as well, in that further "desolations are decreed." Jesus said, "There will be famines and earthquakes in various places" (Matt. 24:7). Jesus further taught, "All these [wars and natural disasters] are but the beginning of the birth pains" (Matt. 24:8). That is because they are leading up to the full labor of tribulation that will be experienced during the final week.

The Final Week

The final seven-year period starts when the desolator makes "a strong covenant with many for one week, and for half of the week he shall put an end to sacrifice and offering" (9:27). The phrase "a strong covenant with many" means to make a strong agreement between many parties. This is probably a peace agreement that the desolator negotiates between Israel and the many warring countries hostile to Jerusalem.

At some point Israel will build another temple in Jerusalem. I believe this will cause another war in the region, for I cannot imagine the Palestinians or the Muslim nations allowing this to happen peacefully. The Antichrist will then establish a peace treaty between Israel and her enemies that will initially protect Jerusalem and its newly rebuilt temple.

But three and a half years into the treaty, the Antichrist is going to let this accomplishment go to his head. He will become delusional, believing he is the world's savior, and will enter the temple, making himself out to be God. He "puts an end to sacrifice and offering" and demands to be worshiped as God. This desolation of the temple is an abomination to God.

It is then that the Great Tribulation begins, taking place over the final three and a half years: "on the wing of abominations shall come one who makes desolate." This matches what Jesus preached:

> So when you see the abomination of desolation spoken of by the prophet Daniel, standing in the holy place, ... For then there will be great tribulation, such as has not been from the beginning of the world until now, no, and never will be. (Matt. 24:15–21)

Satan causes a powerful delusion to come upon unbelieving Jews and Gentiles; they will believe that the Antichrist is God incarnate. The Antichrist then enters a rebuilt temple claiming he is God and sets up an idol of himself in the temple. This brings another form of desolation to the temple and even greater tribulation upon Israel and the world for the next three and a half years.

The final week comes to an end when the short reign of the Antichrist or the desolator comes to an end: "And on the wing of abominations shall come one who makes desolate, until the decreed end is poured out on the desolator." The "decreed end," according to another vision of Daniel's, is when the desolator is destroyed by fire:

> And as I looked, the beast was killed, and its body destroyed and given over to be burned with fire.... and his dominion shall be taken away, to be consumed and destroyed to the end. (Dan. 7:11, 26)

And according to Revelation, the "decreed end" is the lake of fire: "And the beast was captured, and with it the false prophet ... These two were thrown alive into the lake of fire that burns with sulfur" (19:20). Satan is then bound, and the millennial reign of Christ begins.

The completion of the last seven-year week brings the seventy weeks to a conclusion, which leads to the restoration of Israel and the beginning of the reign of the Messiah. The Anointed One, previously cut off after he atoned for iniquity and ascended to the Ancient of Days, now establishes his kingdom of righteousness on this earth. Christ sits on his throne and governs Israel and the world from the right hand of the Father. The "most holy place" is finally restored and anointed for priestly services.

This follows the same pattern established in prior visions of Daniel, whereby the destruction of the desolator marks the time when the Anointed One begins his reign:

> But the court shall sit in judgment, and his dominion [Satan and the Antichrist's] shall be taken away, to be consumed and destroyed to the end. And the kingdom and the dominion and the greatness of the kingdoms under the whole heaven shall be given to the people of the saints of the Most High. (7:26–27)

Or, after the last of the five satanic empires comes to an end:

> As you looked, a stone was cut out by no human hand, and it struck the image on its feet of iron and clay, and broke them in pieces. . . . the stone that struck the image became a great mountain and filled the whole earth. . . . the God of heaven will set up a kingdom that shall never be destroyed. (2:34–35, 44)

But how are "the saints of the Most High" going to inherit Christ's kingdom if they have already died or are killed by the Antichrist? For the departed saints to participate in his messianic kingdom, they will need to be resurrected. That, of course, is what Ezekiel 37, known as the valley of dry bones, envisions with the resurrection of the Jewish saints to reinhabit the restored nation of Israel. This is also the pattern found in Revelation 20, where John envisions the saints from all nations experiencing the first resurrection in order to inherit the millennial reign of Christ.

With these interpretations in mind, let's revisit this vision of the seventy weeks and see how well it harmonizes with the Olivet Discourse. Daniel prayed for the Jews to be given new hearts and for the restoration of Jerusalem and its temple after seventy years of captivity, only to be told by the angel Gabriel that it will take seventy weeks of years to complete this restoration and usher in the messianic kingdom:

THE SEVENTY WEEKS IN DANIEL | 299

- **Seventy weeks are decreed about your people and your holy city** [before Israel, Jerusalem, and its temple will be truly restored in the messianic kingdom],
- **to finish the transgression, to put an end to sin** [for the punishment of repeatedly breaking their covenant with God],
- **and to atone for iniquity** [through the Messiah's atoning sacrifice],
- **to bring in everlasting righteousness** [the messianic kingdom],
- **to seal both vision and prophet** [to fulfill this vision and all the other messianic prophecies pertaining to Israel, Jerusalem, and its temple],
- **and to anoint a most holy place** [establish the Ezekiel temple in the messianic kingdom]. [*End of overview*]
- **Know therefore and understand that from the going out of the word to restore and build Jerusalem** [as foretold by Jeremiah] **to the coming of an anointed one, a prince** [the Messiah],
- **there shall be seven weeks. Then for sixty-two weeks it shall be built again with squares and moat** [After forty-nine years, Jerusalem and the temple are rebuilt by Nehemiah and Ezra, with priestly functions restored in 408 BC],
- **but in a troubled time** [Nehemiah and Ezra experienced great opposition during the rebuilding of Jerusalem and the temple].
- **And after the sixty-two weeks, an anointed one shall be cut off** [After 434 years in AD 26, the Messiah will come, but he will be rejected and crucified to "atone for iniquity"]
- **and shall have nothing** [He did not rule the world at that time—the world remains Satan's unrighteous regime. He then ascended to heaven: "with the clouds of heaven there came one like a son of man, and he came to the Ancient of Days" (Dan. 7:13). The Son of Man is Lord-elect and sits and waits for the Ancient of Days to determine when his reign begins].
- **And the people** [unbelieving Jews and pagan Romans] **of the prince** [Satan] **who is to come** [in the future desolation of the temple] **shall destroy the city and the sanctuary. Its end shall come with a flood** [Roman troops poured into Jerusalem in AD 70, bringing utter desolation to the city and the temple],

- **and to the end** [of Satan's reign over this world of wicked, warring kingdoms] **there shall be war** ["For nation will rise against nation, and kingdom against kingdom" (Matt. 24:7)].
- **Desolations are decreed** ["There will be famines and earthquakes in various places" (Matt. 24:7)].
- **And he** [the Antichrist] **shall make a strong covenant with many for one week** [a peace agreement between Israel and the many warring countries hostile to Israel],
- **and for half of the week he shall put an end to sacrifice and offering** [After three and a half years, the Antichrist puts an end to temple sacrifice because he enters the temple and declares himself to be God: "So when you see the abomination of desolation spoken of by the prophet Daniel, standing in the holy place" (Matt. 24:15)].
- **And on the wing of abominations shall come one who makes desolate** [the Antichrist] [As Jesus taught, "For then there will be great tribulation, such as has not been from the beginning of the world until now, no, and never will be" (Matt. 24:21)],
- **until the decreed end is poured out on the desolator** [as Daniel taught, "And as I looked, the beast was killed, and its body destroyed and given over to be burned with fire. . . . and his dominion shall be taken away, to be consumed and destroyed to the end (Dan. 7:11, 26).

This completes the seventy weeks and brings us full circle to the events laid out in the overview. The Messiah has made atonement for their sins. The transgressions of the Jewish people have come to an end, and the temple is restored. The Messiah rules the world during an age of righteous humanity. All prophecies and visions pertaining to the messianic kingdom are fulfilled. After the fulfillment of all these prophecies, it is the close of the age, when "the Son of Man comes in his glory" to rapture the saints into the clouds to the Father's heavenly kingdom, where, in the very presence of the Ancient of Days, there will no longer be a temple.

The Two Gospel Accounts of the Olivet Discourse

One of the difficulties theologians have in interpreting Christ's Olivet Discourse on Daniel's vision is that Luke's account is noticeably different from Matthew's account. For example, Luke emphasized the first desolation when the temple is destroyed by the Romans. He never used the phrase "the abomination of desolation" that refers to the seventieth week when the Antichrist enters the temple claiming he is God. In contrast, Matthew emphasized the second desolation by the Antichrist. The Antichrist does not destroy the temple; rather, he desolates the temple by entering the Holy of Holies claiming to be God. He then directs his war against the saints during the Great Tribulation.

Luke's audience was mainly Greco-Roman, whereas Matthew's was a more Jewish one, so they probably had their reasons for emphasizing the different desolations of the temple. Let's first see how Luke referenced the first desolation of Daniel, and then we will look at how Matthew referenced the second desolation that occurs in the seventieth week. Each desolation has its own distinctive characteristics, so it is fairly easy to see which of the two desolations they emphasize.

Let's compare Luke's account to Daniel's.

The first desolation of Daniel:
And after the sixty-two weeks, an anointed one shall be cut off and shall have nothing. And the people of the prince who is to come shall destroy the city and the sanctuary. Its end shall come with a flood. (9:26)

Luke's account of the first desolation:
And they asked him, "Teacher, ... what will be the sign when these things are about to take place [the destruction of the temple]?" And he said, ... "when you see Jerusalem surrounded by armies, then know that its desolation has come near. Then let those who are in Judea flee to the mountains, and let those who are inside the city depart, and let not those who are out in the country enter it, for these are days of vengeance, to fulfill all that is written. ... For there will be great distress upon the earth and wrath against this people [the unbelieving Jews]. They will fall by the edge of the sword and be led captive among all nations, and Jerusalem will be trampled underfoot by the Gentiles, until the times of the Gentiles are fulfilled." (21:7–24)

During the First Jewish-Roman War (AD 66–73), the Roman armies surrounded Jerusalem, and both the city and the temple were destroyed. In the aftermath of this desolation, Luke recorded Christ describing Jerusalem and its temple as being "trampled underfoot by the Gentiles, until the times of the Gentiles are fulfilled." Since AD 70, Jerusalem has truly been trampled on by a succession of invading Gentile nations. Even today, much of East Jerusalem and the temple mount remain occupied by Gentile Palestinians.

Also notice that in Luke's account, the destruction of the temple by the Romans is part of God's vengeance toward the Jews for having rejected their Messiah. This wrath was not directed against the saints:

> For these are days of vengeance, to fulfill all that is written. . . . For there will be great distress upon the earth and wrath against this people [the generation of Jews who rejected Christ]. (21:22–23)

In fact, Luke informed the saints that when they see an army amassing around Jerusalem, they can easily escape the tribulation that will fall on the city by fleeing to the mountains. The Jewish saints of the first century heeded Christ's warning. They fled the region and escaped the tribulation that fell on those who remained in Jerusalem. Unbelieving Jews did not follow Christ's advice; they experienced horrible tribulation during the siege and were either killed by the soldiers or captured and sold as slaves to other regions of the empire. Again, the saints who wisely fled Jerusalem did not experience this tribulation because this wrath was not directed against them.

In contrast, Matthew's account of the Olivet Discourse matches the final week of Daniel's second desolation, which involves the Antichrist. Matthew recorded Christ as making specific reference to the "abomination of desolation spoken of by the prophet Daniel" that occurs in the final week. This tribulation will be directed against the saints. Also notice that Jesus did not warn the saints to be on the lookout for armies surrounding the city to destroy it. Rather, he said to be on the lookout for the time when the desolator appears within the temple "standing in the holy place." The temple itself is not destroyed but is instead used as a place of worship of the false messiah.

Moreover, in Daniel's vision, there is no evidence that the Antichrist brings an army against Jerusalem when he enters the temple claiming to be God. Daniel described this second desolation as occurring during a period of peace after a strong covenant is made between Israel and her enemies. We get the impression that the Antichrist and his false prophets will be accepted by the deceived people. He will simply walk into the temple to desecrate it. The warning to be on the lookout for the Antichrist entering the temple is directed to the saints so they can at least attempt to hide from him.

Let's compare Matthew's account to Daniel's.

The second desolation of Daniel:
And he shall make a strong covenant with many for one week, and for half of the week he shall put an end to sacrifice and offering [when he enters the temple]. And on the wing of abominations shall come one who makes desolate, until the decreed end is poured out on the desolator. (9:27)

Matthew's account of the second desolation:
So when you see the abomination of desolation spoken of by the prophet Daniel, standing in the holy place (let the reader understand), then let those who are in Judea flee to the mountains. . . . For then there will be great tribulation [against the saints], such as has not been from the beginning of the world until now, no, and never will be. (24:15–21)

In Daniel's other description of the Great Tribulation, he taught that, rather than the unbelieving Jews being the object of this persecution, the saints will be targeted by the Antichrist and will be unable to escape this time of trial:

As I looked, this horn [the Antichrist] *made war with the saints and prevailed over them*, . . . He shall speak words against the Most High, and shall wear out the saints of the Most High, . . . and they shall be given into his hand for a time, times, and half a time [three and a half years]. (7:21–25)

In Revelation, John made the same observation:

And the beast [the Antichrist] was given a mouth uttering haughty and blasphemous words, and it was allowed to exercise authority for forty-two months [three and a half years]. . . . it was allowed *to make war on the saints and to conquer them*. . . . If anyone is to be taken captive, to captivity he goes; if anyone is to be slain with the sword, with the sword must he be slain. Here is a call for the endurance and faith of the saints. (13:5–10)

According to Matthew's account, Jesus also warned the saints in Judea to flee to the mountains when this war against the saints unfolds. But he indicated that the saints will not be able to escape this tribulation as easily as they did during the Roman desolation: "For then there will be great tribulation [against the saints], such as has not been from the beginning of the world until now, no, and never will be" (24:21).

The first desolation Luke emphasized is directed against the unbelieving Jews who rejected their Messiah. Jerusalem and the temple will be surrounded by armies, and the temple utterly destroyed, similar to the Babylonian invasion and destruction. The saints can easily escape this persecution by getting out of Jerusalem when they hear of the approaching armies. And the Gentiles will continue to trample on Jerusalem and the temple mount for some time.

The second desolation emphasized by Matthew is when a rebuilt temple is desolated by the Antichrist when he enters the temple claiming to be God. It is not destroyed by an invading army; rather, it is used as a place of worship by the Antichrist. The extreme persecution that follows will be directed against the saints, who will not be able to easily escape this war against them. According to Daniel's vision, immediately after the Antichrist is destroyed and the Tribulation comes to an end, the messianic kingdom will begin. The Son of Man's age of righteous humanity will be established by the Ancient of Days. All nations will experience peace on earth when Israel and Jerusalem are restored and its temple is anointed as the most holy place—never to be desecrated again by any demonic empire.

Many theologians have failed to recognize these obvious distinctions between the two desolations. They assert that there is only one desolation that already occurred in AD 70. Therefore, there is no future Great Tribulation. This is a serious mistake because many Christians under their influence will not be prepared for this period of human history if it occurs in their lifetimes.

Summary

Daniel's vision of the seventy weeks and Christ's discourse on this vision are undoubtedly quite complex and involved. And having a restored temple as described by Ezekiel in the messianic kingdom presents numerous theological problems. But the restored temple is an inseparable feature of numerous Old Testament prophecies, and it plays a central role in God's endgame. The vision of the seventy weeks revolves around Israel and the Jewish temple.

Daniel and Christ envisioned two future desolations of the temple. The first desolation corresponds to the sixty-ninth week of Daniel and occurred in AD 70 during the fourth-kingdom Roman Empire, or the "legs of iron," when the temple was destroyed.

Christ taught that during the first desolation, the destruction of the temple by the Romans will be directed against the unrepentant Jews for their transgression of having rejected their Messiah. The Jewish saints, who have accepted their Messiah, can easily escape this persecution by getting out of Jerusalem when they hear of the approaching armies. After this destruction, the temple mount will be trampled on by the Gentiles for some time. Only the Father knows when the final week will unfold and the reign of Christ will begin.

The second desolation occurs during the fifth kingdom of the "feet of iron and clay" and corresponds to the seventieth week of the seven-year Tribulation. Christ taught that during this desolation, the Antichrist will use the temple as a place of worship. And the Antichrist will go to war against the saints because they will refuse to worship Satan and the false messiah. Christ warned that it will be extremely difficult for the saints to escape this period of great persecution. After the Antichrist is destroyed and the Tribulation comes to an end, the seventy weeks are complete and the messianic kingdom will begin.

In the next chapter, I will examine the meaning of Christ's reference to "this generation" when referring to the Jews in the Olivet Discourse. The generation of his day will see the destruction of the temple in their lifetimes, but there is a future generation that will experience the messianic kingdom.

18

This Generation

Review

In the last chapter, I described Daniel's vision of the seventy weeks as it relates to Christ's Olivet Discourse. I made the case that Daniel's vision covered a wide range of prophetic events on this earth as they relate to Jerusalem and its temple. I demonstrated that Daniel's vision of the seventy weeks and Christ's sermon detailed two separate occasions when the temple will be desolated. The first desolation corresponds to the sixty-ninth week of Daniel and occurred during the fourth-kingdom Roman Empire, or the "legs of iron," in AD 70 when the temple was destroyed. This was a manifestation of God-ordained wrath directed against the unbelieving Jews who rejected their Messiah. This desolation was similar to the destruction of the first temple by the Babylonians and is emphasized in Luke's account of the Olivet Discourse.

The second desolation emphasized in Matthew's account corresponds to the seventieth week of the seven-year Tribulation. This is when the desolator, or the Antichrist, enters a rebuilt temple claiming to be God and suspends all sacrifices. When Christians refuse to worship this false god, the Antichrist will make war against the saints during the Great Tribulation. After three and a half years, the Antichrist is destroyed and his reign of terror comes to an end. The completion of the seventy weeks culminates in Christ exercising his reign over this earth during an age of righteous humanity.

This Generation of Jews

Another often misunderstood section of the Olivet Discourse deals with the reference to "this generation" by Christ:

> From the fig tree learn its lesson: as soon as its branch becomes tender and puts out its leaves, you know that summer is near. So also, when you see all these things, you know that he is near, at the very gates. Truly, I say to you, *this generation will not pass away until all these things take place.* Heaven and earth will pass away, but my words will not pass away. But concerning that day and hour [of his second coming] no one knows, not even the angels of heaven, nor the Son, but the Father only. (Matt. 24:32–36)

Many theologians believe that the reference to all these things occurring in "this generation" is a reference to only the Jews of Christ's generation who witnessed the temple's destruction in AD 70. Therefore, there is only one desolation, and the Great Tribulation has already occurred. These theologians are known as partial preterists.

In one section of his Olivet Discourse, Christ is clearly addressing the Jews of his generation in reference to the temple being destroyed during their lifetime. This is indicated by his lament and pronouncement of judgment on the Jews for their rejection of him:

> Truly, I say to you, all these things will come upon *this generation* [the current generation]. Oh Jerusalem, Jerusalem, the city that kills the prophets . . . See, your house [the temple] is left to you desolate. For I tell you, you will not see me again, until you say, "Blessed is he who comes in the name of the Lord." (Matt. 23:36–39)

The temple was destroyed about forty years later in AD 70, which would have been within the lifetime of the generation of unfaithful Jews who heard Christ's lament and judgment. But as has been demonstrated in previous chapters, Daniel's vision and the Olivet Discourse cover a much broader range of events than merely the destruction of the Second Temple. Daniel's vision of the seventy weeks also includes the second desolation by the Antichrist when he enters another temple, and the ultimate restoration of the Ezekiel temple in the messianic kingdom. The reference to "this generation," therefore, is a reference to both the unfaithful generation in Christ's day *as well as* a future generation of believing Jews who will experience the messianic kingdom.

Notice that in Christ's pronouncement of judgment on the Jews of his generation for their unbelief, Christ includes a future generation of Jews who will repent and believe in him:

> See, your house is left to you desolate [unbelieving Jews of Christ's generation]. For I tell you, you will not see me again, until you say, "Blessed is he who comes in the name of the Lord [a future generation of believing Jews]." (Matt. 23:39)

Indeed, there will be a future generation of Jews who will be "blessed" when they, too, believe in Christ.

Jeremiah

We know that Christ was preaching from the book of Daniel, but there is every reason to believe that he was also preaching from the book of Jeremiah in his extended discourse on the events that will occur on this earth before he comes again. In fact, Christ was probably referring to Jeremiah's understanding of the Jews when he used the phrase "this generation." Jeremiah described two generations of the Jews. The generation of his day was hardhearted and unfaithful to their covenant with God. They refused to listen to him and to the other prophets God sent. Their transgressions would lead to the destruction of its temple and to their exile. But Jeremiah described another future generation of Jews that will be blessed by God. These "offspring" will be given a new heart under a new covenant. As faithful believers, they will prosper in a restored Jerusalem in the messianic kingdom. In the following passage, Jeremiah described these two different kinds of generations of Jews, beginning with the unfaithful Jews of his generation:

> "And it shall come to pass that as I have watched over them to pluck up and break down, to overthrow, destroy, and bring harm [unfaithful generation attacked by the Babylonians and sent into

> exile], ... Behold, the days are coming, declares the Lord, when I will make a new covenant with the house of Israel and the house of Judah [a faithful generation], ... For this is the covenant that I will make with the house of Israel after those days, declares the Lord: I will put my law within them, and I will write it on their hearts. And I will be their God, and they shall be my people. ... For I will forgive their iniquity, and I will remember their sin no more." Thus says the Lord, who gives the sun for light by day and the fixed order of the moon and the stars for light by night, who stirs up the sea so that its waves roar—the Lord of hosts is his name: "If this fixed order departs from before me, declares the Lord, then shall the offspring of Israel cease from being a nation before me forever." ... "Behold, the days are coming, declares the Lord, when the city shall be rebuilt for the Lord [Jerusalem restored in the messianic kingdom]." (Jer. 31:28–38)

Despite God having brought them out of bondage in Egypt into the promised land, the Jews in Jeremiah's day proved to be unfaithful to their covenant with God. As a result, God disciplined them by allowing the Babylonians to sack Jerusalem, destroy their temple, and take them into exile. A similar generation of unfaithful Jews existed in Jesus' day. When they rejected the Messiah that God sent to them, God used the Romans to sack Jerusalem and destroy the Second Temple.

But someday "the offspring of Israel," or another generation of Jews, will have faith and will believe in their Messiah. They will experience a new covenant of forgiveness and righteousness springing from a new heart. In this "new covenant with the house of Israel and the house of Judah," God will forgive their iniquity, forget their past sins, and put his law within their hearts so they can obey his commandments. As a result of this change of heart and spiritual transformation, he will be their God, and they will be his righteous people. This leads to the nation's restoration in the messianic kingdom and an age of righteous humanity "when the city [and its temple] shall be rebuilt for the Lord." These prophecies concerning this future generation of the righteous "offspring of Israel" inheriting the messianic kingdom are as certain to occur as the fixed operation of the sun, moon, and stars of the heavens and of the earth.

Notice the striking similarities between Jeremiah's reference to the certainty of these prophecies and Christ's:

> **Jeremiah said:** "Thus says the Lord, who gives the sun for light by day and the fixed order of the moon and the stars for light by night, . . . 'If this fixed order departs from before me, declares the Lord, then shall the offspring of Israel cease from being a nation before me forever.'" (Jer. 31:35-36)
>
> **Jesus said:** "Truly, I say to you, this generation [of unfaithful and faithful Jews] will not pass away until all these things take place. Heaven and earth will pass away, but my words will not pass away." (Matt. 24:34-35)

Christ assigns the highest degree of certainty to the fulfillment of these prophecies, for he proclaims that all the prophecies related to unfaithful and faithful generations of Israel are as certain to be fulfilled on this earth as the continued existence and operation of the Genesis heavens and earth!

There was a remnant of faithful Jews in Jesus' day but most of that generation of Jews was hardhearted, blind, unregenerate, and unfaithful. This was true despite the many miraculous signs and wonders that Christ performed. He also demonstrated his love, compassion, and forgiveness in numerous ways and revealed to them an extensive knowledge of the truth about God and the Scriptures. Jesus warned them that it will be more bearable for the people of Sodom and Gomorrah on the day of judgment than for the Jews who ignored this overwhelming evidence and refused to believe in him.

Based on the book of Jeremiah, Christ was saying there are two generations of Israel related to Jerusalem, its temple, and the future. The generation of his day, like the one in Jeremiah's day, killed the prophets sent to them and remained unfaithful. As a result of their hardness of heart, that generation of unfaithful Israel would experience the destruction of their temple in their lifetime as foretold by Daniel. This would be for the horrible transgression of having rejected their own Messiah despite clear evidence that he was in their midst. In the meantime, the baton has passed to believing Gentiles who are experiencing the new covenant.

Another generation, their offspring, however, will respond to the gospel and experience the "new covenant" as faithful believers in the Lord when they say, "Blessed is he who comes in the name of the Lord" (Matt. 23:39). They will experience the restoration of Israel, Jerusalem, and its temple in the messianic kingdom. The nation of Israel will continue to play a strategic role in God's endgame as long as this Genesis creation exists.

Isaiah also foresaw a future generation of the offspring of Israel who will be given new hearts, which leads to the restoration:

> "And a Redeemer will come to Zion, to those in Jacob *who turn from transgression*," declares the Lord. "And as for me, this is my covenant with them," says the Lord: "My Spirit that is upon you, and my words that I have put in your mouth, shall not depart out of your mouth, or out of the mouth of your offspring, or out of the mouth of your children's offspring," says the Lord, "from this time forth and forevermore." (Isa. 59:20–21)

Isaiah foresaw a future generation of faithful Jews who will "turn from transgression." They will become believers filled with the Holy Spirit. This will lead to the redemption of Israel and the messianic kingdom.

Paul also wrote that the Jews in his day were an unbelieving generation. But based on his reading of Isaiah, Paul foresaw the day when the "offspring of Israel" will experience the new covenant and be given new hearts and minds:

> For if you [repentant Gentiles] were cut from what is by nature a wild olive tree, and grafted, contrary to nature, into a cultivated olive tree, how much more will these [repentant Jews], the natural branches, be grafted back into their own olive tree. Lest you be wise in your own sight, I do not want you to be unaware of this mystery, brothers: a partial hardening has come upon Israel [unrepentant Jews], until the fullness of the Gentiles has come in. And in this way all Israel will be saved, as it is written [in Isaiah], "The Deliverer will come from Zion, he will banish ungodliness from Jacob; and this will be my covenant with them when I take away their sins [repentant Jews]." (Rom. 11:24–27)

Based on his reading of Isaiah, Paul described two generations of his fellow Jews: the Jews of his day, who were largely unrepentant and hostile to Christ and the gospel, and a future generation of Jews, who will repent and believe in their Messiah. Paul connected this future generation of repentant Jews to the time when Christ will deliver Israel. And, as predicted by Isaiah, they will then experience the messianic kingdom of righteousness. After the fulfillment of all these things pertaining to Israel and this age, the end of the age is at hand and the second coming "is near, at the very gates"—when heaven and earth will disappear and be replaced with the eternal new heavens and new earth.

Summary

Christ taught that there are two generations of Israel related to Jerusalem, its temple, and the future. The generation of his day, like the one in Jeremiah's day, was unregenerate and unrepentant and killed the prophets sent to them. As foretold by Daniel, this unfaithful generation will see another destruction of their temple in their lifetime. Another generation, their offspring, will repent and respond to the gospel. They will experience the "new covenant" and be filled with the Holy Spirit. This generation will be blessed when they experience the restoration of Israel, Jerusalem, and its temple in the messianic kingdom during an age of righteous humanity. These prophecies relative to Israel and their offspring are as certain to occur as the fixed operations of the sun and the moon.

19

The Cosmic Changes in the Heavens

Review

In the last chapter, I made the case that in the Olivet Discourse, Christ's understanding of the words "this generation" was based on his reading of Isaiah, Jeremiah, and Daniel. Christ taught that there are two generations of Israel related to Jerusalem, its temple, and the future. There was the generation of unfaithful Jews of his day, like the Jews in Jeremiah's day, who were unrepentant and killed the prophets sent to them. Those Jews would see a destruction of their temple by the Romans in their lifetimes, similar to the destruction of the first temple by the Babylonians.

But there will be another generation, their offspring, who will repent and respond to the gospel and experience the "new covenant," just as the Gentiles have. This future generation of Jews will have new hearts filled with the Holy Spirit. They will then experience the restoration of Israel, Jerusalem, and its temple in the messianic kingdom.

Paul, like Isaiah, also described two generations of his fellow Jews. The Jews of his day were largely unrepentant and hostile to Christ and the gospel. Yet, Paul foresaw a future generation of repentant Jews who will indeed believe in their Messiah, which ushers in the messianic kingdom.

All these events foretold by the prophets and confirmed by Jesus are as certain to occur on this Genesis earth as the fixed operations of the sun and the moon. These events pertain to this earth and will not go unfulfilled as long as this earth exists.

The Cosmic Realm

The word *heaven* is sometimes used in the Scriptures to describe the Genesis cosmos or the sky and solar system. It is also used to describe God's eternal home and dwelling place. Christ ascended into the sky, but he also ascended into heaven to be with his Father. Satan and the fallen angels are described as the cosmic powers of the demonic world in the heavenly realm. Paul taught:

> Put on the whole armor of God, that you may be able to stand against the schemes of the devil. For we do not wrestle against flesh and blood, but against the rulers, against the authorities, *against the cosmic powers over this present darkness, against the spiritual forces of evil in the heavenly places.* (Eph. 6:11–12)

Major events in the spiritual realm can also be reflected by events in the physical realm. For example, Christ's crucifixion for our sins was a cosmic event in the spiritual realm in that it overcame Satan's power of sin and death over us. This cosmic spiritual event was reflected in the physical realm by an earthquake that shook Jerusalem the moment Christ died on the cross: "And Jesus cried out again with a loud voice and yielded up his spirit. . . . And the earth shook, and the rocks were split" (Matt. 27:50–51).

As he was about to breathe his last breath, the sun was also darkened:

> It was now about the sixth hour, and there was darkness over the whole land until the ninth hour, while the sun's light failed. And the curtain of the temple was torn in two. (Luke 23:44–45)

Christ also taught that he will literally return in the clouds when he comes again to gather his saints, just as he ascended in the clouds when he returned to his Father in the celestial realm of heaven. When he returns, the whole Genesis cosmos will be destroyed and replaced with an entirely new cosmos: "From his presence earth and sky fled away [the Genesis cosmos], and no place was found for them.... Then I saw a new heaven and new earth" (Rev. 20:11—21:1).

In the Olivet Discourse, Christ taught:

> Immediately after the tribulation of those days the sun will be darkened, and the moon will not give its light, and the stars will fall from heaven, and the powers of the heavens will be shaken. Then will appear in heaven the sign of the Son of Man. (Matt. 24:29-30)

The cosmic changes occur immediately after the Great Tribulation—followed by Christ's second coming. Based on their version of God's endgame, there are two ways theologians interpret these verses. Some amillennialists assert that immediately after the Tribulation, Christ comes again at the end of this Genesis creation. He destroys this Genesis cosmos and takes the raptured saints to the Father's eternal kingdom of heaven.

Premillennialists assert that Christ comes again immediately after the Tribulation to set up his 1,000-year messianic kingdom. The cosmic changes in the heavens are figurative in that they reflect the transition from Satan and the demonic host ruling this fallen world to Christ ruling this world. And the shaking of the earth reflects the transition from unrighteous men ruling the world to righteous men ruling the world. The world transitions from being ruled by Satan and his Antichrist to being ruled by Christ. The cosmic changes in the heavens are a metaphorical depiction of this major regime change.

Postrestorationalism agrees with the view that there is a cosmic regime change immediately after the Tribulation when Satan is removed and Christ begins his reign over this world from his throne in heaven. But this view asserts that Christ's second coming occurs *after* the millennium, not immediately after the Tribulation.

So how do we make sense out of these verses? Notice that the very next events that occur immediately after the Tribulation are the cosmic changes that take place when "the powers of the heavens will be shaken." After these cosmic changes take place and Christ rules the world, "*then* will appear in heaven the sign of the Son of Man" on Judgment Day to rapture the saints and take them to heaven. In other words, the second coming occurs *after* this cosmic regime change in who rules this world—not immediately after the Tribulation. Let's read these verses again with this interpretation in mind:

> *Immediately after the tribulation* of those days the sun will be darkened, and the moon will not give its light, and the stars will fall from heaven, and the *powers of the heavens will be shaken* [cosmic changes in the spiritual realm]. *Then* [after these cosmic changes and Christ's reign] will appear in heaven the sign of the Son of Man, and then all the tribes of the earth will mourn, and *they will see the Son of Man coming on the clouds of heaven with power and great glory* [the second coming on the last day]. And he will send out his angels with a loud trumpet call, and they will gather his elect from the four winds, from one end of heaven to the other [the rapture of the saints]. (Matt. 24:29–31)

Therefore, the cosmic changes in the heavens described by Christ reflect the changes in the governance of this world from Satan to Christ when he removes the demonic "forces of evil" and establishes his messianic kingdom. After these cosmic changes take place and Christ has established his kingdom, *then* the second coming occurs.

This can be outlined as follows:
- The Great Tribulation takes place during an unprecedented age of demonic humanity.
- The Tribulation comes to an immediate end when the Antichrist is destroyed and Satan and all his cosmic forces of evil are removed from this world.
- Christ then rules the world with his saints during the millennium, establishing an age of righteous humanity.
- Then, *after* his 1,000-year messianic kingdom, the second coming occurs to gather his elect on Judgment Day.

Cosmic Changes According to the Prophets

These figures of speech related to the cosmic changes in the heavens and on the earth metaphorically describe God's judgment on demonic humanity and the cosmic changes in who rules this world. This is borne out by many Old Testament visions and prophecies. Christ probably expected us to understand his teachings in the light of these prophecies. The prophet Joel, for example, used similar language to describe God's judgment on the world at the end of the Tribulation when he ushers in the messianic kingdom:

The earth quakes before them; the heavens tremble. The sun and the moon are darkened, and the stars withdraw their shining [cosmic changes in the heavens and on the earth]. The Lord utters his voice before his army, for his camp is exceedingly great; he who executes his word is powerful. For the day of the Lord is great and very awesome; who can endure it [the battle of Armageddon]? . . . Then the Lord became jealous for his land and had pity on his people. The Lord answered and said to his people, "Behold, I am sending to you grain, wine, and oil, and you will be satisfied; and I will no more make you a reproach among the nations [the messianic kingdom]." (Joel 2:10–19)

Notice the striking parallels to Christ's teaching:

> **Joel taught**: "The sun and the moon are darkened."
> **Jesus taught**: "The sun will be darkened, and the moon will not give its light."
> **Joel taught**: "The stars withdraw their shining."
> **Jesus taught**: "The stars will fall from heaven."

According to Joel, this is followed by the messianic kingdom, when Israel is restored and experiences an abundant life on this earth—not the end of the world.

Also notice the striking parallels between Joel's prophecy and John's vision of the cosmic battle of Armageddon in Revelation 19:

> **Joel taught**: "The Lord utters his voice *before his army*, for his camp is exceedingly great."
> **John taught**: "Then I saw heaven opened, . . . a white horse! The one sitting on it is called Faithful and True, and in righteousness he judges and makes war. . . . And the *armies of heaven*, . . . were following him on white horses."
> **Joel taught**: "He who executes *his word* is powerful."
> **John taught**: "From *his mouth* comes a sharp sword with which to strike down the nations."

Like Joel, John described *a cosmic battle in heaven* between Christ and Satan or "the powers of the heavens." John also described *a cosmic battle on earth* between Christ and his army of saints against the Antichrist and his human armies on the earth. According to John, the conclusion of *this cosmic battle in heaven and on earth* leads immediately to the 1,000-year messianic kingdom described by Joel.

The prophet Haggai used similar language to describe God's cosmic judgments on this world as the transition to the inauguration of the Messiah's reign over this earth:

> For thus says the Lord of hosts: Yet once more, in a little while, I will shake the heavens and the earth and the sea and the dry land [cosmic changes in the heavens and on the earth]. And I will shake all nations, so that the treasures of all nations shall come in, and I will fill this house with glory, says the Lord of hosts. . . . And in this place I will give peace, declares the Lord of hosts [the messianic kingdom]. (Hag. 2:6–9)

Daniel envisioned this cosmic regime change as well:

> But the court shall sit in judgment, and his dominion shall be taken away [Satan and his Antichrist], to be consumed and destroyed to the end [in the lake of fire]. And the kingdom and the dominion and the greatness of the kingdoms under *the whole heaven* [the cosmic change in dominion] shall be given to the people of the saints of the Most High [during Christ's reign]. (Dan. 7:26–27)

The cosmic changes described by the prophets reflect a cosmic regime change from Satan as the ruler of this dominion of darkness to Christ as the ruler of this world. The world goes from being characterized by strife, war, injustice, and unrighteousness under Satan's dominion to being characterized by peace, justice, and righteousness under Christ's dominion.

One of the most extraordinary prophecies in the Bible that deals with these cosmic forces of evil in the spiritual realm can be found in Isaiah, which describes the cosmic release of Satan and his demonic host during the Great Tribulation. This results in a great deal of evil on the earth. Isaiah alluded to Satan's subsequent imprisonment as described in Revelation. He even alluded to Satan's final release after Christ's millennial reign. With the help of Revelation, one can understand this prophecy:

THE COSMIC CHANGES IN THE HEAVENS | 321

For the windows of heaven are opened [Satan is released], and the foundations of the earth tremble. The earth is utterly broken, the earth is split apart, the earth is violently shaken [cosmic forces of evil on the earth]. The earth staggers like a drunken man; it sways like a hut; its transgression lies heavy upon it [the extreme evil during the Tribulation], and it falls, and will not rise again [the Tribulation comes to an end]. On that day the Lord will punish the host of heaven, in heaven, [Satan and his demons] and the kings of the earth, on the earth [the Antichrist and the kings with their armies that follow him]. They [the demonic host of heaven] will be gathered together as prisoners in a pit; they will be shut up in a prison [Satan and the demons are seized, bound, and thrown into a pit, which is sealed], and after many days [one thousand years] they will be punished [after Satan's final release, he and all demons will be captured and thrown into the lake of fire]. Then [Isaiah returns to describing Christ's reign] the moon will be confounded and the sun ashamed [cosmic regime change], for the Lord of hosts reigns on Mount Zion and in Jerusalem [Christ's reign], and his glory will be before his elders [resurrected saints who sit on thrones as ruling elders]. (Isa. 24:18–23)

Isaiah's prophecy can be outlined as follows:
- "The windows of heaven are opened" when Satan and his cosmic forces of evil are released on the earth.
- "The earth is utterly broken, the earth is split apart, the earth is violently shaken" when extreme transgression occurs during this period of demonic activity.
- The demonic forces of evil are then imprisoned.
- Cosmic changes to the sun and moon reflect the cosmic regime change when "the Lord of hosts reigns" over the earth with his elders.
- After many days (one thousand years), Satan is released for a short time, but then he is eternally punished in the lake of fire.

Isaiah, Joel, Haggai, and Daniel all used similar language as Jesus to describe the cosmic changes in the heavens and on the earth to reflect this incredible regime change. The Antichrist is destroyed, Satan is removed from this world, and Christ establishes his reign as the true King and Lord of this restored Genesis earth. Christ described this change of governance as truly earth-shattering.

When Christ referred to the cosmic changes that take place immediately after the Great Tribulation, he was referring to these prophecies being fulfilled during his reign as the Messiah *before* he comes again on the last day to take his followers to heaven.

Summary

Jesus taught that immediately after the Great Tribulation comes to an end, there will be a cosmic change in rulership over this world from Satan to Christ when the messianic kingdom is realized on the earth. After Christ has established his messianic kingdom, then he comes again on the clouds at the end of the age to literally destroy this Genesis cosmos, gather his elect, and take them to his Father's eternal kingdom of heaven.

20

The Stealthy Restoration

Review

Chapter 19 examined Christ's reference in the Olivet Discourse to the cosmic changes in the heavens that take place immediately after the Great Tribulation. These cosmic changes represent a regime change in the rulership of this world, from Satan to Christ, when the messianic kingdom is realized on the earth. After Christ establishes his messianic kingdom, he will come again to destroy this Genesis cosmos, rapture the saints, judge the world, and usher in the eternal age to come.

The Obscure Kingdom of Christ

Admittedly, this reference to the cosmic changes in the heavens to describe Christ's earthly kingdom is rather obscure. In fact, discerning how and when Christ will establish his kingdom on this earth requires a synthesis of numerous obscure Old Testament prophecies and visions. Christ's Olivet Discourse must also be harmonized with Daniel's complex vision of the seventy weeks and the stealthy book of Revelation.

The word *stealthy* describes something intended to be secretive in order to escape detection or observation. For example, the stealth bomber is a military aircraft designed to deflect radar signals, enabling it to deliver its payload without being detected by the enemy.

Revelation is stealthy by design. God intended it to be difficult to understand for unbelievers. It is an apocalyptic form of literature that God used to reveal the truth about Christ's 1,000-year messianic kingdom to believers while obscuring it from the Roman authorities.

But why would God intentionally make the messianic kingdom difficult for the Roman authorities to comprehend by putting most of the information about it in books such as Daniel and Revelation? Because if the Roman authorities had easily understood these teachings about this earthly kingdom, they would have felt threatened by the contents and predictions of these books that foretold a Jewish-led messianic kingdom. In contrast, a gospel message that emphasized a heavenly kingdom that is not of this world did not pose a geopolitical threat to the Roman Empire.

The Nature of the Messianic Kingdom

It is important to remember that the Old Testament vision of the messianic kingdom involves more than the political entity of the nation of Israel. Daniel and the prophets present a vision of a worldwide empire in which the Messiah uses Israel to rule over all other nations. As Daniel foresaw, the Messiah will rule every nation on this earth: "The greatness of the kingdoms under the whole heaven [all nations] shall be given to the people of the saints of the Most High" (Dan. 7:27). The Jewish Messiah and his ruling elders will rule the whole world as a global empire, with Jerusalem as its capital.

Pagan Rome had expanded its empire to include Israel and many other nations. Whenever they conquered a nation, they would bring the captured king back to Rome through the gates of the city in a triumphal procession through the streets. They would parade both their captives and the loot they had seized. They even built triumphal arches at these gates to commemorate many of these victories. The Arch of Titus was constructed in AD 81 by Emperor Domitian to commemorate the sack of Jerusalem in AD 70. A portion of the relief on the inside of the arch depicts the spoils of Jerusalem and the temple. During the Roman Empire, all roads led to Rome, bringing the wealth of the conquered nations.

In the Jewish vision of the Messiah's empire, all roads will lead to Jerusalem, bringing the wealth of the nations: "Your gates shall be open continually; day and night they shall not be shut, that people may bring to you the wealth of the nations, with their kings led in procession" (Isa. 60:11). In the messianic kingdom, Rome will be subservient to the Jewish empire centered in Jerusalem! In contrast to the stolen wealth brought to Rome, the riches that will be brought to Jerusalem will be graciously offered by nations out of appreciation for an era of peace and prosperity.

The Romans knew enough about the Jewish concept of a messianic kingdom to be hypersensitive to any talk about a Jewish Messiah who would overthrow their empire and set up a Jewish empire in its place. As such, the Romans would have been very hostile to any gospel message that foretold a Jewish Messiah ruling over their nation. That is why the New Testament authors remained focused on a gospel that emphasized the kingdom of heaven.

It also explains the stealthy book of Revelation, which reintroduces the messianic kingdom described by the Jewish prophets and informs us that it will last for a thousand years. But Revelation would be like one enormous parable to the Roman authorities. They could read the book all day long and still be unable to comprehend it. Revelation is difficult for believers to decipher; for unbelievers, understanding it would have been an almost impossible task.

Prophetic books, such as Revelation, provide an effective way for God to deliver his message about Christ's earthly kingdom to his discerning followers, while disguising it from hostile unbelievers. But did God make it a little too stealthy? Theologians today continue to struggle to understand the book and remain divided on its interpretation.

The reason the Roman Empire conquered nations such as Israel was not to spread their pagan religion but to enrich themselves with the resources and tribute from the nations they conquered. Israel was a rather prosperous country and produced an abundance of olive oil and some of the finest wines in the Mediterranean region. Through Roman taxation, Israel also produced a good deal of revenue to fill their treasury. The Romans appointed governors over Israel and stationed military garrisons in the country to maintain this source of goods and revenue.

The Romans wisely allowed, however, some measure of religious liberty in Israel. They did not impose emperor worship or pagan worship on the Jewish people as they did in other pagan nations they conquered. But the Romans were utterly ruthless in their repression of any threat to their empire. And they remained on the lookout for any would-be Messiah who would threaten their empire and its source of great wealth.

During the years of his public ministry, Christ intentionally avoided disputes over Roman taxation and domination. And he carefully navigated the subject of his future reign over this world. He would cleverly refer to his coming kingdom as a cosmic change in the sun, moon, and stars, when "the powers of the heavens will be shaken." Consider his stealthy answer to Pilate when asked about his earthly kingdom:

> So Pilate . . . called Jesus and said to him, "Are you the King of the Jews?" . . . Jesus answered, "*My kingdom is not of this world.* If my kingdom were of this world, my servants would have been fighting, that I might not be delivered over to the Jews. . . ." Then Pilate said to him, "So you are a king?" Jesus answered, "You say that I am a king. For this purpose I was born and for this purpose I have come into the world." . . . [Pilate then] went back outside to the Jews and told them, "I find no guilt in him." (John 18:33–38)

Christ admitted that he was the Messiah, or the King of the Jews. But he said his kingdom is "not of this world," and his servants would not fight for him to establish it. Therefore, Pilate had no reason to fear him. Pilate recognized that Christ was not guilty of leading an insurrection against the Roman Empire and attempting to set up a Jewish-led messianic kingdom in its place. As a result, Pilate found him innocent of these charges and tried to free him. This strange man only talked of a celestial kingdom—one that is not of this world.

But what did Christ mean when he said that his kingdom is "not of this world"? This seems to imply that there is no earthly kingdom. Amillennialists interpret this statement to mean there is no earthly kingdom, only the heavenly kingdom on the last day.

Christ, however, was being clever when he answered that his kingdom is "not of this world." In Pilate's sinful world, unrighteous and greedy rulers enlisted armies of men to fight, murder, and conquer other nations to gain power and glory. Their rulers lorded their power over their subjects, unjustly exploiting them to enrich themselves.

Pilate and his Roman overlords were tyrannical rulers, and many of their subjects were reduced to poverty or slavery so that the powerful could live lives of luxury. But the problems in this world are not simply the result of unjust earthly rulers. Behind these unjust rulers stands Satan, who rules over this dominion of darkness. The ungodly rulers are *his* people.

Christ teaches that the world needs a cosmic regime change *in heaven and on earth* before it becomes his righteous world. When this occurs, Christ's earthly kingdom will be a very different kind of kingdom from that of Pilate's world. Christ will truly lead an insurrection against Satan and the demonic host in this world. As the true King of this world, he will overthrow Satan and banish him from this earth for a thousand years. His angelic servants will then fight and destroy the Antichrist and the evil rulers of this world at the battle of Armageddon. He will then rule this world from his throne in heaven, using the saints whom he will resurrect to rule with him. All the rulers under his authority will be true servants to those they govern, according to the example their master set. His earthly kingdom will be one of peace, justice, righteousness, and abundant prosperity for all mankind. As Jesus said, his messianic kingdom *will not be* of this fallen, satanic world that is characterized by greed, unjust invasions, and exploitation. When his earthly kingdom comes to an end, he will return to take his people to his Father's eternal kingdom in heaven—which is also not of this world!

Christ was a skillful master of words. While affirming in his answer to Pilate that he was indeed the Messiah, he also refuted his accusers and spoke the truth about his future kingdoms—the one on this earth and the one in heaven—neither of which is of "this world." Sadly, Pilate was so lost in demonic lies and deceptions that he doubted if truth even existed.

Paul's Gospel

The apostle Paul was also very careful in his approach to Christ's earthly kingdom. It is important to remember that he was a Jewish missionary sent by God primarily to the Gentiles throughout the Roman Empire. He understood their world well, having been born, raised, and educated in the Roman city of Tarsus. Paul knew that the Romans were familiar with the messianic prophecies and that he would be operating in a hostile environment. He knew that the Roman authorities would be deeply concerned about any Jewish evangelist traveling throughout their empire preaching that a Jew from Nazareth was the long-promised Messiah. Preaching such a message could be very dangerous.

Therefore, during the formative years of the church, Paul seems to have intentionally avoided the subject of Christ's earthly kingdom. Paul preached and wrote that Jesus of Nazareth was indeed the Jewish Messiah, but that he had come to liberate his people from Satan's dominion of darkness. Roman citizens who responded to his gospel were rescued from Satan's dominion and became citizens of heaven. They were to wait for Christ to return from heaven, resurrect them, and take them to the eternal kingdom of heaven. Paul's gospel message was truly heaven-centric:

> But our citizenship is in heaven. And we eagerly await a Savior from there, the Lord Jesus Christ, who, by the power that enables him to bring everything under his control, will transform our lowly bodies so that they will be like his glorious body. (Phil. 3:20–21 NIV)

Paul's message centered on the saints being resurrected so they could inherit the kingdom of heaven—not his earthly kingdom or empire. The Romans, however, did not believe in a resurrection of the body. They viewed it as a resuscitation of a corpse, a notion which they found repugnant. Upon investigating Paul's teachings, the Roman authorities would have considered the idea of a citizenship in heaven obtained through a resurrection bizarre, even nonsensical. As such, they considered his gospel message essentially harmless and not a real geopolitical threat to their great empire.

Most important, the Roman authorities could not accuse Paul of promoting an insurrection because he never emphasized the fact that Jesus Christ would someday establish a worldwide kingdom on this earth. Besides, from their perspective, Paul's Jewish Messiah was dead because they had crucified him. How could a dead Jew from Nazareth overthrow the Roman Empire and become the ruler of the world?

THE STEALTHY RESTORATION | 329

The Romans were not overly concerned about Jews or Gentiles in their kingdom following a dead Jew who claimed to be the Messiah. They were, however, very concerned about other living Jews who kept popping up claiming to be the Messiah and leading revolts against Roman dominance. This is exactly what happened in the First Jewish-Roman War (AD 66–73) when certain Jewish leaders arose claiming to be the Messiah who would liberate Israel from Rome. The Romans sent three legions to surround Jerusalem and put down this rebellion. And they ruthlessly sacked Jerusalem and destroyed the temple. Another insurrection occurred during the Second Jewish-Roman War (AD 132–135). The Romans crushed the Jewish insurrectionists and killed the so-called messiahs. The Romans grew weary of these insurrections, and they dissolved the nation of Israel.

As a Jewish evangelist within the Roman Empire, Paul knew he was operating in hostile territory and had to be very careful in his description of Christ's kingdom. He would preach that Jesus of Nazareth was the Messiah according to the Jewish prophets, but he avoided a discussion of his earthly kingdom. Instead, he remained focused on his eternal kingdom in heaven with the Father.

Even though Paul avoided the subject of Christ's earthly kingdom, the Jews who were hostile to his gospel message knew that if they could distort his teachings to include a message of insurrection, the Roman authorities would have him arrested. This occurred in Thessalonica when Paul first began preaching that Jesus of Nazareth was the Messiah.

> They came to Thessalonica, where there was a synagogue of the Jews. And Paul went in, . . . saying, "This Jesus, whom I proclaim to you, is the Christ." And some of them were persuaded and . . . a great many of the devout Greeks . . . But the Jews were jealous, . . . [and they brought some of Paul's recent converts before the Roman authorities and said] "They are all acting against the decrees of Caesar, saying that there is another king, Jesus." And the people and the city authorities were disturbed when they heard these things. (Acts 17:1–8)

The Roman authorities were understandably disturbed by this false portrayal of Paul's message. This episode in Thessalonica reveals what Paul was up against as he traveled throughout the Roman Empire preaching that Jesus of Nazareth was the Jewish Messiah. What if Paul's sermons and writings had included a clear message about the future messianic kingdom on this earth when Christ would rule this world through Israel? Imagine how the Roman authorities would have reacted to Paul had he entered a Roman city and preached from the following messianic psalm:

> May he have dominion from sea to sea, and from the River to the ends of the earth! May desert tribes bow down before him, and his enemies lick the dust! May the kings of Tarshish and of the coastlines render him tribute; may the kings of Sheba and Seba bring gifts! May all kings fall down before him, all nations serve him! (Ps. 72:8–11)

The Roman authorities would not have embraced the idea that they would one day be ruled by a Jewish king who would require them to serve him, bow down to him, "lick the dust" under his feet, or "render him tribute" in order to enrich Jerusalem instead of Rome. The Old Testament contains numerous messianic prophecies of this nature.

Therefore, for strategic reasons, Paul wisely avoided preaching on Christ's earthly kingdom. Instead, his gospel message focused on repentance and regeneration, being rescued from Satan's dominion of darkness, living a life of faith, escaping God's wrath on Judgment Day, looking forward to Christ's return and the resurrection of an eternal body, and entering the eternal kingdom of heaven.

In his letters to the Thessalonians, Paul described many eschatological events such as the coming Tribulation, the second coming, Judgment Day, and the kingdom of heaven. He made no mention, however, of the earthly kingdom of Christ. Paul's objective was to bring as many Gentiles as possible into the kingdom of heaven. He may have figured that if he could get the pagan Gentiles to believe in Christ and make it to heaven, the messianic kingdom would come with the territory—whether they knew about it or not.

Because Paul's gospel focused on the heavenly kingdom, the early church was not persecuted for instigating a Jewish insurrection. The apostles admonished the young converts to become respectable citizens, pay their taxes, and to obey Roman law whenever possible.

It is important to remember that Rome was not a secular state with religious liberty; it was a state with an established pagan religion with laws intended to enforce the worship of their emperors and their pagan gods. As a result, Christianity was considered unpatriotic, even if it did not advocate a competing earthly kingdom. The Romans believed the Gentile Christians were being disloyal to their country.

The Roman authorities often unjustly persecuted the Gentile Christians for refusing to worship the emperor and abandoning pagan idol worship. This was unavoidable, but the early church surely did not need the added persecution that would have come had they advocated the overthrow of Rome for a coming messianic kingdom.

As an Old Testament scholar, Paul probably knew much more about the future reign of Christ than he revealed. Paul's one direct reference to the restoration of Israel is in Romans 11, which seems intentionally obscure. He taught that after the Jews finally repent and are grafted back in as believers in their own Messiah, then "the Deliverer will come from Zion, he will banish ungodliness from Jacob; and this will be my covenant with them when I take away their sins" (Rom. 11:26–27).

Paul was quoting from a section of Isaiah (59:20–21) that is surrounded by a description of the messianic kingdom. But after the Deliverer forgives their sins, how will he deliver Israel and establish his kingdom? Paul does not answer this question. He leaves it to the reader to search Isaiah and figure out how Christ will deliver Israel and set up his messianic kingdom. Paul's unique mission to the Gentiles required him to avoid any clear presentation of Christ's earthy kingdom. Therefore, if one wants to learn about Christ's reign over this earth, Paul's letters are not the best resource.

Some theologians believe the book of Acts was written by Luke specifically to prove that Paul and the followers of Christ were not advocating the overthrow of the Roman Empire:

> We think of Acts as the great missionary book of the Bible. . . . But in addition to being a narrative of great missionary advance, Acts was written as a legal defense. Luke was at pains to demonstrate to most excellent Theophilus (likely a Roman official or a member of the societal elite) that Christianity was not hellbent

on overthrowing Roman rule and was not in violation of the religious provisions of Roman law.[12]

The Messianic Kingdom in the Gospels

Even the Gospels avoid the subject of Christ's earthly kingdom. They include only a limited number of Jesus' teachings that refer to his reign over this world. The best example can be found in Matthew 19. Christ has a conversation with a rich man and a follow-up conversation with his disciples, who were willing to sacrifice everything to follow him. Christ taught that one day he will indeed sit on his throne in heaven, restore this Genesis creation to its Edenic condition, and install his disciples on twelve thrones to assist him in ruling over the twelve tribes of Israel. Jesus promised the disciples that during his reign they will receive a hundredfold reward in this Genesis age *before* they inherit eternal life in the age to come.

But there are only a few references of this kind to his earthly kingdom in the Gospels. And they are not easily understood without a good understanding of the stealthy book of Revelation. The emphasis in the New Testament is clearly on the eternal kingdom of heaven, which posed no real threat to the Romans. The apostles who wrote the Gospels knew that the church had to first be established in the hostile Roman Empire that dominated their world at the time. Christ sent his apostles on a missionary journey with the following advice:

> Behold, I am sending you out as sheep in the midst of wolves, so be wise as serpents and innocent as doves. . . . And you will be dragged before governors and kings for my sake, to bear witness before them and the Gentiles. (Matt. 10:16–18)

As the disciples spread the message that Jesus was the Jewish Messiah, they wisely avoided a clear presentation of Christ's earthly kingdom so that the Roman wolves would not devour them. And although they were innocent of advocating a Jewish insurrection against Rome, Jesus

---

12 Kevin DeYoung, "Is It Wrong for Christians to Defend Their Rights?," *The Gospel Coalition* (blog), October 24, 2014, https://blogs.thegospelcoalition.org/kevindeyoung/2014/10/24/is-it-wrong-for-christians-to-defend-their-rights/.

told them they should still anticipate being brought before the Roman authorities for questioning as to the nature of Christ's kingdom.

Emperor Domitian's Interrogation

One can get a sense of the apprehension of the Roman authorities toward a Jewish messianic kingdom from an incident recorded by the church historian Eusebius, who lived from AD 263 to 339. The Christian grandchildren of Jude, the brother of Christ, were brought before Emperor Domitian, who reigned from AD 81 to 96. The emperor interrogated them about their beliefs regarding the earthly reign of Christ:

> They were brought to the Emperor Domitian by the Evocatus [a re-enlisted veteran soldier]. For Domitian feared the coming of Christ as Herod also had feared it. And he asked them if they were descendants of David, and they confessed that they were. . . . And when they were asked concerning Christ and his kingdom, of what sort it was and where and when it was to appear, they answered that it was not a temporal nor an earthly kingdom, but a heavenly and angelic one, which would appear at the end of the world, when he should come in glory to judge the quick and the dead, and to give unto every one according to his works. Upon hearing this, Domitian did not pass judgment against them, but, despising them as of no account, he let them go, and by a decree put a stop to the persecution of the Church.[13]

This interrogation is very revealing. Concerning the nature of Christ's kingdom, the emperor asked:
- Is it an earthly kingdom? "And when they were asked concerning Christ and his kingdom, of what sort it was"
- Would it start in Jerusalem? "And where it was to appear"
- Would it occur during his reign? "And when it was to appear"

---

13   Eusebius, *Church History*, III.20.1–7. (Note: All quotes of early church fathers from A. Roberts, J. Donaldson, and A. C. Coxe, eds., 1997.)

These are important questions that pertain to the what, where, and when of Christ's kingdom.

Jude's grandchildren wisely answered, "It was not a temporal nor an earthly kingdom, but a heavenly and angelic one." It would appear "at the end of the world" when Christ comes in glory on Judgment Day "to judge the quick and the dead." Their answers correspond to the gospel message of Paul and the apostles, which emphasized Christ's second coming on Judgment Day, when all mankind will be resurrected from the dead. The saints will inherit eternal life in a heavenly kingdom, while unbelievers will be sent to the lake of fire. The grandchildren's gospel message informed the emperor that he should stop worrying about threats to his temporal worldly empire and start worrying about Judgment Day and eternity!

Yet, Emperor Domitian considered their other-world beliefs "as of no account" and essentially harmless. As a result, he simply let them go because they did not present a geopolitical threat to his empire. He even issued an order to put a stop to the persecution of the church. Conversely, had Jude's grandchildren articulated a clear message about the earthly kingdom of Christ, the persecution of the church would have intensified. And the growth of the church would have been severely stunted at this critical stage.

This interrogation probably occurred before the book of Revelation was written in AD 90, so Jude's grandchildren likely had no knowledge of the millennial reign of Christ described by John. Without this information to draw from, they might not have had a full understanding of the future 1,000-year messianic kingdom. Or, if they did believe in an earthly kingdom, maybe they wisely chose not to say anything about it at that time.

This interrogation by the Roman emperor, however, clearly reveals why God may have kept the truth about the earthly kingdom of Christ cleverly hidden in stealthy books like Revelation during the embryonic stages of the early church. The gospel revealing Jesus as the Jewish Messiah had to be spread throughout the Roman Empire initially by Jewish missionaries, like Peter and Paul. The nation of Israel, which rejected Jesus as their Messiah, was still looking for a Messiah to liberate them from Roman domination. Therefore, the Romans were understandably hypersensitive to any talk of a messiah who might overthrow their empire and set up a Jewish-led empire in its place. As such, the Jewish apostles wisely avoided the subject of Christ's earthly kingdom and focused their gospel message on the Father's kingdom of heaven.

Materialism

Another reason Christ may have downplayed his earthly kingdom was because of mankind's tendency to be worldly and materialistic. The Old Testament prophets described the restoration as an earthly paradise with incredible abundance and material prosperity. Had Christ emphasized this prosperity, many people would have been drawn to him for the wrong reasons. The situation that Christ faced after he had made bread and fish for the five thousand serves as a good example of this tendency. John recorded the crowd's reaction to Christ's miracle:

> When the people saw the sign that he had done, they said, "This is indeed the Prophet who is to come into the world!" Perceiving then that they were about to come and take him by force to make him king, Jesus withdrew again to the mountains by himself. (John 6:14–15)

The crowd wanted to force Christ to establish his earthly kingdom at that time, for they believed he would continue to miraculously provide them with an abundance of food—like manna from heaven—and they would never have to work the ground again. Sadly, they looked to Christ to provide only material things to sustain the physical body. They were searching for life in the pleasures of this world—not in Christ himself, who is the source of true spiritual life. Christ told them to get their priorities in order and to stop focusing on the material blessings of the kingdom. They should not labor in vain for the food that perishes but for the food that endures to eternal life. He taught them that the Spirit, not the flesh, offers true life. Christ wanted them to be drawn to a restored relationship with God—who is the source of spiritual life. And he wanted them to be drawn to God's eternal home in heaven, where they will experience this life with God for eternity. But as the reaction to the feeding of the five thousand reveals, humans tend to set their hearts on the worldly aspects of the messianic kingdom and ignore the most important thing missing in our lives—spiritual life derived from a restored relationship with our Creator. Humans miss the garden of Eden but not its Creator.

Admittedly, Christ's earthly reign is a somewhat vague biblical teaching. Premillennialists sometimes act as if Christ's millennial reign is so obvious that it practically jumps off the pages of Scripture. But it really isn't that obvious. To understand God's endgame, we have to work our way through numerous obscure passages in the New Testament and synthesize them with the Old Testament vision of the messianic kingdom.

Amillennialists, on the other hand, interpret this lack of clear reference to Christ's earthly kingdom in the New Testament to mean that there is no millennial reign of Christ on this earth before the eternal kingdom. But that is a serious mistake. They are failing to take into consideration God's strategic reasons for keeping Christ's earthly kingdom hidden from the pagan Roman authorities, who would have felt threatened by a gospel that included a clear description of Christ's messianic kingdom.

Summary

Christ intentionally downplayed his earthly kingdom and remained focused on the Father's future eternal kingdom of heaven. The most definitive statement about Christ's reign over this earth occurs in the apocalyptic book of Revelation, which speaks volumes about God's intention to make it difficult to discern and to keep it hidden from those hostile to the church.

And Paul, like Jesus, focused on our rescue from the tyranny of Satan's dominion of darkness—not a rescue from the tyranny of the Roman Empire. Paul must have realized that had he articulated a clear vision of a Jewish Messiah who would someday rule the world with all nations subservient to this Jewish King, there would have been a severe backlash against him and the young Christian church. This would have stunted the growth of the church at this critical stage of its development.

But God did not leave later generations in the dark. Without alarming the Roman authorities of a competing world empire, the stealthy book of Revelation conveys the truth to discerning believers about Christ's future millennial reign. Through the book of Revelation,

God gives us a window into the Old Testament, which contains an extensive description of Christ's earthly kingdom.

The subject of Christ's earthly kingdom was reserved for a later day, after the church was more firmly established. This is exactly what happened during the next few hundred years of the church, as Christianity made significant inroads into all strata of Roman society. The early church fathers began putting the pieces of the puzzle together. They began to link the millennium described in Revelation to the teachings of Isaiah and the prophets that describe Christ's earthly kingdom. As a result, many important church fathers began to articulate a literal millennial reign of Christ before the eternal kingdom of heaven.

21

The Early Church Millennialists

Review

In the last chapter, I made the case that the 1,000-year messianic kingdom has a stealthy quality about it. This is because much of the information about Christ's earthly kingdom is found in obscure and complex books of the Bible, such as Daniel and Revelation.

The messianic kingdom described by the prophets will be an earthly kingdom with all nations subservient to the Jewish Messiah. The Romans were understandably hypersensitive to any talk of a Jewish Messiah. Any proclamation of this coming kingdom by Jewish missionaries like Paul would have surely caused the Roman authorities to react violently against them and against those who followed their teachings. These were dangerous times to be speaking and writing about an earthly messianic kingdom in which Christ would rule the world as King of kings and Lord of lords. Therefore, the apostles wisely focused on the eternal kingdom of heaven, which did not pose a geopolitical threat to the Romans.

If Roman authorities had obtained a copy of the book of Revelation, they probably would have read a small portion and thrown the book down in exasperation, unable to comprehend it! But in the book of Revelation, God provides his saints a window into the Old Testament, which contains an extensive description of the messianic kingdom on this earth.

The Early Church Fathers

The apostles' strategy of avoiding the subject of Christ's earthly kingdom and emphasizing the heavenly kingdom paid off. Despite periodic episodes of severe persecution, the church grew rapidly, extending into all socioeconomic levels of Roman society. The church leadership also shifted to Gentile believers, who were in a much better position to read the book of Revelation and openly discuss the existence of a future messianic kingdom. These Gentile Christians were not Jewish missionaries and were loyal Roman citizens. Most of the early church fathers were writing after the Second Jewish-Roman War when Israel was dissolved as a nation. The Romans would be hard-pressed to accuse these Gentile leaders of leading a Jewish insurrection, since the nation of Israel no longer existed.

These Gentile Christian leaders began to decipher the book of Revelation and to connect it to other scriptures. They linked Christ's reference to a hundredfold reward in this age, when he sits on his throne and rules the world, to the millennial reign of Christ described by John. They linked Christ's reference to the disciples sitting on twelve thrones, judging Israel during Christ's reign, to the thrones that will rule the nations in the millennium. As a result, a significant number of well-respected early church fathers became millennialists.

Scholars use the First Council of Nicaea in AD 325 in dating the church fathers. The church fathers who lived before the First Council of Nicaea are referred to as ante-Nicene fathers. Those who lived after the First Council of Nicaea are referred to as post-Nicene fathers. Irenaeus (AD 120–202) is an ante-Nicene father, for he lived before AD 325, whereas Augustine (AD 354–430) is a post-Nicene father. In my opinion, when it comes to the correct interpretation of the millennium, the teachings of the ante-Nicene millennialists are more important than those of Augustine because they lived closer to the time of the apostles and had access to their oral testimonies.

Papias (c. AD 60–130)

The early church historians indicate that those closest to John developed a robust form of millennialism. Papias is an early church father who was one of John's disciples. Papias was so intrigued by John's description of Christ's millennial reign that he wrote a book on the subject. Papias gathered material from John's oral testimony and other knowledgeable sources for his book. This is like the way Luke gathered oral testimonies from those who knew Christ to write his gospel. Papias's book had a profound impact on other church fathers, such as Irenaeus, who lived not long after him. Unfortunately, Papias's book was lost in antiquity, and we only have fragments of his writings. But we do have written testimonies about his book by other church fathers.

Historian Brian E. Daley describes Papias's endeavor to write about the millennium in the book *The Hope of the Early Church*:

> Papias, bishop of Hierapolis in Phrygia in the early second century, apparently also had had close contact with the community in which the Johannine writings were produced. He is known to have collected material about Jesus and his disciples from oral sources, and to have arranged it in five books entitled Explanations of the Words of the Lord. According to Irenaeus (AH 5.33.3-4), book 4 of Papias' collection contained, among teachings attributed to Jesus, a vivid description of a coming millennial kingdom, in which the fruitfulness of the earth will be increased to staggering proportions for the sake of the risen saints. Papias' authority became the basis of Irenaeus' own millennial expectations at the end of the second century.[14]

The apostle John had spent several years listening to Christ's teachings. Like an investigative journalist, Papias probably peppered John with questions regarding the millennium. He could ask John about other things that Christ had taught him about the future millennial kingdom when the risen saints will experience the incredible "fruitfulness of the earth." Revelation only contains one short paragraph describing the millennium, but with his access to the oral history of Jesus' teachings from the apostle John, Papias was able write an entire book vividly describing the millennium. This indicates that the twelve apostles were exposed to much more information about the earthly kingdom of Christ than what is revealed in the Gospels. But for the

---

14 Brian E. Daley, *The Hope of the Early Church* (Peabody, MA: Hendrickson Publishers, 2003), 18.

reasons noted in the previous chapter, the Holy Spirit probably had the Gospel writers downplay Christ's earthly kingdom and remain focused on the eternal heavenly kingdom.

We read modern commentaries on the book of Revelation by biblical scholars who inform us what *they think* John meant by the "first resurrection." But Papias could ask John in person about his opinion of the nature of this resurrection. It is a fair assumption, therefore, that Papias's views on these subjects would be close to what John believed. His direct access to the apostle John gives Papias's teachings great credibility when he expounds on the meaning of the millennium. We should pay close attention to how Papias and these early millennialists understood Christ's millennial reign.

Scholars cannot agree on what percentage of the ante-Nicene fathers were millennialists. But they do agree that a significant and highly respected number of them did believe in a literal millennium. And we have a sufficient collection of their writings to be able to understand their views on the subject.

Early Millennialism versus Modern Premillennialism

Because of the inherent credibility of the teachings of the ante-Nicene millennialists, premillennialists often lend support to their eschatology by referencing what they taught. Modern premillennialists believe Christ physically returns to the earth at the beginning of the millennium to establish his 1,000-year messianic kingdom. They also believe the first resurrection at the beginning of the millennium represents the saints in their raptured eternal bodies that are no longer given in marriage. Only human survivors of the Tribulation remain in their natural bodies and continue to experience marriage and reproduction. The raptured saints in their glorified bodies comingle with natural human beings during the millennium.

Like modern premillennialists, these early millennialists believed that Christ physically returns to this earth at the beginning of the millennium to establish his kingdom. Regarding the first resurrection at the beginning of the millennium, however, they did *not* believe it would be of raptured, glorified bodies. Rather, they believed the first resurrection in conjunction with Christ's return would be of natural bodies, which would experience marriage and procreation. The early millennialists placed the rapture *after* the millennium at the final resurrection, when the glorified saints inherit the Father's eternal new heavens and new earth.

The early millennialists' view of the two resurrections can be outlined as follows:

- The **first resurrection** will be of the natural bodies of the departed saints to inherit the restored natural earth during Christ's reign.
- The **final resurrection** after the millennium will be of the raptured or eternal bodies of the saints to inherit the Father's eternal new heavens and new earth.

We will be resurrected into natural bodies for a restored natural earth and into eternal bodies for an eternal new earth.

When I first formulated the view of postrestorationalism, I extensively researched the millennial views of the early church fathers. I was very encouraged when I discovered that they had the same understanding of the nature of the two resurrections as I do. The only real difference between their view of God's endgame and the one presented in this book is that I believe the Scriptures teach that Christ rules the world during the millennium from his throne in heaven, where he already has all the authority and power necessary to establish his earthly kingdom. His second coming *and* the rapture would be after the millennium at the end of the world, when he takes the raptured saints to his Father's heavenly kingdom. Christ, as the all-powerful Son of God, through whom and for whom this Genesis creation was made, does not need to physically return to this earth to rule over his own creation.

As I read their writings, I noticed that when they assume Christ's second coming is at the beginning of the millennium, they do not reference any oral history from the apostles to support this claim. Nor do they offer any biblical justification for this teaching. On the other hand, when they teach about the nature of the two resurrections, they do support these teachings with oral history as well as the Scriptures.

The early millennialists made one critical mistake. They placed the second coming at the beginning of the millennium instead of on the last day. Other than the misplaced second coming, I discovered that postrestorationalism is remarkably like the historical teachings of these early millennialists. I am convinced that if they had not made this mistake, this view of God's endgame would have been the orthodox teaching for the last two thousand years and we never would have heard of premillennialism or amillennialism.

The following charts compare these three views.

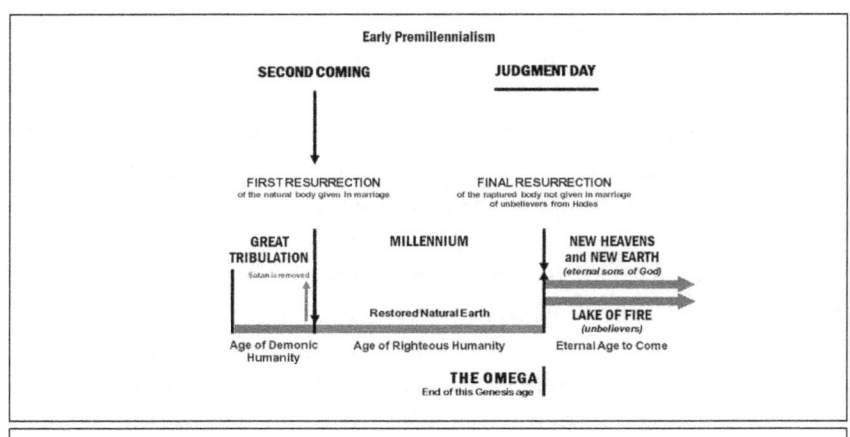

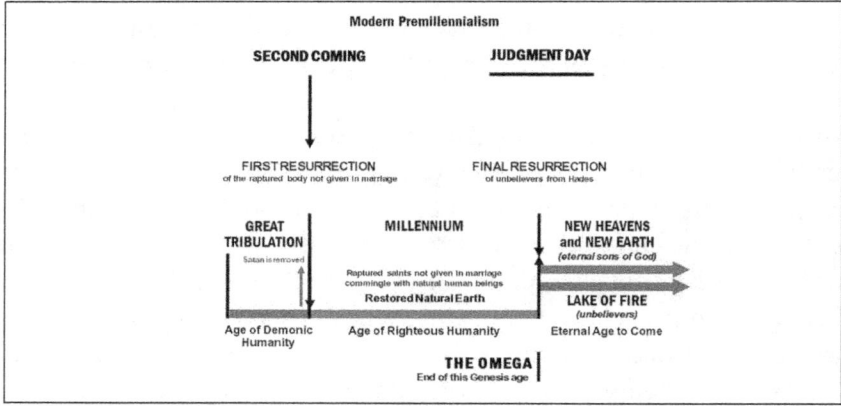

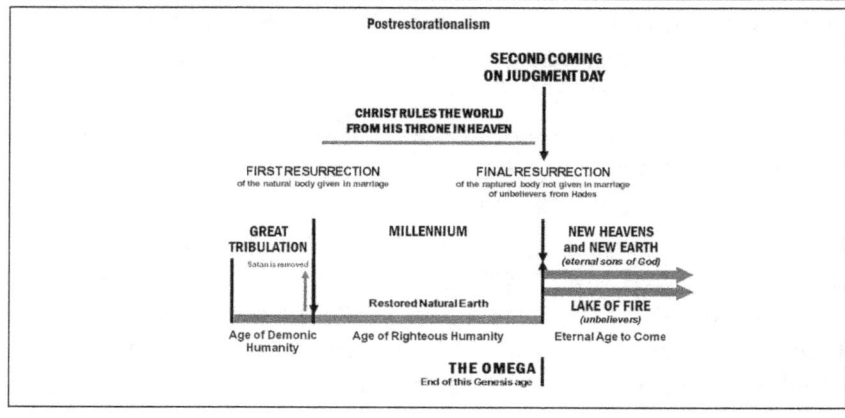

Some theologians have accused me of introducing a new doctrine on eschatology. Theologians are usually apprehensive of new doctrines because they are often harbingers of a new heresy. The historical teachings of the church are given great weight. My view of God's endgame, however, is not really new. It is a revival of the millennialism of the early church. It is a rediscovered and slightly modified version of their teachings. In fact, as this chapter will demonstrate, postrestorationalism is closer to the views of the early millennialists than any modern form of premillennialism, which gives this view of God's endgame great historic credibility.

The Two Resurrections

The key to understanding the eschatology of the early millennialists is understanding their view of the nature of the first and final resurrections, so let's look at their teachings relative to the nature of these two resurrections. The Scriptures define two kinds of resurrected bodies—the natural body, which experiences marriage, and the immortal body, which does not experience marriage. Lazarus was resurrected into his natural body, whereas Jesus was resurrected into his immortal body.

There are two ways to determine how the early millennialists understood the first and final resurrections:
1. Study which Scriptures they link to these two resurrections
2. Study when they describe the resurrected saints as experiencing marriage, and when they describe them as not experiencing marriage

The early millennialists linked the first resurrection to Ezekiel 37 and the valley of dry bones. Ezekiel experienced a graphic vision of the resurrection of the natural, Adamic bodies of the departed Jewish saints, reconstituted with bones, muscles, tendons, and skin. The saints are given the breath of life in the manner of the creation of Adam and Eve and experience marriage and reproduction as they dwell in the restored nation of Israel on the restored Edenic earth.

The early millennialists also understood that Ezekiel, Isaiah, and the prophets envisioned the messianic kingdom on this earth as an age of righteous humanity with resurrected humans living with houses, land, and extended human families on a restored natural earth. They linked these prophecies to Jesus' promise of a hundredfold reward in this age when he regenerates the earth to its Edenic condition.

Modern theologians typically interpret Ezekiel 37 metaphorically. But unlike modern theologians, the ante-Nicene millennialists interpreted Ezekiel literally. They believed that to inherit an Adamic paradise on a restored Edenic earth in this age, the saints must come back to life in their natural bodies. And to inherit an eternal kingdom in the age to come, the saints will need eternal bodies.

The early millennialists linked the final resurrection to Christ's description of the immortal bodies of the sons of God in his answer to the Sadducees:

> The sons of this age marry and are given in marriage [natural human beings in this Genesis age], but those who are considered worthy to attain to that age [believers] and to the resurrection from the dead [on the last day] neither marry nor are given in marriage, for they cannot die anymore [immortal bodies], because they are equal to angels and are sons of God, being sons of the resurrection [destined for the eternal age to come]. (Luke 20:34–36)

In the resurrection of the sons of God in the eternal kingdom, we will no longer experience the Adamic function of marriage. Our mortal or natural Adamic bodies will be transformed into immortal bodies. Our existence in heaven will be like that of angels, who are immortal creatures that do not experience marriage. Unlike angels, who are only living spirits, we will remain eternally embodied creatures, like the ascended Christ.

The question of when immortality begins—at the first resurrection or at the final resurrection—is ambiguous in early millennialists' writings. That is because they often describe the first resurrection as of an *immortal* natural body. Perhaps this is because they believed the saints who experience the first resurrection would live for the entire one thousand years, possessing a form of immortality. If Adam had not sinned, his natural body would still be alive today and would be thousands of years old, possessing a form of immortality.

Since the beginning of immortality is ambiguous in their writings, one can simply follow the existence of marriage in their descriptions of the resurrected saints to understand how they defined the nature of the two resurrections. They consistently describe the first resurrection as of a natural body that experiences marriage, and the final resurrection as of the kind of body that does not experience marriage.

Justin (c. AD 100–165)

Justin, another well-known early millennialist, is sometimes referred to as Justin Martyr because he was killed by the Romans for his faith. He was born shortly after John wrote the book of Revelation. He was thirty years old when Papias died and most likely had access to his books. Justin's teachings on the millennium can be found in his book *Dialogue with Trypho*. Justin believed in a premillennial return of Christ to destroy the Antichrist and set up his millennial kingdom. But he described the saints who are martyred during the Great Tribulation and resurrected as experiencing marriage and procreation in the millennium. Justin is not the most lucid communicator, so his writings can be difficult to read and understand. Hopefully, my comments in brackets will add some clarity to his teachings. Justin wrote:

> Two advents of Christ have been announced: the one, in which He is set forth as suffering, inglorious, dishonoured, and crucified [the first coming]; but the other, in which He shall come from heaven with glory [the second coming to this earth], when the man of apostasy [the Antichrist], who speaks strange things against the Most High, shall venture to do unlawful deeds on the earth against us the Christians, . . . and we who were filled with war, and mutual slaughter, and every wickedness [Christians are martyred during the Tribulation], have [he now transitions to the millennium] each through the whole earth changed our warlike weapons,—our swords into ploughshares, and our spears into implements of tillage [peace on earth],—and we [the resurrected martyred saints] cultivate piety, righteousness, philanthropy, faith, and hope, . . . and sitting each under his vine, i.e., each man possessing his own married wife. For you are aware that the prophetic word says, "And his wife shall be like a fruitful vine."[15]

---

15 Justin, *Dialogue with Trypho*, 110.1.

Justin taught that for the departed saints to inherit the millennial age of peace and righteousness, the first resurrection will be of the natural, Adamic body of flesh and blood that can marry, be fruitful, and multiply. Each man will possess "his own married wife," who shall be "like a fruitful vine" as the saints fill the earth with their offspring.

In the following quote, notice that Justin linked the first resurrection to the teachings of Ezekiel, Isaiah, and the prophets:

> But I and others, who are right-minded Christians on all points, are assured that there will be a resurrection of the dead [the first resurrection], and a thousand years in Jerusalem, which will then be built, adorned, and enlarged, [as] the prophets Ezekiel and Isaiah and others declare.[16]

Justin made a direct correspondence between the "resurrection of the dead" at the beginning of the millennium to the teachings of Ezekiel and Isaiah to show how the resurrected saints will inherit the restored Jerusalem in the messianic kingdom. Justin did not need to provide details about the nature of the first resurrection being of the natural body because Ezekiel had already given us a graphic picture of the resurrection of the natural bodies of the departed saints.

In his book, Justin also described the final resurrection after the millennium on Judgment Day. This is when the sons of God will no longer experience marriage, as Jesus taught in his answer to the Sadducees:

> And further, there was a certain man with us, whose name was John, one of the apostles of Christ, who prophesied, by a revelation that was made to him, that those who believed in our Christ would dwell a thousand years in Jerusalem [through the first resurrection]; and that thereafter [after the millennium] the general, and, in short, the eternal resurrection [the final resurrection of an eternal body] and judgment of all men would likewise take place [Great White Throne judgment]. Just as our Lord also said [to the Sadducees], "They shall neither marry nor

---

16 Justin, *Dialogue*, 80.2.

be given in marriage, but shall be equal to the angels, the children of the God of the resurrection."[17]

Whereas Justin linked the first resurrection to the kind of resurrection the prophets described, he linked the final resurrection on Judgment Day to the type of resurrection Christ described. There are two different kinds of resurrections because the saints are destined to inherit two kingdoms of the triune God—one on the *restored natural earth* for a thousand years and the other in the *eternal kingdom*.

Justin's views on the two resurrections of the saints can be summarized as follows:

- First resurrection to inherit the Son's restored natural earth: natural bodies as defined by Ezekiel, that will experience marriage ("each man possessing his own married wife") and reproduction ("his wife shall be like a fruitful vine")
- Final resurrection to inherit the Father's eternal kingdom: eternal bodies as defined by Jesus ("the eternal resurrection . . . Just as our Lord also said, 'They shall neither marry nor be given in marriage, but shall be equal to the angels.'")

Tertullian (c. AD 160–220)

Tertullian, another famous early millennialist, believed that the departed saints experience the first resurrection gradually, based on how righteous and faithful they were during their lives. Once this prolonged process of rewarding the saints is complete and the millennium comes to an end, the saints are raptured into incorruptible bodies not to be given in marriage and are then taken to heaven. Tertullian was somewhat unclear as to the nature of the first resurrection at the beginning of the millennium, but he definitely placed the rapture of the saints destined for heaven *after the millennium* at the final resurrection:

> Of the heavenly kingdom this is the process. After its thousand years are over, within which period is completed the resurrection of the saints [nature not clear], who rise sooner or later according to their deserts [good deeds] there will ensue the destruction of

---

17 Ibid., 81.1.

the world [the last day] and the conflagration of all things [by fire] at the judgment [Judgment Day]: we shall then be changed in a moment ["in the twinkling of the eye"] into the substance of angels [as described by Jesus], even by the investiture of an incorruptible nature [the eternal body no longer given in marriage], and so be removed to that kingdom in heaven.[18]

According to Tertullian, the final resurrection occurs on the last day in conjunction with "the destruction of the world and the conflagration of all things at the judgment" of mankind. This resurrection will be a sudden transformation of our bodies "into the substance of angels," no longer given in marriage. Our bodies will take on an "incorruptible nature" and will be transported to the eternal kingdom of heaven. Tertullian linked this resurrection and rapture of the saints directly to Jesus' answer to the Sadducees, when we shall be "changed in a moment," and given "an incorruptible nature" like that of the angels.

Commodianus (AD 240)

Tertullian may be unclear as to the nature of the first resurrection, but Commodianus, a North African bishop, is very clear. Only two poems remain from his writings, which are dated sometime around AD 240. These poems only address the nature of the first resurrection and the millennium. It should be noted, however, that his sequence of events surrounding the millennium do not match the sequence found in Revelation. For example, Commodianus taught that the New Jerusalem descends to this Genesis earth at the beginning of the millennium. John, however, clearly taught that after the Genesis earth is destroyed, the New Jerusalem comes down to the new eternal earth—not to the restored earth.

Commodianus also taught that during the millennium the resurrected saints will experience natural lives of marriage and reproduction in an Edenic paradise, as described by Isaiah and the prophets. The saints will possess a form of immortality in that they will live for a thousand years:

---

18 Tertullian, *Against Marcion*, III.25.

From heaven will descend the city in the first resurrection; this is what we may tell of such a celestial fabric. We shall arise again to Him, who have been devoted to Him. And they shall be incorruptible, even already living without death [immortal natural bodies]. And neither will there be any grief nor any groaning in that city. They shall come also who overcame cruel martyrdom under Antichrist, and they themselves live for the whole time [entire millennium], and receive blessings because they have suffered evil things; and they themselves marrying, beget for a thousand years. There are prepared all the revenues of the earth, because the earth renewed without end pours forth abundantly.[19]

According to Commodianus, the devoted followers of Christ who experience the first resurrection will be raised into incorruptible bodies that will no longer experience death and will live for the entire millennium. They will continue to experience marriage and reproduction during the millennium. And they will no longer experience grief but will enjoy an abundant life as restored human beings on the renewed Edenic earth.

If we combine Commodianus's teachings on the first resurrection with Tertullian's teachings on the final resurrection, they would be formulated as follows:

- First resurrection: natural bodies of the departed saints in Christ's messianic kingdom, or "We shall arise again . . . marrying, beget for a thousand years"
- Final resurrection: the raptured bodies of the saints taken "to that kingdom in heaven," when "we shall then be changed in a moment into the substance of angels, even by the investiture of an incorruptible nature [no longer given in marriage]"

Modern premillennialists claim that their understanding of God's endgame accurately reflects the teachings of the early millennialists. This is only partially true. Yes, the early millennialists believed Christ would return at the beginning of the millennium. But rather than the

---

19 Commodianus, *The Instructions of Commodianus in Favour of Christian Discipline. Against the Gods of the Heathens*, XLIV.

first resurrection being of the raptured bodies of the departed saints, as modern premillennialists teach, they taught that the first resurrection will be of the *natural* bodies of the saints that will marry and reproduce. As resurrected male and female human beings, the saints will experience an abundant life on the renewed natural earth for a thousand years. They taught that after the millennium, the saints will experience the final resurrection, which occurs on Judgment Day. This is when the current Genesis earth transitions to the eternal earth and the sons of God are raptured into eternal bodies no longer given in marriage to inherit the Father's eternal kingdom of heaven.

Because the early millennialists had access to the important oral teachings of Christ and the apostles, their views on eschatology have an inherent credibility. This should give premillennialists pause when they so confidently claim that the New Testament teaches that the first resurrection will be of the raptured saints.

Summary

The ante-Nicene millennialists were not under the same constraints as the Jewish apostles when writing about Christ's earthly kingdom. For this reason, they began to connect the messianic kingdom Ezekiel and the prophets described to the millennium John described in the book of Revelation. Because of this synthesis, they developed a robust form of early millennialism.

Some of the early millennialists, including Papias, knew John personally. John, in turn, had direct access to the oral teachings of Christ. With this oral history, Papias could compose a book devoted to Christ's millennial kingdom in which he described the millennium as an Edenic paradise.

The best way to understand how the early millennialists understood the nature of the two resurrections is to observe which Scriptures they link to these two resurrections. They created a direct link between:
- The **first resurrection** and the resurrection of the natural body described by Ezekiel (which experiences marriage)
- The **final resurrection** and the resurrection of the eternal body described by Jesus (which does not experience marriage)

This correspondence to these Scriptures should erase any doubt as to how they understood the nature of these two resurrections.

In the next chapter, we will continue to explore the important teachings of the ante-Nicene millennialists by examining the teachings of Irenaeus. He is one of the most prominent early church fathers and wrote extensively on the nature of the millennium.

22

Irenaeus and the Two Resurrections

Review

Chapter 21 surveyed the teachings of some of the early millennialists, such as Papias, Justin, and Tertullian. Papias was a disciple of John and was able to ask John what he meant by some of the things he wrote in the stealthy book of Revelation. Papias also gathered oral history from others who knew Jesus, and with this information he composed an entire book describing the millennial kingdom of Christ.

Because of this access to an oral history of the teachings of Christ and the apostles, the views of these early millennialists have an inherent credibility. These early millennialists created a direct link between the first resurrection and the resurrection of a natural body that would inherit the messianic kingdom, as described by Ezekiel (Ezek. 37). And they linked the final resurrection to the resurrection of an eternal body not given in marriage that would inherit the Father's eternal kingdom of heaven, as described by Jesus in his answer to the Sadducees (Luke 20:34–36). This correspondence to these Scriptures should erase any doubt as to how they understood the two resurrections.

Irenaeus (c. AD 120–202)

Irenaeus was a prominent ante-Nicene millennialist who lived not long after John. Irenaeus did not know John, but as a teenager he was taught by Polycarp (c. AD 69–160), who was discipled by John. Polycarp was in the unique position to be able to ask John exactly what he meant by the millennial reign of Christ. We do not have any surviving writings by Polycarp that reveal his view of the millennium, but we do have a large collection of the writings of his student, Irenaeus, who was only one generation removed from John. Irenaeus's teachings on the millennial kingdom are found in his books *Against Heresies*. These books can be difficult to read because their primary purpose was to refute the strange and heretical Gnostic teachings that were negatively influencing the church in his day.

Gnosticism

The following is a short summary of the Gnostics' beliefs. They believed the human body and the material world were created by an inferior god or angel. As a result, the material world is flawed and the human body is inherently evil and defective, which explains why it has so many carnal and sinful passions. One day, a superior God will annihilate this defective creation and our evil physical bodies. Only our liberated human spirits will ascend to the mysterious spiritual realms of heaven. The spirits of the more "enlightened" Christians will ascend to the higher levels of heavenly paradise. Christ, a highly enlightened man, did not experience a resurrection of his evil body; only his enlightened spirit ascended to heaven. Thus, Christ escaped his evil body and this flawed creation.

Irenaeus agreed that our human spirits are contained in sinful human bodies of flesh and blood, but he refuted Gnosticism by affirming that before the fall the Genesis creation and the human body created by the sovereign God were indeed "good." Further proof of their inherent goodness is the fact that this same Creator will restore this Genesis creation *and* our natural Adamic bodies in the millennium. If the natural body and this creation are so intrinsically evil, then why would God the Creator, as the superior God, affirm their goodness by restoring them to their Edenic condition in Christ's future millennial kingdom? Why not just destroy our bodies and this defective creation and take our liberated spirits to heaven?

Even further proof of the inherent goodness of the body is demonstrated when God resurrects it once again after the 1,000-year restoration at the final resurrection, which is another resurrection of the human body. It will be transformed into an incorruptible body and will reside on a real eternal earth. Irenaeus believed that the current Genesis earth is only purged by fire when it transitions to the eternal new earth.

Irenaeus and the First Resurrection

Like other early millennialists, Irenaeus linked the first resurrection and the millennium described by John directly to the Old Testament prophets Isaiah and Ezekiel and their visions of a resurrection of the natural body residing on a restored natural earth. Irenaeus's favorite expression for the first resurrection is "the resurrection of the just." Notice in the following excerpt how he created a direct correspondence between the nature of the first resurrection to the type of resurrection defined by Isaiah and Ezekiel when the saints inherit the messianic kingdom:

> Then, too, Isaiah himself has plainly declared that there shall be joy of this nature at the resurrection of the just, when he says: "The dead shall rise again; those, too, who are in the tombs shall arise, and those who are in the earth shall rejoice. . . ." [a reference to Isa. 26:19]. And this again Ezekiel also says: "Behold, I will open your tombs, and will bring you forth out of your graves; when I will draw my people from the sepulchres [tombs], and I will put breath in you, and ye shall live; and I will place you on your own land, and ye shall know that I am the LORD" [a reference to Ezek. 37:12–13]. . . . "And they shall dwell in it in peace; and they shall build houses, and plant vineyards, and dwell in hope" [a reference to Isa. 65 and the renewed earth during the messianic kingdom]. . . . "God will remove men far away [evil men], and those that are left [who inherit the renewed earth] shall multiply in the earth [marriage and reproduction]. And they shall build houses, and shall inhabit them themselves: and plant vineyards, and eat of them themselves" [a reference to Isa. 65]. For all these and other words [of the prophets] were unquestionably spoken in reference to the resurrection of the just [the first resurrection], which takes place after the coming of Antichrist, and the destruction of all

nations under his rule; in which the righteous shall reign in the earth [during the subsequent millennial reign of Christ].[20]

Irenaeus connected John's teachings in Revelation 20 with the teachings of Isaiah and Ezekiel. The millennium corresponds to the messianic kingdom described by these prophets, and the first resurrection corresponds to the kind of resurrection they described so that the departed saints can inherit Christ's earthly kingdom. When Christ rules the world during the millennium, an age of righteous humanity will dawn, and the resurrected saints in their natural bodies will multiply, build houses, and plant vineyards on a restored Edenic earth.

In the next excerpt, Irenaeus observed that believers often experience a great deal of misery on this earth and are sometimes martyred for their faith. It is definitely not paradise on earth. In "the resurrection of the just," however, they will inherit a paradise on a restored Edenic earth as a reward for their faith. They will come back to life in the same kind of natural bodies they had before they died. The first resurrection has to be of the natural body because it is destined for the restored natural earth:

> . . . of the resurrection of the just, . . . when they rise again to behold God in this creation which is renovated, . . . For it is just that in that very creation in which they toiled or were afflicted [in natural bodies on this Genesis earth], . . . they should receive the reward of their suffering; and that in the creation in which they were slain because of their love to God, in that they should be revived again [in the same Adamic bodies in the same Genesis creation]; . . . It is fitting, therefore, that the creation itself, being restored to its primeval condition [restored Edenic earth], should without restraint be under the dominion of the righteous.[21]

The saints were in their natural bodies when they toiled, suffered, and, in some cases, were slain on this earth. When the creation is renovated and "restored to its primeval condition," the saints will be "revived again" at the first resurrection. They will have restored natural

---

20 Irenaeus, *Against Heresies*, V.34.1—V.35.6.
21 Ibid., V.32.1.

bodies for a restored natural earth and will fulfill the original creation mandate by subduing the earth "under the dominion of the righteous." The millennium is a restored Edenic paradise for the resurrected saints.

Irenaeus also linked the millennium to the conversation Christ had with the disciples when he promised them that they would one day drink wine with him in his kingdom (Matt. 26:29). And Irenaeus referenced the conversation Christ had with the disciples when he promised them a hundredfold reward in this age as their reward for sacrificially following him. In that conversation, Jesus also taught that the disciples will occupy twelve thrones to assist him in ruling Israel (Matt. 19:28–29). Irenaeus connected these thrones to the thrones described by John in Revelation 20.

In interpreting these promises, Irenaeus taught that in order for the disciples to drink wine with Christ in his kingdom and inherit the hundredfold reward in this age with houses, land, and extended human families, they must be resurrected into the same kind of natural bodies they had while they were with Christ on the earth:

> He promised to drink of the fruit of the vine with His disciples, thus indicating both these points: the inheritance of the earth in which the new fruit of the vine is drunk, and the resurrection of His disciples in the flesh [real bodies for real wine]. For the new flesh which rises again is the same which also received the new cup [both are natural Adamic bodies of flesh and blood capable of drinking real wine].... And again He says, "Whosoever shall have left lands, or houses, or parents, or brethren, or children because of Me, he shall receive in this world a hundred-fold, and in that to come he shall inherit eternal life." For what are the hundred-fold in this world, ... The predicted blessing therefore, belongs unquestionably to the times of the kingdom [the millennial reign of Christ], when the righteous shall bear rule upon their rising from the dead [the first resurrection of the disciples when they will sit on twelve thrones ruling over Israel]; when also the creation, having been renovated and set free, shall fructify with an abundance of all kinds of food, from the dew of heaven, and from the fertility of the earth [the regenerated earth].[22]

---

22 Ibid., V.33.1–3.

During Christ's millennial kingdom, the disciples will drink wine with Christ again in an age of righteous humanity. When the disciples are resurrected into their natural bodies, they will experience "the inheritance of the earth" and will inherit a hundredfold reward in this age as restored human beings in the same kind of natural bodies they had when they were on this earth. In fact, the resurrected bodies of the departed disciples at the beginning of the millennium must "unquestionably" be of their natural bodies because the resurrected disciples will experience an Adamic paradise with houses, land, and children on a fertile earth with "an abundance of all kinds of food." This occurs when this Genesis creation is "renovated and set free" from the curse and is "under the dominion of the righteous" again, as it was in the beginning before the fall.

Irenaeus uses almost identical phrasing ("the new flesh which rises again is the same") when he described the resurrection of the natural bodies of both the widow's son and Lazarus:

> The widow's dead son, . . . and Lazarus, who had lain four days in the tomb—in what bodies did they rise again? In those same, no doubt, in which they had also died.[23]

The widow's son and Lazarus had natural bodies when they died, and they had the same kind of natural bodies when they were resurrected. Likewise, at the first resurrection, all the saints will have the same kind of natural bodies they had before they died.

Oral History from Christ

Irenaeus affirms that these teachings of an Edenic paradise on this earth came directly from elders such as Papias and Polycarp, who learned these truths from the apostle John, who, in turn, learned them from Jesus. Irenaeus claimed that the teachings of a literal messianic kingdom inherited through a resurrection of a natural body came directly from Christ himself:

---

23 Ibid., V.13.1.

> The predicted blessing, therefore, belongs unquestionably to the times of the kingdom, when the righteous shall bear rule upon their rising from the dead; ... as the elders who saw John [likely Papias and Polycarp], the disciple of the Lord, related that they had heard from him [John] how the Lord used to teach in regard to these times [Jesus taught John about his earthly kingdom], ... [the Lord taught] that a grain of wheat would produce ten thousand ears, ... and that all other fruit-bearing trees, and seeds and grass, would produce in similar proportions; and that all animals feeding [only] on the productions of the earth, should [in those days] become peaceful and harmonious among each other, ... when the creation is restored, all the animals should obey and be in subjection to man, and revert to the food originally given by God, ... the lion shall [then] feed on straw.[24]

According to the elders instructed by John, Jesus taught that the restored earth will produce great quantities of wheat, fruit-bearing trees, and wine, in keeping with the vision of the messianic kingdom. Seeds and grasses will become so nutritious and abundant that animals will no longer feed on each other. The earth will revert to the garden of Eden ruled by righteous humans, when animals lived peacefully together.

Irenaeus claimed that these oral teachings that the saints will be resurrected into natural bodies to experience the restored Edenic creation came directly from John, who in turn learned them directly from Christ. This is an extraordinary claim! And it should compel any amillennial theologian to reconsider his position that there is no literal millennial restoration of this Genesis creation before the eternal kingdom of heaven.

Irenaeus also alluded to an incident that Papias recorded in his fourth book, which was devoted to the millennium. Papias wrote of a discussion between Jesus and the disciples in which Judas found these teachings about a future paradise on earth incredulous. Irenaeus wrote:

> And these things are borne witness to in writing by Papias, the hearer of John, and a companion of Polycarp, in his fourth book; ... And he says in addition, "Now these things [about the restored

---

24 Ibid., V.33.3–4.

earth and its incredible abundance] are credible to believers." And he says that, "when the traitor Judas did not give credit to them, and put the question, 'How then can things about to bring forth so abundantly be wrought by the Lord?' the Lord declared, 'They who shall come to these [times] shall see.'"[25]

As this conversation indicates, Jesus probably taught the disciples a great deal about the future restoration and the hundredfold reward on the regenerated earth. But much of this material was not included in the New Testament for reasons alluded to in chapter 20, which explores the stealthy nature of his earthly kingdom. Had the apostles emphasized Christ's future reign over the nations, it would have posed a serious geopolitical threat to the Romans. And had they focused on the material blessings of Christ's earthly kingdom, people might have been attracted to the material pleasures of the kingdom rather than to God himself.

Fortunately, Papias was able to question John and others who had known Christ in person, and with that oral history he wrote an entire book about the future restoration. I find this truly remarkable, and it is a tragedy that this book was lost in antiquity.

The Promises to Abraham

When developing his theology of the future, Irenaeus linked all these promises of resurrection and restoration found in Revelation and in the Gospels to the promises made to Abraham and his spiritual descendants:

> Now God made promise of the earth to Abraham and his seed; yet neither Abraham nor his seed, that is, those who are justified by faith, do now receive any inheritance in it [in today's cursed creation]; but they shall receive it at the resurrection of the just [when Abraham and his spiritual seed are resurrected in the millennium]. For God is true and faithful; and on this account He said, "Blessed are the meek, for they shall inherit the earth."[26]

---

25 Ibid., V.33.4.
26 Ibid., V.32.2.

Irenaeus reasoned that all spiritual *and* material blessings promised to Abraham are extended to his seed, which is made up of all believers of all time who have been justified by faith. The restored earth during the millennium that the prophets described is the land promised to Abraham and his seed. All these promises of a restored earth made to Abraham and his spiritual descendants are confirmed by Jesus' promise that the meek shall inherit the earth.

But Abraham and his faithful descendants died before this restoration has taken place. How, then, can they inherit Christ's kingdom? According to Irenaeus, the only way Abraham and the departed meek of all nations can inherit the promised restored earth is through the first resurrection of their natural bodies. That is because God is "true and faithful" to all the promises he has made to his people.

Origen's Observations

One of the early critics of millennialism was Origen, a famous amillennialist who lived from AD 185 to 254. He was a highly educated man and started a famous school of theology in Alexandria. Origen held some Gnostic beliefs and frowned upon the pleasures of the flesh and any worldly kingdom, particularly one that was Jewish in nature. The Jewish prophets described the messianic kingdom as an earthly kingdom accessed through a resurrected natural body. Origen read much of the Bible allegorically, and he seemingly arbitrarily decided that the Old Testament Jewish vision of an earthly messianic kingdom should be interpreted metaphorically without any corresponding reality on this Genesis earth. He believed that Christ's eternal kingdom will be a *spiritual* kingdom accessed through a *spiritual* body, not a material body.

Origen was a brilliant man, however, and it helps to read what he wrote about the millennialists of his day to further confirm what they actually taught. He was a young man when Irenaeus was getting old, but he surely would have been familiar with Irenaeus's teachings. In the following quote, it is clear that Origen believed Irenaeus and the other millennialists of his day were teaching that the first resurrection would be of a natural body given in marriage:

> Certain persons . . . are of opinion that the fulfillment of the promises of the future [millennium] are to be looked for in bodily pleasure and luxury [a worldly kingdom]; . . . after the resurrection [the first resurrection], such bodily structures as may never be without the power of eating, and drinking, and performing all the functions of flesh and blood, . . . that after the resurrection there will be marriages, and the begetting of children [natural human body], . . . Such are the views of those who, while believing in Christ [true Christians], understand the divine Scriptures in a sort of Jewish sense.[27]

Origen understood that the millennialists of his day believed that the first resurrection will be of the natural bodies of the departed saints. These resurrected saints will experience all the normal functions of the human body, including "marriages, and the begetting of children." These millennialists adhered to a literal interpretation of both the promises to Abraham and the Jewish prophets' vision of an earthly paradise.

The Final Resurrection

Irenaeus believed that God has a predetermined number of people who will become his children and that once that number is reached, this Adamic creation will come to an end on Judgment Day. He believed the final resurrection will include believers and unbelievers who will inherit their eternal destinies. Irenaeus also taught that the transformed saints will no longer be given in marriage on the eternal new earth. Surprisingly, he taught that unbelievers will also no longer experience marriage and reproduction when they are resurrected and sent to hell, which seems obvious, since they are destined for eternal destruction. Yet, Irenaeus clearly placed the rapture of the saints after the millennium on the last day at the final or general resurrection:

> And therefore, when the number [of saints] is completed, which He [the Father] had predetermined in His own counsel, all those who have been enrolled for [eternal] life shall rise again [at the

---

27 Origen, *De Principiis*, II.11.2.

final resurrection], having their own bodies, and having also their own souls, and their own spirits, in which they had pleased God [body, soul, and spirit united in resurrected bodies]. Those, on the other hand, who are worthy of punishment [unbelievers], shall go away into it [the lake of fire], they too having their own souls, and their own bodies [body and soul], in which they stood apart from the grace of God. Both classes [resurrected believers and resurrected unbelievers] shall then cease from any longer begetting and being begotten, from marrying and being given in marriage.[28]

Once the Father's predetermined number of saints has been reached, reproduction of our kind as human beings comes to an end. After the final resurrection on the last day of the human experience, resurrected believers and unbelievers will no longer marry and reproduce children in the eternal age to come. Most important, according to Irenaeus, the rapture of the immortal children of God who are no longer given in marriage will occur on Judgment Day at the final resurrection—not at the first resurrection at the beginning of the millennium, as claimed by modern premillennialists.

Irenaeus's understanding of the two resurrections in Revelation 20 can be summarized as follows:

First resurrection: This resurrection will be of the natural bodies of the departed saints when they inherit the messianic kingdom, as defined by Christ, Ezekiel, Isaiah, and the prophets = "The inheritance of the earth . . . and the resurrection of His disciples in the flesh. For the new flesh which rises again is the same which also received the new cup." + "'And they shall build houses, and shall inhabit them themselves: and plant vineyards, and eat of them themselves.' For all these and other words were unquestionably spoken in reference to the resurrection of the just."

Final resurrection: This resurrection will be of the eternal bodies of the sons of God, as defined by Jesus in his answer to the Sadducees = "All those who have been enrolled for [eternal] life

---

[28] Irenaeus, *Against Heresies*, II.33.5.

shall rise again, having their own bodies, and . . . shall then cease from any longer begetting and being begotten, from marrying and being given in marriage."

The only significant difference between Irenaeus's view of God's endgame and the view presented in this book is that instead of Christ returning to this earth to rule the world, postrestorationalism proposes that Christ will rule the world during the millennium *from his throne in heaven*. The second coming will occur *after* the millennium on Judgment Day in conjunction with the final resurrection, when the raptured saints inherit the Father's eternal kingdom.

Summary

The Gnostics claimed that a superior God will one day save our enlightened spirits from our evil bodies and this defective earth when we ascend to the super-spiritual realm of heaven. Irenaeus built his biblical case against these heresies by teaching that both this current Genesis earth and the human body are inherently good as the Creator originally created them. Proof of their goodness is borne out by the fact that God plans to resurrect this same kind of human body when the saints inherit the restored Edenic earth in the millennium.

In fact, God never abandons the good body he created for his people. Instead, he resurrects the body twice—once as a restored natural body to experience the Son's messianic kingdom, and then again as a new kind of incorruptible body no longer given in marriage at the final resurrection on Judgment Day. On Judgment Day, the predetermined number of saints chosen by grace will be taken to be in the presence of God the Father for eternity.

23

Lactantius and the Two Resurrections

Review

Chapter 22 explored the teachings of Irenaeus, a prominent early millennialist. To refute the Gnostic teachings of his day that devalued the human body and the material world, Irenaeus made his case for the inherent goodness of this Genesis creation by alluding to the fact that the supreme Creator of this world will restore this cursed creation to its Edenic condition during Christ's future millennial reign over this earth. The departed saints who have experienced hardship and sometimes martyrdom in this fallen world will inherit this material paradise on earth through the first resurrection of their natural bodies. Our bodies and this creation may currently be under a curse, but God's plan of redemption of our bodies *and* this creation during the millennium proves that our bodies and this creation are indeed good.

Irenaeus linked the first resurrection of the natural body and the millennial age of paradise to a resurrection and restoration described by the prophets Isaiah and Ezekiel. Irenaeus traced these teachings of a future restoration directly to oral history emanating from Jesus himself. To inherit the eternal new earth, Irenaeus taught that the saints will experience yet another resurrection and transformation of their natural bodies into eternal bodies not given in marriage on Judgment Day, when the saints inherit God the Father's eternal new earth. These two resurrections prove that the Gnostics were wrong when they asserted that our human bodies are an inferior dwelling place for our inner spirits.

Lactantius

Lactantius, who lived between AD 245 and 325, is another well-known early millennialist. Highly educated, he was an important historian of the period who wrote toward the end of the ante-Nicene period. He was an accomplished orator as well as a skillful writer and tutored Emperor Constantine's eldest son, Crispus.

Like other early millennialists, Lactantius believed that the first resurrection of the departed saints will be of their natural bodies. They will experience marriage and bear godly children. Some of these resurrected saints will sit on thrones and rule over the survivors of the Tribulation. Lactantius was also premillennial in that he believed Christ will return to the earth and dwell in the midst of all mortal human beings. Following is his description of the millennium when Christ returns to destroy the Antichrist and rule the world:

> But He, when He shall have destroyed unrighteousness, and executed His great judgment [against the Antichrist at his second coming], and shall have recalled to life the righteous [the first resurrection], who have lived from the beginning [all the departed saints], will be engaged among men [survivors of the Tribulation] a thousand years, and will rule them with most just command [the resurrected saints will sit on thrones to reign with Christ over the nations].... Then they who shall be alive in their bodies shall not die [the risen saints will live for the entire thousand years], but during those thousand years shall produce an infinite multitude [marriage and reproduction], and their offspring shall be holy, and beloved by God; ... About the same time also the prince of the devils, who is the contriver of all evils, shall be bound with chains, and shall be imprisoned during the thousand years of the heavenly rule in which righteousness shall reign in the world [an age of righteous humanity], so that he may contrive no evil against the people of God.... the earth will open its fruitfulness, and bring forth most abundant fruits of its own accord; the rocky mountains shall drip with honey; streams of wine shall run down, and rivers flow with

milk [the earth is regenerated to its Edenic condition]: in short, the world itself shall rejoice, and all nature exult, being rescued and set free from the dominion of evil and impiety, and guilt and error.[29]

Lactantius described the millennial kingdom as an Edenic paradise experienced by mortals who survive the Tribulation and by the risen saints from all ages. All the departed saints "who have lived from the beginning" will be "recalled to life" through the first resurrection to take part in this paradise, where they will experience marriage and an almost "infinite multitude" of godly offspring.

The Eternal Kingdom

Lactantius proceeded to describe the transition of this creation to the eternal new earth and the final resurrection, when the saints will receive immortal bodies that no longer experience marriage. It is also Judgment Day for resurrected unbelievers.

> But when the thousand years shall be completed, the world shall be renewed by God, and the heavens shall be folded together, and the earth shall be changed [the new heavens and new earth], and God shall transform men into the similitude of angels [the final transformation of the sons of God into immortal bodies not given in marriage], and they shall be white as snow [holy and pure]; and they shall always be employed in the sight of the Almighty, and shall make offerings to their Lord, and serve Him forever [in the eternal kingdom]. At the same time shall take place that second and public resurrection of all [unbelievers on Judgment Day], in which the unrighteous shall be raised to everlasting punishments [in the lake of fire] (*DI* VII.26.2).
> ... After these things [the destruction of this Genesis creation, the final resurrection, and Judgment Day] God will renew the world [the new heavens and new earth], and transform the righteous into the forms of angels [immortal sons of God], that, being presented with the garment of immortality, they may serve God forever; and this will be the kingdom of God, which shall have no end. (*DI* VII.72)

---

29 Lactantius, *The Divine Institutes*, VII.24.1–4.

Lactantius links the final resurrection to Jesus' answer to the Sadducees when Jesus taught that the resurrected immortal sons of God will be like the angels, who do not experience marriage. Lactantius taught that "the thousand years shall be completed" at the final resurrection, when God will "transform the righteous into the forms of angels" so they can serve God forever in his eternal kingdom.

In summary, Lactantius believed that the first resurrection is of natural bodies that will produce godly children because the saints are destined for the regenerated earth during the millennial reign of Christ. And he believed the final resurrection will be of the raptured immortal bodies because the glorified saints are destined for the eternal new heavens and new earth. Like the other early millennialists, Lactantius clearly placed the rapture of the saints *after* the millennium on the very last day of this Genesis creation—not at the beginning of the millennium in conjunction with Christ's second coming.

The early millennialists' timing of the rapture of the saints is very different from that of modern premillennialists, who place the rapture of the eternal bodies not given in marriage sometime *before* the millennium—either before the Great Tribulation (pre-tribulation), midway through the Great Tribulation (mid-tribulation), or after the Great Tribulation (post-tribulation). Regardless of where they place the rapture, modern premillennialists believe the resurrected saints will be in their raptured, glorified bodies when they re-inhabit the earth. This comingling of raptured saints with mortal survivors of the Tribulation would have made no sense to these early millennialists. They believed the first resurrection had to be of the saints' natural bodies as described by the prophets because they are destined to inherit the restored natural earth—an Edenic paradise for real human beings.

Creating a Biblical Theology

Early millennialists understood the distinction between the two orders of being—the Adamic order of being and the new order of being as sons of God. And they used these two orders of being and their corresponding characteristics to interpret and organize the Scriptures to understand God's endgame. Using these hermeneutical principles, early millennialists were able to comprehend the nature of the millennium as the Son's kingdom on earth for the restoration of the Adamic order of being and the Father's kingdom in heaven as the subsequent eternal new heavens and earth for the eternal sons of God.

In the modern era of the Internet, we create hyperlinks on web pages to link a particular word or subject to related in-depth information found on other websites. In like manner, the early millennialists linked Revelation 20 to other Scriptures to make sense of John's teachings and to create a logical biblical theology of the future. They created a hyperlink between the first resurrection and the millennium to the following key sections of Scripture to make their case for the 1,000-year messianic kingdom:

- Ezekiel 37: the departed saints will inherit the messianic kingdom through a resurrection of their natural bodies.
- Isaiah 65: the wolf and the lamb will graze together in a restored Edenic paradise in God's kingdom of peace, justice, righteousness, and prosperity.
- Matthew 19: Christ promised his faithful disciples a hundredfold reward in this Genesis age, when he rules the world and the earth is regenerated to its Edenic condition.

They also linked these Scriptures to oral apostolic teachings passed along from elders such as Papias and Polycarp, who learned them directly from John and other apostles. This recorded oral history indicates that Christ probably spoke at length about the future restoration of this Genesis creation to an Edenic paradise. Papias gathered so much material that he was able to write a book about these teachings of Christ.

The only major problem with the early millennialists' system of eschatology is that they placed Christ's second coming in conjunction with the first resurrection of the natural bodies of the saints instead of in conjunction with the rapture of their immortal bodies after the millennium on the last day. Paul plainly teaches that Christ's second coming is associated with the rapture of the immortal bodies of the saints, not with the rapture of their natural bodies. This mistake is easily corrected, however, by realizing that it is not necessary for Christ to return to this world to rule over it. As the Son of God, he can simply rule his creation from his throne in heaven, seated at the right hand of the Father, where after his ascension he said he would be seated "from now on" (Luke 22:69). His reign will begin when the Father says it is time for Satan to be bound and for Christ to use his power to govern this world.

When early millennialists assume that Christ returns to this earth at the beginning of the millennium, they never offer biblical justification for this belief. Neither do they refer to John's oral teachings to confirm this assumption. Their mistake concerning the second coming is understandable. The church was young; these budding theologians were just beginning to grapple with the complex book of Revelation and to learn how to create a systematic and logical set of beliefs from what John and other Old and New Testament writers had revealed.

Revelation was the first book of the Bible to reveal the existence of a millennial reign of Christ and to teach that there are two distinct resurrections—one to inherit Christ's millennial kingdom, and another to inherit the new heavens and new earth. These teachings also had to be harmonized with the oral history and the information from other complex books of the Bible, such as Daniel, Ezekiel, and Isaiah, as well as the New Testament Scriptures. This was no small task as evidenced by the fact that almost two thousand years later, theologians are still endeavoring to navigate this revelation and make sense out of all the relevant biblical data.

Summary

Theologians continue to debate three very different eschatological views: amillennialism, postmillennialism, and premillennialism. None of these views can be legitimized by referencing the teachings of the early millennialists. Premillennialism is the closest to their teachings, but the premillennial assertion that the first resurrection will be of the raptured saints directly opposes the teachings of the ante-Nicene millennialists.

Postrestorationalism, however, is the eschatology that is closest to the teachings of the ante-Nicene millennialists, which gives this view of God's endgame great credibility. The early millennialists understood that the first resurrection will be of the natural bodies of the departed saints because they are destined to inherit the restored natural earth during Christ's millennial reign. They also understood that the final resurrection of the saints after the millennium on Judgment Day will be of the eternal bodies of the sons of God because they are destined to inherit eternal life in the Father's kingdom of heaven. The only major modification to their eschatology that I have made is that instead of Christ returning to this earth to establish his dominion over this creation for a thousand years, he remains seated on his throne in heaven while he rules the world. Christ's second coming is after the millennium on the last day.

Before the fall, the world was the Son of God's dominion, for this Genesis creation was uniquely created through, by, and for him. As Adam and Eve multiplied and filled an Edenic earth, the Son would have ruled over his wonderful creation from heaven. After the fall, God cursed the earth, and the world became Satan's dominion. When Satan is removed from this world, Christ, as the Son of God, will restore this creation to its Edenic condition and will reestablish his dominion over it from his throne in heaven for a thousand years. When he returns, he will rapture the saints into eternal bodies and will usher in the Father's eternal kingdom.

24

Augustine's Theology of the Future

Review

In the last chapter, I explored the teachings of Lactantius, a prominent early millennialist and important historian living at the time of Emperor Constantine. Like the rest of the early millennialists, he, too, believed the departed saints will inherit the 1,000-year messianic kingdom through the resurrection of their natural bodies. When this Edenic paradise comes to an end, the sons of God will experience a transformation and resurrection to eternal bodies at the final resurrection on the last day so they can inherit eternal paradise in the Father's kingdom. Lactantius taught that there are two resurrections because we are destined to inherit two kingdoms of God—one on the Son's restored earth as restored human beings who experience marriage and reproduction, and another on the Father's new earth as sons of God who will no longer experience marriage.

Millennialism Fell out of Favor

During the first few hundred years of the church, the Christian faith continued to grow, gaining credibility among all strata of Roman society, despite periodic persecution from the Roman Empire. Millennialism, however, gradually fell out of favor. There were obvious theological problems with this eschatology. Critics could easily refer to

Scriptures that taught that the second coming will be in conjunction with the resurrection of the eternal bodies of the saints, not of their natural bodies.

Critics also found fault with their emphasis on the pleasures of the body and the material world during the millennium. The Romans had a strong tradition of hedonism and some early millennialists from this background distorted the millennium by overemphasizing the earthly aspects of it. They envisioned it as an almost carnal period of intense pleasures of the flesh, with extravagant feasts bordering on gluttony. The produce of the earth would be so abundant that they would not have to work the fields; they could simply sit around all day feasting on the earth's bounty. Mature Christians in that day would naturally be repulsed by these distortions and excesses. Moreover, many Gentile Christians came from a more Neoplatonic background. They would have frowned upon views of a kingdom of Christ that focused on the pleasures of the body and not of the mind. Returning to this earth after tasting of the paradise of heaven was also considered retrogressive. As a result, many turned against the idea of an Edenic paradise before the eternal kingdom.

The dissolution of Israel also posed a problem for a future 1,000-year messianic kingdom. The Old Testament prophecies were framed around the restoration of Israel. The Messiah was supposed to rule all nations through the nation of Israel. But Israel had rejected their Messiah and as a result, Christ rejected them when he pronounced judgment on Jerusalem and its temple. In the First Jewish-Roman War (AD 66–73), the temple was destroyed. During the Second Jewish-Roman War (AD 132–135), the nation itself was dissolved by the Romans. So how could there be a Jewish-led messianic kingdom if the nation of Israel no longer existed?

The Rise of the Christian Emperors

Another pivotal event in the history of the understanding of the millennium was the unexpected conversion of some important Roman emperors. Emperor Constantine, who reigned from AD 306 to 337, converted to Christianity in AD 312, and he made Christianity the official religion of his army. He established another important precedent thirteen years later, in AD 325, when he convened the Council of Nicaea to resolve a doctrinal dispute among the church fathers over the nature of Christ as fully human and fully God. Constantine presided over the council, and the rulings then became a form of state law. Bishops or pastors who continued to promote heretical beliefs were arrested and punished by the civil authorities. The emperor was now ruling over the beliefs and affairs of the church, as he had ruled over the pagan priests and temples.

Emperor Theodosius, who reigned from AD 379 to 395, also converted to Christianity. During his reign, he made Christianity the official religion of the empire. He condoned the tearing down of pagan temples and began banning many of the pagan rituals. He made the church a department of the state, and Roman taxes were collected to build churches and support bishops and pastors.

This was a remarkable turn of events. Christianity had once been regarded as an illegal religion, often persecuted by the state because its followers refused to worship the deified emperor and the pagan gods of the empire. Now it was the official religion of the empire! Amillennialism began to morph into postmillennialism, which asserts that Christ's reign over the nations begins when the nations are Christianized through effective evangelism and the work of the Holy Spirit. Pagan Rome was being Christianized, which led many theologians to believe that the messianic kingdom had begun.

Augustine (c. AD 354–430)

Augustine is one of the most brilliant and important theologians in church history. He lived during this period of the Christianization of the Roman Empire and was twenty-six when Emperor Theodosius made Christianity the official religion of the empire. Before Augustine became a Christian, he had explored the heathen pleasures of the flesh, including sexual orgies. After he became a Christian, he rejected his former lifestyle and became celibate, frowning upon bodily pleasures. He considered that sex between married partners was only for procreation—sex for the sake of pleasure was sinful. He initially entertained millennialism, as taught by the early millennialists, but he found its emphasis on the pleasures of this world unspiritual.

Augustine interpreted Revelation 20 as follows. The first resurrection is not of the actual body; rather, it is of the regenerated spirit of the believer upon conversion.[30] Satan is already bound, so God can now rescue pagans from bondage to sin, and they can be resurrected from spiritual death and be brought into Christ's kingdom. With the emergence of Christian Rome, the millennium had begun. The Christian rulers and church leaders are those sitting on thrones to reign with Christ over this earth. As John taught, "Then I saw thrones, and seated on them were those to whom the authority to judge was committed" (Rev. 20:4). These Christian Roman rulers have the "authority" of Christ to judge or rule the Christianized nations on his behalf. From Augustine's perspective, Israel could not become the center of the messianic kingdom because the nation of Israel no longer existed. But the Romans had accepted Christ, and Rome was already a world empire ruling over the nations.

The Roman Empire was evolving into a Christian empire ruled by Christian emperors, so the Old Testament messianic prophecies that described the Messiah as ruling all nations was being fulfilled. But they were being fulfilled through Christian Rome and the Gentile church instead of through Israel and the unrepentant Jews. The messianic kingdom would be a theocratic kingdom, with Christ ruling the world through his agents sitting on these thrones.

To understand Augustine's view of church and state during Christ's reign over the world through Rome, it is important to understand the concept of the Jewish theocracy. Through Moses, God had established a spiritual-civil covenant with the Jewish people that made Israel a religious state, or theocracy. This covenant was much like a constitution in that it laid out Israel's form of government. The Jewish state was to rule over both the civil *and* spiritual affairs of the Jewish people to ensure that only the one true God was worshiped. The Jewish kings were to enforce with the sword the religion of Judaism by tearing down any pagan temples and punishing any false teachers or false prophets that arose. Judaism was to be the only religion allowed in Israel. Israel was a religious state, not a secular state. There was no religious freedom in Israel. The first part of the Ten Commandments was indeed an establishment clause:

---

30 Augustine, *The City of God*, trans. Marcus Dods (New York: Random House, 1950), 20.6.

> You shall have no other gods before me. You shall not make for yourself a carved image, or any likeness of anything that is in heaven above, or that is on the earth beneath, or that is in the water under the earth. You shall not bow down to them or serve them. (Deut. 5:7-9)

Judaism, with its worship of Yahweh, was the established religion in this spiritual-civil covenant between Yahweh and the people of Israel.

Israel struggled to remain faithful to this covenant in an age of unrighteous humanity. The messianic kingdom, however, is structured around the concept of a restored Israel worshiping the true God in an age of righteous humanity. All the nations will be theocratic states during the millennium. With Satan removed, Israel and the whole world will worship its Creator. All the nations will be true Christian nations. Until then, the church best operates under a secular or civil government where religious freedom is a civil right.

Religious Liberty in a Secular State

In stark contrast to the Jewish covenant, the U.S. Constitution created a secular state among its citizens without any established religion:

> Congress shall make no law respecting an establishment of religion, or prohibiting the free exercise thereof; or abridging the freedom of speech, or of the press; or the right of the people peaceably to assemble, and to petition the Government for a redress of grievances.[31]

Whereas Israel was a religious state ordained by God, the U.S. federal government has no role to play in regulating the religious thought and behavior of its citizens. Religion operates in a free marketplace of ideas, and different religions can compete for the hearts and minds of the people. "We the People" are free to decide for ourselves what is the truth and can assemble into our own congregations of like belief (freedom to assemble). We have the freedom to preach what we believe

---

31 U.S. Constitution, Amendment I.

(freedom of speech). And we have the freedom to publish our beliefs (freedom of the press). The U.S. federal government is a secular or civil state that is responsible for the material well-being of its citizens—not for their spiritual well-being. Christians do not have to fear the government accusing them of heretical beliefs and prosecuting them in court for their faith. The government will neither punish them with fines, imprisonment, or execution for their faith; nor will it tear down their places of worship. This seminal freedom of religion forms the basis for civil liberties for other civic groups, such as political parties. They, too, can freely assemble, speak, and publish their beliefs in a free marketplace of ideas.

Roman Theocracy

Augustine was operating from a very different worldview. The Gentile rulers and their people had accepted the Jewish Messiah, and the Christian rulers had established Christianity as the official religion of the state. The *Christian* empire in Rome, therefore, was the fulfillment of the messianic prophecies, not Israel. These rulers should govern Christ's kingdom in much the same manner as the Jewish kings and priests had governed the theocratic nation of Israel. Augustine made this claim in his famous book *The City of God*:

> But while the devil is bound, the saints reign with Christ during the same thousand years... in the words, "And I saw seats and them that sat upon them, and judgment was given." It is not to be supposed that this refers to the last judgment [after the millennium], but to the seats of the rulers and to the rulers themselves by whom the Church is now governed [by the Christian emperors and church leaders]. And no better interpretation of judgment being given can be produced than that which we have in the words [to Peter], "What ye bind on earth shall be bound in heaven; and what ye loose on earth shall be loosed in heaven."[32]

According to Augustine, the millennial reign of Christ had begun. The Christian civil and religious rulers are those seated on the thrones

---

32 Augustine, *The City of God*, 20.9.

described by John in Revelation 20. They now have the authority to reign with Christ over the state *and* the church in Christ's earthly kingdom. They are to rule as judges over his kingdom. Jesus' prophecy to Peter had predicted a day when Christ would rule the world through Rome.

The rule of the Christian Roman authorities over the affairs of the church included the state convening church councils, as Constantine did, and writing laws based on sound Christian doctrines. The state would enforce these binding laws by punishing heretics and false teachers who violated these doctrines. This is similar to the way the Jewish kings opposed pagan worship and enforced Mosaic law by punishing false prophets and false teachers who led the nation astray. Augustine taught:

> But these emperors [civil authorities], whatever the occasion of their becoming acquainted with the crime of your schism [heresy] might be, frame against you such decrees as their zeal and their office demand. For they bear not the sword in vain; they are ministers of God to execute wrath upon those that do evil. (*Letters* 87.1.7–9)[33]

The evil in this case is not criminal behavior, like burglary. Rather, it is heretical beliefs that are harmful to the spiritual well-being of the nation. The Christian emperors are the ministers of God's wrath against anyone who would corrupt the Christian empire with their heretical teachings.

Augustine's assumption that the state possessed the power to regulate the affairs of the church was extraordinary. Can you imagine the U.S. Congress convening theologians to a special council to define orthodox Christian doctrine and then making those doctrines the law of the land? Or the Department of Justice prosecuting and punishing any professor or pastor who deviated from those doctrines? It is hard to imagine, but that is precisely what Augustine advocated. Just as King David was a minister of God in Israel, so, too, the Christian emperors were to be ministers of God's wrath against false teachers who might corrupt the Christian empire.

---

33 Henry Paolucci, *The Political Writings of St. Augustine* (Chicago: Henry Regnery Company, 1962), 192.

Augustine received opposition from some fellow Christians for his assertion that the state had jurisdiction over the affairs and teachings of the church. These Christians argued that Paul and the apostles did not set out on their missionary journeys to turn the pagan Roman Empire into a Christian theocracy modeled on Israel. Their gospel focused on the heavenly kingdom, not on the earthly kingdom of Christ. The apostles set out to establish the church as a peaceful assembly of God's people, not a theocratic state ruled by Christians. They hoped and prayed that the church would be granted some religious liberty by the pagan Roman authorities so that they would be free to assemble and to spread the gospel to all peoples and nations. The apostles never intended to establish Christ's kingdom on this earth until the Father determined it was the right time.

Augustine's rebuttal to their argument was that Christ's reign over the nations did not occur during the time of the early church because Rome had not yet become a Christian kingdom. Once the pagan Gentiles and their rulers received Christ, his reign described by the prophets had begun. In the following quote, Augustine connects the thrones described in Revelation 20 to these messianic prophecies, which describe the kings ruling the world on Christ's behalf:

> But as to the argument of those men who are unwilling that their impious deeds should be checked by the enactment of righteous laws [by the state], when they say that the apostles never sought such measures from the kings of the earth, they do not consider the different character of that age, and that everything comes in its own season. For what emperor had as yet believed in Christ [the emperors were still pagan], so as to serve Him in the cause of piety by enacting laws against impiety [false teachings], when as yet the declaration of the prophet was only in the course of its fulfillment [the messianic kingdom had not yet begun], "Why do the heathen rage, . . . and their rulers take counsel together, against the Lord, and against His Anointed;" and there was as yet no sign of that which is spoken a little later in the same psalm: "Be wise now, therefore, O ye kings; be instructed, ye judges of the earth. Serve the Lord with fear, and rejoice with trembling [during the messianic kingdom]." How then are kings to serve the Lord with fear, . . . he serves Him by enforcing with suitable rigour

such laws as ordain what is righteous [Christian rulers enforce Christian thought and behavior during the reign of Christ], ... Even as Hezekiah served Him, by destroying the groves and the temples of the idols, and the high places which had been built in violation of the commandments of God [the Gentile messianic kingdom is modeled on Israel's theocracy]. (*Letters* 185.19–36)[34]

According to Augustine, the messianic kingdom did not occur in Peter's day, but with the Christianization of Rome, Christ's reign had begun. The rulers had the authority and the God-given responsibility to reign with Christ over the state and the church during Christ's earthly kingdom. Christian kings were to serve the Lord with fear as they enacted laws to establish an age of righteousness on this earth during his reign. Just as Judaism was the established religion of the nation of Israel, so, too, Christianity was to be the established religion of the Christian state of Rome. The Roman king under Christ's reign was to act in the same manner as the God-fearing Jewish kings by destroying the pagan temples and killing the false teachers. There would be no religious freedom in the messianic kingdom, just as there was none in Israel.

Augustine applied another messianic prophecy, Psalm 72, to the Roman emperors now reigning with Christ. This psalm describes Christ's reign in the future restoration, when he will rule the whole world:

May he have dominion from sea to sea, and from the River to the ends of the earth! ... Blessed be his glorious name forever; may the whole earth be filled with his glory! Amen and Amen! (vv. 8–19)

Quoting from this psalm, Augustine wrote:

... Christ from the kingdom bought with His blood, which extends from sea to sea, and from the river to the ends of the earth? Nay verily; *let the kings of the earth serve Christ by making laws for Him and for His cause.* (*Letters* 93.16–19)[35]

---

34 Ibid., 211–212.
35 Ibid., 206.

Augustine believed the Christian kings were to serve Christ by "making laws for Him and for His cause." They would rule with Christ over his earthly kingdom that, through Rome's vast empire, extended from sea to sea and to the ends of the earth.

In stark contrast, the early millennialists, such as Justin and Irenaeus, linked the messianic prophecies of Ezekiel and Isaiah to the *future* millennium described by John. Christ's reign will not occur until Satan is completely removed from this world and the earth is regenerated to its Edenic condition.

Rejecting these early millennial views, Augustine linked the Old Testament messianic prophecies to the theocratic kingdom of Christian Rome in his day. Satan was partially bound, so Christ could rescue sinners from his kingdom of darkness through the first resurrection of their spirits. But Satan was not completely removed from this world. He continued to influence unbelievers in a competing kingdom, and the curse remained on this earth. This was a radically different understanding of God's endgame from that of the early millennialists.

I have often wondered how history would have been different if Emperors Constantine and Theodosius had been advised by millennialists, such as Irenaeus. They would have likely counseled the emperors to decriminalize Christianity and disestablish the pagan religions from the Roman state. They would have advocated for a truly secular state with no established religion. The church could then have competed freely for the hearts and minds of the Roman people. The pagan gods were devious, unloving, and unpredictable creatures. They were no match for the God of the Bible, who is all-powerful, personal, and loving.

Unfortunately, millennialism had fallen out of favor when these emperors became believers. Postmillennial theologians like Augustine persuaded the Christian rulers and church leaders to view the Christian Roman Empire as a fulfillment of the messianic prophecies. Augustine gave theological justification for this faulty eschatology. His brilliance and the sheer breadth of his writings carried the day. Augustine's interpretation of Revelation 20 and his theory of the relationship between church and state became the paradigm for the Roman Empire and, subsequently, Medieval Europe, when Christ's kingdom on earth became known as Christendom. The Catholic

Church was considered the one and only true universal church during Christ's reign. The pope, cardinals, and bishops, along with kings and princes, were those seated with Christ on the thrones described in Revelation 20.

Throughout this period, there was a great deal of wrangling over who was actually sovereign over matters of faith—the civil authorities or the church authorities. At times, the state had the upper hand and had the authority to appoint key church officials, such as bishops. At other times, the Catholic Church was responsible for appointing these key officials. The pope eventually claimed that he was the successor to Peter, who could bind anything on this earth related to matters of the faith. The pope even had the authority to excommunicate the civil king if he strayed too far from the faith.

Ironically, Augustine's flawed understanding of Revelation provided Satan the ideal opportunity to delude sinful church and civil rulers into believing that they were on the thrones set up to reign with Christ. Since these rulers could use the sword to rule over the spiritual affairs of their nations, this led to much tyranny and the tragic loss of religious liberty for centuries. The punishment by the theocratic state of those deemed heretical and unrepentant was considered a sacred duty of these civil authorities, and the punishment often included execution.

This view of eschatology also led to the loss of all civil liberties, including the freedoms of assembly, speech, and the press. Scientists, including Galileo, were required to get the pope's blessing before publishing any new theories on nature. When Galileo defied the pope's orders by announcing his proof that the earth moves around the sun, he was convicted of heresy and punished with house arrest for the rest of his life. He would have been burned at the stake had he not recanted his findings at the end of his trial.

Augustine's interpretation of Revelation 20 and the Old Testament messianic prophecies is obviously wrong, and it led to a seriously flawed view of the functions of church and state during this interim period leading up to Christ's millennial reign. Clearly, Satan is still operational in this world, and with a theocratic form of government all he had to do to corrupt the church was to influence a few key people at the top of this hierarchy. Until Christ removes Satan, however, the state has no right to rule this world on Christ's behalf.

Calvin and the Reformers corrected many of these unbiblical doctrines of the Catholic Church, but they did not reject the Catholic Church's eschatology. They largely accepted Augustine's understanding of the role of church and state during Christ's reign over this world.

25

Calvin's Theology of the Future

Review

Chapter 24 examined Augustine's interpretation of the millennium. When the Roman emperors became Christians, they imagined their enormous empire as a Christian theocracy ruling over the spiritual affairs of the church. They governed their empire as the Jewish kings had governed Israel. Augustine gave theological justification to this turn of events based on his distorted interpretation of Revelation 20. He believed the first resurrection is of the regenerated spirits of the believers upon conversion; it is not a resurrection of their physical bodies. He also believed Satan was already bound and that God could now rescue pagans from bondage to sin and spiritual death. With the emergence of Christ's kingdom of believers on this earth, the millennium had begun. The Christian Roman rulers and the church leaders were those sitting on thrones to rule the world on Christ's behalf during his messianic kingdom. Augustine modeled this Roman theocracy on Israel's theocracy and looked to the messianic prophecies to describe how the Gentile messianic kingdom should rule the world on Christ's behalf.

John Calvin (1509–1564)

During the Middle Ages, the Catholic Church grew more powerful, wealthy, and centralized. But it also became corrupt, and its beliefs became more heretical. The Reformation was a revolution against this corruption and the heretical doctrines. Calvin and the early Reformers may have wanted to reform many of the teachings of the Catholic Church, but they did not reject its eschatology. They accepted Augustine's interpretation of Revelation and the prophets and his understanding of the role of church and state during Christ's reign over this world. They also agreed with Augustine's postmillennial eschatology. Calvin rejected a future millennium based on a literal interpretation of Revelation 20. He called that interpretation so childish as to not warrant a rebuttal.[36]

Calvin, too, believed the reign of Christ had already begun with the messianic kingdom being realized in his day. But he believed that the state and church rulers seated on the thrones described in Revelation 20 were Protestant rulers, not Catholic rulers. Since the Catholic and Protestant theocracies were both operating with the use of the sword, religious wars were often necessary to make the transition from the Catholic kingdom of Christ to the Protestant kingdom of Christ.

Calvin quoted many of the same messianic psalms that Augustine quoted when he attempted to justify the role of the civil magistrates over the affairs of the church. He had no qualms about having heretics arrested and prosecuted by the civil authorities. If the heresy was serious and the heretic unrepentant, he supported capital punishment. There was no religious liberty in Calvin's Geneva, just as there was none in the theocratic nation of Israel.

In his book *Institutes of the Christian Religion*, Calvin taught that civil government is responsible for the citizens' material well-being *and* their spiritual well-being. Just as the Old Testament kings were responsible for the religious purity of the Jewish people, so, too, the Protestant states should prevent false teachings among the people. In chapter 20 of book IV, titled "The Chief Tasks and Burdens of Civil Government," Calvin explains their role over the spiritual affairs of the people:

> For it [civil government] does not merely see to it, as all these serve to do, that men breathe, eat, drink, and are kept warm, . . .

---

36 John Calvin, *Institutes of the Christian Religion*, ed. John T. McNeill, trans. Ford Lewis Battles (Philadelphia: The Westminster Press, 1967), Book III.25.5.

It does not, I repeat, look to this only, but also prevents idolatry, sacrilege against God's name, blasphemies against his truth, and other public offenses against religion from arising and spreading among the people.... Let no man be disturbed that I now commit to civil government the duty of rightly establishing religion.[37]

Calvin made himself quite clear that the function of a Christian state under Christ's reign was to use the coercive force of law to rule over the spiritual affairs of its citizens to establish a godly kingdom. To assign to the state only the responsibility of the material well-being of the citizens is to not understand Christ's current reign. Calvin drew heavily from the Old Testament model when explaining the relationship of church and state in his day. Calvin's Geneva was modeled after the Jewish theocracy.

Believing that the church and state were already experiencing the messianic kingdom, Calvin, like Augustine, applied the following psalm of David to his day:

I will tell of the decree: The Lord said to me, "You are my Son; today I have begotten you. Ask of me, and I will make the nations your heritage, and the ends of the earth your possession...." Now therefore, O kings, be wise; be warned, O rulers of the earth. Serve the Lord with fear, and rejoice with trembling. Kiss the Son, lest he be angry, and you perish in the way, for his wrath is quickly kindled. Blessed are all who take refuge in him." (Ps. 2:7–12)

Calvin believed that this psalm describing the future messianic kingdom pertained to the civil authorities of his day:

For where David urges all kings and rulers to kiss the Son of God (Ps. 2:12), he does not bid them lay aside their authority and retire to private life, but submit to Christ the power with which they have been invested, that he alone may tower over all.[38]

---

37 Ibid., Book IV.20.3.
38 Ibid., *Inst.* IV.20.5.

Since Christ's reign had begun, Calvin believed that the nations to "the ends of the earth" had become Christ's possession. The kings and rulers of these nations, therefore, should submit to Christ and enforce Christianity in their kingdoms. They should use their authority and power to serve Christ by establishing his righteous kingdom on this earth.

In Calvin's day, some people were disturbed that he advocated using the civil government to establish Christianity as the religion of the state. They argued for religious freedom, even for heretics, and believed the state should only concern itself with civil affairs—not with religious affairs. Calvin considered this concept of religious freedom in civil society as folly and believed it would lead to anarchy. If the state did not fulfill its responsibility to serve Christ and to regulate the spiritual affairs of its people, evil would spread throughout the nations. Calvin looked to the Jewish kings in the theocratic nation of Israel as the model for how the civil rulers should rule over Christ's kingdom. Note that when I quote Calvin, all copy in parentheses, including Old Testament citations, is in the original text of Calvin's writings. My comments are always bracketed. Calvin wrote:

> Also, holy kings are greatly praised in Scripture because they restored the worship of God when it was corrupted or destroyed, or took care of religion that under them it might flourish pure and unblemished. . . . the Sacred History places anarchies among things evil: because there was no king in Israel, each man did as he pleased (Judg. 21:25). This proves the folly of those who would neglect the concern for God and would give [civil authorities] attention only to rendering justice among men. As if God appointed rulers in his name to decide earthly controversies [civil disputes] but overlooked what was of far greater importance—that he himself should be purely worshiped according to the prescription of his law.[39]

The holy kings of Israel "took care of religion," which was under their jurisdiction. It was the king's responsibility to make sure the nation worshiped God properly, "according to the prescription of his

---

39 Ibid., *Inst.* IV.20.9.

law." The Jewish nation flourished spiritually when the kings were faithful to their spiritual covenant with God. When they were unfaithful, evil prevailed as "each man did as he pleased." These kings were responsible for settling civil disputes among the people, but it was far more important that they made sure God would "be purely worshiped" during this time of Christ's reign. They believed that those who advocate religious freedom, and the anarchy that comes with it, are teaching folly, which can only lead to a morally corrupt nation. Like the Jewish kings in theocratic Israel, the civil authorities in Geneva had a God-given duty to render justice in civil affairs for their citizens *and* to establish state laws to ensure God was properly worshiped.

Calvin drew heavily from the Old Testament to prove that the civil authorities had a duty to serve Christ by appointing judges to rule over spiritual matters:

> What is this, except that God has entrusted to them [Jewish civil authorities] the business of serving him in their office [over spiritual affairs], and (as Moses and Jehoshaphat said to the judges whom they appointed in every city of Judah) of exercising judgment not for man but for God (Deut. 1:16–17; 2 Chron. 19:6)?[40]

Teachings in Deuteronomy and the two books of Chronicles are the basis upon which Calvin determined that the Christian state should govern the religious affairs of its citizens.

Romans

Calvin struggled to find New Testament support for this Christian theocracy, which is why he mainly referenced the Old Testament. One section of the New Testament, however, that he did focus on was a teaching in Paul's letter to the Romans in which Paul admonishes the Gentile believers to obey the civil authorities.

When the early Gentile converts abandoned pagan temple worship and emperor worship, they faced a great deal of persecution by the Roman authorities. Pagan worship was required by Roman law, so the practice of Christianity was, in effect, criminal behavior. Paul

---

40 Ibid., *Inst.* IV.20.4.

taught these Roman believers to be good law-abiding citizens, despite their ill treatment by the civil authorities for violating these laws. Paul was obviously referring to the involvement of the civil authorities in the civil affairs of the believers. The last thing he would have condoned was Roman rulers governing the spiritual affairs of the church. That, in fact, was the problem because the Romans were attempting to force paganism on them. Paul wrote:

> Let every person be subject to the governing authorities. For there is no authority except from God, and those that exist have been instituted by God. . . . For rulers are not a terror to good conduct, but to bad. Would you have no fear of the one who is in authority? Then do what is good, and you will receive his approval, for he is God's servant for your good. But if you do wrong, be afraid, for he does not bear the sword in vain. For he is the servant of God, an avenger who carries out God's wrath on the wrongdoer. (Rom. 13:1–4)

Yet, Calvin asserted that Paul intended this obedience to civil authorities to include religious affairs now that the rulers had become Christians. Calvin believed that governing authorities have been "instituted by God." Wayward Christians should fear these authorities, for they "bear the sword" to punish bad behavior. The question, of course, is what does Paul mean by bad behavior and wrongdoing? Was Paul referring to civil affairs, such as stealing bread from a market or burglarizing a house? Or was he referring to spiritual affairs, such as the proper worship of God? Did Paul envision these authorities, instituted by God, ruling over the religious beliefs and practices of their people?

In his interpretation of Romans 13, Calvin extended the right of the civil authorities to govern the spiritual affairs of the people and to use the sword, if necessary. The civil authorities, as servants of God, were God's means of avenging the heretic and carrying out God's wrath on wrongdoers in the church. Calvin linked this role of civil authorities ruling over the church to the Old Testament rulers. Again, the Scripture references in parentheses are in Calvin's original text:

> But Paul speaks much more clearly when he undertakes a just discussion of this matter [the role of civil authorities to rule over

matters of the faith]. For he states both that power [with the sword] is an ordinance of God (Rom. 13:2), and that there are no powers except those ordained by God (Rom. 13:1). Further, that princes are ministers of God, for those doing good unto praise; for those doing evil, avengers unto wrath (Rom. 13:3–4). To this may be added the examples of holy men, of whom some possessed kingdoms, as David, Josiah, and Hezekiah.[41]

According to Calvin, "Paul speaks much more clearly" when he teaches that Christian rulers are ministers of God over civil matters *and* spiritual beliefs and practices. Their powers *over the church* are ordained by God. When someone advocates false doctrines or unChristian conduct, the rulers are God's agents as "avengers unto wrath" upon the evildoer. King David and the other godly Jewish kings during Israel's theocracy are good examples of what Paul was advocating.

Paul wrote his letter to the Roman Christians in AD 56 in a specific historical context. Calvin took Paul's letter out of context and distorted it to support his false teachings regarding a Christian theocracy. It is absurd for Calvin to assert that Paul had wanted the pagan Roman authorities of his day to govern the teachings and practices of the church and to use the sword as an instrument of God's wrath over the church.

On numerous occasions, Paul and the church had suffered greatly from the unjust use of the Roman sword against them for their religious beliefs and practices. The last thing Paul would have advocated was that Roman authorities police the doctrines of the church. He was merely instructing the Roman Christians to be law-abiding citizens—not criminals, and definitely not insurrectionists.

In Romans 13, Paul described how government authorities should *ideally* function in regard to civilian affairs. Note his careful choice of words: "For rulers are not a terror to good conduct, but to bad." Paul knew firsthand that the Roman government could be a real terror to good Christian citizens who simply followed Christ. He also knew these Roman Christians might be tempted to lash out against the Roman authorities for the abuse they were experiencing. To prevent such retaliation, Paul admonished them to "bless those who persecute you;

---

41 Ibid., *Inst.* IV.20.4.

bless and do not curse them" (Rom. 12:14); "Repay no one evil for evil" (v. 17); "Never avenge yourselves, but leave it to the wrath of God" (v. 19); "Do not be overcome by evil, but overcome evil with good" (v. 21). Paul was also concerned that they would refuse to pay taxes as a form of protest for the unjust abuse they were receiving. He instructed them: "Pay to all what is owed to them: taxes to whom taxes are owed, revenue to whom revenue is owed, respect to whom respect is owed, honor to whom honor is owed" (13:7). Paul knew that not paying taxes would provide the Romans with another excuse to terrorize them even more.

There is no New Testament support for Calvin's concept of a Christian theocracy. Calvin misinterpreted Romans 13 to mean that the civil authorities should govern the doctrines and affairs of the church. He operated from this premise because he believed the messianic reign of Christ had begun, with Christian rulers sitting on thrones ruling the nations on Christ's behalf. That is why they should emulate the kings of Israel. Paul, however, made it clear that he did not use the weapons of the civil realm to advance Christ's kingdom. Rather, he used the power of persuasion of the truth combined with the conviction of the Holy Spirit:

> For though we walk in the flesh, we are not waging war according to the flesh. For the weapons of our warfare are not of the flesh but have divine power to destroy strongholds. We destroy arguments and every lofty opinion raised against the knowledge of God, and take every thought captive to obey Christ. (2 Cor. 10:3–5)

Paul even urged the church to pray for religious liberty so that the church could assemble peacefully without interference or persecution from the state:

> First of all, then, I urge that supplications, prayers, intercessions, and thanksgivings be made for all people, for kings and all who are in high positions, that we may lead a peaceful and quiet life, godly and dignified in every way. (1 Tim. 2:1–2)

This is a prayer for both religious freedom and freedom of assembly. Because the early church did not set out to establish a theocracy through the use of the sword, the disciples and the early church were no real threat to the Roman state. Their only weapons were the Holy Spirit, the preaching of truth, and rational discourse to persuade the Gentiles to join them in peaceful assembly in worshiping God.

Calvin challenged many of the doctrines of the Catholic Church, rightfully relying on the Scriptures as the sole authority for Christian doctrine. And he was correct in his assessment of many of those doctrines. Unfortunately, he did not take the opportunity to revisit Augustine's flawed eschatology. Calvin wrote commentaries on many books of the Bible, but he never wrote one on Revelation—a book he seemingly did not understand and essentially ignored. As a result of Augustine's and Calvin's flawed interpretations of Revelation 20, the Western world lost religious liberty for centuries.

The Puritan Reformers in Scotland created the famous Westminster Confession of Faith, which was commissioned by an act of the English Parliament in 1647. Although never officially approved by Parliament and the Church of England, it became the de facto official statement of faith for the churches in Scotland. Religious liberty was not to be allowed, and the state had a major role in maintaining the purity of the church:

> And because the powers which God hath ordained, and the liberty which Christ hath purchased, are not intended by God to destroy, but mutually to uphold and preserve one another; they who, upon pretense of Christian liberty, shall oppose any lawful power, or the lawful exercise of it, whether it be civil or ecclesiastical, resist the ordinance of God. And, for their publishing of such opinions, or maintaining of such practices, as are contrary to the light of nature, or to the known principles of Christianity, whether concerning faith, worship, or conversation; or, to the power of godliness; or, such erroneous opinions or practices, as either in their own nature, or in the manner of publishing or maintaining them, are destructive to the external peace and order which Christ hath established in the Church, they may lawfully be called to account, and proceeded against, by the censures of the Church, and by the power of the civil magistrate.[42]

---

42 *The Westminster Confession of Faith*, 1646 (Glasgow: Free Presbyterian Publications, reprinted, 2003), chapter 20, "Of Christian Liberty, and Liberty of Conscience," para. 4, pp. 87–88.

In the footnote to this section of the Confession, the authors refer to Paul's instructions in Romans 13 to obey the civil authorities, extending to them the authority to rule over spiritual matters of the people and the church—just as Calvin did. The church and the civil authorities had a God-given duty to ensure that erroneous beliefs and practices would be prosecuted by the censures of the church and the civil magistrates. The idea of expounding false beliefs "upon the pretense of Christian liberty" was, in reality, a false teaching and a form of resistance against God, and it was not to be tolerated by the church or the state.

The civil authorities may not be the church, nor can they administer Holy Communion, but they do have the authority and power *to regulate* the church, to call for special councils to establish orthodox matters of faith, and to prevent heresies with the sword:

> The civil magistrate may not assume to himself the administration of the Word and sacraments, or the power of the keys of the kingdom of heaven: yet he hath authority, and it is his duty, to take order, that unity and peace be preserved in the Church, that the truth of God be kept pure and entire; that all blasphemies and heresies be suppressed; all corruptions and abuses in worship and discipline prevented or reformed; and all the ordinances of God duly settled, administered, and observed. For the better effecting whereof, he hath power to call synods, to be present at them, and to provide that whatsoever is transacted in them be according to the mind of God.[43]

The footnote to this section of the Confession references multiple Old Testament Scriptures that served as guidelines for the theocratic nation of Israel in which the Jewish kings, magistrates, and judges were to enforce the Mosaic law with the sword. Violators were to have their goods confiscated, and they would be banished or, in some cases, put to death. Even blasphemers were to be put to death.

---

43 Ibid., chapter 23, "Of the Civil Magistrate," para. 3, pp. 100–101.

Religious Liberty

Because both the Catholic and Protestant theocracies were operating with the use of the sword, the era was plagued by religious wars as they battled over doctrine, authority, and territory. When the conflicts in England and Scotland grew ugly, protestant Puritans came to Colonial America to escape the conflicts and to establish the Massachusetts colony in 1629 as a shining example of a Christian theocracy. The colony would demonstrate to Europe what Christ's righteous kingdom should really look like on this earth.

But Puritan separatists like Roger Williams (1603-1684) began to question the concept of a Christian theocracy. As Williams searched the New Testament, he concluded that Christ's millennial reign over the nations had not yet begun. Moreover, the church was not a theocratic version of Israel because it did not have a spiritual-civil covenant with God. Williams contended that the state had no right to rule over the affairs of the church and that the state should only be concerned with the material well-being of its citizens until Christ returned. Christ did not use the sword to establish his kingdom, and neither did his disciples. The church should only use rational persuasion and the power of the Holy Spirit to bring people into Christ's kingdom. The church promotes its gospel message best in a free marketplace of ideas where it can compete freely for the hearts and minds of the people.

Williams broke away from the Massachusetts colony and established Rhode Island in 1637 as the first truly secular state with religious liberty in history. Rhode Island became the model for the U.S. Constitution, ratified in 1789. Thomas Jefferson and the humanists were also tired of the centuries of religious wars and tyranny, and they formed an alliance with the Puritan separatists when framing the Bill of Rights, creating a federal constitution that ensured the federal government would not rule over the spiritual affairs of its citizens. The state and the church were considered separate entities with different functions. They were not hostile to each other; they merely operated in different realms—one in the civil and material realm, and the other in the religious or spiritual realm. Churches could influence civil laws, but they could not leverage the state to establish orthodox doctrines and police the churches. Evangelists could compete for converts in a free marketplace of ideas and would have to use the power of rational discourse and the power of the Holy Spirit to persuade converts to join them in worshiping God, just as Paul had advocated.

Calvin's view of a Christian theocracy continued to influence many Reformed theologians in America in the late 1700s, but their version of postmillennialism was not as theocratic as Calvin's. They adapted their views to the American context of a secular state with religious freedom. For example, the previously quoted sections of the Westminster Confession of Faith dealing with the role of the civil magistrate were modified after the American Revolution by the American Presbyterian Assembly of 1789 to remove the language concerning the authority of the civil magistrate to rule over the spiritual affairs of the people. This modified form of postmillennialism taught that we can Christianize the nations on a social and cultural level when our civil laws reflect a righteous nation. This view continued to be popular during the Industrial Revolution (1760–1840) due to the considerable improvement of the material well-being of the people. After World Wars I and II, however, postmillennialism suffered a major blow to its unfounded optimism, when it became obvious that Satan was not bound but was very much alive and active. As a result of the Industrial Revolution, instruments of war became more cruel and lethal. Horrible wars continued, just as Christ predicted.

Christian Nation

This modified form of postmillennialism is still popular in America, although it often takes the form of neo-Puritanism. Pastors preach that we should return to the day when America was a Christian nation. They are not advocating the return to a Christian theocracy, however, as defined by Calvin. Rather, they preach for the return to a nation that has Christian values and morals. But with the historical baggage associated with the term "Christian nation" when it was used by the Reformers to refer to a true theocracy, it is probably not a good idea for pastors to harken back to a "Christian nation."

It would also be wise for neo-Puritan Christians to stop clamoring for symbols of a Christian nation to be displayed in the public square. Neo-Puritans want nativity scenes to be displayed on public grounds, and so forth. But wouldn't a church be the best place to display a nativity scene, with Christians on hand to explain the true meaning of the virgin birth and God incarnate? Nor is it the responsibility of the secular state to propagate the gospel. The Great Commission is the responsibility of the church.

The demands made by neo-Puritan Christians on issues such as these are counterproductive and give secular humanists and naturalists another excuse to keep discussions of biblical ideology out of the public domain. We are losing the battle for the hearts and minds of people in this country because we are fighting the wrong battles with the wrong objectives. We should be fighting for a true secular public domain with true religious liberty, where free speech and free press can operate. Christ wants us to use the church to spread our message to the world, not some pseudo-Christian nation run by leaders who may or may not be Christians.

When Christ was on this earth, he refused to get involved in the civil affairs of man because it was not time for his reign as Messiah to begin. It was difficult for even the disciples to wait for his reign. They hated the tyranny, injustice, and evil around them and desired for God's will to be done on earth as it is in heaven. They also hated the false religions around them and sincerely wanted people to worship the true God. Many Christians today seem to be just as impatient as the disciples were. We have an innate desire for Christ to rule the world and for God's will to be done on earth. We desire justice, and we naturally react against false teachings that bring spiritual harm. Unfortunately, we often let this desire control our reasoning when we press forward in our timing by attempting to establish Christian nations, instead of waiting on the Father's timing.

Today, most Reformed theologians and pastors are amillennialists. They do not believe there will be a messianic kingdom on this earth. They believe the world remains an evil age under Satan's dominion until Christ comes again and ushers in the eternal new earth. In the meantime, they believe religious liberty allows for the greatest advancement of the gospel throughout the world.

Summary

Augustine and Calvin did not see a future for the restoration of the nation of Israel. They contended that unrepentant Israel would never be restored to the promised land during the messianic kingdom. They believed the Christian Gentile nations had replaced Israel as the heir of the messianic promises.

The next chapter will explore the Scriptures as they relate to the future of the nation of Israel. I will make the biblical case that one day Israel will become a nation of believers, which will lead to the restored nation of Israel in the messianic kingdom.

26

The Future of Israel

Review

The previous chapter examined Calvin's interpretation of Revelation 20. Like Augustine, Calvin was a postmillennialist and believed the 1,000-year messianic kingdom had already begun, now that the nations were becoming Christian nations. Those seated on thrones reigning with Christ were civil and church rulers who were to rule over Christ's kingdom on his behalf. He modeled this Christian theocracy on Israel's theocracy. The spiritual-civil covenant that God had with Israel had transferred to the Gentile Christian nations. Calvin saw the faithful Jewish kings as role models for how the Christian civil rulers in his day should govern the affairs of the church and the state. He believed the Christian civil rulers had a God-given duty to establish his messianic kingdom on this earth. Just as there was no religious freedom in Israel, there should be no religious freedom in the Christian nations. Those deemed heretics should be treated as criminals.

The Reformers revisited many Catholic doctrines that had evolved over the centuries, using the Scriptures as the sole authority to determine their truthfulness. Unfortunately, they did not revisit Augustine's flawed interpretation of the millennial reign of Christ. Because the Catholics and the Reformers both believed in the use of the sword to establish Christ's reign on this earth, many brutal wars resulted between Catholic and Protestant territories. These doctrines of a Christian theocracy changed dramatically when countries like the

United States set up truly secular states with religious groups free to establish their own beliefs and practices.

Rejection of Israel

Modern amillennialists no longer believe in a Christian theocracy, but they continue to believe there is no future for the nation of Israel in God's plan of redemption. They claim that the promise to the Jews of an earthly messianic kingdom centered in Israel was a conditional covenant subject to Israel's faithfulness in receiving their Messiah when he came into the world. They believe that since the Jews rejected their Messiah, Christ rejected the nation of Israel and terminated the promises of a Jewish-led messianic kingdom on the earth. Therefore. Israel will not play a significant role in God's endgame. There will not be a 1,000-year messianic kingdom on this earth that revolves around Israel before the eternal kingdom. Paradise is never restored on this earth. A large number of Jews might repent in the future and join the church, but that simply means they are destined to inherit the eternal kingdom of heaven, like all believers.

A Holy Nation

Many amillennialists believe that the church, as the body of Christ, is now the new "Israel" and, in effect, replaces the nation of Israel. They base this belief on the following teaching:

> Blessed be the God and Father of our Lord Jesus Christ! According to his great mercy, he has caused us to be born again to a living hope . . . to an inheritance that is imperishable, . . . kept in heaven for you, . . . But you are a chosen race, a royal priesthood, *a holy nation*, a people for his own possession, . . . Once you were not a people, but now you are God's people. (1 Peter 1:3–5; 2:9–10)

The amillennial interpretation of this text can be formulated as follows:
- The church as "God's people" = "a holy nation" as the new Israel

The new nation of Israel, whose citizens are made up of Jewish and Gentile believers, will inherit the imperishable kingdom of heaven— not the Jewish-led messianic kingdom on this earth.

In these verses, however, Peter is simply making an analogy between two types of God's chosen people: (1) the nation of Israel as "God's people," when the Jews were faithful to their spiritual-civil covenant with God; and (2) the church as "God's people," when they, too, are faithful to their spiritual covenant with God.

When Peter referred to the believing church as "a chosen race," he was not designating the body of Christ as a literal race. And when he referred to the church as "a holy nation," he was not defining the church as a civil nation like Israel. The church is made up of people from all races and nations, and it does not have a civil covenant with God that involves an ethnic group within a nation with geographic boundaries.

The New Testament metaphorically compares the church to many things, such as a chosen nation, a city, a bride, a temple, a house, and even a human body with its many parts. Amillennialists are often accused of not taking the Scriptures literally. In this case, however, they are guilty of taking Peter's description of the church as a holy nation far too literally. The idea that the church replaces the nation of Israel is not a valid deduction from these verses.

Galatians

Amillennialists also claim that the church has become a new form of Israel based on Galatians 6:15–16:

> For neither circumcision counts for anything, nor uncircumcision, but a new creation. And as for all who walk by this rule, peace and mercy be upon them, and upon *the Israel of God.*

Amillennialists assert that "the Israel of God" refers to the church, made up of Jewish and Gentile believers. Therefore, there is no future restoration of the kingdom to the civil nation of believing Israel. But this is an odd interpretation, for nowhere does the New Testament teach that the church is the new Israel. The church is always treated as a spiritual body of believers in assembly, and Israel is always treated as a civil nation.

To understand the historical setting in which Paul wrote to the Galatians, it is important to remember the unique relationship the Jews had with the Romans. Unlike other pagan cultures the Romans had conquered and easily assimilated into their pagan Roman culture, the conquered Jews remained fiercely devoted to a monotheistic God and would riot if forced to worship the emperors or the Roman gods. As a result, the Romans wisely gave the Jewish people in Israel and those dispersed throughout the empire a pass—they were not forced to worship the emperor and the empire's pagan gods. The Jews were given an important cloak of immunity, as long as they could identify themselves as circumcised Jews.

Then entered Paul, convincing the Gentiles to believe in the Jewish Messiah from Galilee and not requiring them to be circumcised. They did not have to become Jews to join the Messiah's kingdom. This, obviously, left them outside this cloak of immunity and subjected them to great persecution when they refused to worship the emperor and the empire's pagan gods. Paul's letters contain numerous descriptions of the hardships the uncircumcised Gentile converts faced, as well as the hardships Paul faced for advocating such a doctrine.

The Judaizers, or the "circumcision party" as Paul referred to them (2:12), had infiltrated the church in Jerusalem and then began traveling around to the churches Paul had established in an attempt to persuade the Gentile converts to be circumcised. They offered a tempting proposition: be circumcised and then they, too, would fall under the Jewish cloak of immunity. In effect, they would be Jews in the eyes of the Romans and would no longer be persecuted. And the Jewish evangelists would no longer fear persecution for instigating this Gentile insubordination against the Romans. The "circumcision party" offered a compelling opportunity: be circumcised and everyone would be spared persecution by the Romans.

Paul resisted this temptation, however, and insisted that the Gentiles not be circumcised, even if this meant severe persecution:

> You were running well. Who hindered you from obeying the truth? . . . But if I, brothers, still preach circumcision, why am I still being persecuted? In that case the offense of the cross has

been removed. . . . It is those who want to make a good showing in the flesh who would force you to be circumcised, and only *in order that they may not be persecuted for the cross of Christ.* (5:7–11, 6:12)

Paul strongly opposed the teachings of the "circumcision party" and told the Gentiles that they could become members of Christ's kingdom without converting to Judaism and following its rules and regulations, particularly circumcision. He realized that following Jewish customs would be a serious impediment to Gentiles becoming Christians. Jews were circumcised as infants, but these Gentile converts would have to be circumcised as adults.

Paul recognized that once the converted Gentiles were circumcised to avoid persecution, they would begin following other Jewish laws and customs: "You observe days and months and seasons and years!" (4:10). And once they began to operate under Mosaic law, they would be obligated to follow the whole law:

"Look: I, Paul, say to you that if you accept circumcision, Christ will be of no advantage to you. I testify again to every man who accepts circumcision that he is obligated to keep the whole law." (5:2–3)

Many Gentile believers would be averse to changing their eating habits to follow Jewish dietary law. Imagine a Jewish evangelist like Paul going to the state of Louisiana and telling the heathens there that to become Christians, they would have to conform to Jewish dietary laws and could no longer eat crawfish, shrimp, crabs, oysters, seafood gumbo, red beans and rice (seasoned with ham), and many other beloved native foods. He would not attract many converts. Believe me, I know. I'm originally from Louisiana and continue to enjoy this cuisine.

The centerpiece of Paul's teaching is that the new creation as children of God is attained not by birthright as a Jew or by conversion to Judaism. Rather, it is attained by simple faith in Christ, for both the circumcised Jews like Paul and the uncircumcised Gentiles in Galatia. Notice how Paul identified believing Jews like himself who adhere to this truth:

> We ourselves are Jews by birth and not Gentile sinners; yet we [Jewish believers] know that a person is not justified by works of the law but through faith in Jesus Christ, so we [Jewish believers] also have believed in Christ Jesus, in order to be justified by faith in Christ and not by works of the law, because by works of the law no one will be justified. (2:15–16)

The key to understanding Paul's concluding remarks in his letter to the Galatians when he uses the phrase "the Israel of God" is to remember his definition of true Jewish believers like himself. Paul is wishing peace and mercy on both the uncircumcised Gentile believers who have accepted his gospel of justification by faith without being compelled to convert to Judaism, as well as the circumcised Jewish believers like himself, or "the Israel of God," who also understand that they are justified by faith, not as a result of their being circumcised as Jews and obeying the law. When reading Galatians, it is critical to distinguish when Paul is referring to Jewish believers like himself and when he is referring to uncircumcised Gentile believers. Let's read Galatians 2:15–16 and 6:15–16 again consecutively to grasp the meaning of Paul's use of the phrase "the Israel of God":

> We ourselves are Jews by birth and not Gentile sinners; yet we [Jewish believers] know that a person is not justified by works of the law but through faith in Jesus Christ, so we [Jewish believers] also have believed in Christ Jesus, in order to be justified by faith in Christ and not by works of the law, because by works of the law no one will be justified. . . . For neither circumcision [as Jewish believers] counts for anything, nor uncircumcision [as Gentile believers], but a new creation. And as for all who walk by this rule [of justification by faith], peace and mercy be upon them [believing Gentiles], *and upon the Israel of God* [believing Jews].

The phrase "the Israel of God" clearly refers to believing Jews like Paul, Peter, James, Barnabas, and many other Jewish believers who knew that "a person is not justified by works of the law but through faith in Jesus Christ." The phrase "the Israel of God" does not refer to the church as a new form of Israel. Thus, the church, made up of circumcised and uncircumcised believers, does not become or replace the nation of Israel.

Jesus himself used a similar expression to describe the Jewish disciple Nathanael: "Jesus saw Nathanael coming toward him and said of him, 'Behold, an Israelite indeed, in whom there is no deceit!'" (John 1:47). A true Israelite would be a Jew with a sincere heart who believed in the God of Abraham. Nathanael was a physical *and* spiritual descendant of Abraham. Like Paul, he was a part of "the Israel of God" who understood that he was justified by faith.

In contrast to "the Israel of God" who understood justification by faith, Paul described the Judaizers as "false brothers" and the "circumcision party" who taught that works of the law were essential for justification (2:4, 12). They distorted the gospel of Christ and were "accursed" (1:7, 9). Paul wished they "would emasculate themselves," or castrate themselves, for their distortion of the gospel of justification by faith (5:12).

Paul's use of the phrase "the Israel of God" unquestionably refers to Jewish believers like himself who knew that it was circumcision of the heart that justified a person. Paul never forsook his heritage as a Jewish believer, and he repeatedly said that he was a believing Jew who had been justified by the grace of God and that he was a member of the true "Israel of God." When amillennial theologians claim that Paul was describing the church as the new "Israel of God" that replaces Israel, they are completely missing the meaning of Paul's teachings. One day the restored nation of Israel will play a strategic role during Christ's reign over the nations.

Much of the confusion over this issue stems from the failure of amillennial theologians to understand and maintain a distinction between the Adamic order of being and the new order of being as children of God. Anyone, Jew or Gentile, who believes in Christ and is justified by faith is born of God and becomes a new creation as a child of God. In this new order of being, there is no distinction between Jew and Gentile, just as there is no distinction between male and female:

> For in Christ Jesus you are all sons of God, through faith. For as many of you as were baptized into Christ have put on Christ. There is neither Jew nor Greek, there is neither slave nor free, there is no male and female, for you are all one in Christ Jesus. (Gal. 3:26–28)

A Gentile does not have to be circumcised or convert to Judaism to become a son of God and inherit eternal life in God's eternal kingdom of heaven. While we are on this earth operating in the Adamic order of being, however, the distinctions between Jew and Gentile remain, just as they do between male and female. The Jews, as an Adamic people, will continue to play a strategic role in God's plans to restore this Genesis creation to its Edenic condition in the messianic kingdom. God used the nation of Israel to bring the Messiah into this world, and someday God will use the *believing* nation of Israel again to bring Christ's messianic kingdom to this world, which leads to a restoration of the Adamic order of being during an age of righteous humanity.

Only after the millennium at the final resurrection when the sons of God inherit the Father's eternal kingdom will the distinctions between Jew and Gentile come to an end, just as they will between male and female. Until then, the distinctions remain, and they are highly relevant to God's plan of redemption.

Jesus Predicted the Restoration of Israel

Even though the Jews of Jesus' day largely rejected Christ, Jesus predicted a future day of repentance and restoration for Israel:

> See, your house [the temple] is left to you desolate [unbelieving Jews]. For I tell you, you will not see me again, until you say, "Blessed is he who comes in the name of the Lord [believing Jews]." (Matt. 23:38–39)

As noted in chapter 18, "This Generation," the prophet Jeremiah linked this offspring of believing Jews given new hearts to the beginning of the messianic kingdom. Right before Christ ascended to heaven, he again confirmed there would be a future restoration of the nation of Israel in the messianic kingdom:

> So when they had come together, they asked him, "Lord, will you at this time restore the kingdom to Israel?" He said to them, "It is not for you to know times or seasons that the Father has fixed by his own authority." (Acts 1:6–7)

The disciples knew their Scriptures. Now that he was resurrected, they legitimately asked him when he would liberate Israel and establish his messianic kingdom. Yes, in the future, the Jews will repent and believe in their Messiah. And, at a time determined by the Father, there will indeed be a restoration of the nation. The disciples will even serve as rulers over the twelve tribes of Israel.

Romans

Let's examine Paul's letter to the Romans to see how he understood the future of Israel. Paul distinguished between two groups of people and a subgroup within each group:

- Ethnic Jews (believers and unbelievers)
- Gentiles (believers and unbelievers)

The Jewish and Gentile believers are the people of God destined for eternal life. The Jewish and Gentile unbelievers are not God's people and are destined for condemnation.

A major theme of the book of Romans is that God's methodology for justifying sinners and bringing them into his holy kingdom as his people is the same for Jews and for Gentiles. All Jews and all Gentiles are ungodly people before God and are justified before God solely by faith in Jesus Christ. It is God's grace alone that brings both Jews and Gentiles to faith in Christ. This grace is determined by a sovereign God whose mind and will are unsearchable.

Once God has brought his predetermined number of Gentiles into his kingdom and the gift of faith finally comes to the Jews, the messianic kingdom that Isaiah and the prophets described will unfold. As we survey Romans, notice that Paul maintained a clear distinction between Jews and Gentiles and that the justification of the repentant Jews ultimately leads to the restoration of Israel:

> For I am not ashamed of the gospel, for it is the power of God for salvation to everyone who believes, to the Jew first and also to the Greek. For in it the righteousness of God is revealed from faith for faith, as it is written, "The righteous shall live by faith." (1:16–17)

> For we hold that one is justified by faith apart from works of the law. Or is God the God of Jews only? Is he not the God of Gentiles also? Yes, of Gentiles also, since God is one—who will justify the circumcised by faith and the uncircumcised through faith. (3:28–30)

> For the promise to Abraham and his offspring [Jew and Gentile believers] that he would be heir of the world did not come through the law but through the righteousness of faith. . . . That is why it depends on faith, in order that the promise may rest on grace and be guaranteed to all his offspring—not only to the adherent of the law [believing Jews] but also to the one who shares the faith of Abraham [believing Gentiles], who is the father of us all [Jew and Gentile]. (4:13, 16)

When it comes to salvation, Jews and Gentiles are all in the same boat. The boat contains two types of passengers, believing Jews justified by faith and believing Gentiles justified by faith. It is critical to note, however, that even though Paul said all people are in the same boat when it comes to being justified by faith, he continues to maintain a clear distinction between Jews and Gentiles as fellow passengers in that boat. Simply because Jews and Gentiles are both justified by faith does not mean that Jews cease to exist as a distinctive group with a specific eschatological future.

When the full number of Gentiles that God has chosen to enter his kingdom is reached, then we should expect that the natural heirs of the Jewish Messiah will respond en masse. Paul was certain of this, despite his great sorrow and anguish over the Jews' current hardness of heart:

> I ask, then, has God rejected his people? By no means! . . . For if their rejection means the reconciliation of the world, what will their acceptance mean but life from the dead? . . . For the gifts and the calling of God are irrevocable. For just as you were at one time disobedient to God but now have received mercy because of their disobedience, so they too have now been disobedient in order that by the mercy shown to you they also may now receive mercy. (11:1–31)

The Jews' rejection of their Messiah is not permanent, for the day is coming when the natural recipients of the Messiah will also receive God's mercy when they, too, are justified by faith in Christ. This eventual "calling of God" of the Jews is "irrevocable." It will happen even though most of the Jews of Paul's generation rejected their Messiah, had him crucified, and continued to be hostile to the gospel.

Paul further taught that their "inclusion" will lead to the realization of the messianic kingdom as described by the prophets:

> So I ask, did they stumble in order that they might fall? By no means! Rather through their trespass salvation has come to the Gentiles, so as to make Israel jealous. Now if their trespass means riches for the world, and if their failure means riches for the Gentiles, how much more will their full inclusion mean! . . . all Israel will be saved, as it is written, "The Deliverer will come from Zion, he will banish ungodliness from Jacob; and this will be my covenant with them when I take away their sins." (11:11–12, 26–27)

God has an irrevocable covenant with the Jewish people. One day they will believe in Christ, and God will deliver them from sin, just as he has delivered believing Gentiles.

But does this repentance lead to a revival among the Jews whereby they are delivered from their bondage to sin and simply become a part of the church destined for heaven? Or does this revival have far greater geopolitical ramifications for this world whereby the Messiah from Zion delivers the nation of Israel itself from this fallen world? Paul did not directly answer these questions.

As addressed in chapter 20, "The Stealthy Restoration," there is an intentional stealthy nature about Christ's earthly kingdom in the New Testament. Paul and the Jewish apostles had to be careful in preaching a gospel throughout the Roman Empire that foretold an earthly messianic kingdom in which Rome would be subservient to the Jewish Messiah. But the prophets definitely taught that the Jewish repentance will one day lead to a real messianic kingdom on this earth.

The phrase "the Deliverer will come from Zion" is a subtle hyperlink to these messianic prophecies. Paul intended this phrase to be a window into the prophets' vision of the Son's messianic kingdom on this earth. In the following passages, notice how Isaiah described the redemption of Israel as leading to the messianic kingdom on this earth:

> "I will rejoice in Jerusalem and be glad in my people; no more shall be heard in it the sound of weeping and the cry of distress.... They shall build houses and inhabit them; they shall plant vineyards and eat their fruit.... They shall not labor in vain or bear children for calamity, ... The wolf and the lamb shall graze together; the lion shall eat straw like the ox [restored Genesis creation], ... They shall not hurt or destroy in all my holy mountain," says the Lord [peace and prosperity in Jerusalem]. (Isa. 65:19–25)

The messianic kingdom established through Israel is also a major theme of the psalms. Notice in the following psalm that the eventual righteousness of the house of Israel is more than an inner spiritual reality. It also leads to an age of righteous humanity throughout the world when the Messiah finally judges the world:

> The Lord has made known his salvation; he has revealed his righteousness in the sight of the nations. He has remembered his steadfast love and faithfulness to the house of Israel [Israel restored]. All the ends of the earth have seen the salvation of our God [a global redemption]. ... He will judge the world with righteousness, and the peoples with equity [the messianic kingdom realized]. (Ps. 98:2–9)

Paul taught, "Now if their trespass means riches for the world, and if their failure means riches for the Gentiles, how much more will their full inclusion mean!" (Rom. 11:12). Paul left it to the reader to combine his teachings with Isaiah and the prophets to determine what happens when the Jews finally repent and believe. According to the prophets, this "full inclusion" leads to the messianic kingdom when Christ "will judge the world with righteousness, and the peoples with equity," such that "all the ends of the earth" will experience salvation and restoration. When we examine the prophets, we can conclude that once the Jews finally repent en masse, the Messiah from Zion will deliver all mankind from Satan's regime, and we will enter into the long-promised messianic kingdom on this earth. The Messiah will banish all ungodliness in this world when he establishes an age of peace and righteousness for Israel and all nations.

Paul quoted Isaiah so extensively throughout his letter to the Romans that it seems he was writing an exposition on Isaiah. Here are a few other striking similarities between Isaiah and Romans:

Isaiah taught how God has temporarily abandoned Israel:
"'For a brief moment I deserted you, . . . In overflowing anger for a moment I hid my face from you, but with everlasting love I will have compassion on you,' says the Lord, your Redeemer." (Isa. 54:7–8)

Paul taught the same:
"Lest you be wise in your own sight, I do not want you to be unaware of this mystery, brothers: a partial hardening has come upon Israel, until the fullness of the Gentiles has come in. . . . as it is written, 'The Deliverer will come from Zion [to establish his kingdom].'" (Rom. 11:25–26)

Isaiah taught that God's love for Israel is irrevocable:
"'For the mountains may depart and the hills be removed, but my steadfast love shall not depart from you, and my covenant of peace shall not be removed,' says the Lord, who has compassion on you." (Isa. 54:10)

Paul taught the same:
"I ask, then, has God rejected his people? By no means! . . . God has not rejected his people whom he foreknew. . . . For the gifts and the calling of God are irrevocable." (Rom. 11:1–11, 29)

According to Isaiah and Paul, there should be no doubt that God will bring about this future period when the Jews repent and believe in their own Messiah. Once God delivers the Jews, "the Deliverer will come from Zion" and the messianic kingdom will begin. All the nations of the world will share in the abundance of Israel's restoration.

Paul's teachings can be outlined as follows. The Jews are the ethnic descendants of Abraham, and the Gentiles are not. The Jews are circumcised, and the Gentiles are not. The Jews were entrusted with the law and the temple and with bringing the Jewish Messiah into the world, and the Gentiles were not. Jesus is the Jewish sacrificial lamb; he is not the product of a pagan sacrificial system. Jesus is the seed of

Abraham and is the fulfillment of the Jewish religious system. Salvation is from the Jews.

The Jews and Gentiles alike are sinners and are justified by faith in the blood of Jesus Christ by the grace of God through his sovereign election. Justification by faith is the only way that all human beings (Jew and Gentile)—past, present, and future—can be reconciled to God the Father.

Once the complete number of Jews and Gentiles have been brought into his kingdom, "the Deliverer will come from Zion," and Christ will establish his messianic kingdom on this earth. Isaiah taught that because of God's character and promises, the messianic kingdom will most certainly occur. He even taught that it will be established quickly:

> "Shall a land be born in one day? Shall a nation be brought forth in one moment? . . . Shall I bring to the point of birth and not cause to bring forth?" says the Lord; . . . "Rejoice with Jerusalem, and be glad for her, all you who love her; rejoice with her in joy, all you who mourn over her; . . . that you may drink deeply with delight from her glorious abundance [in the restoration]." For thus says the Lord: "Behold, I will extend peace to her like a river, and the glory of the nations like an overflowing stream." (Isa. 66:8–12)

When the Jews repent, Israel and all nations will experience joy, abundance, and peace during the Messiah's glorious reign over the world. But how can "a land be born in one day" and "a nation be brought forth in one moment"? The answers can be found in Revelation 20 and Matthew 19. When Satan is bound and Christ sits on his throne to govern the world, Christ will regenerate the earth to its Edenic condition in a single day. He will resurrect all the deceased Jewish saints at once, "in one moment," at the first resurrection, and the nation of believing Israel will be reconstituted. That is how "all Israel will be saved." Literally in one day all believing Jews since Abraham will come to life as a holy nation on the regenerated earth in the 1,000-year messianic kingdom!

Summary

It is important to recognize the New Testament writers' ongoing distinction between Israel and the church. There are several instances when the church is compared to Israel, as the people of God, and both are referred to as "a holy nation." These comparisons, however, are only analogies between the church, a non-civil institution, and Israel, a civil nation. The church may be the current means by which God relates to this world, but that does not mean he will not use the believing nation of Israel once again to carry out his mission to deliver this world from Satan. In fact, the complete deliverance of this world from Satan's regime is tied to the period when the Jews ultimately repent and believe in their Messiah.

Just as we remain male and female when we believe in Christ, we also remain Jew and Gentile. And there is a great deal of prophetic truth built around these remaining distinctions. God used Israel to bring the Messiah into the world, and he will use the regenerated Jewish people and their nation again to bring blessings to all nations. Israel will indeed play a strategic role in God's endgame. Isaiah and Paul taught that God's promise to Israel of a messianic kingdom is an irrevocable covenant.

27

The Four Forms of Resurrection

Review

In the last chapter, I made the biblical case that neither Christ nor the church replaces Israel. Jesus taught that one day the Jews will repent, and on a day determined by the Father, Israel will be restored in the messianic kingdom. God used Israel to bring the Messiah into the world, and he will use the regenerated Jewish saints and their nation once again when he establishes the messianic kingdom. God's plan for the redemption of this Genesis creation is built around the restoration of Israel. In his letter to the Galatians, Paul maintained a clear distinction between believing Jews and believing Gentiles, all of whom are justified by faith. And based on Isaiah, the eventual repentance of the Jews leads to the messianic kingdom as described by the prophets. Isaiah and Paul both taught that God's promises to Israel of a messianic kingdom on this earth are irrevocable.

Unfulfilled Human Aspirations

I am surprised how angry with God some people, including Christians, become when something bad happens to them or their families or friends. Why would a gracious and loving God allow this to happen? In fact, the hardships we experience are evidence that our Creator is not happy with mankind. He is demonstrating his anger with Adam and his descendants. God altered nature to cause death and destruction, and the tragic things that happen to us are reminders, or wakeup calls, that something is dreadfully wrong with the relationship between God and man. God is not pleased with mankind.

Nature communicates two very different messages to mankind. One, there is enough residual beauty, joy, and life to hear the echo of the garden of Eden and know there must be a Creator of this wonderful Genesis creation. Two, there is something fundamentally wrong with this creation for there to be so much misery and death, and for our lives to fall so far short of our human aspirations. The loving Creator of this remarkable creation, in his anger, must have directed his wrath toward man and nature.

When we break a bone in our foot, our nervous system sends us a message of pain alerting us to stop walking on our foot and to seek treatment. With the pain and misery in this world, God is also trying to send us a message. Natural disasters, disease, and death are alerting us that something is dreadfully wrong with this creation. Instead of getting angry with God when life is cruel, it would be much wiser to stop and examine why God is angry with mankind.

The ancient pagans understood that something was wrong with this creation. One year they might have a bountiful harvest and eat well. But the next year, a drought or a flood might devastate their crops, or an invading army might steal their produce and destroy their fields. Their first child might have been healthy and lived well into adulthood, but their second child died at birth. They recognized the discrepancy between their human aspirations for an abundant and fulfilling life and the reality of this unstable and ultimately tragic world. They understood that the God or gods in control of this world must be angry and had to be appeased through some kind of sacrifice. So they developed elaborate rituals for all aspects of their lives to appease the many pagan gods. They called upon gods that they believed controlled the sun, the rain, the harvest, and even fertility.

For many of us today, modern medicine, technology, and material improvements have taken the edge off our short existence. Some of us can live a little longer in a more comfortable and entertaining world. But every year, there are new reminders—in the form of sickness, death, and natural disasters—that our aspirations and expectations are often unfulfilled. The death of a close friend or family member never comes naturally to us, for we are struck with grief and often anger.

Something must have gone terribly wrong. Since the original Genesis creation was created as good, we could say that it is unnatural for man and nature to be in such a fallen condition.

There is a major discrepancy between our aspirations for a healthy and abundant life on this earth and the unreliable condition of nature, our fragile bodies, and our dysfunctional societies. This discrepancy should lead us to search for the cause and for the solution to the human condition and predicament we are in. Yes, we should stop and smell the roses as we take time to enjoy this creation. But we cannot avoid the smell of sickness and death along the way, which should lead us to make an honest assessment of our deeply disturbed world.

Neither philosophers nor scientists nor spiritualists have been able to explain or solve mankind's problems. Darwinian naturalists claim we are trapped in this hostile, natural world of misery and death with no hope of life after death. In some ways, the ancient pagans had a better grasp on reality than modern naturalists. At least they realized the gods were angry and there was an underlying spiritual reason for the world's condition.

Scientific discoveries and advances in technology today can make life a little more pleasant on this earth, but all the scientists and engineers in the world cannot remove the curse on nature and our bodies. Philosophers can come up with some good insights into life on this earth, but all the philosophers in the world cannot come up with a solution to mortal death. Spiritualists believe we can manipulate the gods into providing material prosperity, but they offer no real hope for life after death. As a result, mankind remains lost and confused by its predicament.

If our Creator is the one who put the curse of death on mankind and the curse on this earth, then God is the only one who can restore mankind and this creation. If we are going to escape this tragic world, we will need divine intervention and supernatural help from God. Fortunately, through the Scriptures and divine revelation, God provided some real answers and offered some real solutions.

The Scriptures reveal that mankind used to live in fellowship with the Creator in an Edenic paradise without death and destruction. That is why we have such deep aspirations for an abundant life on this earth. We perceive vestiges of the good creation now, and we subconsciously miss Eden. But why did God become so angry with mankind that he banished us from Eden and put a curse on this creation in the first place? The Scriptures inform us that the misery and death in this world are a result of Adam and Eve's rebellion against God. They succumbed to Satan's temptation by eating of the tree of the knowledge of good and evil, believing that by gaining the knowledge of good and evil they could become self-sufficient. With this knowledge, they could define for themselves what was the right and wrong way to function. They could live autonomous from God and be their own gods, no longer subject to God.

Their rebellion infuriated God and brought about his curse on this creation, which dramatically changed the world. Mankind's good nature became a sinful nature hostile to God. God also allowed Satan and his demonic host to enter the world, influencing all aspects of human thought and behavior. The world became Satan's dominion over fallen mankind instead of God's dominion over righteous mankind.

As spiritual descendants of Adam and Eve, we have inherited their insubordinate nature that is inherently hostile to God. We have a god-self complex that deludes us into believing we can be self-sufficient and have no need for God. We do not need to be dependent on God for truth and life. And we surely do not want to be submissive to him. We are hostile to God, and he is hostile toward us. The death of our mortal bodies is evidence of God's wrath. But this broken relationship is our fault, not God's. Humanity and this creation are in desperate need of redemption, resurrection, and restoration—which only God can accomplish.

God's Options for Fallen Man

After the fall and God's judgment against mankind, God had several ways he could have responded to sinful humanity. To understand God's plan of redemption, it is helpful to explore these options. God could have let man go the way of the fallen angels, with no hope of salvation, and destroyed mankind and this Genesis creation. He could have started over and created the children of God as spiritual creatures with nonsexual bodies that do not experience marriage and reproduction, and he could have created an entirely new kind of heaven and earth as their eternal habitat.

Or, God could have provided a way to redeem mankind and restore humanity to the Edenic paradise he had originally created. After a process of salvation, he could have forgiven mankind of their sins and removed their sinful natures. They would be saved from Satan's dominion and restored to the original good creation that began in Eden. These saints would be resurrected into their natural Adamic bodies as male and female given in marriage and would live forever on a restored natural earth. The human experience would be restored.

In his divine wisdom, however, God chose to institute a plan of redemption that includes a combination of two of these options. He will first restore the human experience to an Edenic paradise for a thousand years. Jesus revealed that after this restoration, the Adamic creation will come to an end. God will then establish a new creation for his redeemed people by transforming their natural Adamic bodies into nonsexual, eternal bodies as sons of God. Christ will then create a new kind of heaven and earth as their eternal habitat. This is an amazing plan of redemption! As Paul wrote:

> But, as it is written, "What no eye has seen, nor ear heard, nor the heart of man imagined, what God has prepared for those who love him"—these things God has revealed to us through the Spirit. For the Spirit searches everything, even the depths of God. (1 Cor. 2:9–10)

But why didn't God simply restore humanity to its pre-fallen state of paradise? Why create a new being as sons of God? I do not know the answer to these questions, but it is God's prerogative to do what he wants.

In his divine wisdom, God decided to have pity on mankind and instituted a plan of redemption. When the time was right, God sent his Son into this world as a human being. Whereas the first Adam did not pass the test of obedience and was insubordinate, Christ, although fully tempted and tested as a human being, passed the test and did not sin. He never yielded to Satan's schemes, and he remained fully submissive to God. Because of his perfect obedience, he did not deserve to be under the curse of death, as Adam. Yet, in a manner of substitution prefigured by the Jewish sacrificial system, he was cursed on the cross by the Father for *our* insubordination and sin. Through Christ's death and resurrection, God created a way to justify the ungodly and overcome death for his people.

Three Forms of Death

Fallen man experiences three forms of death:
1. Because sinful man is alienated from God who is Spirit and Life, natural man experiences a form of *spiritual death* during his lifetime on this earth.
2. The second form of death is *mortal death*, when the natural body dies and the spirit of an unrepentant person is sent to hades and is held there until Judgment Day.
3. The third form of death is *"the second death"* of the body and soul, which occurs on Judgment Day when unbelievers are resurrected from hades and sent to the lake of fire. This final form of death is irreversible and eternal.

Four Forms of Resurrection

God's plan of redemption for those who receive his Son is structured around saving us from these three forms of death and is achieved through four forms of resurrection—two of the spirit and two of the body.

1. Resurrection from Spiritual Death

The first form of resurrection is of the spirit of a person and takes place when we receive Christ. We are born as sinners and are dead spiritually because we are alienated from the life of God. But when we repent and believe in Christ, we experience regeneration and are reconciled to the living God. Our fallen spirits are raised from spiritual death, and we become spiritually alive again. The Holy Spirit indwells our hearts, and we are reconnected to the living God, who is Life. Paul taught that at the moment of conversion, we are somehow miraculously joined with Christ in his crucifixion *and* his resurrection:

> Do you not know that all of us who have been baptized into Christ Jesus were baptized into his death? We were buried therefore with him by baptism into death, in order that, just as Christ was raised

from the dead by the glory of the Father, we too might walk in newness of life [as we live resurrected lives with God]. (Rom. 6:3–4)

Our sins are punished through his crucifixion. God justifies the ungodly, and we are made holy like Christ. We are then joined with Christ in his resurrection, which enables us to be reconciled to a holy God who is Life. Satan's power of sin and death over us is broken. We experience a resurrection from spiritual death and become living beings again, as Adam and Eve were spiritually alive before the fall. We become restored men and women of God in a proper relationship with our Creator. As we walk through this life, we fellowship with the living God through the indwelling of the Holy Spirit. But we still experience mortal death, even as Christians.

2. Resurrection of the Reborn Spirit to Heaven

The second form of resurrection of the spirit takes place when our natural bodies die and our regenerated spirits are raised up to be with the Lord in heaven. In his encounter with the Sadducees, Jesus discussed this type of resurrection. The Sadducees did not believe in a resurrection of the body, nor did they believe in a resurrection of the spirit or soul of a deceased person—nothing survived after the death of the body. They believed we only live for this life. Jesus refuted these false teachings by referencing Abraham, Isaac, and Jacob as examples of the resurrected, living spirits of the saints who have departed this world:

> And as for the resurrection of the dead, have you not read what was said to you by God: "I am the God of Abraham, and the God of Isaac, and the God of Jacob"? He is not God of the dead, but of the living. (Matt. 22:31–32)

Even though these saints have died, their risen spirits remain alive with God. Hebrews also refers to the spirits of the departed saints as having been resurrected to heaven:

Therefore, since we are surrounded by so great a cloud of witnesses [in heaven], . . . let us run with endurance the race that is set before us, . . . But you have come to Mount Zion and to the city of the living God, the heavenly Jerusalem, . . . and *to the spirits* of the righteous made perfect. (Heb. 12:1, 22–23)

God is a living being who dwells in heaven, and the spirits of his departed people have been raised to spiritual life to dwell with him in heaven. The risen saints are described as witnessing the events on earth from heaven. Their bodies may be asleep on the earth, but their spirits are very much alive and awake in heaven.

But how are these disembodied spirits going to inherit the restored Edenic paradise on this earth?

3. Resurrection of the Natural Body

The third form of resurrection in God's plan of redemption is the first to involve the human body. John referred to it in Revelation 20 as "the first resurrection." It occurs at the beginning of the 1,000-year restoration when Christ sits on his throne in heaven and rules over the restored Edenic earth. The spirits of the departed saints come down from heaven to reenter their regenerated natural Adamic bodies and physically reside again on the restored earth. This is a resurrection of the natural Adamic body because it is destined for a regenerated natural earth. The resurrected saints can marry and have children, and they will experience an abundant life on the restored earth with Christ ruling the world, not Satan.

God's plan of redemption also includes the saints experiencing an eternal paradise in heaven as his immortal children. But how are we going to inherit the Father's eternal kingdom of heaven on the last day if we are still in mortal bodies of flesh and blood?

4. Resurrection of the Eternal Body

The fourth form of resurrection is a transformation of the natural body into an eternal body adapted for the eternal new heavens and new earth. This occurs after the millennium at the final resurrection when Christ comes again to rapture the saints into transformed, glorified, spiritual bodies like his resurrected body. He then takes the saints to the Father's imperishable kingdom of heaven, or the new heavens and new earth. The Adamic order of being comes to an end, and the sons of God will be immortal and will no longer experience marriage and reproduction. Christ referred to this form of resurrection when he responded to the Sadducees:

> The sons of this age marry and are given in marriage [the Adamic order of being], but those who are considered worthy to attain to that age and to the resurrection from the dead [God's people] neither marry nor are given in marriage [non-sexual bodies], for they cannot die anymore [immortal bodies], because they are equal to angels and are sons of God, being sons of the resurrection [a new creation for a new habitat on the eternal new heavens and new earth]. (Luke 20:34–36)

Paul, too, described this same kind of resurrection:

> Behold! I tell you a mystery. We shall not all sleep, but we shall all be changed, in a moment, in the twinkling of an eye, at the last trumpet. For the trumpet will sound, and the dead will be raised imperishable, and we shall be changed. For this perishable body must put on the imperishable, and this mortal body must put on immortality. (1 Cor. 15:51–53)

To inherit the Father's eternal kingdom as sons of God, our natural bodies will have to be raised and transformed into a new kind of immortal and imperishable body—eternal bodies for an eternal new earth.

As Jesus taught Martha through the power of resurrection, whoever believes in him overcomes the three forms of death:

> Jesus said to her, "Your brother will rise again." Martha said to him, "I know that he will rise again in the resurrection on the last day [at the final resurrection]." Jesus said to her, "I am the resurrection and the life [as God, he has the divine power of resurrection]. Whoever believes in me, though he die, yet shall he live, and everyone who lives and believes in me shall never die." (John 11:23–26)

In effect, because of these four forms of resurrection, believers will never really experience death—nothing can separate us from the life of God. Our bodies may die a mortal death, like Lazarus, but our spirits will be raised to heaven, where they will remain alive with God. Christ's resurrection of Lazarus's natural body foreshadows the first resurrection of the natural body at the beginning of the millennium.

Summary

Nature communicates two different messages to mankind. One, because of the remarkable natural beauty and complexity of this world, there must be a Creator of this creation. Two, because nature can be so cruel and cause so much misery and death, this same Creator must be angry with mankind. Many of our deepest human aspirations for joy and happiness go unfulfilled in this life. We long for a return to the paradise of the garden of Eden.

The good news is that God's divine power of resurrection resolves mankind's predicament of death and paradise lost. The four forms of resurrection are the basic framework within God's plan of redemption to save us from the three forms of death. Through the first resurrection of the spirit, we are born again and become the living children of God while we walk with God on this earth during our short lives. Through the second resurrection of the spirit when our mortal bodies die, our individual spirits are raised up to join Christ in heaven while our bodies sleep on the earth.

Through the first resurrection of the natural body at the beginning of the millennium, the spirits of the departed saints will reenter regenerated Adamic bodies to experience the 1,000-year paradise on this restored Edenic earth. And through the final resurrection when Christ returns on the last day, our natural Adamic bodies will be transformed into immortal spiritual bodies (that neither marry nor reproduce) so that we can inherit the eternal new heavens and new earth as sons of God. To inherit eternal life in an eternal kingdom, we will need eternal bodies.

28

God's Plan of Redemption

Review

In the previous chapter we explored how we can easily perceive that the current world falls far short of our human aspirations. God became angry with Adam and Eve when they revolted against him, so he banished them from the garden of Eden and put a curse on the human body and on nature. As their descendants, we have inherited their sinful nature and this fallen world. And we remain under God's anger and wrath. As a result of the fall, sinful human beings experience three forms of death:

1. Spiritual death while we live out our short lives alienated from the life of God
2. The death of our mortal bodies
3. The second death of our bodies and souls in the lake of fire on Judgment Day

When we repent and receive Christ, however, we overcome God's wrath and are reconciled to him. To overcome these forms of death, God's plan of redemption is structured around four forms of resurrection:

1. The resurrection of our dead spirits upon conversion
2. The resurrection of our spirits to heaven upon the death of our mortal bodies

3. The resurrection of our natural bodies to inherit the restored natural earth during the millennium
4. The resurrection of our eternal bodies to inherit eternal life in the new heavens and new earth as sons of God

Because of these resurrections, believers never really die.

Restored Creation

This final chapter is a review of the major themes in this book based on the postrestorational view of God's endgame.

There are four fundamental reasons why our human aspirations for an abundant life on this earth fall so far short of our expectations:
1. Humans have a sinful nature that separates us from God.
2. Unrighteous rulers govern the nations.
3. The world remains Satan's dominion as demons operate throughout this world.
4. Nature remains under a curse.

During the millennial reign of Christ, all these conditions will be dramatically changed. Righteous humans will reinhabit the restored earth through the first resurrection of their natural bodies. Righteous men and women will become rulers over their respective nations. Satan and all demons will be removed from this world. The curse on this creation will be removed, and the earth will be regenerated to its Edenic condition. This leads to a restored human paradise, where all our unfulfilled aspirations for an abundant life will be fulfilled.

God's plan of redemption unfolds while Christ remains on his throne in heaven. After his resurrection and ascension, Jesus taught, "But *from now on* the Son of Man shall be seated at the right hand of the power of God" (Luke 22:69). Postrestorationalism proposes that instead of Christ returning to the earth to establish his millennial kingdom, he rules the world from his exalted throne in heaven.

In fact, nowhere in chapters 19 and 20 of Revelation is Christ described as residing on this earth. When Christ is described as riding on a white horse engaged in the battle of Armageddon, no mention is made of Christ descending to the plane of this earth. Later, when the beginning of the millennium is described, there is no mention of

Christ sitting on a throne on this earth to establish his reign. All these thrones are described as being occupied by humans who are resurrected to reign with Christ over the nations. The first resurrection is not of the raptured body. Rather, it is of the natural body in the manner of Lazarus. The saints will receive restored human bodies of flesh and blood and will marry and fulfill the original creation mandate to fill and subdue the restored Genesis creation.

Christ's Second Coming

After the millennium, Christ returns at the final resurrection on Judgment Day, known as the Great White Throne judgment. The saints are raptured into their eternal bodies and inherit the Father's eternal kingdom at the same time that unbelievers are resurrected from hades to face eternal condemnation. The books are opened to determine rewards for the saints on the new earth and the level of punishment for unbelievers in the lake of fire.

Christ's return on Judgment Day is also when the Genesis earth is burned up and perishes and we inherit the eternal new heavens and new earth. Peter taught this doctrine concerning Judgment Day:

> According to his great mercy, he [the Father] has caused us to be born again to a living hope through the resurrection of Jesus Christ from the dead [we hope for a resurrected eternal body like Christ's resurrected body], to an inheritance that is imperishable, undefiled, and unfading, kept in heaven for you [in the new heavens and new earth], who by God's power are being guarded through faith for a salvation ready to be revealed in the last time. . . . at the revelation of Jesus Christ [when Christ comes again]. (1 Peter 1:3–7)

> But the day of the Lord will come like a thief, and then the heavens will pass away with a roar, and the heavenly bodies will be burned up and dissolved [the Genesis earth is destroyed], and the earth and the works that are done on it will be exposed [when the books are opened]. . . . But according to his promise [of an eternal body to be taken to an eternal kingdom] we are waiting for new heavens and a new earth in which righteousness dwells. (2 Peter 3:10–13)

Peter revealed that when Christ returns on the last day, the current Genesis creation will be destroyed and the saints will be resurrected into eternal bodies like Christ's resurrected body. It is Judgment Day, when our works are rewarded or punished. The immortal sons of God will inherit the imperishable new heavens and new earth. In short, Peter places the second coming *and* the rapture at the end of the world—not at the beginning of the millennium, as claimed by premillennialists.

The Ante-Nicene Millennialists

Like modern premillennialists, the early church millennialists such as Irenaeus and Lactantius may have mistakenly taught that Christ returned at the beginning of the millennium. But unlike today's premillennialists, they did not place the rapture before the Tribulation, midway through the Tribulation, or after the Tribulation in conjunction with the second coming of Christ. Rather, they placed the rapture *after* the millennium at the final resurrection on the last day.

These early millennialists also taught that the first resurrection of the departed saints is of their natural bodies that will experience marriage and reproduction. That is because they are destined for a restored Edenic earth—natural bodies for a restored natural earth. They linked this resurrection to the resurrection described in Ezekiel 37, known as the valley of dry bones. They also linked this kind of resurrection to the resurrection of Lazarus, who came back to life in his mortal body.

They taught that the final resurrection had to be of the eternal body not given in marriage because the sons of God are destined for the eternal new heavens and new earth—an eternal body for the Father's eternal kingdom. They linked this resurrection to the resurrection Jesus described in his answer to the Sadducees. Jesus told the Sadducees that unlike the Adamic creation, the sons of God will have immortal bodies that, like the angels, will not be given in marriage.

The teachings of the early millennialists are important because some of these men were in the unique position to know disciples of John who could have asked John what he had meant by the first resurrection. From oral testimony such as this, Papias was able to write an entire book on the millennium as a restored Edenic paradise.

The only major difference between postrestorational eschatology and the eschatology of the early millennialists is that postrestorationalism has Christ ruling this world during the millennium from his throne in heaven at the right hand of God the Father, rather than having Christ physically return to this earth to establish his kingdom. Even with this important correction, however, out of all the prevailing views on eschatology today, postrestorationalism is undoubtedly the closest to the teachings of the early church millennialists, which gives this eschatology great credibility.

The Stealthy Restoration

It is important to remember that the prophets described the messianic kingdom as an earthly kingdom, with the rulers of all nations subject to the Jewish Messiah. The Messiah will be King and Lord of all nations, and all roads will lead to Jerusalem, not Rome. This vision of Christ's earthly kingdom would have presented a geopolitical threat to the Roman Empire, which is likely the reason why the New Testament authors and Jewish missionaries downplayed the Messiah's reign as they evangelized the Roman world. The apostles wisely focused their gospel message on the eternal kingdom of heaven during this embryonic stage of the church's growth. This posed no real threat to the Roman authorities. This approach also explains why God used the stealthy book of Revelation to inform us of his future reign. Like a complex parable, Revelation revealed the truth about Christ's earthly kingdom to the believer, but it remained cleverly hidden from the Romans. Maybe it was a little too stealthy because theologians struggle even today to understand God's endgame.

Understanding the Two Orders of Being

I believe much of the confusion that surrounds the subject of eschatology can be attributed to the failure of theologians to understand and differentiate between the two orders of being and their corresponding kingdoms that are described in the Scriptures. The Adamic order of being is defined as man as male and female in natural bodies being given in marriage and reproducing their kind as they fill and subdue the earth. The restoration of humanity corresponds to God the Son's 1,000-year restoration of this Genesis earth. Through the first resurrection of their natural Adamic bodies, the saints will experience an abundant life on an Edenic earth during an age of righteous humanity.

The new order of being as children of God is defined in the Scriptures as a new creation that is neither male nor female. The new creation as sons of God corresponds to the Father's heavenly kingdom, or the new heavens and new earth in the eternal age to come. Through the final resurrection of their eternal bodies, the saints will experience a new kind of eternal paradise in heaven as immortal sons of God. There are two resurrections of the body because the saints are destined to inherit two different kingdoms of the triune God—one on earth and the other in heaven.

Using this method of interpretation, one can read the Bible and easily determine when the authors are describing a future Adamic paradise and when they are describing the children of God's eternal paradise in heaven. For example, in Ezekiel 37, the prophet describes a valley of dry bones that are resurrected into natural bodies in order to inherit the messianic kingdom of peace, justice, righteousness, and prosperity. This corresponds to John's description in Revelation 20 of the first resurrection at the beginning of the millennium. It can also be linked to Jesus' promise to the disciples of a hundredfold reward in this Genesis age described in Matthew 19, Mark 10, and Luke 18, when Christ sits on his throne in heaven and rules over the regenerated earth.

In contrast, Paul described the resurrection of a new kind of eternal body destined for the Father's eternal kingdom when Christ returns (1 Corinthians 15). Paul taught that the nature of our eternal bodies at the final resurrection remains a mystery at this time. A pecan planted into the ground does not germinate into another pecan; rather, it is transformed into a pecan tree. One cannot examine the pecan and know in advance what the resulting tree will be like. Likewise, one cannot examine the current human body and know in advance what the future eternal body will be like. The human body will be transformed into a new kind of body adapted for the eternal new earth.

Paul also taught that the Genesis creation will somehow be brought into the eternal kingdom, just as our transformed bodies will be brought into the eternal new earth. The continuity between this Genesis creation and the eternal new earth, however, also remains a mystery at this time. Paul instructed us to trust God to create a new habitat suitable for the transformed sons of God. God has already demonstrated his awesome creativity with this current creation, and he will use this same creativity when he creates our new kind of bodies adapted for the new heavens and new earth.

Four Forms of Sitting on His Throne

Jesus taught that after his ascension, "*from now on* the Son of Man shall be seated at the right hand of the power of God" (Luke 22:69). Distinguishing between the different forms of Christ sitting on his throne in heaven after his ascension helps in discerning God's endgame.

1. Sitting and Waiting

Christ is currently waiting on the Father to say when it is time for him to establish his kingdom and dominion over this world:

> But when Christ had offered for all time a single sacrifice for sins, he sat down at the right hand of God, **waiting** from that time until his enemies should be made a footstool for his feet. (Heb. 10:12–13)

In the meantime, he is gathering people out of Satan's dominion of darkness into his kingdom. His people, however, remain in a hostile, demonic world full of the cosmic spiritual forces of evil. It is definitely not paradise on earth.

2. Sitting to Rule

One day, Christ will indeed sit on his throne and rule the world:

> Jesus said to them, "Truly, I say to you, in the new world [regenerated earth], when the Son of Man will sit on his glorious throne [to rule the world from his throne in heaven], you who have followed me will also sit on twelve thrones, judging the twelve tribes of Israel [on earth through the resurrection of their natural bodies]. And everyone who has left houses or brothers or sisters or father or mother or children or lands, for my name's sake, will receive a hundredfold [during the restoration in this age] and [in addition] will inherit eternal life [in the eternal kingdom of heaven in the age come]." (Matt. 19:28–29)

When Christ sits on his throne in heaven and rules the world, the Genesis creation will be renewed, restored, or regenerated. The disciples will inherit a life on the restored earth that is a hundred times better than the rich man's life, with houses, lands, and extended human families. They will even assist Christ by ruling over the restored nation of Israel.

Notice that Christ characterizes this hundredfold reward in this age as an Adamic existence. These are human habitats (houses and lands) and human relationships derived from marriage (brothers or sisters or father or mother or children). With this description of his kingdom on earth, Jesus is probably alluding to Isaiah and the prophets, who described the messianic kingdom as an Adamic paradise. Isaiah wrote:

> "They shall build houses and inhabit them; they shall plant vineyards and eat their fruit [lands]. . . . They shall not labor in vain or bear children for calamity [extended human families], . . . The wolf and the lamb shall graze together; the lion shall eat straw like the ox [on an earth restored to an Edenic paradise], ..." says the LORD. (Isa. 65:21–25)

To establish his messianic kingdom, Christ simply binds Satan and exercises his reign over this world from heaven. Peter and all followers of Christ will be resurrected into natural bodies at the first resurrection. We will marry and reproduce, have extended human families, live in human habitats, and experience fruitful lands. We will reinhabit the regenerated earth and experience a hundredfold reward as Adamic creatures in an Edenic paradise. Our human aspirations will indeed be fulfilled, and we will experience an abundant life on this earth as Christ, the Good Shepherd and rightful God of this creation, exercises his reign. Satan will no longer be able to rob us of the joys of life on the redeemed earth.

Christ is making a clear distinction between the two types of kingdoms the disciples will inherit. One is Adamic and of this Genesis creation—"houses or brothers or sisters or father or mother or children or lands," which corresponds to the Son's restored paradise on the regenerated earth. The other is of the eternal new creation as God's immortal children, which corresponds to the Father's eternal paradise in the new heavens and new earth.

GOD'S PLAN OF REDEMPTION | 435

3. Sitting to Judge

After experiencing this restoration, we will inherit eternal life in the age to come. This occurs at the end of the Genesis age when Christ returns and sits on his throne to judge the world:

> When the Son of Man comes in his glory, and all the angels with him, then **he will sit on his glorious throne** [the Great White Throne]. Before him will be gathered all the nations [at the final resurrection], and he will separate people one from another as a shepherd separates the sheep from the goats. . . . Then the King will say to those on his right, "Come, you who are blessed by my Father, inherit the kingdom prepared for you from the foundation of the world." . . . Then he will say to those on his left, "Depart from me, you cursed, into the eternal fire prepared for the devil and his angels [the lake of fire]." (Matt. 25:31–41)

The second coming on Judgment Day ushers in the Father's eternal kingdom—not the Son's millennial kingdom.

4. Sitting to Create

The final form of Christ "sitting" on his throne in heaven is when he creates the new heavens and new earth as the eternal home for the sons of God. John wrote:

> Then I saw a new heaven and a new earth, for the first heaven and the first earth had passed away, . . . **And he who was seated on the throne said**, "Behold, I am making all things new." (Rev. 21:1–5)

The Son of God was the unique person of the Trinity who created this heavens and earth. He is also the person of the Trinity tasked with creating the new heavens and new earth as the eternal home for the sons of God.

In summary, after ascending to heaven, Christ sat down at the Father's right hand, where he currently waits for the Father to say it is time for his reign to begin. When Satan is bound and removed, Christ will govern the world as he sits on his throne in heaven. When Christ returns on Judgment Day, he will judge the world while sitting on his Great White Throne in heaven. After he destroys this Genesis creation, he will create the eternal new earth while he sits on his throne. All four forms of sitting occur from his throne in heaven, where he said he would remain seated at the right hand of God the Father.

The Gospel of the Kingdom

On the Mount of Olives, the disciples asked Jesus, "What will be the sign of your coming and of the end of the age?" (Matt. 24:3). Jesus answered, "And this gospel of the kingdom will be proclaimed throughout the whole world as a testimony to all nations, and then the end will come" (Matt. 24:14). Most theologians believe Christ is referring to the Great Commission being fulfilled before he comes again. But he is not describing the proclamation of the gospel. Rather, based on Isaiah, Christ is teaching that the messianic kingdom of peace, justice, righteousness, and prosperity *must be realized* on this earth "as a testimony to all nations" before he comes again. Isaiah taught:

> How beautiful upon the mountains are the feet of him who brings good news, who publishes peace, who brings good news of happiness, who publishes salvation, who says to Zion, "***Your God reigns***" [the gospel realized when the Messiah exercises his reign as Lord]. The voice of your watchmen—they lift up their voice; together they sing for joy; for eye to eye they see the return of the Lord to Zion. Break forth together into singing, you waste places of Jerusalem, for the Lord has comforted his people; he has redeemed Jerusalem. The Lord has bared his holy arm before the eyes of all the nations, and all the ends of the earth shall see the salvation of our God [as "a testimony to all nations"]. (Isa. 52:7–10)

Isaiah equated the "good news" with the implementation of Christ's future reign when the whole world actually hears, sees, and experiences his messianic kingdom. The messianic kingdom will demonstrate to the world that Jesus of Nazareth is indeed the Messiah and the true God of this creation. Through the 1,000-year restoration, God wants to demonstrate to mankind and the heavenly witnesses what God's kingdom on this earth would have been like if Adam and Eve had not sinned. We will witness righteous humanity as he had originally planned when he created the garden of Eden under the Lordship of the Son of God.

Jesus taught that after this "gospel of the kingdom" is accomplished, "then the end will come," when he comes again at the end of the age to destroy this Genesis creation, judge the world, separate the sheep from the goats, and usher in the Father's eternal kingdom.

In heaven, we will always remember that we were at one time fallen Adamic creatures destined for judgment and destruction, just like the demons. We will be eternally grateful that God in his mercy instituted a means of salvation for us, whereby we would be saved from his final wrath and brought into his eternal kingdom as his beloved children. God's plan of redemption will reveal something about his character for all eternity.

A Trinitarian Eschatology

Jesus Christ was more than a Jewish king. The Jewish Messiah was none other than the eternal Son of God incarnate. Within the Trinity, this creation was specifically created through, by, and for the Son of God. Therefore, Christ has a divine right to rule over the whole world.

Before the fall, the world was the Son's kingdom on earth. When Adam and Eve sinned, they let Satan into our world, and the world became Satan's kingdom. When Satan is completely removed from this world, there will be a regime change, and the world will once again become the Son's dominion and kingdom.

We tend to think that the thousand years of paradise on earth is for our pleasure. But, in fact, the restoration is primarily for the Son's pleasure and glory. He wants to delight in his restored creation during an age of righteous humanity, as he did in the beginning when he celebrated his creation as good. What better way to glorify Christ than by fulfilling the human experience as men and women of God as intended before the fall.

After this 1,000-year restoration, Christ will come again to take us to be with him in heaven in his Father's house for eternity. There we will experience a completely new order of being even more glorious than restored humanity. God's endgame revolves around this fascinating interplay between the members of the Godhead.

With this understanding of God's endgame, we discover that the Lord's Prayer covers a great deal of the major events that will occur in the future. Jesus taught us to pray like this:

> **Our Father in heaven** [as children of God, we call him Father], **hallowed be your name** [as a first priority, we worship him].
> **Your kingdom come** [we look forward to the Father's heavenly kingdom in the eternal age to come], **your will be done, on earth as it is in heaven** [in the Son's kingdom when he establishes a reign of righteousness].
> **Give us this day our daily bread** [we should live a daily life of dependence on God while we wait for these events], **and forgive us our debts, as we also have forgiven our debtors** [and live a life of love and mercy toward our neighbors].
> **And lead us not into temptation, but deliver us from evil** [today, and during the Great Tribulation]. (Matt. 6:9–13)

Jesus taught how we should live today as we wait for the following major events to unfold in the future:

- The Father's kingdom of heaven
- The Son's kingdom on this earth
- The Great Tribulation

In the meantime, we should:

- Learn to worship the Father to whom we have been reconciled
- Learn to depend on him for our daily sustenance
- Learn to forgive and love our neighbors

Being Prepared for the Tribulation

If postrestorationalism is the correct interpretation of the Scriptures, the next major eschatological event facing the church is the Great Tribulation. The church needs to be spiritually and physically prepared for this period of demonic humanity. Fortunately, the New Testament has a lot to say about enduring suffering by looking forward to the reward set before us. (Unfortunately, many theologians either

GOD'S PLAN OF REDEMPTION | 439

believe the Great Tribulation already took place in AD 70 or that the church is raptured before the Tribulation occurs.)

At some point the Tribulation will be on the horizon, and the church will need to start making physical preparations to hide in wilderness areas from the Antichrist and his followers for more than three and a half years. The logistics involved in such an endeavor are almost insurmountable. It will not be easy to blaze trails to remote hiding places that cannot be traced. Most likely not every person will have left his or her smartphone or other digital devices behind to avoid being traced. Going completely off the grid will be difficult.

My suggestion is to form wilderness survival organizations with a dual purpose: to teach members about nature and teamwork in the wild, and at the same time prepare hiding places for small groups when the Tribulation approaches. The Tribulation, however, is not imminent because there is no temple for the Antichrist to enter and present himself as God. But when the temple rebuilding program starts, either on the current temple mount or in another location in the old City of David, it will be time for churches to begin preparations.

Today's Confusion

Each of the current views on God's endgame has its strengths and weaknesses. But none of them provide a logical biblical theology of the future based on the relevant biblical data.

- *Premillennialists* affirm a literal millennium, but they have the second coming and the rapture in the wrong time frame.
- *Postmillennialists* affirm that Christ can rule this world from his throne in heaven, but they are under the false impression that sinful man can usher in an age of righteous humanity with Satan still operational in the world.
- *Amillennialists* affirm the second coming and the rapture on the last day to usher in the Father's kingdom, but they boldly claim there is no 1,000-year messianic kingdom on this earth before the eternal kingdom of heaven.

Amillennialists claim that Satan continues to rule this evil age until the end of the world when Christ comes again. But Christ has a divine right to rule this creation before he comes again to take us to his Father's kingdom because the world was the Son's kingdom before the fall. And the Father has promised his Son that one day he will remove Satan and his demonic hosts and restore this creation to his Son, who is its rightful Lord: "The Lord [God the Father] said to my Lord [God the Son], 'Sit at my right hand, until I [the Father] put your enemies under your feet'" (Matt. 22:44). This is an unconditional covenant between the Father and the Son.

If amillennialists are correct and the Son of God never gets his creation back free of Satan, then Satan will have robbed the Son of his right to delight in his own Genesis creation. Christ will never be restored as the true God of this world—his very own creation. From a human perspective, the suffering caused by human sin, demons, and the curse is heart-breaking. But our Creator, too, is heartbroken and greatly distressed by the thoughts and actions of sinful mankind. He has been cheated out of the joy and delight of his good creation. The Son of God, however, has the divine right, power, and authority to restore this Genesis creation to himself in its original glory and rule over this world. According to the Scriptures, this *must* be accomplished before he comes again, destroys this Adamic creation, and takes his people to the Father's kingdom.

In Revelation, John describes the saints in heaven singing praises to God when Christ's reign over this earth unfolds:

> And ***they sang a new song***, saying, "Worthy are you to take the scroll and to open its seals, for you were slain, and by your blood you ransomed people for God from every tribe and language and people and nation, and you have made them a kingdom and priests to our God, and ***they shall reign on the earth***." . . . and there were loud voices in heaven, saying, "***The kingdom of the world has become the kingdom of our Lord and of his Christ***," . . . And the twenty-four elders who sit on their thrones before God fell on their faces and worshiped God, saying, "We give thanks to you, Lord God Almighty, who is and who was, for ***you have taken your great power and begun to reign*** [over this earth]." (Rev. 5:9–10; 11:15–17)

John hears a song in heaven celebrating Christ's future messianic kingdom on this earth. For some reason, amillennialists cannot hear this music. They claim that Christ never gets his Genesis kingdom back and that there is never an age of righteous humanity. They deny the Son the divine right, joy, and glory of delighting in his own restored creation. Yet, Jesus, himself, insists that we listen to all God's promises that must be fulfilled before he returns:

> Then he said to them, "These are my words that I spoke to you while I was still with you, *that everything written about me in the Law of Moses and the Prophets and the Psalms must be fulfilled.*" Then he opened their minds to understand the Scriptures. (Luke 24:44–45)

All the prophetic verses about Christ and his messianic kingdom "must be fulfilled" before he returns. Amillennialists need to open their minds so they can understand the Scriptures and hear the music in Revelation.

Many theologians like to organize the flow of biblical history by describing different dispensations or covenants described in the Bible. These methods have merit, but I prefer to use the following ages of mankind to describe the overall flow of biblical history:

The seven ages:
- An age of righteous humanity in the garden of Eden
- An age of unrighteous humanity after the fall
- An age of violent and corrupt humanity in Noah's day
- An age of demonic humanity during the Great Tribulation
- An age of restored righteous humanity during the millennial reign of Christ
- The end of this Genesis age when this creation perishes
- The eternal age and the beginning of the new creation as sons of God on the eternal new earth

Faith in God

The Bible informs us of what God has done in the past, is doing today, *and will do* in the future. It will not just all "pan out" in the end, as some Bible teachers like to say. Disciples of Christ should be able to speak intelligently about what Christ *will do* in the future. Believing in these promises requires *faith* in a God whom we can trust to keep his word about what he will do to establish his future kingdom on earth and in heaven. Theologian and author Donald E. Hartley paraphrased Hebrews 11:1–6 and described this kind of faith:

> So what is faith? Faith is really the heart-felt confidence of coming to pass all that is rightfully hoped for, the deep seated certitude that untranspired but promised events will eventually take place. And without this type of faith, it is impossible to please God. Why? Because when approaching God, only this faith treats him as absolutely trustworthy to keep his promises and he must therefore be a rewarder to those who earnestly seek him.[44]

If we are to please God by having faith in him and his promises, then we certainly need to understand what he has promised he will do. Christians should not consider the subject of eschatology or the kingdom of God an elective. It is the study of the very gospel itself, for it gets to the heart of what God as the Father, Son, and Holy Spirit has done, is doing, *and promised he will do*.

Conclusion

Now that Christ has come to this earth, has been crucified for our sins, has been resurrected, and has ascended to the right hand of the Father, I propose that the biblical data supports the proposition that **he will do** the following to establish God's kingdom on earth and then in heaven:

- Christ will continue to gather those whom the Father has given him out of Satan's dominion of darkness into his kingdom through our work of evangelism and the power of the Holy Spirit.
- Christ will one day bring repentant Jews into his kingdom.

---

44 Donald E. Hartley, "Heb. 11:6 – A Reassessment of the Translation 'God Exists,'" *Trinity Journal* 27.2 (Fall 2006): 307.

- Christ will remove Michael, the archangel who restrains Satan, and the Great Tribulation against his people will begin.
- Christ will pour out his wrath against those who worship Satan and his Antichrist during the Tribulation.
- Christ will destroy the Antichrist and his false prophet at the battle of Armageddon to bring the Tribulation to an end.
- Christ will send an angel to bind Satan at the beginning of the millennium at a time set by the Father.
- Christ will remove the curse and regenerate the earth to its Edenic condition.
- Christ will sit on his throne in heaven at the right hand of the Father and will rule over the restored earth for one thousand years.
- Christ will resurrect all deceased saints into their natural bodies to reinhabit the restored natural earth as restored human beings during his millennial reign.
- Christ will designate some resurrected saints from all nations to sit on thrones to assist him in governing the nations during this age of righteous humanity.
- Christ will release Satan for a short time after the millennium to command one last rebellion on the earth, leading to the battle of Gog and Magog.
- Christ will put down this rebellion and destroy Satan by sending him to the lake of fire for eternity.
- Christ will return on the last day of this Genesis creation.
- Christ will destroy the heavens and earth with fire.
- Christ will then make all things new when he creates the new heavens and new earth.
- Christ will sit on his Great White Throne and judge every human being.
- Christ will resurrect unbelievers from hades, punish them according to their evil deeds, and send them to the lake of fire.
- Christ will gather all believers, whether asleep or alive, and transform their bodies to be like his resurrected and glorified body—immortal and imperishable.

- Christ will reward the glorified saints for their good deeds and give them eternal life in the Father's eternal kingdom of heaven.
- Christ will consummate the marriage with the church, his bride, in the New Jerusalem.
- Christ, as the Alpha and Omega of this Genesis creation, will then say, "It is done!"
- Christ will have completed the work of redemption that the Father has given him.
- Christ will turn his kingdom over to his Father and be subject to the Father.

By faith we can be certain that God is absolutely trustworthy to keep all these promises concerning what he will do in the future.

SCRIPTURE INDEX

Genesis
Gen. 1:1 *91, 244*
Gen. 1:1–2 *76*
Gen. 1:26–28 *92*
Gen. 1:26—2:24 *50*
Gen. 1:29–30 *206*
Gen. 2:7 *91*
Gen. 2:8–15 *22, 91, 249*
Gen. 2:15–17 *93*
Gen. 2:18–24 *92*
Gen. 3:4–5 *93*
Gen. 3:6 *93*
Gen. 3:14–15 *95*
Gen. 3:16–23 *94*
Gen. 3:17–19 *52*
Gen. 6:5, 11 *233*
Gen. 9:3 *206*
Gen. 12:1–3 *95*
Gen. 13:10 *23*
Gen. 50:26 *22*

Deuteronomy
Deut. 1:8 *96*
Deut. 1:16–17 *391*
Deut. 5:7–9 *379*

Judges
Judg. 21:25 *390*

1 Samuel
1 Sam. 26:9–10 *174*

2 Samuel
2 Sam. 7:12–13 *96*

1 Kings
1 Kings 18:37–39 *262*

2 Kings
2 Kings 6:15–17 *272*
2 Kings 6:17–18 *131*
2 Kings 19 *272*

2 Chronicles
2 Chron. 19:6 *391*

Ezra
Ezra 4 *294*
Ezra 7:11–16 *294*

Nehemiah
Neh. 4—6 *294*

Psalms
Ps. 2:6–8 *12, 108*
Ps. 2:7–12 *389*
Ps. 37:7–11 *235*
Ps. 72:8–19 *330, 383*
Ps. 98:1–9 *108, 109, 207–208, 212, 412*
Ps. 110:1 *12, 78, 154*

Isaiah
Isa. 9:6–7 *25, 77, 96, 152, 176*
Isa. 11 *206*
Isa. 24:18–23 *107, 321*
Isa. 24:22 *119*
Isa. 26:19 *357*
Isa. 33:24; 35:4–6 *199*
Isa. 52:7–10 *109, 212, 214, 215, 413*
Isa. 53:3–13 *98*
Isa. 54:7–14 *45, 236, 436*
Isa. 54:10 *413*
Isa. 59:20–21 *312, 331*
Isa. 60:11 *324, 325*
Isa. 65:17–25 *81, 110, 150, 185, 198, 280, 371, 412, 434*
Isa. 65:20 *65*
Isa. 66:1–2 *84*
Isa. 66:8–12 *414*
Isa. 66:12–21 *280*

Jeremiah
Jer. 25:11 *291*
Jer. 30:1, 3, 8–9; 33:14–16 *28*
Jer. 31:17–33 *291*
Jer. 31:28–38 *309, 311*

Ezekiel
Ezek. 34:25–31; 36:35 *111, 204*
Ezek. 36:26–28 *207*
Ezek. 36:30, 35 *54*
Ezek. 37:5–26 *54, 186, 371*
Ezek. 37:12–13 *357*
Ezek. 38:1–12 *275*
Ezek. 38:22 *275*
Ezek. 39:9–10 *238*
Ezek. 39:29 *207*

Daniel
Dan. 2:31–45 *283, 285, 298*
Dan. 7:11, 26 *297, 300*
Dan. 7:13–14 *99, 171*
Dan. 7:19–25 *104, 172, 286, 303*
Dan. 7:25–27 *171, 286, 298, 320, 324*
Dan. 9:21–24 *290, 292*
Dan. 9:25–27 *261, 293, 295, 296, 301, 303*
Dan. 11:36 *105, 258*
Dan. 12:1 *105, 258*
Dan. 12:6–11 *258*

Joel
Joel 2:10–19 *319*

Micah
Mic. 4:1–3 *109, 280*

Haggai
Hag. 2:6–9 *320*

Zechariah
Zech. 5:1–4 *122*
Zech. 5:5–10 *122*
Zech. 6:1–8 *122*
Zech. 12:10 *123*
Zech. 13:1 *123*
Zech. 14:4–9 *122*

Malachi
Mal. 4:5–6 *262*

Matthew
Matt. 5:5–10 *214*
Matt. 6:9–13 *86, 438*
Matt. 6:33 *101*
Matt. 10:16–18 *332*
Matt. 11:3–5 *29*
Matt. 12:29 *147*
Matt. 13:27–30 *239*
Matt. 13:36–43 *136*
Matt. 13:39 *139*
Matt. 13:41–42 *240*
Matt. 16:27—17:2 *220*
Matt. 19:27–29 *31, 111, 157, 176, 196, 359, 371, 433*
Matt. 20:20–23 *30, 31*
Matt. 22:31–32 *423*
Matt. 22:41–44 *12, 78, 171, 440*
Matt. 23:36–39 *103, 281, 308, 309, 312, 408*
Matt. 24:1–3 *139, 146, 157, 278, 282, 436*
Matt. 24:7–8 *102, 103, 296, 300*
Matt. 24:9–13 *265*
Matt. 24:13–14 *110, 211, 213, 436*
Matt. 24:15 *279, 290, 300*
Matt. 24:15–21 *106, 297, 303*
Matt. 24:21 *262, 300, 304*
Matt. 24:21–29 *108, 132*
Matt. 24:29–31 *142, 317, 318*
Matt. 24:31 *240*
Matt. 24:32–36 *308, 311*
Matt. 24:33 *275*
Matt. 25: 1–13 *239*
Matt. 25:31–46 *136, 180, 435*
Matt. 26:29 *359*
Matt. 26:53 *273*
Matt. 26:64–65 *100*
Matt. 27:50–51 *316*
Matt. 28:19–20 *112*

Mark
Mark 10:28–30 *111, 156, 196*

Luke
Luke 1:30–35 *97*
Luke 4:18–19 *29*
Luke 11: 21–22 *43*
Luke 17:22–36 *233, 234, 239*
Luke 18:29–30 *156, 196*
Luke 20:34–36 *13, 55, 346, 355, 425*
Luke 20:42–43 *154*
Luke 21:7–24 *103, 301, 302*
Luke 22:24 *30*
Luke 22:69 *169, 170, 183, 193, 371, 371, 428, 433*
Luke 23:44–45 *316*
Luke 24:19–27 *98*
Luke 24:36–43 *218*
Luke 24:44–45 *441*

John
John 1:1–14 *74, 97*
John 1:10–11 *97*
John 1:43–45 *27*
John 1:47 *407*
John 3:16–17 *97*
John 5:22 *240*
John 5:28–29 *115, 135*
John 6:14–15 *335*
John 6:40 *139*
John 7:37–39 *76, 250*
John 10:10, 14 *204*
John 11:23–26 *425*
John 12:31 *147*
John 14:1–3 *126*
John 17:4–5, 24 *243*
John 18:33–38 *326*
John 19:19 *285*
John 21:18–19 *48, 236*
John 21:21–23 *236*

Acts
Acts 1:6–9 *32, 80, 99, 153, 170, 296, 408*
Acts 1:8–9 *32*
Acts 1:9–11 *141*
Acts 3:20–21 *101*
Acts 7:54–56 *130, 173*
Acts 9:4 *173*
Acts 17:1–8 *329*
Acts 26:13–15 *221*

Romans
Rom. 1:1–4 *78, 97*
Rom. 1:16–17 *409*
Rom. 3:28–30 *410*
Rom. 4:13, 16 *410*
Rom. 6:3–4 *422*
Rom. 8:14–23 *60*
Rom. 8:19–22 *102, 114, 182*
Rom. 8:29 *58*
Rom. 11:1–31 *410, 413*
Rom. 11:11–12 *411, 412*
Rom. 11:24–27 *45, 312, 331, 411, 413*
Rom. 11:29 *413*
Rom. 12:14–21 *393, 394*
Rom. 13:1–4 *392, 393*
Rom. 13:7 *394*

1 Corinthians
1 Cor. 2:9–10 *421*
1 Cor. 3:11–15 *240*
1 Cor. 4:1–6 *61, 223*
1 Cor. 6:15–17 *251*
1 Cor. 7:1–4 *59*
1 Cor. 15:23–28 *74, 140, 179, 197, 213, 214, 240*
1 Cor. 15:35–53 *61, 224, 226*
1 Cor. 15:51–53 *240, 425*

2 Corinthians
2 Cor. 5:1, 16–17 *58*
2 Cor. 10:3–5 *394*
2 Cor. 11:23–27 *194*
2 Cor. 12:1–4 *61*

Galatians
Gal. 1:3–4 *146*
Gal. 1:7, 9 *407*
Gal. 2:4 *407*
Gal. 2:12 *404, 407*
Gal. 2:15–16 *406*
Gal. 3:26–28 *58, 407*
Gal. 4:10 *405*
Gal. 5:2–3 *405*
Gal. 5:7–11 *404*
Gal. 5:12 *407*
Gal. 6:12 *404*
Gal. 6:15–16 *403, 406*

Ephesians
Eph. 1:19–21 *100, 170*
Eph. 2:1–2 *94*
Eph. 2:4–7 *70*
Eph. 4:10 *169*
Eph. 6:11–12 *102, 171, 316*

Philippians
Phil. 3:10 *263*
Phil. 3:20–21 *126, 189, 218, 328*

Colossians
Col. 1:13–14 *102*
Col. 1:16 *75, 93*
Col. 1:21–22; 2:13–14 *98*
Col. 1:24 *263*
Col. 3:18–19 *59*

1 Thessalonians
1 Thess. 1:9–10 *133, 141*
1 Thess. 4:15–17—5:2 *47, 121, 141, 240*

2 Thessalonians
2 Thess. 1:7—2:8 *124*
2 Thess. 2:3–9 *106, 259*

1 Timothy
1 Tim. 2:1–2 *394*
1 Tim. 2:9 *252*
1 Tim. 6:14–16 *62, 222*

Titus
Titus 3:4–5 *76*

Hebrews
Heb. 1:2–10 *74, 93*
Heb. 2:7–8 *80, 100, 155, 172*
Heb. 9:27 *262*
Heb. 9:28 *138*
Heb. 10:12–13 *80, 101, 170, 433*
Heb. 10:26–27 *138*
Heb. 11:1 *4*
Heb. 11:1–6 *442*
Heb. 11:17–19 *189*
Heb. 11:35–38 *195*
Heb. 12:1–2 *265, 267, 424*
Heb. 12:22–23 *188, 424*
Heb. 12:26–29 *138*

1 Peter
1 Peter 1:3–7 *101, 127, 402, 439*
1 Peter 2:9–10 *402*
1 Peter 4:17 *240*
1 Peter 5:8 *104*

2 Peter
2 Peter 2:7 *194*
2 Peter 3:3–13 *137, 245*
2 Peter 3:7–10 *9*
2 Peter 3:10–13 *69, 240, 429*

1 John
1 John 3:1–2 *46, 62, 220, 240*
1 John 5:19 *33, 256*

Revelation
Rev. 1:1 *198*
Rev. 5:9–10 *33, 112, 152, 183, 440*
Rev. 7:9–14 *151, 268*
Rev. 9:4 *267*
Rev. 11:15–17 *108, 110, 155, 176, 440*
Rev. 12:7–12 *105, 259*
Rev. 12:12 *262*
Rev. 13:1–10 *105, 265, 304*
Rev. 13:2–4 *105, 261*
Rev. 13:11–14 *263*
Rev. 13:16–17 *266*
Rev. 14:12–13 *267*
Rev. 16:2–11 *266, 267*
Rev. 17:6 *263*
Rev. 19:1–2 *151*
Rev. 19:7–8 *251*
Rev. 19:11–21 *106, 129, 272*
Rev. 19:14 *273*
Rev. 19:15 *133, 177*
Rev. 19:16 *180*
Rev. 19:20 *297*
Rev. 20:1–3 *42, 107, 131, 148, 175*
Rev. 20:4–6 *34, 112, 131, 151, 180, 183, 187, 188, 199, 378*
Rev. 20:7–10 *113, 274, 275*
Rev. 20:11 *69, 149, 240, 244*
Rev. 20:11–15 *115, 181, 240*
Rev. 20:11—21:1–6 *81, 114, 134, 135, 316*
Rev. 20:11—21:27 *82*
Rev. 21:1 *240*
Rev. 21:1–6 *34, 69, 75, 76, 149, 182, 240, 246, 247, 435*
Rev. 21:1–22 *116, 245*
Rev. 21:2–11 *115, 252*
Rev. 21:6 *240, 249*
Rev. 21:19–21 *253*
Rev. 22:1–2 *76, 249*
Rev. 22:4–5 *241*
Rev. 22:7 *235*
Rev. 22:12–14 *34, 69, 75, 134, 135, 181, 232*
Rev. 22:14–15 *248*

www.ingramcontent.com/pod-product-compliance
Lightning Source LLC
Chambersburg PA
CBHW022055150426
43195CB00008B/150